Theories of Counseling
and Therapy

Theories of Counseling and Therapy

AN EXPERIENTIAL APPROACH

THIRD EDITION

Jeffrey A. Kottler and Marilyn J. Montgomery

cognella® | ACADEMIC PUBLISHING

Bassim Hamadeh, CEO and Publisher
Amy Smith, Project Editor
Casey Hands, Associate Production Editor
Jess Estrella, Senior Graphic Designer
Sara Schennum, Licensing Associate
Jessica Hillstrom, Interior Designer
Natalie Piccotti, Director of Marketing
Kassie Graves, Vice President of Editorial
Jamie Giganti, Director of Academic Publishing

Cover image: Copyright © 2014 Depositphotos/Zakharova.
Cover/Interior design image: Copyright © 2017 iStockphoto LP/Benjavisa.

Printed in the United States of America.

ISBN: 978-1-5165-2421-1 (pbk) / 978-1-5165-2422-8 (br) / 978-1-5165-8362-1 (al)

Brief Contents

Preface   xv

1   A Personal Introduction to Theory   1

2   Theory in Context   12

3   Theory in a Clinician's Life   35

4   Look to the Past to Set You Free:
    Psychodynamic Approaches   53

5   What Is Learned Can Be Unlearned:
    Behavioral Approaches   87

6   The Primacy of Personal Experience:
    Humanistic Approaches   118

7   Thoughts Before Feelings: Cognitive
    Approaches   159

8   All in the Family: Systemic Approaches   199

9   Shift Your Perspective: Constructivist
    Approaches   230

10 Brief and Action-Oriented Approaches:
    Just Do It   255

11 Mind–Body and Experiential
    Approaches: Just Breathe   285

12 Integrative Approaches to
    Doing Therapy   311

13 Personalizing and Customizing Theory
    for Clients and Settings   341

References   366

Index   394

Detailed Contents

Preface   xv

1 A Personal Introduction to Theory   1
Evolving Theoretical Journeys   2
  Jeffrey's Story   2
  Marilyn's Story   3
So Many Choices, So Little Time   4
  Jeffrey's Story   4
  Marilyn's Story   6
How to Get the Most From This Course and Text   8
An Experiential Approach to Your Personal Theory   10
Suggested Readings   12

2 Theory in Context   12
A Narrative of Theory-in-Action   14
What Theory Will Do for You   15
Is a Theories Course Obsolete?   17
A Review of Basic History   18
Points of Agreement   21
  Ethical Practice   21
  Cultural Diversity   23
  Assessment and Diagnosis   25
  The Impact of Managed Care   26
  Working Efficiently   26
Contemporary Trends   28
  The Impact of Technology on Clients   28
  The Impact of Technology on Therapists   30
  Unique Advantages and Disadvantages   31
  Integration and Synthesis   32
Suggested Readings   33

3 Theory in a Clinician's Life   35
   Three Theories, Three Lives   36
   Personal and Professional Interactions   38
      Theories and the Developing Person   39
      Cultural Worldviews   42
   The Next Steps in Your Understanding   45
      Confusion and Ambiguity   45
      Fervor and Zeal   46
      Points of Departure   47
      Expanding Your Options   49
      The Main Attraction   51
   Suggested Readings   52

4 Look to the Past to Set You Free:
   Psychodynamic Approaches   53
   Early Background   54
   Psychoanalytic Disciples and Revisionists   55
   Basic Principles of Psychoanalytic Theory   56
      The Unconscious   56
      Driven by Drives   57
      Intrapsychic Conflicts   58
      Psychosexual Stages   59
      Exploring the Past   60
      Resistance   61
      Defense Mechanisms   62
      Dreams   63
      Catharsis   64
      Corrective Emotional Experience   65
   Treatment Procedures   66
      Evenly Hovering Attention   66
      Transference   67
      Countertransference   70
   Psychoanalytic Innovators   72
      Object Relations Theory   72
      Self-Psychology Theory   74
      Interpersonal Psychoanalysis and Interpersonal Psychotherapy   74
   Contemporary Developments   76
      Relational Psychoanalysis   77
      Brief Psychodynamic Psychotherapy   78
   Strengths and Limitations   80
   Suggested Readings   86

5 What Is Learned Can Be Unlearned: Behavioral Approaches   87

  History of the Behaviorism Movement   88

    Ivan Pavlov and Classical Conditioning   89

    John Watson and Learned Neuroses   90

    B. F. Skinner and Operant Conditioning   90

    The First Behavior Therapies   91

  Basic Principles and Techniques   95

    Reinforcing and Discouraging Certain Target Behaviors   96

    Shaping Behavior Incrementally   97

    Measurement of Progress and Outcomes   98

    It's Action That Counts   98

  Behavioral Techniques   100

    Goal Setting   101

    Relaxation Training   104

    Sensate Focus Exercises   107

    Contingency Contracting   108

    Behavioral Intervention Plans   111

  Contemporary Developments   112

    Strengths and Limitations   114

  Suggested Readings   117

6 The Primacy of Personal Experience: Humanistic Approaches   118

  Some Shared Beliefs   119

    Basic Assumptions   120

    The Healing Relationship   120

  Background and History   122

  Existential Theory   123

    Background and History   123

    Victor Frankl and Logotherapy   124

    Existential Principles   125

    Existential Therapy   127

    A Different Sort of Relationship   128

    The Therapeutic Process   129

    Some Recent Developments   131

    Some Strengths and Limitations   132

  Person-Centered Theory   133

    Basic Assumptions   134

    Core Conditions   136

    Features of a Client-Centered Session   139

Contemporary Revisions — 143
Some Strengths and Limitations — 144
Gestalt Theory — 145
Early Background — 145
A Theory of Being and Doing — 147
Gestalt Techniques — 148
Some Strengths and Limitations — 150
Contemporary Extensions of Humanistic Theory — 150
Applying the Skills of Humanism — 151
Focusing — 153
Pre-therapy — 153
Emotion-Focused Therapy — 155
Back to the Personal Dimensions of the Therapist — 156
Concerns and Criticism of Humanistic Approaches — 157
Suggested Readings — 158

7 Thoughts Before Feelings:
Cognitive Approaches — 159
Aaron Beck and Cognitive Therapy — 160
Dysfunctional Styles of Thinking — 161
Principles of Cognitive Therapy — 164
Applications to Specific Problems — 165
Some Limitations — 166
Cognitive Behavioral Therapy (CBT) — 167
Strengths and Limitations — 168
Albert Ellis and Rational Emotive Behavior Therapy (REBT) — 169
Background of REBT — 170
Basic Ideas — 171
The ABC Theory — 173
Specific Disputing Strategies — 176
Some Strengths and Limitations — 179
Adlerian Therapy — 180
Background — 181
Basic Concepts — 182
Social Interest and Mutual Respect — 183
Birth Order — 183
The Helping Process — 184
Core Fears — 187
A Plan of Action — 188
Strength and Flexibility — 189
Some Limitations — 189

Reality Therapy	191
Underlying Assumptions	192
"Is That Working for You?"	192
No Excuses	193
The Therapeutic Process	194
Strengths and Limitations	195
In Conclusion	196
Suggested Readings	198

8 All in the Family: Systemic Approaches | **199** |
Thinking in Circles Rather Than in Straight Lines	200
The Emergence of Systemic Thinking	201
Natural Science	202
Mathematics	202
Physics	203
Systems Theory	203
Psychoanalysis	203
Anthropology	204
Some Principles of Systemic Thinking	205
Circular Causality	205
Rules of Relationships	207
A Quick Review of Some Options Available	209
Psychodynamic Influences and Bowen Family Therapy	210
Humanistic/Experiential Approaches	211
Structural Approaches	212
Strategic Approaches	214
Multicultural Family Therapy and Sociocultural Approaches	215
A Unified Front	216
Doing Family Therapy	220
Stages in the Process	222
In Conclusion	226
Suggested Readings	228

9 Shift Your Perspective: Constructivist Approaches | **230** |
Constructivist Theories	230
Constructivist Assumptions	231
Narrative Therapy	232
Stages in the Narrative Process	235
The Problem Is the Problem	237
Strengths and Limitations	238

Feminist Approaches 239
   Gender and Mental Health 241
   Feminist Therapy 243
Relational Cultural Therapy 246
Solution-Focused Therapy249
   Major Premises 248
   Staying Flexible 248
   Discovering Patterns and Constructing New Ones 250
   The Miracle Question 251
   Scaling 252
   Strengths and Limitations 253
Some Final Thoughts 253
Suggested Readings 253

10 Brief and Action-Oriented Approaches: Just Do It 255

Brief Therapy Defined 256
   The Theory Behind Brief Therapies 257
   Insight Versus Action 259
   Some Background and Brief History 261
Ericksonian Therapy 262
   A Typical Erickson Story 263
   The Antitheorist 264
   Contributions, Limitations, and Contraindications 266
Strategic Therapy 267
   Reframing the Problem 268
   Advance Preparation 270
   Directives 270
   Accentuate the Positive 271
   Remind Clients That Therapy Will End 272
   Predict a Relapse 272
   Strengths and Limitations 273
Single-Session Therapy 274
   Advantages and Special Problems 275
The Best Candidates for Brief, Action-Oriented Therapy 276
   Stages of Readiness for Change 277
Motivational Interviewing 278
   OARS 279
   Decisional Balance 279
   Scaling to Target Small Changes 280
   Rolling With Resistance 281

Some Final Thoughts 282
Suggested Readings 283

11 Mind–Body and Experiential Approaches: Just Breathe 285

Neurologically Informed Approaches 287
  Early Trauma and Attachment Issues 289
Mindfulness Approaches 289
Emotional and Behavioral Regulation Therapies 291
  Acceptance and Commitment Therapy 292
  Dialectical Behavioral Therapy 293
  Eye Movement Desensitization and Reprocessing (EMDR) Therapy 257
  Body and Energy Psychotherapies 298
Expressive Therapies 299
  Drama Therapy 300
  Art Therapy 303
  Dance and Movement Therapy 304
  Play Therapy 305
  Filial Play Therapy 306
  Sandplay Therapy 307
Animal-Assisted Therapy 308
  In Summary 309
Suggested Readings 309

12 Integrative Approaches to Doing Therapy 311

Arnold Lazarus and Multimodal Therapy 313
  Foundational Ideas 313
Theoretical Integration: Blended Families 316
Assimilative Integration: Borrowing an Idea Now and Then 316
Technical Eclectisim: The Toolbox Approach 317
  Evidence-Based Eclecticism 318
Common Factors: The Heart of the Matter 320
  Therapist Presence 321
  Use of Self 322
  The Placebo Effect 322
  Altered States 323
  Helping Relationship 323
  Feedback 325
  Finding Meaning 326
  Rehearsal 327
  The Process 328

Finding Your Own Way   329
  There's Too Much Good Stuff Out There   330
  Sending Recall Notices   331
How to Be Integrative   334
  But What's the Right Answer?   333
  There is Value in Most Approaches   335
  Be Skeptical of Truth   336
  Get Outside Your Discipline   336
  Get Outside Your Culture   337
  Avoid Thinking in Boxes   338
  Resist the Urge to Label Yourself   338
  One Additional Thought   339
Suggested Readings   340

13 Personalizing and Customizing Theory
   for Clients and Settings   341
  It All Looks the Same to Me: Comparisons and Differences   343
    Insight Versus Action   345
    Cognitive Versus Affective   346
    Present Versus Past   347
    Flexible Versus Rigid Roles   348
    Making Further Comparisons   348
  A Custom Fit   349
    Clients Have Theories, Too   352
    The Real-Time Practice of Therapy   354
    Your Own Inimitable Style   356
  Deciding on a Starting Point   357
  Limitations of Theory   360
  Moving On   361
    A Final Thought   363
  Suggested Readings   364

References   366
Index   394

Preface

This is a text for a *very* challenging course—not only for students but also for the instructor. There is *so* much material to cover and so many complex and confusing ideas to review that most people involved in the experience often feel overwhelmed and bewildered. Names start to sound the same. Various theories all run together. Rather than feeling excited and stimulated by the wonderful theoretical background of the field, both students and faculty often keep their heads to the ground, grimly marching toward the distant goal of conceptual mastery. It's the theory-of-the-week club, and every seven days force the abandonment of one set of ideas for the next ones waiting around the corner.

This text will not only supply the background material that is needed for a first course on theory in counseling and therapy, but it will also provide a structure for the experience that will keep things fun, stimulating, and personally meaningful. Similar to any experiential approach to a subject, the emphasis throughout this book is on *applying* concepts not only to your future professional practice but also to your personal life. One of the incredible joys and gifts of this career is that almost everything you learn in your classes, supervision, and clinical work has direct applications to your personal life. Our interactive approach will keep you actively involved in the learning process and help you develop ways for synthesizing the material in a personally meaningful way.

WHO THIS TEXT IS FOR

This is a text for both undergraduate and graduate classes in psychology, counseling, social work, human services, family therapy, and related helping professions. It draws on theories from *all* these disciplines, as well as contributions from medicine, education, philosophy, and the social sciences. It is intended to be the primary text for courses such as Theories of Counseling and Theory and Practice of Psychotherapy. It is also suitable for a number of other courses that introduce students to the conceptual background of helping.

Because of its experiential format, this text is especially appropriate for instructors whose teaching style involves lots of class discussions, debates, simulations, role playing, small group work, personal applications, interactive exercises, and demonstrations. Lectures and readings can carry even the most eager students only so far in such a content-rich course. At some point, there must be opportunities for more active learning structures, especially since most people are able to sustain attention on one thing while sitting passively for only about 20 minutes.

This text is designed to help you personalize and integrate what you learn in a meaningful way. It speaks to you as a trusted companion who not only whispers in your ear the important things you will need to know, but also advises you on the best ways to use these ideas in your life and work.

You'll notice that we take on the role of a tour guide as we explore the territory within each theoretical model. Even if you are already familiar with some of the approaches, our goal is to give you a tantalizing review of the most important, useful, and interesting features of each theory, rather than to cover it comprehensively. Instead of overwhelming you with content you can't possibly digest meaningfully in a single semester, we help you focus on the salient features that may be most clinically useful. It has often been the tradition that students are introduced to a new theory each week, expected to master its core ideas, memorize a bunch of names and terms, pass a quiz on the material, and then quickly move on to the next theory the following week. Instead, we have tried to stimulate your curiosity about some of the models that you find most attractive and interesting, knowing that later in your studies and practice you will likely hone in on the few that are most relevant and compatible with your own style and clinical practice.

STRUCTURE OF THE BOOK

The book is divided into three main parts. An introductory section provides the background you need to understand the theories that follow, a middle section is composed of the chapters that discuss the main theory "families," and a final section helps you synthesize and apply what you've learned and chose where you'd like to go next. You'll finish by choosing the theory or theories you especially resonate with, which will make you ready to articulate the main approach you'd like to take with clients.

In this new edition, we integrate samples of historically significant writing from the influential "giants" in each family of therapies into our reviews of the most approaches. These "voices from the past" introduce you to the historical figures who have been most persuasive in the development of our field. Robert Burton, one of the first cognitive theorists writing as early as the 17th century, observed that each of us is able to see further by standing on the shoulders of giants, and we want you to catch a glimpse of some of those shoulders we are standing on. In addition, we include several "cutting edge" theorists in counseling and therapy, those who break new ground by building on what has been constructed before. We also present "voices from the field" in most chapters: beginning and experienced clinicians talking about the realities of using theory in their daily practices. This integration of the old with the new makes this book unique, allowing you to form your own informed decisions about which conceptual models seem most appropriate for your individual personality, style, attitudes, beliefs, and work setting. In this book, we hope to surprise you with the best of the past, excite you with the vitality of the present, prepare you for the future you will encounter, and give you tools for negotiating a professional terrain that you will see as both novel and familiar.

Throughout the text are a collection of experiential activities that include (a) reflective exercises, (b) class or group activities, (c) field studies, (d) homework assignments, and (e) personal applications. These are not the sorts of projects that you would want to skip in order to get to the real meat of things—they *are* the central focus of this text. When this course is over, you should be able to understand the major conceptual ideas of the field, be able to talk about them intelligently, and apply them in your life and work.

The Way Things Are Organized

There is considerable debate in the field about the best way to classify theories or to organize them according to their essential features. To make matters more complex, there is the practical problem of squeezing all the major models currently in use into a single course. Although there are hundreds of different theories favored by practicing counselors and therapists, only about two dozen of the models would be considered mainstream, and just a handful of those in common practice. The challenge we face is how to organize all these different theories into reasonably sized packages that you can digest in limited time. We found this task to be both frustrating and unsatisfying no matter which framework we selected. Take the Adlerian model for instance, a theoretical structure that was devised by Alfred Adler in the previous century. He was originally a disciple of Sigmund Freud, so one might categorize him within that family. Yet most Adlerians would strenuously disagree, arguing that this approach is "systemic," or "cognitive," "humanistic," or "psychoeducational." It is for this very reason that we had no choice but to consider it "integrative" in the sense that it has been the foundation for many other approaches that followed, as well as contemporary practitioners expanding ideas way beyond their original conceptualization. We struggled with making decisions about other theories, and often just made rather arbitrary choices. So, if you wish to argue with us that a theory should have been placed in another chapter, we surrender and likely agree with you.

Instructors of this course have their own strong opinions about which theories should be featured and which ones should be excluded. It is likely your instructor will focus on a few favorites and choose theories that will be most relevant for your setting and future population. That is one of the beauties of this field—you have a great deal of independence, and so much is up to interpretation based on your own understanding of the literature, research evidence, and experiences as a clinician. We encourage instructors to choose the chapters and sections of chapters that best align with what students need most. We anticipate that some areas of content will be considerably expanded, while others may be skipped altogether because of time limitations.

We think one of the best parts of your education as a practitioner involves being exposed to divergent viewpoints and then forming your own ideas based on research and practice. So, be prepared to hear considerable disagreement among your instructors (and textbook authors) about some of the ideas presented here. The good news is that most of us have reached consensus about the basic ideas in the field, such as what clinicians need to know so they can be "theory literate" in their future practice situations.

We chose to organize the theories according to broad families rather than discrete entities for a number of reason. For one, if each theory had its own chapter, you would feel even more overwhelmed with all the material to master! Instead, we have covered the principal approaches in nine chapters, each one including conceptual frameworks that share some common ancestors and basic ideas. For instance, it is common in theories texts to have separate chapters covering existential, person-centered, Gestalt, and perhaps emotion-focused therapies, yet we see them as part of the same "family," sharing certain philosophical ideas even though their practice and applications are dramatically different. Although we will discuss their distinct differences and unique features, we want you to understand the broad themes that tie them together in some ways. This will make your job so much easier as you are trying to figure out what fits best with your own values, style, personality, setting, and future practice. Since this course is intended as an *overview* of theories, there will be plenty of time later in your program— and in your career—to study a few of your favorite approaches in greater depth.

CONTENTS OF THE BOOK

In the first three chapters, the stage is set for the main acts that follow. The book begins with a very personal introduction to the subject of theory in Chapter 1, reviewing the processes and experiences that you might reasonably expect to encounter during this journey. As you will soon learn, for therapy to work well, clients must be inducted into appropriate roles. They must learn what to expect, how to behave, and how to get the most from their experience. The same holds true for your role as a student of theory.

In Chapter 2, the context for the ways that practitioners use theories in their work is described. Some of the major trends in the profession are highlighted, with an emphasis on the realities of contemporary practice, including the current emphasis on evidence-based practice and how "the golden thread" of theory can assist in treatment planning, the importance of sensitivity to diversity, and the way in which the use of technology is changing both our clients and our practice.

Chapter 3 talks about the distinctly individualized aspects of theory development and application. Each practitioner develops an approach to helping that closely matches his or her own client populations, personality, values, philosophy of life, and preferences, and in this chapter, we invite you to think about these before you begin your tour of theories. Furthermore, you will be expected not only to integrate a therapeutic approach into your work but also to combine it with a number of other theories about how people learn, develop, and grow. This first section ends by providing a particular set of lenses through which to look critically at each model you will study. Flexibility and fluidity are extremely crucial for you to adapt theories to fit the diverse cultures and backgrounds of each client you will see.

In Chapter 4, the psychoanalytic family of theories is covered. Although hardly a cohesive, high-functioning group of siblings (more like feuding cousins), these frameworks do share a common heritage that emerged from Sigmund Freud's original work. The Vienna Psychoanalytic Society was at one time composed of the likes of Alfred Adler, Carl Jung, and others who went on to found their own schools of thought. Other related theories developed by Melanie Klein, Erich Fromm, and Wilhelm Reich are mentioned, as are a number of contemporary revisions proposed by so-called self-psychologists or ego theorists. The briefer forms of psychoanalytic treatment that are becoming increasingly common are discussed.

In comparison to the breadth of psychoanalytic approaches, Chapter 5 on behavioral approaches is fairly homogeneous. The basic tenets of behavioral theory are introduced, along with the generic interventions that have now become part of standard practice for most practitioners. Thus, the methods of relaxation training, systematic desensitization, and behavioral contracting will be familiar to you. We also describe how behavioral approaches can be applied to school settings, child issues, and sexual difficulties.

The humanistic family of theories in Chapter 6 are also diverse. Naturally, Carl Rogers and his client-centered approach are covered. But so are existential theory and Gestalt therapy, which are often afforded their own separate chapters. As different as these three theories might be, they share a core set of beliefs about the nature of human beings. They all value a particular kind of helping relationship that is genuine, authentic, and caring. A modern theoretical approach that began with humanistic premises, emotion-focused therapy, is also discussed.

Chapter 7 offers a review of cognitive approaches; it contains not only the standard entries of cognitive therapy and rational emotive behavior therapy, but also Adlerian therapy, which has some cognitive features. Reality therapy is also included here because of convergences in Glasser's work with that of other cognitive theorists (such integration between different theories is occurring with increasing regularity).

Chapter 8 on systemic theories will feel very different from the other theories in this book. This is because they differ from those theories that were devised from an individual person's perspective; instead, they focus on the family system as the meaningful unit.

Chapter 9 contains an introduction to constructivist therapies that have become so influential. We include narrative therapy here, as well as feminist therapy and solution-focused therapy, because all these models are founded on postmodern assumptions that are very different from other theories. These approaches emphasize how individuals construct meaning and choose goals and actions from within particular contexts, and they approach clients' problems very differently. Relational cultural theory, a feminist and culturally sensitive adaptation of some traditional theoretical approaches, is also described in this chapter.

Chapter 10, on models of brief and action-oriented therapy, describes the changing landscape of our profession, showing how more and more we will be expected to make a difference in people's lives in briefer periods of time. The most prominent models of brief therapy are presented, including Ericksonian therapy, strategic therapy, problem-solving therapy, single-session therapy, and a generic model that combines the best features of all.

Chapter 11 presents some approaches that are receiving growing attention: mind–body and experiential approaches. The main emphasis for this chapter is on approaches that conceptualize emotional reactivity to life events as influenced by deeply embedded neurological patterns. From these perspectives, actions and bodily experiences can influence our mental health in a "bottom-up" way, whereas most theories assume that change happens in a "top-down" way with the mind directing the show. Also reviewed are mindfulness-based approaches, trauma-based theories including modern versions of attachment-based therapy, as well other modern integrative approaches that help clients deal with distress and pain, such as acceptance and commitment therapy. Expressive therapies that employ music, drama, art, and movement are also included.

The final section of the book helps integrate what was learned. Chapter 12 compares the theories that have been covered and looks at the common factors of all theoretical approaches that are close to the heart of all therapeutic work. It also sets the common notion of "evidence-based practice" in the context of the theories reviewed, illustrating what this common term can and can't tell us about choosing a theory from which to work. Chapter 13 discusses what it takes to develop therapeutic expertise and encourages an introspective, critical process of personalizing the material from the whole book and will help you pull it all together as you design your first personalized model of working with clients.

SOME ADVICE ON READING THIS BOOK

The first thing we should admit is that giving advice is not usually a very effective strategy to influence people. First, hardly anyone actually listens to advice; if that were the case then therapy would simply unfold something like this:

CLIENT:	"So, as much as I would love to stop getting myself into these situations where I feel forced to do what my parents insist I do, it's just that. ..."
COUNSELOR:	"Just tell them no."
CLIENT:	"Excuse me?"
COUNSELOR:	"I just said that you need to tell them no, not let them control your life like that."
CLIENT:	"Just like that?"
COUNSELOR:	"That's about it. I think we're done here. Have a good life."

This is ridiculous, of course, because problems are never that simple and people usually already know what they need to do to fix them, whether to stand up for themselves, eat less and exercise more, stop drinking so much, quit their job, or whatever. So, just giving you advice probably isn't all that effective either, but we thought we'd give it a try, for no other reason that you are likely to be tested on this material later.

FOR REFLECTION

Besides the idea that giving advice is usually futile, why do you suppose that it is generally a problematic approach to helping?

    If the advice doesn't work out, guess who gets blamed? The client is therefore able to avoid responsibility and perhaps blame you for ruining their lives. The only thing worse than giving bad advice is giving good advice. Why is that? Because telling clients (or students) what to do only reinforces that they are not able to work out problems on their own. It leads to dependence and encourages clients to come back again and again since they are not able to figure things out on their own.

Primarily, we encourage you to respect the strenuous nature of this journey and the impact of what it means to you. This class is among the most intellectually challenging academic experiences in your program. It requires you to do a fair degree of deep reflection about some very thorny issues that have plagued scientists, philosophers, and theoreticians throughout the ages. What gives life its greatest meaning? What leads people to develop problems? How can we best influence people to change lifelong dysfunctional patterns? What makes changes last? Given the complexity of these questions, be prepared to live with a certain amount of confusion.

Next, to hold onto the ideas, theories, and concepts in this text (and class) it is imperative that you become an active learner. That means personalizing everything, applying concepts to your daily life. It also means devising as many ways possible that you can *engage* with the content. Try some of the techniques you'll read about at home! The experiential activities will help with this task, but it is up to *you* to find other ways to make the theories part of you, especially those that offer an approach most compatible with the ways you relate to the world.

We consider it particularly important for you to talk about what you are learning to your friends and families. There is a danger in a training program like this to leave loved ones behind. You are working on yourself, studying complex ideas, improving your interpersonal skills, digging deeply into your personal issues, and establishing higher standards for intimacy and connection. Unless you talk about what you are learning to those who mean the most to you, there may eventually be some increased distance between you.

It's one of the most remarkable aspects of programs like this, that you are the "designated student," the one from your family and friendship circle who is attending classes and reading texts, but it is your whole systemic community that is being influenced and impacted as well.

It's also important to get together with classmates and debate differences of opinions. We don't mean only through social media and messaging on your mobile devices but rather spending quality time together to talk through areas of confusion and make sense of what you are learning. Try to explain the theories to others in comprehensible language. Challenge ideas that don't make sense. Push yourself to be as active as possible in class, even though this may not ordinarily be the way you behave.

Our final piece of advice? Ask questions. Ask *lots* of questions.

ACKNOWLEDGMENTS

We both wish to thank Kassie Graves, acquisitions editor at Cognella, for her encouragement and her enthusiasm for completing this project. We are also grateful to our own students who are creating the conceptual models for the next generation, just as you will do someday.

Jeffrey Kottler
Houston, Texas

Marilyn Montgomery
Georgetown, Texas

CHAPTER 1

A Personal Introduction to Theory

LEARNING OBJECTIVES

After reading this chapter, you should be able to do the following:

1. Describe how theories of counseling develop from theorists' personal motives and passions.
2. Articulate how a practitioner's theoretical journey evolves across the course of a career.
3. Identify key practices that help you gain the most from studying theories of counseling and therapy.
4. Describe how an experiential approach to learning adds value to the study of theories.

It may seem like theories arise solely from academic and intellectual sources, but there are a number of very personal motives that lead practitioners of any profession to select and develop the theoretical constructs that guide their work. Albert Ellis, a founder of cognitive therapy, for example, developed his unique form of therapy because of his attraction to logic and more direct confrontation. He admitted that at one point he got tired of his clients droning on and on and decided to interrupt them in frustration, much later discovering that actively challenging thinking patterns was essential for change to take place. Carl Rogers, who developed the person-centered approach, spent much of his life searching for deep understanding in relationships and so evolved a style of therapy that was compatible with this journey. Rogers never felt truly understood in his life and so evolved a theory that emphasized empathic connection, compassion engagement, and deep understanding. Karen Horney explored how parental indifference toward a child sets up the development of neurosis after trying for years to win the love of her father, who, as a ship captain, was frequently absent. Likewise, many of the other theorists developed models that best reflected their unique personalities, solutions to personal pain, interpersonal styles, beliefs, values, and preferences.

Before we begin this journey together, we would like to introduce ourselves because, whether you realize it or not, our relationship with you is critical. It is important that we develop some level of trust with you so that our voices are heard and respected. It's also useful for you to better understand some of our personal experiences that shape our ideas about theories and inform our practice and daily lives. These introductions will thus give you some clues to how we see the world, how we believe change best takes place, and what we think is most useful to guide helping endeavors. So, we will begin by telling you about the relationship each of us has developed with theory over the years. We hope this will encourage you to do the same with each other.

EVOLVING THEORETICAL JOURNEYS

Jeffrey's Story

Throughout my training as a counselor and therapist, theory was the scourge of my life. I wanted to help people. I'm impatient, so I wanted to learn practical things that I could use *immediately* to make a difference in others' lives. Just as importantly, I hoped that I could use much of what I was learning to improve my own personal relationships, some of which were rather challenging during my days as a student. I was in active conflict with my father over my choice of a profession. My mother was dying of cancer. One of my brothers had been hospitalized for a mental illness. And I was engaged to someone I decided was not right for me. I was a mess and was desperately searching for quick answers.

I had visions that once I became proficient in the basic skills I could get people to like me more, understand better why people act the way they do, and be more effective in my daily interactions—and, most of all, unravel the difficulties I was facing at this stage of my life. I was also concerned about dwindling finances and whether I'd ever be able to pay off my debt and support myself in this new profession.

Although theory could be useful in reaching these goals, I was ready to get going already. I could not see a clear connection between what I was learning in school and what I was expected to do in my work and in my life. When reading class assignments, I often found it difficult to concentrate on the words. All the names seemed to run together. And I could not figure out the point of learning so many different theories when they all seemed to contradict one another.

I was a very impressionable student, eager to learn as much as I could and motivated to impress my teachers. Each instructor would present a particular theory that he or she believed was *the* answer. Research would be supplied to support the particular choice. Case examples of miracle cures further impressed me with how superior this theory was to all others. In no time, I was convinced that I had finally found *the truth*.

My moments of revelation would last about as long as it took to arrive at my next class in which the instructor would be equally persuasive. An alternative theory would be presented that directly refuted the premises of the previous one. Naturally, I would resist attempts to convert me to the enemy camp, but I soon found myself a true believer of another theory.

I won't bore you with the lengthy journey I have traveled down the road to theory enlightenment. When you consider that there are hundreds of distinct theories that have been catalogued you can appreciate just how long it would take to sample all of them. Even if you narrow the choices to the dozen most popular approaches, you would still need a few lifetimes to do them justice.

I am not exaggerating when I say that, at one time or another, I have followed the tenets of at least a dozen or more of the theories contained in this book. I loved them all! And I found they all worked most of the time.

I've long found it amusing when I have read reviews of my books and found myself classified as psychodynamic, while another reviewer called me existential, and still another labeled me cognitive behavioral. I have been introduced at conferences where I speak as a noted feminist or humanistic or social justice advocate. I was once invited to demonstrate my theory of counseling on in a video series and, although flattered, started to panic because I didn't know what my theory was called.

"Well, Kottler," the producer said, "you are sort of existential, kind of humanistic, but also cognitive ..."

"Yeah," I interrupted, "so what do we *call* my theory?"

It was eventually called "integrative counseling" because, after all, that is really what most practitioners actually do behind closed doors: We use whatever fits the situation, whatever the client needs, and whatever might work given the client's background, culture, presenting complaints, and particular needs.

Marilyn's Story

In some ways, Jeffrey and I are like two sides of a coin—and this is one of them. Rather than being the scourge of my life, theories, and theory per se, intrigue me.

I had a meandering career as a clerk in a tire factory, a secondary teacher, a private music teacher, and a freelance writer before I went to graduate school and officially got into the business of research, writing, and higher education. During that early time, "theory" and all things related to it were usually referred to by my acquaintances in terms of gentle derision; references to "theory" were usually paired with an image of someone so lost in abstract ideas that they would forget to tie their shoes or bore other people to death when they talked. My own understanding of theory came on slowly—and later.

As a young adult, I lived in a small rural town for a number of years. There was not much to do and no work in my field, so I started reading every book in the library (which was not hard—and yes, this was before the Internet) on development and human meaning. I had lots of questions—what makes a good life? What is "normal"? How do people turn out the way they do? Can they change? What, in the range of human potentials, is noble and worth aspiring to? Is that potential there for all? What does experience and life circumstance have to do with it?

I overwhelmed myself pretty fast because I found out that there were as many different answers to these questions as there were books in the library. But then I realized that many different views could be grouped together in their similarities, and that made it a little easier. I started to see that assumptions or "big ideas" lay under each writer's propositions, such as "humans are basically good" versus "humans are neither bad nor good; their experiences make them what they are." Then, I could think about whether I agreed or disagreed with that—which allowed me to gradually narrow down what I really wanted to learn more about, and from whom. Thus, theory was a thread that I could follow through the dense and sometimes scary forest of contradictory ideas. Now, I find theory to be both an exciting and comforting thing. A theory gives you a structure from which to tell a story. It helps you notice important things and leave other things in the background. It highlights how things are connected—which is more tasteful to me than gazing at chaos. I tend to like "grand theories" that explain a whole lot, probably because I also like epic movies and novels with a broad sweep of history, characters, and history-changing events. And I love how, in the end, you can see all the connections.

FOR PERSONAL REFLECTION or CLASS ACTIVITY

Either in your journal or with a small group of peers, talk about the reactions you have to the authors' confessions. How do they compare with what you have experienced thus far in your life and in your training? Talk about your own journey toward theory development, including your major points of confusion and frustration.

SO MANY CHOICES, SO LITTLE TIME

Jeffrey's Story

I started with psychoanalytic theory because that was the approach taken by the first therapist I saw while I was a college student. I had been heart-broken by a girlfriend, so depressed I could barely get out of bed. I visited the counseling center on campus in a last, desperate effort to prevent myself from dropping out of school. The therapist was so understanding, so responsive—the mother I had always wanted. We spent a lot of time talking about my childhood and how those experiences shaped the problems I was encountering in the present. After reading the collected works of Freud and many of his disciples, I decided to follow in the footsteps of my therapist and become a psychoanalytic therapist.

My first job as a crisis intervention counselor was quite at odds with the theory to which I had decided to devote my life. Here, I was in a situation trying to help people who were overdosing on drugs or trying to kill themselves. Even if I could get them to pay attention for more than a minute at a time, they had very little interest in their dreams, unconscious, or repressed impulses; all they wanted was a little relief from their suffering—and they wanted it immediately.

I became a behaviorist within days of starting my job. I usually had only one session, or maybe two—sometimes just a brief phone call—in which to offer help. I learned rather quickly to identify specific treatment goals, identify effective reinforcers, and help people to set up some self-management plan to deal with their problems. Then I would refer them to a support group.

I read everything I could get my hands on about behavioral theory. I loved its specificity and concreteness. I felt so grateful for the structure that it offered, especially for a beginner like me who was trying to make sense of this mysterious process that everyone explained so differently. Moreover, I liked the way I could define specific goals and then measure the extent to which my efforts were helpful.

When I began graduate school, my advisor was a cognitive therapist, so that is what I became next. I desperately wanted his approval, and because he believed that behavioral theory was so limited, I could not help but agree with him. Once he demonstrated the theory in action by helping me work through a long-standing family problem in a single hour, I was truly blown away. I went to workshops on cognitive approaches and did my best to become an expert, even volunteering to be a client with Albert Ellis on stage during demonstrations. Just as convincing was how effective the approach seemed to be with the clients I was beginning to see as part of my training.

If we had more time together, I could elaborate further about how many theories I have followed during my career. From cognitive theory, I adopted the person-centered approach and then Gestalt therapy and existential therapy. I loved each of them—loved them all!

In later years, as I progressed through a master's and doctoral program and worked in a dozen different jobs, I became a full-fledged, card-carrying, transpersonal, strategic, and constructivist practitioner. I have attended workshops on a dozen other conceptual approaches, finding all of them useful with my clients. As my work evolved from individual and group sessions to community activism and advocacy programs in remote villages around the world, and as I began focusing on refugee trauma, I necessarily adapted all I had learned previously to settings in which traditional interventions and mainstream theories would have been useless and inappropriate. I am a work in progress, always evolving what I know and understand as my work demands it—and as my life priorities change.

Marilyn's Story

As I mentioned before, I like epic movies and novels (with the scope and reach of *Star Wars*); this has been true since I was a teenager. So, I have always liked grand theories and would be happy if someday those following in Albert Einstein's or Stephen Hawking's footsteps do indeed come up with a theory of everything.

While I began building on my previous careers to become a counselor, I was also caring for my own young children. Their development—and their similarities and differences—fascinated me, so developmental theories were my first love. I found Erikson's lifespan development theory to make a lot of sense as I watched my children grow; Bowenian family systems ideas did too, as I saw how all the individuals in my family impacted each other across generations. I did a lot of parent education training (this naturally followed from trying to do a better job with my own kids) and this led me into Adlerian theory. I followed the roots of all three of these theories back to psychodynamic theories, where I found explanations for why people are who they are and do what they do.

In addition to having a taste for breadth and depth, I am also pragmatic and I like simple, elegant solutions to problems when they can be found. In graduate school, I found myself hanging around the family therapy training clinic where there was a strong emphasis on brief approaches; I began experimenting with those and got good results. Later, while working with teenage girls using alcohol and other drugs, I became intrigued with approaches that help people *want* to change. Living in the midst of tremendous diversity, relational cultural theory gave me an aspirational roadmap for how I want my close relationships, classes, and workgroups to be. And lately I have been thinking a lot about the heart of the matter, of life and of this profession, which leads me to an appreciation for the existential and humanistic theories that prize deep and genuine contact with self and others. While this probably sounds "hodgepodge," it all comes together into a good working base that feels like "me" and helps me be my best with others.

FOR PERSONAL REFLECTION

You must already have some hunches about the kinds of theories, or explanations, you tend to like. You may already be very familiar with some. Share with your classmates what you already know about and what would make a theory personally appealing to you.

We are both now rather integrative therapists as far as theory goes, but earlier there were points where confusion settled in. You will probably feel the same as you read this book and take in one good theory after another. All these theories seem so different, yet they all seem to work well. How can this possibly be true? To make matters worse, at times all the theories sound the same—it is hard to keep them separate and remember where one ends and the other begins.

Like most experienced practitioners, we have tried to integrate the best features of each theory we studied. We have each borrowed a little here, changed a few ideas there, and combined the parts we liked most into frameworks that seemed to work best with our personality and style, as well as with our clients. Since beginning this synthesis many years ago, we are still making refinements in our personal "working" theories in light of new ideas that emerge, new research that is published, and new experiences we accumulate with our clients. In Jeffrey's case, the changes have been so vast that clients he saw 10 years ago might not recognize his work today! In Marilyn's case, there is a recognizable thread that runs through her work with clients, but her thinking about how and why her techniques work has evolved. Rather than apologizing for this evolution, we are proud, delighted, and challenged by the ever-changing nature of this profession. You will be too—once you overcome some of your confusion, uncertainty, doubts, and fears.

FOR A FIELD STUDY

Approach several practitioners who are doing what you hope to do someday. Ask them about the evolution of their conceptual development. Rather than keeping the conversation solely on an intellectual level, as if their theories were selected purely based on logical choices, inquire about the personal motives and factors that influenced their theoretical development. Find out what critical incidents shaped their ideas about how therapy works best.

HOW TO GET THE MOST FROM THIS COURSE AND TEXT

The main challenge of this course is that there is *so* much material to learn and so little time in which to learn it. You will be studying theories not only to understand their roots, to pass an exam, or to write a paper, but also to *apply* them effectively. Very soon you will be sitting opposite clients who look to you for relief from their pain. They want you to explain what is wrong with them. They expect you to make their problems go away. They demand to know what you are going to do and how you are going to do it. And you had better have some answers—not only in addressing their concerns, but also in delivering what you promise. Unless you have mastered a theory to make sense of what is happening and organize your interventions, not only won't you help people, but you can also make things a lot worse.

We will do our best to "sell" each of the theories in this text. We will be as persuasive as we can to convince you why a theory is wonderful, how much it offers, and all the neat stuff it provides in the way of guidance. Then, in the very next chapter, we will present *another* theory that sounds just as good. Then another, and another.

Our recommendation is to treat each of the theories as valuable and important. Assume that every prominent approach is popular because many experienced professionals have found it effective. Know that current research has failed to support the superiority of any one of these theories over all the rest (although some are better than others for some situations and issues). That is not to say that you will *like* each of them; on the contrary, some will immediately attract you and others will strike you as silly or irrelevant or not at all representative of your experience. That is very good news because it will make your job so much easier in narrowing down the options to those that fit best with your interests, specialty, personality, and desired job setting.

As you read this text, we invite you to consider the following advice about approaching this subject:

1. *Think critically about what you read.* Don't take our word for what is presented. Compare the ideas to your own experience. But don't argue with us or your instructor; argue with yourself.
2. *Notice what you resonate with and what you don't.* Pay attention to your gut-level feelings as you learn about a theory or see it in action. These feelings are related to your core beliefs and assumptions about which deserve to be honored.

3. *Talk about the concepts with family members and friends.* Take the ideas home with you. Don't just compartmentalize what you are learning; if you do, you may end up leaving loved ones behind.

4. *Keep up with your reading.* This is not the sort of course in which you can wait until the last minute to prepare for a test or assignment.

5. *Form a study group with classmates.* It is important for you to find and create opportunities to talk about what you are learning and to apply ideas to your work and life.

6. *Do the exercises and activities.* Throughout the text there are numerous "time-outs" for reflection, field studies, class activities, and homework assignments. If your goal is to make this stuff part of you, you must make an effort to personalize the concepts.

7. *Manage your frustration and stress levels.* There is far too much content in this book for any one human being to master in a lifetime, much less in a single semester. Be patient and realistic with yourself about what you can do.

8. *Understand that you have the rest of your career to study a few of these theories in depth.* For now, your job is to get the basics down so that you have a working background in which to apply one or two theories with reasonable effectiveness.

9. *Make learning an active process.* Take responsibility for applying what you read and do in class to your daily life.

Keep in mind that one of the consequences of training to be a counselor or therapist is that you will change fairly dramatically. In this theory course alone, you will be exposed to many new ideas that will reshape the way you look at the world and yourself. In addition, therapist preparation places great emphasis on developing greater intimacy in relationships, being more honest and direct, and using a variety of interpersonal skills to communicate more powerfully and persuasively. If you don't think this will change all your relationships, you aren't paying attention.

This book is subtitled, "an experiential approach" because we believe that it is through direct, meaningful, personal experiences that you are most likely to internalize and apply the ideas that are presented. When the course is over, you will discard your notes (and perhaps this book) and move on to the next semester. You will have new and more advanced topics to consider. Yet the theoretical concepts introduced to you during the next weeks provide the foundation for all that will follow. For that reason, it is important to actively engage with others—classmates, family, friends—about what you are learning. Find reasons and excuses to talk about those concepts you find intriguing, as well as those that are most perplexing.

FOR HOMEWORK

Sometime in the next 24 hours, initiate a conversation with a friend or family member, preferably in person rather than on the phone, about something interesting you learned in class or in the text this week. Make sure this is an interactive encounter in which you not only talk about your experience, but you also invite the other(s) to share his or her ideas, thoughts, or feelings on the subject.

AN EXPERIENTIAL APPROACH TO YOUR PERSONAL THEORY

As we've mentioned, this text takes a very personal approach to the subject of theory. We favor this method not only because it makes learning fun, but also because active involvement is required to help the ideas stick with you over time. After all, you won't do your clients much good if sometime in the future you have only vague notions about how to make sound clinical decisions. With active involvement, you might not remember all the names of things, but you'll recall the principles that guide your professional choices.

This sort of experiential approach is consistent with what is known about how human learning takes place. Real change don't only occur on an intellectual level, but it also involves a person's whole being. This is the case not only with how you do counseling and therapy, but also how you learn to do it.

In order for you to become thoroughly familiar with the major theoretical structures that guide therapeutic action, you will need to study the material so that it becomes personally meaningful to you. First, as you are well aware, you tend to remember those ideas that seem most relevant as well as those that you can use daily. Second, you will need to understand the theories to the point that you can talk about them intelligently to colleagues, explain them to clients, and combine the best features of divergent approaches into a coherent framework to guide your actions.

An experiential approach to this subject means that you must have direct and intimate connections with the content, not as something that is "out there," but as something that is part of you. It is not enough to *know* the ideas; you must use them in your daily functioning. The theories become integrated into the routine and normal ways that you relate to the world.

How does this transformation occur that transcends mere superficial learning such as memorization or recall? Deep learning takes place through direct experience in which you become actively involved in the process. You can't learn this stuff merely by reading about it, or by sitting still in a seat while an instructor—no matter how entertaining and interesting—tells you about it. Seeing demonstrations of the theories in action and watching videos of master practitioners are also extremely useful in making the ideas come alive, but this still doesn't engage you actively to personalize what you are learning.

FOR A CLASS ACTIVITY

Talk to one another about the ways you find most effective for learning new, complex ideas. Think about one specific instance in which you felt particularly successful in this regard and provide examples of what helped you the most to retain the learning.

As a counterpoint, talk about times that you learned things to pass an exam or get through a series of obstacles, but the results were not enduring. Compare the two experiences and come to your own conclusions about what matters most for your learning.

In order for you to hold onto this content for the rest of your life, you must integrate the new material with what you already know. Then you have to figure out ways to combine the material with reality-based practice. The theories that will be most enduring in your work will be those that fit with your experience. They explain things that make sense to you. They predict behavior accurately. They are congruent with the ways you view the world. Finally, the theories you integrate in making good decisions and doing your job most effectively will make you a convincing and effective therapist.

To aid you with this challenging mission, each chapter contains a number of experientially based activities, assignments, and reflective exercises that are designed to help you not only remember the theories, but also apply them where they can help the most. We can't stress how important it is that you complete these assignments so that the active process of learning continues even when you aren't studying the text.

To help you begin the difficult job of organizing the material you read and linking related concepts from different approaches, this text treats various theories in broad categories. Throughout your exposure to each individual approach, you will also begin looking at how it is similar to and different from others.

We will do our best to maintain your interest by including lots of stories, case examples, practical applications, and humor. It will be your job to relate what you learn to what you already know, what you are doing in your life, and what you hope to do in the future.

REMINDERS OF HOW TO STUDY THEORY

1. Read consistently and steadily throughout the semester.
2. Think critically about what you read, and pay attention to how you resonate with it, too.
3. Talk about the concepts with family members and friends.
4. Form a study group with classmates to talk about the ideas.
5. Complete the exercises and activities.
6. Manage your frustration and stress levels so that you remain patient and realistic about what can be done.
7. Get the basics down and then focus on a few theories that appeal most to you.
8. Take responsibility for applying what you read and do in class to your daily life.

SUGGESTED READINGS

Halbur, D., & Halbur, K. V. (2014). *Developing your theoretical orientation in counseling and psychotherapy* (3rd ed.). Upper Saddle River, NJ: Pearson.

Kottler, J. A. (2017). *On being a therapist* (5th ed.). New York, NY: Oxford University Press.

Pipher, M. (2016). *Letters to a young therapist: Stories of hope and healing.* New York, NY: Basic Books.

Yalom, I. (2017). *The gift of therapy: An open letter to a new generation of therapists and their patients.* New York, NY: Harper Collins.

CHAPTER 2

Theory in Context

LEARNING OBJECTIVES

After reading this chapter, you should be able to do the following:

1. Sketch the changes of theoretical notions of healing across history.
2. List specific ways that working from a theory helps practitioners.
3. Describe how theories are applied in treatment planning and current clinical contexts.
4. Identify key tenets of ethical practice that apply across theoretical approaches.
5. Describe how client diversity requires adjustments in the application of theoretical approaches.
6. Recount how diverse aspects of your own culture, values, and traits influence your theoretical preferences.
7. Identify ways in which managed care practices and pressures work efficiently influence theory choice.
8. Articulate the association between assessment and diagnostic requirements that impact theory choice.
9. Evaluate the impact of technology on contemporary clients and counselors' approach.
10. Describe trends toward integration and synthesis of theories that influence current practice.

You are sitting in session with a client who does not seem to be cooperating with your best efforts to get him talking about his childhood abuse. In previous sessions he has been quite willing to explore his traumatic past; in fact, he brought up the issue as something he wanted to work on. In the last meeting, you experienced a bit of a breakthrough as the man was able to recover lots of memories that had previously been buried. But now he seems reluctant to continue further. He appears listless and depressed, not at all like his usual demeanor. Finally, after sitting quietly for some minutes, he suddenly looks up at you and starts screaming that you've betrayed him. Quick! What do you do?

This five-minute scenario is not unlike any critical incident that will arise in a session. Something happens that seems puzzling, or at least unanticipated. You know you have to do something to intervene, but you can't act until you first figure out what is going on. In other words, you rely on some theory to account for the phenomenon and then to guide your efforts to intervene most effectively.

FOR PERSONAL REFLECTION

What do you think transpired in this brief episode to explain why this client returned so uncooperative and volatile? Although you have limited information and don't know the context for the behavior, that does not stop you from form- ing hypotheses to explain confusing situations.

Someone may cut you off on the freeway, and although you don't know the first thing about this person, you still have a theory to explain the erratic behavior—he didn't see you, he was drunk, or he's the sort of person who doesn't care about others. Someone else does you a favor and you also have a theory to explain the gesture, even with limited data.

Based on the sparse information at your disposal in this therapeutic scenario, what is your best guess about what may be going on?

How do you trace the origins of this belief—from what reasoning did it evolve?

There are many legitimate hypotheses that might explain this client's behavior. Perhaps things got a little too threatening last time and defenses are kicking in to protect him from further perceived assaults. Or maybe he is mad at you about something else that is completely unrelated to the prior incidents. Another possibility is that something came up during the week that led him to mistrust you. Maybe he went home, talked about the session, and his spouse told him it was all bunk and he'd need to stop his therapy. There are probably a hundred other possibilities, each of which might logically follow the reasoning of a practitioner who identifies those factors that seem most significant and relevant.

All actions taken by a therapist depend on the particular theory that is adopted as an organizing framework. In this example, the clinician happens to hold some strong beliefs about what is good for people, how they best change, and what interferes with that progress. Furthermore, there are very well-developed conceptions about what causes resistance and how it must be overcome. Even the belief that resistance is something that exists in reality stems from a theory that is being followed.

A NARRATIVE OF THEORY-IN-ACTION

This chapter continues with a description and review of what counseling and psychotherapy are all about and what practitioners actually do. Based on interviews with therapists in a variety of settings, the concepts in this chapter are highlighted with first-person narratives about the ways that theory is most often employed.

In the opening example that began the chapter, the therapist shares what she was thinking at the time:

> *If you want to know the truth, I don't know what was going on inside my head when this happened. I felt scared. I was so disappointed and hurt that the progress I thought we'd made was now washed out. I also felt misunderstood and attacked.*
>
> *After I calmed down—and I knew I had to do this because he was getting progressively more agitated—I tried to reason through what he might be saying, or really, what he wanted from me. I had to stall first to buy some time.*
>
> *It's hard, really, to sort out what I was thinking at the time versus what I thought afterward. I've had lots of time to think about this case and talked to lots of colleagues about it to get their perspective on things. You can't believe how many different opinions I've gotten. … Okay, maybe you can imagine it.*
>
> *In the session itself, I went back to basics, which is what I always do when I'm stuck or feel panicky. I reflected what I was feeling and sensing from him, hoping not only to gather my wits about me, but also to clarify further what he might be experiencing. He had obviously been having trouble putting it into words.*

Let's interrupt the narrative at this point to highlight how different this session would look on the outside from how it feels to the practitioner on the inside. If you were watching this interaction on video, all you'd see in the space of a few minutes is the client yelling at his therapist and the therapist responding calmly and deliberately. Inside, however, the therapist is experiencing a storm of feelings, searching desperately for the "right" handle on what she is facing. Until she can sort out what is really happening, she won't have a remote possibility of choosing the best intervention.

> *I just knew I'd pushed him too far last time. When the previous session was over, I felt so exhilarated about the progress we'd made but I also felt apprehensive because we'd opened up so many doors. All this stuff from the past just flooded out of him. And I had no idea what he'd do with it all after he left.*

Now, here are some clearer inklings of this clinician's theoretical orientation. First, she seems to believe that dealing with material from the past is important to resolve current issues. Not every practitioner subscribes to this theory, but it is not an uncommon way to proceed. Second, she has some relatively clear notions about what might be contributing to his unusual behavior, labeling it "defensive" and "resistant." She is, thus, not taking what is happening at face value but believes that there is some underlying process going on.

The therapist considered other theoretical frameworks as well to explain the situation, those that look at the systemic context of the behavior (its meaning in light of his other relationships) and its secondary gains (the hidden benefits). In other words, in the span of just a few minutes, she reviewed almost everything she could think of that might be useful.

FOR PERSONAL REFLECTION

It is helpful to get into the habit of processing puzzling interactions after they occur. This involves not only playing back what was said and what things looked like, but also how they felt to you inside.

Think of a time recently in which you were involved in some struggle or conflict with someone that ended unsatisfactorily. Review that interaction by focusing on some probable hypotheses to explain why things turned out the way they did. Avoid placing blame on yourself or the other person(s) and instead try to make sense of what happened. Pay particular attention to what you were feeling and thinking at the time.

If time and circumstances permit, share this incident and your analysis with a partner. Recruit his or her assistance in formulating a theory to account for the incident. If you were going to revisit the struggle with the intention of improving the outcome, what might you do that is consistent with your theory?

This sort of internal processing is exactly the kind of thing that you will experience firsthand when you are in the helper's chair. Just about every minute, something will happen that you don't understand. About every two or three minutes, you will have to make some response or therapeutic intervention. In each case, you will need some organizing framework that will guide your thinking and actions.

WHAT THEORY WILL DO FOR YOU

A theory is an organized series of propositions that help you explain phenomena, predict behavior, and inform your decisions. Rather than a stable conception, it constantly undergoes revisions in light of new experiences.

What all this means is that you have a hundred theories that you operate from every day of your life. You have a theory about why you do not always get what you want. You have a theory about why there are lousy drivers on the road. You have theories about the way the world works, the way business gets done, and how people should behave. You even have a theory about the best way to get people to do what you want. The main difference between your theories and those you will read about in this book is that you have not spent the time to research your ideas systematically, to organize and field-test them, and then to record them for others to use. If you are serious about becoming a skilled practitioner, that is going to change.

Theory serves a number of different functions for practitioners of most professions, whether that involves architectural plans, legal cases, or therapeutic relationships. Theory is helpful in that it does the following:

1. Organizes and synthesizes information in such a way to make it more readily accessible
2. Provides a blueprint for action, plotting choices available based on what is believed to be good for people
3. Helps us to stay on track, assessing outcomes in light of stated goals
4. Directs attention to selective data that are deemed most useful
5. Guides the development of new ideas and interventions that are consistent with standard practices
6. Encourages continued research to test hypotheses and formulate new questions for investigation
7. Helps communicate ideas in a cohesive, organized way

As you can see, theory can unify what we do, both as individual practitioners and as experts advancing the field of psychotherapy. Theory is one strand in *the golden thread* that runs through and connects the many activities of the counselor. The metaphor of a golden thread was borrowed from the practice of law (think of the tight chain of evidence that leads to an incontrovertible conviction) and now is applied in many settings to help people connect aims and strategies with results. Figure 2.1 shows how theory can function as the core of the golden thread that tightens and aligns everything counselors do, from assessment and diagnosis, to treatment planning, to delivering interventions and documenting client progress.

In addition, to be perfectly honest (which we will try to be throughout our journey together) theoretical frameworks appease the feelings of uncertainty and anxiety practitioners experience when facing complex, intractable problems during sessions.

FIGURE 2.1. The Golden Thread.

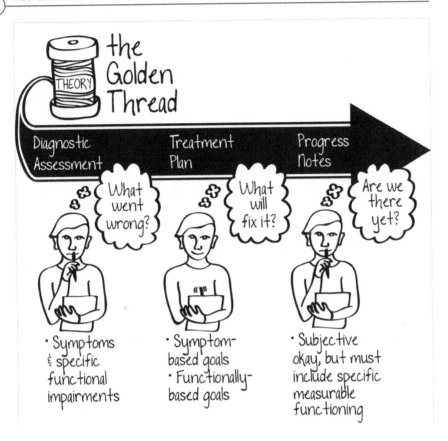

IS A THEORIES COURSE OBSOLETE?

Some would wonder if it is now obsolete to present theories of intervention as discrete entities. For one, most practitioners are eclectic and integrative and tend to borrow strategies from several approaches in their work, depending on what the situation calls for. Second, treatment manuals have been developed to describe specific interventions for particular problems, say, exposure techniques for anxiety or behavioral techniques for sexual dysfunctions. Third, theories are rarely practiced in pure form anymore. The most orthodox psychoanalysts now abbreviate treatment in some cases, as well as employ a variety of methods borrowed from other approaches. In addition, prominent theorists now sit on panel discussions together and interact with one another in spirited debates, all the while incorporating one another's ideas in their own work. There is very little purity any longer, even by the theorists who invented the models.

Finally, the emphasis on more efficient, abbreviated treatments has forced practitioners to be far more flexible, pragmatic, and brief in what they do.

There are limits to any helping approach and there are times when it is neither feasible, nor appropriate, to follow the standard prescribed regimen. We are required to make adjustments, not only to the client and situation, but also to better meld with our own strengths and weaknesses. Some of us just aren't all that comfortable doing some of the things that are considered an integral part of the approach, and so we customize it to make it fit better.

There has also been a consistent movement toward a generic approach to training, driven not only by research but also accrediting bodies that recommend standardized curricula. Any particular course you now take includes facets from many different theoretical families. In a techniques class, for instance, you will most likely learn reflecting feelings (person centered), interpreting (psychoanalytic), goal setting (behavioral), reframing (strategic), role-playing (Gestalt), disputing beliefs (cognitive), and others.

Although there is a push toward finding generic skills and standardized treatments for a host of clinical situations, most practitioners still favor a particular school of thought as a conceptual base. You don't need to be a card-carrying member of a specific school to use the ideas as an organizing framework to assess and treat client complaints. Moreover, the study of the various theories provides a historical context for present standards of practice and future developments.

A REVIEW OF BASIC HISTORY

Reviewing the contents of this or almost any book on theories of psychotherapy, it would appear as if the field began with Sigmund Freud's pioneering efforts to invent what he referred to as "the talking cure." In fact, the next chapter does begin by introducing psychoanalysis as the first "official" systematic model of intervention. But this is a gross simplification. The modern era of psychological helping may have started when Freud and his collaborator Josef Breuer first began experimenting with hypnosis to relieve people of their annoying problems, but the story actually begins a long time prior to that.

We think it is important to share a little about the historical context for the theories you are about to study. We hope that you will see that each theory came to life at a particular time and through particular pressures and opportunities in society that were not available before. Each theorist works out ideas about how change takes place and presents them persuasively, and with great confidence—otherwise they would not have survived. As you read about them, you'll encounter things that seem confusing and contradictory. At times you'll wonder how a particular theory ever made it into the mainstream in the first place! Keep in mind that through the ages there have always been individuals who have believed with all their hearts that they have finally found the path to truth, and others have believed them, too. As you'll see in our field, the drive to invent a new approach is fueled by the desire to help individuals whose cases are most perplexing and resistant to treatments that are known—so far.

When you study the theories that currently exert the most influence on contemporary practice, remember that 100 years from now our colleagues will most likely laugh uproariously at the methods we were using as being primitive and archaic. Remember that our discipline is only a little more than a century old; just a few generations ago our professional forbearers attempted to cure people solely through talking about their dreams on a couch. This was a time before antidepressant medications, before generic helping skills, and before supervision was possible by reviewing recordings. It was a time when progress in sessions was measured in years rather than weeks.

FOR PERSONAL REFLECTION or A GROUP ACTIVITY

Either on your own, or with several partners, make a list of everyday practices that you believe will be laughably obsolete in 20 years. Make some predictions about what you think the future holds for some aspects of our current existence. For instance, do you think we will still be transported from one place to another by automobiles? What will be the state of communication devices? More relevant to our present subject, how so you believe the practice of therapy will become transformed?

As part of our historical review, let's go back a few centuries to a time when there was a major outbreak of disturbing psychological maladies. If you were so unfortunate to have been experiencing these symptoms during the 15th century, it is highly likely that both your diagnosis and your treatment would have consisted of "trial by water." We know this sounds like a better option than being burned at the stake, but only as a matter of personal preference. When someone was suspected of manifesting identifiable signs of weirdness, she would be trussed up and tossed in the nearest lake. If this patient sank to the bottom and drowned, then it was obvious (after the fact) that she had not actually been afflicted with any sort of malady. If, however, the unfortunate subject should float—a most difficult undertaking with one's feet tied to one's hands—then the diagnosis was clear that she was a witch and she was *then* burned at the stake.

This was not the most compassionate of therapies but it was certainly effective in discouraging further outbreaks of the symptoms, or in drawing too much attention to yourself. If you think this treatment was cruel and archaic, consider that in the centuries preceding it, bloodletting was the most reliable cure employed. And before that, going back to ancient times, a whole host of nasty brews were created to cure emotional suffering. Even this would have been a significant improvement over the techniques employed by our cave-dwelling ancestors. Skulls have been found with holes drilled in them, presumably intended to let the demons escape.

It was actually the generation before and during Freud's work when the most dramatic improvement in mental health services was recorded. Philosophers such as John Locke and Jean-Jacques Rousseau were preaching the merits of enlightenment. The scientific method was just coming into its own as a preferred avenue of investigation. Anton Mesmer (recall the term *mesmerized*) and Jean-Martin Charcot (one of Freud's first teachers in medical school) began experimenting with hypnosis as a means for treating mental disorders.

They might have been getting impressive results from their clinical methods, but the theories they advocated to explain the outcomes were somewhat amusing. Mesmer, for example, believed that people were possessed in varying degrees with something called "animal magnetism," a kind of fluid that fills the universe and acts as a conduit between people, the Earth, and heavenly bodies. Using a collection of magnets, flowing water, and a stage that would rival magicians, Mesmer managed to restore the sight of (supposedly) blind people, cure depression, and do anything within the power of a contemporary faith healer. He may not have understood how he worked his healing powers, but he did produce results.

One can only imagine what historians will say about our own theories used to explain how and why people change. In addition, some of our most universally accepted policies, such as the idea that sessions should be 50 minutes in duration, have little empirical support; they are just conventions or habits that have been adopted for convenience because they offer optimal outcomes. We do suggest that you retain a degree of caution, humility, and skepticism as you examine the ideas now believed to form the backbone of helping. It all seems to make sense to us now, but so did bloodletting, witch burning, and animal magnetism to our ancestral therapists.

FOR PERSONAL REFLECTION or DISCUSSION

Even this early in your study of the profession there must be certain aspects of the therapeutic process that strike you as peculiar, if not less than optimally effective. For instance, does it really make sense to you that the best way to learn to be a therapist is reading a book like this or sitting in a classroom listening to someone talk to you about it? Do you think the best way to help someone deal with a lifelong problem is to sit in chairs and talk about these troubles?

What are some of the ideas, concepts, procedures, rituals, or conventions that are part of the profession that you question, or at least wonder, about their validity and appropriateness? If you think creatively, or at least outside the box, what are some other ways you might imagine the helping process could unfold that is different than current accepted standards?

POINTS OF AGREEMENT

You could very well get the idea that practitioners don't agree on very much in this field, that there are a dozen or more different theories to explain most phenomena and apply to most situations. Although that is indeed true to a certain extent, there is also a consensus among practitioners about consistent standards of practice. It's important that we review points of agreement among almost all practitioners before we begin looking at some of the conceptual differences.

Ethical Practice

If you look at the ethical codes of all the different helping professions, whether in counseling, psychology, family therapy, social work, or psychiatry, you will see virtually unanimous agreement about what constitutes appropriate behavior. The basic rule of thumb is that you don't do anything that might harm someone else, either as a result of neglect, incompetence, negligence, or meeting your own needs. Furthermore, therapists are expected to act with the highest standard of moral conviction, fighting against injustice, prejudice, and oppression.

Regardless of the setting in which you practice, the clients with whom you work, and the methods you might employ, your behavior is expected to be consistent with the following ethical principles:

1. *Informed consent.* Clients have a right to make their own choices regarding their treatment, based on accurate information.

2. *Confidentiality.* Conversations are held in the strictest confidence and the client's right to privacy is protected, except under those circumstances in which the client might be a danger to himself or herself or others.

3. *Dual relationships.* Because therapists are in positions of power over clients, such circumstances may lead to exploitation. Therapists are prohibited from taking advantage of their clients in any way.

4. *Competence.* Therapists are not permitted to practice outside the scope of their training and preparation. This means therapists may engage only in those methods for which they are qualified.

5. *Respect for differences.* Each client comes to the relationship with a unique personal and cultural background. Therapists make every effort to respect the client's worldview and to refrain from imposing their personal values on others.

Beyond the general agreement about the ethics of therapy, there are other points that need to be considered about the intersection of theory and good and moral conduct. Does it surprise you to know that particular practices or tenets of some theories might conflict with ethical standards or laws that govern how you practice? For example, narrative therapy holds sacred a belief that an individual's problems are as much a result of internalized scripts from the larger culture as they are some absolute thing in objective reality. This constructivist approach suggests that the stories we hold and tell ourselves are, in a sense, "constructions" that are somewhat limiting. This also holds true with respect to so-called "diagnoses," which are simplified labels that significantly distort and marginalize people. So, here's the problem: You may be required to assign a diagnostic label to a client in order for this person to receive treatment, but in doing so you also violate a core belief that is part of your operating theory. We encourage you to be on the lookout for similar internal conflicts as we move through the theories in this book.

FOR PERSONAL REFLECTION

Among the major ethical challenges you will face are those that involve practicing within the scope of your competence. This means that before you attempt any intervention or therapeutic strategy, you must first receive sufficient training and supervision in its use.

Imagine that an issue comes up in session that leads into an area that you know little about, for instance, impulse disorders or side effects from antidepressants. It is important that you appear to know what you are doing to instill confidence in your ability to be helpful. Yet you also want to be completely honest regarding your relative ignorance about these issues.

The easy part is what you *say* you would do. The correct response, of course, is to admit that this is outside your area of expertise and then to seek additional supervision before the next session. At the very least, you would stall until you could do your homework. Much more challenging, however, is what you would actually do in the session because there is sometimes a large discrepancy between what people say (their espoused theory and beliefs) and what they practice.

Cultural Diversity

As societies the world over have become more culturally diverse, therapists have had to become increasingly flexible, sensitive, and responsive to this variety of backgrounds and experiences. Theories must be elastic enough to accommodate individuals and families who hold very different values and present issues that must be understood within different contexts. In the case example that began this chapter of the angry man who felt betrayed, the way you interpret this behavior may very well be influenced by the cultural background of the participants. What if the client was African American, Native American, or Latino, and the therapist was of European descent? How would that put a different slant on the perception of betrayal? Or what if the differences between client and therapist were reflected in their sexual orientation, socioeconomic status, gender, or religious beliefs? Such client/ therapist cultural differences can both detract from or enhance treatment, and they absolutely must be considered while making sense of the behavior and choosing how to respond.

Imagine, in another example, the ways that two different clients might present symptoms of depression, as well as attempt to cope with the difficulties. The first individual, a white male electrician in his 40s, has been referred because of two convictions of driving while under the influence of alcohol. He does not see himself as depressed even though he hates his job, his youngest child is dying of leukemia, and he drinks himself to sleep each night. The second case involves a 16-year-old Chinese American girl who attempted suicide after receiving a B+ on an assignment in school. "I just can't accept this," she tells you with tears in her eyes, "and neither will my parents." To complicate matters further, imagine a Vietnamese American client who experiences what we call depression as a pain in her chest. She goes to see a cardiologist who can find nothing wrong with her yet she insists her heart aches.

FOR A CLASS ACTIVITY

Talk about the ways you might treat these cases of depression differently. Based on the clients' ages, genders, ethnicity, life situations, and their perceptions, how would you adapt your therapeutic approach to fit their needs?

Just as with any person who might seek your help, theories must be adapted to the client's unique cultural view of the world. Most contemporary books on the subject of theory make some effort to address this challenging issue, even if efforts often fall short. So often culture is spoken of in terms of ethnicity, race, religion, gender, or socioeconomic status. Yet each of us is composed of multiple cultural identities that represent who we are, including all kinds of other factors such as our geography, university alumni, hobbies, interests, social groups, neighborhoods, and families.

As you study the various theories presented in this text and elsewhere in your career, you will want to remember that each of these conceptions represents its own cultural worldview about the nature of reality, what gives life its greatest meaning, and what is good for people. Because these philosophies were developed by theorists who have their own personal notions about the world, they may be at odds with others who come from different backgrounds. This text will discuss this challenge further in almost every chapter that follows.

FOR PERSONAL REFLECTION

Consider the factors that are most influential in shaping your own cultural worldview. If you were going to see a counselor or therapist for help about a personal issue in your life, what would this professional need to know and understand about your own background to be helpful to you?

Fill in the basics about yourself as follows:

1. *Gender.* How was the conception of yourself as a man or woman or non-binary in your life? Who have been your primary role models?

2. *Sexual identity.* What is your sexual identity? This includes your sexual preferences as they have been part of your ongoing development.
3. *Ethnicity and racial heritage.* Going back in your family history, what have been the strongest influences in how you identify yourself culturally? What does this mean to you?
4. *Religious and spiritual beliefs.* This includes your affiliation with those who share your values and also the way you practice these beliefs. Beliefs you feel you have left behind, as well as those you currently hold, are influential.
5. *Geographic background.* How has a sense of place been a strong influence on who you are and what you value? This includes whether you have an urban or rural background and the particular region of the country from which you come.
6. *Socio-economic background.* Did you feel advantaged or disadvantaged while you were growing up? What were aspects of your status that were points of pride in your social group?
7. *Interests and hobbies.* What are the ways you identify yourself as a member of certain groups that are important in your life?

For a class activity: Get together in small groups and share with others which cultural factors have most strongly shaped your worldview. How would counseling theories need to be adapted to respond best to your unique background?

Assessment and Diagnosis

Your first session with a client will likely involve asking lots of questions with the goal of a systematic assessment and diagnosis. After all, how can you be expected to help someone until you have at least a general idea of what's going on, what the presenting complaints might be, and what has led up to these problems? You would also want to know something about the person's background and upbringing and their family and medical history. It would be important to have some notion of how these problems affect your client's life.

You'll be expected to use the *Diagnostic and Statistical Manual (DSM-5)* published by the American Psychiatric Association (2013) to do this. Although developed primarily by psychiatrists, the *DSM-5* is the closest thing to an operating manual that therapists have, at least for getting therapy started and for getting reimbursed for their efforts. It is based primarily on the medical model, which means that it uses an approach that classifies disorders with accompanying symptoms as would be found for any disease. Nevertheless, social workers, nurses, family therapists, and counselors all use the *DSM-5* in their work, making it possible for practitioners to have a common source for assessing and communicating about client problems. We mention this here because it is example of a contribution that is alleged to be *a-theoretical*, meaning that is intended that practitioners from a wide range of orientations to employ its system (that is, if they accept the very idea that mental disorders and diseases really exist—a point that is contested by some).

The diagnostic system currently in use by mental health professionals is only one example of a consistent standard of practice that transcends theoretical allegiances. Despite the theoretical differences among practitioners, there is reasonable agreement on the major diagnostic entities that therapists should look for during initial interviews, and there are a variety of complaints that most practitioners would treat in basically the same way. We say "basically" because it would still be necessary to customize the relationship you develop, as well as the way you implement the interventions, depending on the unique personality, needs, and cultural background of the client.

The Impact of Managed Care

The managed care movement has had a huge impact on the cultural context for the practice of therapy, strongly shaping which theories are favored and used most often. This has spawned much greater emphasis on briefer forms of therapy, especially those that are well suited to measuring outcomes. What this means is that when a new client walks in the door, the choice you make about treatment decisions and plans of action are not only influenced by the supervisors in your organization, but also by case managers (often nurses or administrators) whose main priority is keeping costs under control.

In recent years, and with the burgeoning of treatment planning software used for documentation, review, and supervision of cases, there is more and more emphasis on holding therapists accountable for creating and implementing coherent treatment plans. Although many practitioners resent these intrusions and restrictions on clinical options, this pressure has forced them to develop theories that can be tested by assessing their outcomes.

Working Efficiently

Managed care is not the only reason that therapists feel increasing pressure to employ brief methods. Prospective consumers have become more impatient, wanting quicker results. Whereas in the past it was relatively commonplace to see clients for many months or years, it is now more of a standard to plan for less than a dozen sessions.

"How long will this take?" you will be asked by new clients repeatedly. "I mean, if we can't take care of this today, I am willing to come back for a one more session." This may strike you as humorous, but many people really do expect that you have a magic wand that is capable of fixing lifelong problems by just saying a few incantations or casting a spell.

To put even more pressure on you to work quickly, clients often see therapy as a second choice to taking medication. After all, most antidepressant and anti-anxiety medications are prescribed by primary care physicians who see their patients for less than 20 minutes. During the last decade, new pharmacological advances have made it appear as if these medications will cure every problem, often within a matter of days. In fact, these drugs have often been found to be no more effective than those of previous generations and not any better than therapy for many problems. But there is nothing like aggressive marketing and advertising to convince consumers that there really is a magic cure, especially when many ads are so exaggerated and misleading, promising deliverance from life's problems.

FOR PERSONAL REFLECTION

A person you are helping is not improving as you would expect. As far as you can figure out, you have followed procedures exactly as prescribed. Furthermore, what you have done with this case is the same as you have tried before, always with good results.

You are obviously missing something in this scenario but you can't figure out what that might be. When you are stuck like this, a good place to begin is with the right questions. Many of them are suggested by the various theoretical paradigms.

- What does the literature and research inform you about this situation?
- How have other similar cases that you have worked with proceeded along a different course?
- What are you expecting of this person that he or she is unwilling or unable to do?
- What is it about this person's unique perceptions of the world that are at odds with your favored theoretical approach?
- What is it about this person's cultural background that would be important for you to take into consideration?
- What would the client say is going on and what does he or she think you should be doing differently to be helpful?
- What might you be doing (or not doing) that is creating these difficulties?
- How much empathy do you feel for the client? What might be getting in the way?

CONTEMPORARY TRENDS

One final area to examine the context of theories in the field is the cultural landscape in which therapists must now practice. There are a number of trends that have emerged in recent years that shape not only which theories are rising to greatest prominence but also the ways in which they are applied.

FOR A GROUP ACTIVITY

Working in teams, come up with a list of the major cultural movements, trends, and forces that you believe will most impact the practice of counseling and therapy in the future. Consider such factors as technology, globalization, political climate, economics, ecopsychology, and social values and ethics, as well as cultural trends in music, recreation, entertainment, and lifestyle. Make some predictions about the kinds of theories that will evolve to meet these changing circumstances.

The Impact of Technology on Clients

Your guess is as good as ours about what the future will bring in the ways that technology will affect your life and practice. In the future, will we be using avatars or artificial intelligence or embedded sensors in our work? Will offices become obsolete and all treatments take place via long distance from anywhere in the world? Will we be communicating with one another through messaging systems via mobile devices or even brain implants? Some of these things are already a reality, with a number of clinicians conducting their sessions online with people from all over the world.

Certainly, the increasing use of the Internet, wireless devices, computers, personal tracking devices, social networking sites, artificial intelligence, and such will continue to reshape the world we know. As technology has developed and invaded every aspect of our lives, this has assuredly changed the way people share information about themselves. Furthermore, the sheer magnitude and pace of these changes are staggering. We had to laugh when we reviewed the earlier edition of this book and we talked about Facebook, YouTube, Skype, iPhones, Blackberries, and Twitter as novel innovations that might alter our interpersonal landscape. And who would have predicted that a president of the United States would send out proclamations and policy decisions on his phone while lounging around? What will the next decade bring?

Now that everyone has constant access to social networking sites, people can "reach out and touch someone" with a constancy and impact far beyond what the phone companies (who originated that phrase) ever dreamed of. Feeling down? Post a message on Facebook or Twitter or Tumblr and non-professional counselors will jump right in and give you advice and reassurance. There is always someone to whom you can vent if you are stirred up about a situation. It is too soon in the game to have conclusive studies on this, but some therapists wonder if this 24/7 "free therapy" reduces individuals' perceived need for truly professional help (Russell, 2018).

Technology is also changing the kinds of problems that people present for help. Young children are spending hours each day playing video and computer games, isolating them from peers, and recent studies show increased anxiety and depression in children and teens with online time (Kaliebe & Weigel, 2018). Teenagers and adults become addicted to the Internet, spending as much as 5 to 10 leisure hours each day in front of a screen, and many are involved in the "fantasy obsessions" of Web-based gaming and pornography. Middle-schoolers are sexting in their math classes and checking social media up to 300 times a day as a form of self-defense against things that might be said about them. In-home entertainments systems beam in hundreds of channels, keep families immobile, sitting on their couches every night. Even the tools people use—wireless phones, personal devices, computers, vehicles—are rendered obsolete every few years, requiring more and more energy to be invested in mastering new devices. Jobs are becoming obsolete as often as software versions are updated and digital transformations remake every aspect of business process. New technologies constantly enter the market. All of this has an impact on the wellbeing of therapists and clients alike, as the pace of change in modern life has increased exponentially. Methods and guidelines for addressing these issues in therapy are still emerging.

FOR A CLASS ACTIVITY

How will Web-based approaches impact our field and the ways we think about and do therapy? In small groups, or as a class, talk about your predictions about how therapy and counseling will evolve to meet the needs of a changing world.

Consider how technological advances will alter not only the problems that clients present, but also the ways that therapy will be delivered. How will diagnostic and assessment procedures take place? How will innovations in technology related to simulations, cyberspace, virtual reality, communication devices, neurobiology, and behavioral science change the field?

The Impact of Technology on Therapists

Computers have also vastly affected the way most clinicians practice therapy. Therapists who employ the computer (or their phone, which is really a hand-held computer) to assist in delivering their services are not necessarily following a coherent theory as much as they have adapted their current model to a different means of communication. We are not just talking about one form of therapy, but many kinds that are used in different ways. Officially, computer-assisted (or computer-mediated) therapy is any type of therapy that uses a computer for delivery of services, whether email, chat rooms, messaging apps, online support groups, or video conferencing (Manfrida, Albertini, & Eisenberg, 2018). This might mean any of the following:

1. Web-based interactions in which programmed instructions are followed to gain information or guidance in a specific area, such as online assessments for determining a particular diagnosis, or tried-and-true tips for dealing with specific symptoms
2. Computer simulations in which programs (or avatars) are developed to respond to client written or verbal statements—giving clients experience with a "virtual therapist" whose responses were programmed by actual therapists
3. Internet-based conversations in real time in which clients and therapists conduct a session in a chat room, Internet phone, or through video conferencing
4. Internet-based dialogue in which email messages are sent and responded to, or blog posts are shared with all members of a support group and monitored by the group leader
5. Requiring clients to do Internet-based skill-building modules between sessions
6. Text communications from the therapist with regular encouraging messages to clients

In each of these types of computer-mediated therapy, whichever theory of intervention is being applied must be altered to fit the unique kind of communication taking place. Imagine getting an email communication from a client, for instance, that says the following:

> *I am not sure about what to do about this situation. Sometimes it seems so pointless and I wonder if I should even pursue it further.*

Understandably, there is no context to this message for you to figure out what is going on, but there are also no nonverbal cues or voice tone that lets you "read" what this person is really experiencing. Is he or she a little disappointed, suicidally depressed, or just confused and musing aloud about where to go next? Of course, you can check that out, but you would have to do so in a way that is quite different from how you would proceed in face-to-face therapy.

Unique Advantages and Disadvantages

It is easy to predict that technology and the Internet will only become more important in our lives, including the ways that therapists and clients might communicate with one another. Critics of this technology say that people are already estranged enough in their lives from authentic connections to others and that technology devices only insert another layer of insulation. Instead of venturing out of their homes, people are spending more and more time in front of their screens. They shop on the Web instead of visiting stores, send texts instead of visiting friends in person, work at home instead of commuting to a workplace with other people around, and play video games and use interactive computer media instead of being with real live people in daily interactions. And there is no reason to think that more and more people won't want their therapy on the computer as well.

After all, many people report that computer-based communication is more anonymous, confidential, and private (after all, no one can see you in the therapist's parking lot!) than face-to-face therapy, as well as being far more accessible. Some consumers of computer-based therapy say that it is the only way to go. They feel safer in ways that would never have been possible before. It is certainly more convenient, although that could be a disadvantage as well because change efforts aren't normally associated with comfort. Finally, when therapy involves exchanging written messages, there is a different pace to the communication and a different texture to the interaction that can facilitate thoughtful reflection in between messages. With limited cues, the modality focuses attention on the content of what is communicated in ways that would not ordinarily be practical—and it can be read and re-read.

Of course, it is also much easier for clients to be deceptive and hide. How do you know, for example, that the woman who writes to you about her eating disorder and sexual dysfunction is really who she says she is? There are no nonverbal cues or even a way to confirm her identity (and perhaps "she" is really an underage teenage boy, testing your limits). There are just so few channels of real information available to make sense of what a person is telling you.

Another consideration is the way more and more people are insulating themselves from the world outside computers. One of the fastest-growing psychological problems is Internet addiction, in which people are spending the majority of their waking hours in front of a computer screen. It has even been estimated that between 6% and 38% of the worldwide population have a serious problem of addiction to their computer activities, with this wide variance attributable to differing diagnostic criteria used and the particular group being studied (Kuss & Lopez-Fernandez, 2016; Wiederhold, 2018). Even more alarming is the fact that Internet addiction is associated with higher rates of suicidal ideation and attempts, particularly for children and teens (Cheng et al., 2018). Offering therapy via this medium may then only contribute to clients' further isolation and depression.

Therapists who use technology appreciate all the ways it saves time in taking a history, collecting background information, administering assessment instruments, formulating a diagnosis, and submitting insurance claims—and who doesn't love that! A computer or Web-based format is also great for didactically based tasks such as teaching assertiveness training, relaxation training, or cognitive restructuring. One trend in this area is to blend Internet-delivered cognitive behavioral skill-building modules and offer them in conjunction with a certain number of hours of live therapy. Studies have found this approach to be promising for clients diagnosed with depression (Thase et al., 2017) and schizophrenia (Garrido et al., 2017). It is likely that you'll see more of this blending of therapy with instruction, as it reduces costs and helps clients maintain gains after therapy ends.

Certain ethical issues will continue to make the use of technology challenging for practitioners. Concerns include the potential lack of privacy, the lack of regulation of people who claim to be experts on the Internet, and the lack of research on the effectiveness of computer-mediated psychotherapy for clients with many types of problems (Kramer, Kinn, & Mishkind, 2015). To address these issues, professional ethical codes now provide guidance for distance counseling, social media, and the use of technology (e.g., the 2014 ACA Code of Ethics). Credentials are now available for distance counseling from several professional associations.

What's the "bottom line" for this issue for contemporary practice? The good news is that you are a long way away from having your job replaced by a robot. Rather, your job will stay fresh and interesting as technology continues to introduce innovative ways to support your practice and your clients. However, with every new possibility, we advise you to reflect on how it will impact you, your clients, and your practice, without idealizing something just because it is new.

Integration and Synthesis
There has been a trend developing over the past few decades in which more and more practitioners are describing themselves as eclectic or integrative in their approach, using a variety of approaches depending on what is needed. We'll say much more about this contemporary trend in coming chapters, and we'll give you tools for deciding which approaches you resonate with the most and integrating them yourself.

FOR HOMEWORK

For this exercise, try out therapy with a computer therapist. Look for an artificial intelligence or "AI" therapist favorite browser. Try it out, being authentic about something that is on your mind that you might wish you could talk to a therapist about.

What do you think? How does this "AI" therapist provide elements of counseling or therapy? What is missing? Will a computer therapist replace you?

There's much about this trend that is good; it arises out of dedicated therapists' drive to keep reaching for what will serve their clients the best by integrating new ideas into established ways of doing things. It is human nature to be attracted to new things, and we might naively assume that "newer" is "better"—but then we could be quite wrong! Recall our historical review in this chapter of the many theories of healing that were once the hottest thing going but have since have gone by the wayside. Nearly every day, new approaches are developed (often synthesizing older theories with "new" discoveries); some will become mainstream and others will disappear in less than a decade.

This means a lot more work for you because you will probably not be able to pick only one of the theories in this text and expect to stick with it throughout your career. It requires a high level of conceptual mastery to understand one or more theories and then to combine several of their features into an individualized model. It also requires critical thinking as you coolly and carefully assess each newly proposed synthesis, even as you listen to its cadre of enthusiastic supporters. Yet that is *exactly* the task that we have before us during this journey.

SUGGESTED READINGS

American Psychiatric Association. (2013). *Diagnostic and statistical manual of mental disorders* (*DSM-5*). Washington DC: Author.

Kaliebe, K., & Weigel, P. (2018). *Youth Internet habits and mental health.* Philadelphia, PA: Elsevier.

Kongstvedt, P. R. (2015). *Health insurance and managed care: What they are and how they work* (4th ed). Sudbury, MA: Jones & Bartlett.

Kottler, J. A. (2015). *The therapist in the real world: What you never learn in graduate school (but really need to know).* New York, NY: Norton.

Marzi, A. (2018). *Psychoanalysis, identity, and the Internet: Explorations into cyberspace.* New York, NY: Routledge.

Pope, K. S., & Vasquez, M. J. T. (2016). *Ethics in psychotherapy and counseling: A practical guide* (5th ed.). Hoboken, NJ: Wiley.

Russell, G. I. (2018). *Screen relations: The limits of computer-mediated psychoanalysis and psychotherapy.* New York, NY: Routledge.

Slife, B., O'Grady, K. A. & Kosits, R. D. (2017). *The hidden worldviews of psychology's theory, research, and practice.* New York, NY: Routledge.

IMAGE CREDITS

Fig. 2.1: Illustration by Liesl McCormick.

CHAPTER 3

Theory in a Clinician's Life

LEARNING OBJECTIVES

After reading this chapter, you should be able to do the following:

1. Articulate how personal experiences led the development of several key theorists' approaches.
2. Evaluate the links between developmental theories and counseling theories when developing plans for clients.
3. Articulate how the worldviews, assumptions, and beliefs underlying counseling theories can guide one's choice of preferred theoretical approaches.
4. Identify initial points of alignment between theoretical worldviews and one's own views.
5. Describe how counselors' and client's worldviews are mutually influential in the counseling process.

One of the myths of our profession is that theories are developed purely out of scientific, objective inquiry in which a scholar conducts controlled experiments, slaves over data, analyzes empirical literature, systematically reviews case notes, and then constructs a logical paradigm that sequentially follows the blueprint. In truth, theory construction and development are often messy, springing from chance encounters and intensely personal events in a clinician's life.

Certainly, formal theory emerges and evolves as a result of systematic inquiry, clinical experience, and a synthesis of the literature advancing previous work. But we do not wish to give you the impression that such conceptual frameworks necessarily represent ideas identified purely through neutral scientific inquiry, as many of our field's theoretical innovators were driven by very personal motives. It is very important that you appreciate this point as you begin delving into conceptual ideas that will become a large part of your professional life.

THREE THEORIES, THREE LIVES

In what is certainly the first comprehensive approach to therapy, Sigmund Freud clearly went in the directions he did because of many unresolved issues related to intimacy, sexuality, and his own past (Crews, 2017; Roth, 2016). It was hardly a coincidence, for instance, that his theory followed a path that excavates buried material when his lifelong obsession was with archaeology. Not only did Freud spend his day digging into people's pasts to uncover the meaning of their experiences, but he also spent most of his vacations on archaeological digs, as well as collecting ancient artifacts that adorned his office. This was a man who believed in his soul that the past shapes who we are, and his theory reflected this intensely personal conviction.

Likewise, Victor Frankl, the inventor of one school of existential theory called logotherapy, developed his notions as a result of traumas he suffered in the concentration camps of Nazi Germany (Frankl, 1997). Day after day, as he watched friends, neighbors, and family members give up and die, or actually kill themselves by running into the guarded fence, he searched for some larger purpose to his tortuous existence. This investigation into the meaning of his own suffering gave way to a whole system of helping others that was rooted in the construction of personal meaning.

"He who has a *why* to live for," writes Frankl, paraphrasing Nietzsche, one of his favorite philosophers, "can bear with almost any *how*" (1962, p. 121). Frankl believed that finding the "why" should be the main thrust for any therapeutic effort. Remember, Frankl is not talking about people he has observed in a scientific study or even in his consultation chambers; these are the observations of a man who was a prisoner, who faced death every day, who had already lost everything else in his life except the choice as to how he wanted to view his own predicament.

In a third example of how theories are influenced profoundly by the personal experiences of their inventors, Carl Rogers, the founder of person-centered therapy, developed an approach that followed perfectly his most deeply held convictions. In his autobiography, Rogers (1980) reflects on one of his earliest memories from childhood—the pure pleasure he felt when he could really *hear* someone.

If you ever watch a video of Rogers, you will see the embodiment of the perfect listening being. All his love, his caring and compassion, and his focused attention are directed toward his client. When you watch him work, you may feel a longing to crawl into his lap as the perfect grandparent, to have him hold you and tell you everything will be all right. And you would believe him.

It is hardly surprising that Rogers developed a theory of helping that emphasizes authentic relationships when he felt such an emptiness in his own life growing up. He moved around a lot as a kid, never felt any roots, and admits he never had close friends. "I was socially incompetent," Rogers discloses, "in any but superficial contacts" (1980, p. 30). Yet later in life he develops a theory of helping that holds as its most sacred principle the significance of an accepting, caring, nurturing relationship. He developed a theory that emphasized empathy and compassion because he never felt understood in his own lifetime (Kirschenbaum, 2009).

So, what is the point of including these three examples? This is a reminder that each theory you will study was most likely conceived by someone who was frustrated with the choices already available and sought to develop a framework that would fit better with his or her own values, interests, personality, and life experience. Each theory reflects the personal biases, preferences, and pains of its inventor.

It is hardly a coincidence that someone such as Fritz Perls, once an immigrant with a poor command of the English language, developed Gestalt therapy that emphasized nonverbal forms of communication. Likewise, Albert Ellis grew frustrated with the conventional psychoanalysis he was practicing because he liked to talk a lot rather than sit quietly beside the couch, and his theory was not allowing him that indulgence. So, he developed rational-emotive therapy to express perfectly his love of logical analysis and rational thinking, which he had found so personally helpful in overcoming his difficult childhood and adolescence. In so many other cases, as well, if you take the time to search through their backgrounds, you will find that the architects of various theories were influenced as much by their personal histories as by their professional experiences (Demorest, 2004).

What this means is that if you hope to practice effectively and naturally yourself, you will someday have to become your own theoretician. You will evolve a personal style of practice that adapts what you have learned from your supervisors, mentors, teachers, and theoretical allegiances. Just like your predecessors, you will develop a theory of doing therapy that closely fits your personal and professional style—and makes sense to you in light of the challenges you have encountered.

FOR A FIELD STUDY

Read the biographies or autobiographies of prominent theoreticians in several fields. You might start with those of Sigmund Freud (Roudinesco, 2016; Whitebook, 2017) and Carl Rogers (Thorne, 2013; Kirschenbaum, 2009; Rogers, 1980; Rogers & Russell, 2002), then move on to others that intrigue you, such as Albert Ellis (Carlson & Knaus, 2014), Karen Horney (Paris, 1996), and Anna Freud (Young-Breuhl, 2008). Or read about how some of their lives entwined (Benveniste, 2015).

As you read the stories of their lives, observe the ways their theories evolved from their personal experiences. Trace the roots of their thinking as they emerged in various significant events and critical incidents. Note in particular the ways their theories reflected the context of their times, culture, gender, and home life.

PERSONAL AND PROFESSIONAL INTERACTIONS

It isn't only in the lives of famous therapists that you can witness the interaction between personal and professional lives. In a book edited by Gerson (1996), a number of practicing therapists discuss how various life transitions, crises, and experiences impact their work and influence their theories. They talk about how traumas, transitions, and tragedies they survived helped to shape their views of helping. Not surprisingly, most of the 17 contributors have chosen a psychoanalytic framework that works through past traumas as they are manifested in current problems. One therapist, for example, talks about how losing her father as a child influenced her development as a practitioner. She is big into control issues as a defense against the terror of helplessness. She is mainly focused on the experience of loss in her sessions. And she chose a psychoanalytic framework because of the way it provided the sort of "soothing containing relationship" she missed in her own life. "Undoubtedly," she writes, "my fascination with theory that supported that work was an out-growth of my deeply felt need for missed parenting" (Gerson, 1996, pp. 219–220).

In addition, a series of books coauthored by Jeffrey (Kottler & Carlson, 2003; 2006; 2008; 2009; 2011) offer stories of prominent therapists who were dramatically and profoundly impacted by their clients in such a significant way that it led to the development of their seminal ideas. They had been busily operating in sessions according to the ways they had been originally trained, and then wham!, a client tested them in ways that led to new innovations in their style. Often such theories point to a single client in particular who impacted them in such a powerful way that they changed the ways they thought about their work, and sometimes even their own lives.

Rarely do therapists and counselors admit so honestly the way their professional choices have been influenced by their personal experiences. Other contributors in the volume mention how divorce, pregnancy, parenthood, sexual abuse, death of a child, aging, and obesity have all had a huge impact on the ways they currently operate. You can expect a similar course throughout your own career: Your selection of which theories to employ and the ways you adapt them to your work will be strongly influenced by *everything* you encounter—not only in your work but also in your life.

Theories and the Developing Person

Although this book is focused primarily on theories of intervention, there are many other conceptual frameworks that are part of a therapist's work. For instance, before you can ever hope to select the best treatment strategy for a given client, you will first need to have a thorough understanding of the person's development in a host of areas that include physical, social, emotional, cognitive, and spiritual dimensions, to mention a few.

Social scientists have spent the past century creating and testing theories to describe and predict human behavior in every possible area. Although our efforts will be concentrated theories related to helping strategies, you will also need to be familiar with those that deal with other facets of human conduct. Why? Because we encounter people who are on a journey through a lifespan, and because of the multi-faceted dimensions of human life, therapists often find that their theory of intervention for a client is informed by developmental theories.

FOR PERSONAL REFLECTION

Think of one theory that you find especially useful in your life. This could be related to your job or any other facet of your life.

For instance, I (Jeffrey) am attracted to a theory called evolutionary psychology because of its value in explaining why people do the things they do when surface motives are not apparent. According to this theory, people act in accordance with their drive to increase the likelihood their genes will be passed on to the next generation. This helps explain, for instance, the value of gossip as a source of intelligence, or the reasons why dominance plays such an important part in relationships (holding onto the best resources for one's kin), or even why maternal grandparents often have closer relationships with their grandchildren than do paternal grandparents (because the mother's parents can be certain the offspring has their genetic material but the father's parents can never be sure). There is even some application to therapy in explaining why people so hunger for closeness and affiliation with others, and how therapeutic relationships fill the void left by the disbanding of our tribal heritage.

What are some of your favorite theories that you use every day? Think about what makes them so valuable to you.

It was Robert Havighurst (1972) who popularized the concept of developmental tasks, meaning those challenges that arise at a predictable age that must be met if healthy development is to proceed. For each of several stages in life, people must tackle certain physical, social, and emotional tasks to develop further.

During infancy, for instance, a baby must learn to take solid foods, to sit up, and eventually to crawl and walk if he or she expects to advance much further in life. In middle childhood, or the elementary school years, a child must learn to get along with others, to read and write, to develop a moral system, and so on. Developmental tasks are specified for each stage of life, listing what is absolutely required of the individual to be reasonably competent in our culture. One idea you'll hear a lot, particularly in treatment settings where trauma or addictions are the key issue, is that when psychological problems arise, development gets off track and clients do not complete the necessary developmental tasks. Similarly, when development gets off track, psychological problems arise. Either way, promoting positive development and relieving systems can (and often should) go hand in hand.

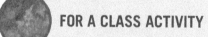

FOR A CLASS ACTIVITY

Divide the class into eight groups. Each group must tackle one of the following six stages of life by listing all its developmental tasks:

- Preschool (3–5)
- Childhood (6–12)
- Adolescence (12–18)
- College or apprentice years (18–22)
- Young adulthood (23–35)
- Adulthood (36–48)
- Middle age (49–65)
- Later maturity (66 and older)

It will help you generate a more complete list of tasks if you think of categories including (a) physical activities, (b) social activities, (c) career-related activities, (d) civic/community activities, (e) family activities, and others that come to mind.

After you are done, talk about how therapists could and should help people achieve the developmental tasks expected of their age group.

Other developmental theories related to cognitive development (Jean Piaget), moral development (Lawrence Kohlberg), ego development (Jane

Loevinger), gender development (Carol Gilligan), personality development (Erik Erikson), cultural identity development (Janet Helms) and career development (Donald Super) provided blueprints to understand and predict the normative challenges people face during their lifetime. Before you start to panic, remember that there are other courses that cover these theories. The key idea here is that it will be useful for you to develop some degree of background knowledge about the ways that people typically develop and integrate this knowledge (to some degree, depending on the client's issues).

Developmental theories help you understand the age-related context of a person's struggles. Once you know the client's approximate life stages, you can make some reasonable predictions about where he or she ought to be operating. This allows you to compare actual functioning to what would be expected. It also makes it possible for you to plan what sorts of interventions would be most likely to stimulate growth to the next successive stage (Jools, Byrne, & Berg, 2017).

FOR PERSONAL REFLECTION or DISCUSSION

A new client is referred to you because of difficulties sleeping and chronic stomachaches. A physical exam has ruled out any physical causes. This young woman is 22 years old, just graduating from a university with a business degree.

Based on this person's age, what are some of the developmental issues that you would expect that she would be struggling with right now? How might these be related to her presenting complaints?

Let's say, for instance, that a 29-year-old client has been having difficulty making commitments to a primary relationship. Although he expresses a deep interest in this love relationship, he senses that things will soon end unless he is prepared to take things to the next step. In conducting an assessment, you discover that his parents were divorced when he was 13 and that he experienced a traumatic breakup in high school, swearing to himself never to get hurt again. As you dig further, you find other significant events in his life that may be related to his present problems: chronic asthma that he developed as a child, as well as a learning disability that interfered with his ability to read. Finally, you note that he is approaching the "age 30 transition" that marks one of the most significant life passages. He must now come to terms with the reality that he will never reach some of his dreams, yet he is still young enough to reassess new priorities.

When you apply developmental theories in this way, you are thinking in terms of how a person is functioning in all the areas of human competence that matter most. You will find this model especially useful when conducting diagnostic and intake interviews, and in anticipating the developmental challenges your client should be prepared for after your time together ends. You can reliably predict some of the most significant tasks that lie ahead and help prepare for them. As one example, imagine you are working with a couple who was having communication issues in their relationship that led to misunderstandings and conflict. They were able to resolve the troubles and strengthen their relationship, enough so that the sessions are coming to an end. However, the couple has recently learned that the wife is pregnant and they are filled with joy and optimism for the future. You happen to know, from developmental theory as well as clinical experience, that one of the most turbulent times in a marriage is during and after the birth of a first child. This is a time when there is constant sleep deprivation, no sex, disrupted intimacy, and often neglect of their own relationship. Knowing this, you can help the couple anticipate and plan for such a transition.

FOR PERSONAL REFLECTION

Often, people report that completing a developmental task feels like a major life turning point because of the new vantages this affords for looking at life and oneself. This is the stuff that novels and films are made of!

Consider the most significant turning points you have had in your life. Either write down in your journal, or talk to a partner, about life's lessons that have been most important to you. For instance, you might mention the time you learned to ride a two-wheel bike without training wheels, when you first understood that rejection is more a state of mind than circumstances, or when you realized for the first time that you might be smart.

Now identify what forces and factors most contributed to these significant learnings. What is it that made the most difference?

As a therapist, what can you do to capitalize most on those elements that you believe are most conducive to promoting significant learning?

Cultural Worldviews

As we mentioned in Chapter 2, a worldview is the way a client makes sense of the world, and it is usually strongly influenced by a person's cultural identity.

It involves a person's basic values and perceptions, the window through which the world is seen and experienced. It is through interactions with others, especially with those of one's identified cultural groups, that views about relationships, family, productivity, control, time, intimacy, love, and similar values are developed (Hays, 2016). It also includes the attitudes one has about seeking assistance from a helping professional.

Therapists and theories work from definite worldviews. Each theory you will study represents its own cultural group. Each has a language, special rituals and customs, and a shared identity that shape values and behavior. You can usually see these differences in the gatherings of different groups at professional conferences. Humanistic practitioners are inclined, for example, to hug a lot and talk in the language of feelings. Their worldview is based on faith and trust in the human capacity for growth and self-healing. On the other hand, attend a gathering of cognitive therapists and you will see interactions that are far more formal. They speak a different language and value other aspects of human experience. They embrace a worldview that is logical, rational, and ordered, based on thinking rather than feeling. They would be less inclined to hug one another and more inclined to talk about what they think about things.

Expressed more systematically, theoretical worldviews give therapists a way to organize their thoughts about what's good for their clients, what can go wrong, and how to get back on track. As we mentioned in Chapter 2, an abbreviated version of the therapist's orientation is expressed in the treatment plans that therapists use to communicate with others. As a taste of what's to come, notice the difference in these four often-encountered ways of thinking:

1. *Existential-humanistic.* Human beings are naturally inclined to grow and develop in positive ways, especially when they experience trusting, caring relationships. It is important to find personal meaning in one's life and to come to terms with one's personal choices. People have problems when something blocks their natural tendency toward self-actualization. The therapist's job is to facilitate this process through a close relationship, exploration of feelings, and search for personal meaning.

2. *Psychoanalytic.* People are ruled by their instincts, especially the drive to need satisfaction. Problems in the present result from unresolved issues in the past, especially those related to early childhood interactions with parents. Analyzing dreams, labeling defenses, and looking for unconscious, repressed material are the best ways to help people resolve their difficulties. The relationship with clients is important mostly as it relates to clients' fantasies and projections.

3. *Cognitive-behavioral.* People get in trouble when they fail to think clearly and logically about their situations. They distort reality and subscribe to beliefs that are self-defeating. Because negative feelings are caused by irrational beliefs, people can alter their moods by choosing alternative interpretations of the situation. To help people, it is necessary to challenge their beliefs and teach them alternative ways of thinking.

4. *Systemic.* Individual problems really represent larger family conflicts. Rather than looking at how the action of one person causes problems for another, therapists should be examining instead the reciprocal, circular exchanges that take place between individuals. This is most effective when therapists work with the whole family and seek to restructure family interactions in a way that is more healthy.

We could have picked any of a dozen other theoretical worldviews to show you how much they can differ, but our point is that you must understand that both the client and therapist enter the encounter with well-developed ideas about the way the world works and the way change should most easily take place. Often, they do not align—at least, initially. If your clients were totally honest with you and you asked them what they wanted to happen in sessions, they would probably tell you something like the following:

> *"I will tell you my troubles. You will listen to me … and agree with me. Then you will tell me what I should do and how to do it."*

This, of course, is a very different view of change than the one that you intend to apply in your work. After all, if your clients' notions of change were working, they wouldn't be seeing you! You assume that using your theoretical perspective you'll have some fresh ideas about what can change, and help convince your client to try them. But notice that this creates an intrinsic conflict that is so often a part of therapist-client relationships: You will each be trying to "sell" one another a particular ideology that you think is optimal. One of four things usually happens:

1. You will be convincing enough that the client buys what you are selling and agrees to adopt your theoretical worldview (at least about the problem at hand) and the features that go along with it.

2. The client insists that you agree with his or her worldview (a not unreasonable request considering who is the "customer").

3. You start with the client's worldview and offer opportunities to expand it with appealing ideas from your own.

4. The client leaves to find satisfaction and agreement elsewhere.

Needless to say, this tension between worldviews presents some interesting challenges to everyone involved and is at the heart of the therapeutic process.

FOR PERSONAL REFLECTION or A CLASS ACTIVITY

Spend a few minutes making a list of the three most significant events that have occurred in your life. These could be traumatic experiences (i.e., loss, physical illness, failure), normal developmental transitions (i.e., riding a two-wheel bike, 21st birthday), or joyful incidents (i.e., marriage, birth of a child, job promotion).

Make a second list of the three most deeply held convictions that guide your life. These should involve those personal values and beliefs that most strongly influence your behavior. They could be related to things such as justice, fate, spirituality, lifestyle, relationships, work, and other related issues.

Find connections between the two lists, noting the ways that your most significant experiences helped you formulate your guiding philosophy.

In small groups, talk to each other about what you discovered. As with any cooperative learning group, (a) allocate your time equitably so that everyone has a chance to speak, (b) show respect and caring for each person's contribution, and (c) stay on task so you complete the assignment.

After all group members have had a chance to share their experiences, look for common themes that emerged.

THE NEXT STEPS IN YOUR UNDERSTANDING

You may already be feeling a little overwhelmed by all the terms, names, and ideas that have been introduced as part of this contextual presentation. Let us remind you that in this course we are after the big picture. Certainly, it is important to learn the central figures and concepts in the field, but unless you can put all of it together into a fairly coherent view of what therapy is all about and why and how it works, you are not going to do your clients much good.

Before beginning an investigation of specific theoretical frameworks covered in the text, there are a few things that you will need to understand first.

Confusion and Ambiguity

If you are looking for truth or even consistent answers to your questions, you won't find them here. If you need clarity or concrete answers, you might try law, engineering, or physics, but you won't encounter much of that in counseling and therapy. For every explanation you hear that makes sense, there will be a dozen other ones that directly contradict it. For every possible course of action you could take with a particular client, afterward there will occur to you several others that seem more advantageous. Once you get input from colleagues and supervisors, you will feel the burden of even more alternatives.

One perspective states that is the client who determines how far progress will go, based on his or her own readiness levels and motivation. The therapist's role is merely to facilitate this process by providing an atmosphere that is rich in both creativity and resources. In fact, there is some compelling evidence that the single best predictor of a successful outcome is what the client brings to the session in terms of personality traits, expectations, motivation, commitment, and attitudes (Wampold & Imel, 2015).

However, as you have no doubt already realized, for every point of view in this field, there is another one that takes the opposite argument. There are other approaches that see the therapist as the expert whose skill determines the outcome. From this point of view, even with so-called resistant or unmotivated clients, strategic maneuverings on the part of the clinician can overcome a client's lack of commitment (Quick, 2011).

Fervor and Zeal

Practitioners become rather attached to their theories. It's like a club, a fraternity or sorority, or even a religious affiliation to which you belong. There are secret handshakes, special code words, designated books, even a particular wardrobe associated with the followers of one theory or another. Furthermore, professionals get upset when you subscribe to another theory that directly contradicts their own preferred ideas.

Often, beginners in their internships are expected to follow the theories of their supervisors who feel a strong commitment to a particular orientation that has been useful to them throughout their careers. This is not altogether a bad idea to start with a theory, *any* theory, that offers sufficient structure and guidance. Having an allegiance to a theory, even for a time, can give you a "tribe" to belong to, and learn from—not a bad place to begin. Learning to speak one theoretical language well can bring lots of advantages in terms of structure and consistency when you are learning this complex practice.

Keep in mind, however, that multiple attempts to demonstrate that one approach is more effective than all others have produced inconclusive results. Even when isolated studies do indicate that one approach might be better for certain kinds of clients or presenting complaints, it is difficult to sort out whether the positive results occurred because the theory was better or because the clinicians selected for one group were more skilled than the others—or because the toughest clients (like the ones we see every day) were left out of the study (Prochaska & Norcross, 2018).

Points of Departure

All the approaches to helping that are covered in this text have points in common, as well as areas where they diverge significantly from one another (see Table 3.1). You will notice that each theory differs primarily in the following dimensions:

1. *Historical context.* From which traditions did this theory emerge? Some are heavily steeped in classical philosophy, others in neurological science, education, anthropology, physics, or humanities. The theory is also influenced by the era in which it was spawned (compare 19th-century Vienna to the '60s in California or the urban settings of contemporary Hong Kong, Mexico City, or Johannesburg).

2. *Underlying philosophy.* Each therapeutic approach follows an organized set of assumptions, as well as a basic philosophy of change. Theories differ in their views of human nature, most legitimate focus of attention and scope of treatment, as well as who has primary responsibility for outcomes, treatment goals, counselor roles, and criteria for success.

TABLE 3.1. Assumptions and Beliefs Underlying Theories of Psychotherapy

People are born good.	People are born neutral.	People are born evil.
Clients control outcomes.	Therapists decide outcomes.	Responsibility is shared.
Feelings are most important.	Thinking is most important.	Behavior is most important.
Focus on the past.	Focus on the present.	Focus on the future.
Goals should be specific.	Broad themes are best.	Concentrate on the process.
Use structuring most often.	Use interpreting most often.	Reflect feelings most often.
Be active.	Be nondirective.	Let client decide what is best.
Function as a friend.	Function as a consultant.	Function as a teacher.
Use one primary theory.	Use several theories.	Combine theories into one.
Theory is most important.	Skills are most important.	Therapist personality is key.

3. *Values held most sacred.* Separate from a guiding philosophy are the values implicit in a particular approach. Therapists who flock together tend to adopt similar attitudes about the work and the best way to do it. Psychoanalytic therapists will be inclined to be more patient, whereas their strategic or brief-oriented colleagues prefer incisive, directive actions. Humanistic practitioners value relationships and process above specific goals and content, whereas behavioral and cognitive therapists emphasize the opposite. You do not have to apologize for identifying with a theory that reflects most closely what you believe is worthwhile and how you tend to approach life—these are among the most important factors to consider.

4. *Types of evidence used to support premises.* Theories cannot evolve and remain influential without compelling evidence to support their claims. They must not only be field tested and found to produce desired results, but also subjected to systemic scrutiny by research efforts. The interesting part, however, is that the practitioners using particular theories tend to collect different types of evidence to support their ideas. Of course, human nature being what it is, all have been accused of hunting for and interpreting results that support their own preferred outcomes. This can be manipulated, to a certain extent, whether measuring outcomes with certain selected criteria and instruments, depending on what is valued; relying on handpicked case examples; or conducting qualitative interviews with participants who are best positioned to provide what is considered most valuable or interesting.

5. *Techniques employed.* Each of the theoretical approaches not only differs in its underlying beliefs but also in the ways it is applied. Sometimes it is difficult to tell what sort of therapy someone is doing simply by watching because we can't really get inside the participants' heads. The skills therapists use are somewhat generic and universal—everyone uses reflection, interpretation, summarization, and so on. Nevertheless, each approach has certain trademark interventions that are immediately identified with that theory. Mention the "hot seat" or "empty chair" and most experienced practitioners will know that they come from Gestalt theory. Disputing beliefs is associated with cognitive theory, dream analysis with psychodynamic approaches, "spitting in the client's soup" as Adlerian, systematic desensitization with behavioral therapy, circular questioning with narrative therapy, and reframing with strategic therapy.

Basically, our point is that it is worth becoming familiar with all the theories in the text (and many others that were left out because of space limitations) so that you can practice shifting perspectives to get a new point of view and collecting a variety of techniques for your arsenal. Being able to shift your viewpoint and flexibly choose what you want to implement with a client means you have a large bag of tricks at your disposal when you are faced with inevitable resistance and challenges. When you try something and it doesn't work, you will always have at your disposal several other alternatives. Of course, this is all predicated on the reality that you have established a solid enough relationship with your clients that they are willing to demonstrate sufficient patience until you both discover the optimal approach.

FOR PERSONAL REFLECTION

Think of something you do well. This could be cooking a favorite dish, engaging in some athletic activity, playing a particular video game, talking convincingly about a subject, or doing anything that stands out as being (in your judgment) exceptional. Now ask yourself how you know you are good at this. What evidence do you have to support this claim?

Perhaps you would say that other people (those whom you trust) tell you that you are good at this (but they may be lying to make you feel good). You may be confident in your competence because you know you are good (but perhaps you are in denial or not seeing things clearly). You could use some more objective measure, such as amount of money won gambling, grade point average, or place you finished in a race (but perhaps the competition was not all that good, you were lucky, or your data are not representative of your total performance). Well, you get the point: It is really hard to determine personal effectiveness and there are so many different ways to do it.

Expanding Your Options

We have heard more than a few instructors who teach this course claim that the whole idea of teaching theories as discrete entities is counterproductive. Why introduce students to a bunch of models that are rarely, if ever, practiced any longer in pure form? It has been widely stated that there are over 400 distinct theories of counseling and therapy and that few of them are clearly better than the others (Wampold & Imel, 2015). The majority of practitioners do not identify with any single theory, calling themselves integrative, pragmatic, or eclectic (Prochaska & Norcross, 2018). This means that they have either combined several approaches into a more personalized approach, used a variety of different theories depending on what is needed, or found common factors that appear universal in all approaches.

To complicate matters further, what professionals say they do in their sessions isn't always what they are really doing. In therapy, just as in life, there is a marked discrepancy between espoused beliefs versus theory in action (Wampold & Imel, 2015). Once in the privacy of their offices, practitioners will try most anything, regardless of its origin, to help their clients who are suffering. In fact, a number of well-known theorists have confessed to Jeffrey during panel discussions that they no longer even use their own models any longer since they have been impacted and influenced by the ideas of their colleagues. If you think about it, this makes perfect sense that behind closed doors you would try most anything to help someone once you have exhausted what is already familiar and comfortable.

Not all the theories are treated equally, nor are they used with equal frequency. Interestingly, the choice one makes often is influenced more by a professional identity than anything else. In a study of the theoretical preferences of various professional groups, the following results were summarized (Prochaska & Norcross, 2018; see Table 3.2):

TABLE 3.2. Preferred Theories of Psychotherapists

Professional Group	First Choice	Second Choice	Third Choice
Clinical psychologists	Cognitive (31%)	Eclectic/Integrative (22%)	Psychodynamic (15%)
Counseling psychologists	Eclectic/Integrative (34%)	Cognitive (19%)	Psychodynamic (12%)
Psychiatrists	Eclectic/Integrative (53%)	Psychoanalytic (35%)	Interpersonal (3%)
Social workers	Eclectic/Integrative (26%)	Cognitive (19%)	Systems (14%)
Counselors	Cognitive (29%)	Eclectic/Integrative (23%)	Rogerian/Person-centered (11%)

You can see from this chart that, hands down, the consistent winner is an eclectic/integrative approach. This means that regardless of training and professional identity, the majority of practitioners combine several different theories in their work or use a variety of methods depending on what is called for. Among those who describe themselves as eclectic or integrative as their dominant approach to therapy, clinicians draw on many different approaches.

What you can't see from this chart is that preferences and practices evolve every decade or so, depending on current trends. This means that as you start your professional practice in a few years, preferences will have already shifted once again. You also don't see that the study found a consistent number of therapists from various backgrounds who still prefer other approaches, such as behavioral (about 10%), existential (about 4%), Gestalt/experiential (about 2%), constructivist (about 2%), and multicultural/feminist (about 1%) approaches as their first choice. Given the low numbers, you might wonder why these theories are even included in this book! But remember this: The growing number of those who say they are eclectic or integrative are integrating *something*—and often it is techniques from these traditional or constructivist approaches blended seamlessly into a widely known approach to fit a particular client's needs. One example might include integrating multicultural therapy perspectives into a person-centered approach when working with a refugee population. A preference for one theoretical orientation does not prevent you from using concepts and techniques from another.

The preceding results are presented not so much to show the winners of a popularity contest, but rather to demonstrate how flexible most practitioners are in the ways they employ theory in their work. You will certainly have your work cut out for you to master the basics of a single theory that you can apply with clients. Augmenting that base with other ideas will usually come later in your career.

We have also personally observed regional preferences among therapists, as well. Marilyn, for example, was recently surprised by how many Jungian psychologists she discovered in the Pacific Northwest and was previously surprised by how many psychoanalysts and psychodynamic therapists were thriving in Florida. Jeffrey has discovered how many narrative therapists there are in New Zealand and emotionally focused therapists in Southern California, and has found that Adlerians enthusiastically practice in the North-Central United States and Canada. The reason for this is good news for you: local expert therapists welcome opportunities to share their favorite theories with you, and this is a great way to learn, now and in the future.

FOR A FIELD STUDY

Watch videos of prominent theoreticians doing therapy. You will find several representative examples in your school or department library that include many of the greatest thinkers in the field demonstrating their ideas in action. Many of these videos are available free online or on the publisher's website.

Observe the ways the theorists appear so effortless and natural in the ways they work with clients. Compare the ways their distinct personalities and personal values reflect the professional styles they have developed.

The Main Attraction

So, enough with the opening acts. Enough with all this preparation for the main attraction. It is time now to begin the study of the principal therapeutic worldviews that are the ones you are mostly likely to encounter. Study them with an open mind. Embrace each theory as if it has something valuable to teach you and something important that you can use to become more effective in your work.

SUGGESTED READINGS

Carlson, J., & Knaus, W. (Eds.) (2011). *Albert Ellis revisited.* New York, NY: Routledge.

Frankl, V. (1962). *Man's search for meaning.* New York, NY: Washington Square.

Jools, P., Byrne, N., & Berg, J. (2017). *Working with developmental anxieties in couple and family psychotherapy: The family within.* New York, NY: Routledge.

Kirschenbaum, H. (2009). *The life and work of Carl Rogers.* Alexandria, VA: American Counseling Association.

Kottler, J. A., & Carlson, J. (2006). *The client who changed me: Stories of therapist personal transformation.* New York, NY: Brunner/Routledge.

Rogers, C. (1980). *A way of being.* Boston, MA: Houghton Mifflin.

Thorne, B. (2013). *Carl Rogers* (3rd Ed.). Thousand Oaks, CA: SAGE.

Wampold, B. E., & Imel, Z. E. (2015). *The great psychotherapy debate: The evidence for what makes psychotherapy work.* New York, NY: Routledge.

Whitebook, J. (2017). *Freud: An intellectual biography.* New York, NY: Cambridge University Press.

CHAPTER 4

Look to the Past to Set You Free: Psychodynamic Approaches

LEARNING OBJECTIVES

After reading this chapter, you should be able to do the following:

1. Describe the early background of psychodynamic therapies.
2. Explain the relationship between the id, ego, and superego.
3. Compare Jungian and Freudian approaches to understanding the unconscious.
4. Identify how drives are related to intrapsychic conflicts, resistance, and defense mechanisms.
5. Contrast the processes and benefits of catharsis and corrective emotional experience.
6. Match Freud's stages of psychosocial development with their erogenous zones, associated physical activities, and potential psychological problems.
7. Describe the psychodynamic therapist's stance and its relationship to transference and countertransference.
8. Differentiate between the key notions of object relations, self-psychology, interpersonal psychotherapy, relational psychoanalysis, and brief psychodynamic psychotherapy.
9. List key contributions and potential limitations of psychodynamic approaches.

Theories differ according to a number of dimensions, as we have seen in previous chapters. Some require a very active therapist role, whereas others put more responsibility on the client to control structure, content, and focus. Some concentrate particularly on changing cognitive activity, whereas others stress observable behavior or inner feelings. And theories vary in where they think most of the action takes place: the present, the past, or the future.

In our first set of therapeutic approaches, the emphasis is clearly on the past. Each of the psychoanalytic conceptions shares a strong belief that until you help people to resolve issues in the past, they will never come to terms fully with what is bothering them in the present.

FOR PERSONAL REFLECTION

Some clients come for help because they see themselves repeating past mistakes over and over again—choosing relationship partners who have problems with addictions or working for a mean boss in every job they take. How do you see your own history repeating itself in some aspect of your life? What are some of the ongoing personal struggles that you have faced? These could involve difficulties with intimacy, authority figures, or poor self-esteem, among others.

What are some possible sources in your early life that could be responsible for these personal struggles? What have you suffered previously that continues to plague you today?

FOR GROUP DISCUSSION

Talk about some of these issues from the past that still make themselves known in your present.

EARLY BACKGROUND

For all practical purposes, the fields of counseling and psychotherapy were launched when a young physician in the middle of the 19th century began using hypnosis to help his patients talk about their difficult problems. Sigmund Freud had been trained as a neurologist with the finest medical scholars of his day. In addition, he had a lifelong interest in reading novels, studying philosophy, and practicing amateur archaeology. In a sense, Freud fancied himself as much a historian and archaeologist as he did a medical practitioner.

In one of his first published papers, Freud collaborated with a mentor, Joseph Breuer, to describe cases of hysteria (physical symptoms of psychological origin) they had treated using hypnosis (see "Voices From the Past" at the end of this chapter). It was their hypothesis that these patients suffered some sort of trauma at an early age and that they attempted to cope with this pain by blocking it out, repressing memories of the events (suspected to be sexual abuse). They theorized that strangling this emotional energy resulted in the development of symptoms that could only be treated by getting at the root of the problem. Although hints of the problem might slip out in dreams and unconscious acts, until the person could be helped to excavate and unearth the buried memories, the symptoms would persist.

During the next 50 years, Freud collaborated with a number of other medical colleagues, as well as students, to formulate a comprehensive theory of human development that included the origins of problems as well as how they might best be resolved. Many of these individuals, whose names may be familiar to you, went on to establish their own unique brand of psychoanalytic theory that better fit their personalities, values, and therapeutic style.

PSYCHOANALYTIC DISCIPLES AND REVISIONISTS

Before we review the core ideas for psychanalytic theories, we must let you know that more than any other approach, this one resembles a "theme and variations" piece of classical music. In the words of one author, "While it is not true that there are as many psychoanalytic theories of personality and treatment as there are psychoanalysts, it often seems that way" (Buirski & Buirski, 1994, p. 1). You have probably heard of many different names in this movement—Carl Jung, Alfred Adler, Eric Erikson, Harry Stack Sullivan, Theodore Reik, Anna Freud, Melanie Klein, Karen Horney, Erich Fromm—all once disciples of Freud who went on to develop their own schools of thought.

Carl Jung and Alfred Adler, for example, were very influential, creating theories that are still quite popular among contemporary practitioners (although Adler is not classified as psychodynamic any longer as he moved in a very different direction). Whereas Freud was big on sexual and biological roots of behavior, Jungian analysts favor more spiritual and cultural factors, which access the collective rather than the individual unconscious. In Jung's theory, he remained true to Freud's original idea about the importance of the past and inaccessible memories, but he expressed these as *archetypes*, which are enduring cultural symbols.

Just as in traditional psychoanalysis, the Jungian therapist encourages clients to talk about their dreams and fantasies, but the interpretations of this material are constructed very differently. That is one of the curious aspects of this field: Jungian patients will dream in Jungian symbols of mythology, folklore, and religious icons, whereas Freudian patients dream in phallic symbols, Oedipal complexes, and wish fulfillment. Does this phenomenon validate the theory or rather reflect that people were indoctrinated into a particular system?

Jungian therapy remains popular precisely because it can be so easily combined with religion, spirituality, and cross-cultural experiences. Because Jung wasn't nearly as sexist, pessimistic, or rigid as Freud (although he has been accused of racism and antisemitism), he is also often embraced as an alternative for therapy focused on exploring aspects of the self that are usually unconscious. I (Marilyn) recently supervised a student who confided to me that she re-reads Jung's classic, *Modern Man in Search of a Soul* (Jung, 1933) once a year to give herself a touchstone and opportunity for reflection as she grows as a therapist.

BASIC PRINCIPLES OF PSYCHOANALYTIC THEORY

It would normally take you at least 5 to 10 years of intensive study at an approved psychoanalytic institute to get a handle on psychoanalytic theory and its nuances. This would include reading the two dozen or more volumes that Freud wrote, plus 10 times that many of other related works. While you were completing this study, you would also be expected to participate in psychoanalysis as a patient for 5 or more years because it is considered crucial that you work through your own issues before you attempt to help anyone else with their problems. Once your training began as a practitioner (traditionally open only to MD's and PhD's, though counselors and social workers have been included more recently), you would then be meeting with your training analyst several times per week to work on cases, as well as attend seminars at the institute.

It might surprise you to know that there are approximately 35 training institutes for psychoanalysis in the United States accredited by the American Psychoanalytic Association (APA), (and there are tens of thousands more psychiatrists with psychoanalytic training, some of whom will likely be your supervisors and colleagues). The International Psychoanalytical Association accredits psychoanalytic training centers throughout the rest of the world, including Austria, France, Germany, Switzerland, Italy, and other countries, and recognizes more than 90 constituent associations and study groups around the world. Institutes often operate low-fee clinics, where people who might not otherwise be able to benefit from analysis can obtain treatment.

Fear not, however, if you have no inclination or intention of making a long-term commitment to the study of Freud. Even a small investment in learning more about his theory will likely pay off in your work. You would certainly be well advised to read a biography about him (see Roudinesco, 2016, or Whitebook, 2017, as examples) because his life's work was so interesting and influential (and he was such a great writer). You would also find it interesting to read a few of his classic works, notably *Interpretation of Dreams*, *The Psychopathology of Everyday Life*, or *An Outline of Psychoanalysis*. Because so many of Freud's original ideas are now part of our universal language and therapeutic principles, you would hardly be considerate literate as a therapist if you didn't at least familiarize yourself with the following basic concepts of the theory. Freud's and his followers' key concepts are explained in a *Comprehensive Dictionary of Psychoanalysis* (Ahktar, 2009). Those most influential in contemporary psychoanalytic thought will be reviewed next.

The Unconscious

As is true for all of us, Freud's ideas evolved with time and experience with his patients. His earliest ideas about consciousness was that it has three realms; the *unconscious* aspects of the psyche (not directly available to us but showing up in dreams and slips of the tongue), the *preconscious* (which includes things we can gain awareness of, perhaps in a well-conducted therapy session) and the *conscious* aspect of us that we usually (and sometimes mistakenly) think directs our lives. Often, the relationship of these aspects of our psyche is portrayed as an iceberg: We see only the tip (the conscious), yet the preconscious is just below the surface of our awareness, and the large, unseen unconscious lurks far beneath in the depths below.

FOR PERSONAL REFLECTION and A FIELD STUDY

Without having to look very hard, you will find evidence for all three levels of consciousness in your own experience, especially if you spend the time interviewing family members to compare what you remember to their own recollections.

For the sake of this exercise, assume that you have buried, repressed, or forgotten some powerful experiences in your life because they were too painful for you to deal with. They might have involved traumatic events about which you have no memory. They could involve abuse you suffered as a child. There could also have been some "convenient" rearranging of facts in which you remember things very differently from others who were around.

Get together with family members and look through old photograph albums together. Before you begin this task, tell yourself that you are going to remember things that you have forgotten previously. Tell stories to one another that are elicited by the photos but resist telling the same old tales. Instead, try to drum up new ones. Compare your different versions of the same events.

Driven by Drives

Freud thought a lot about what makes people behave the ways they do. His answer to that question was to propose two conflicting drives in his book, *Beyond the Pleasure Principle* (1920): the *life drive*, usually called the *libido*, and the *death drive*. You probably instantly think of the sex drive when you hear the word libido, and indeed Freud's theory focused on psychosexual stages and motivations. But the term also encompasses all energies that are expansive and joyful; even babies and toddlers have libido, which keeps them reaching out for pleasurable and growth-producing experiences. We invest our libido in particular people, objects, and activities throughout our life. Though Freud talked a lot about aggression, he did not propose it as a unique drive but rather as libido gone awry, as reflected in Otto Kernberg's book, *The Inseparable Nature of Love and Aggression* (2012).

Similarly, the death drive (later called Thanatos by some analysts, after the "grim reaper" of Greek mythology) is not a literal urge to take one's life, but to "check out," go into oblivion, and reach a state without tension. The two drives balance each other, and Freud thought that we do what we do to keep ourselves in a minimal state of unconscious tension.

Freud proposed an interesting idea about something people often do to keep their drives in an optimal state of balance: the *repetition compulsion*. This behavior is easy to see in young children, who will do something over and over until they master or resolve it. Think of a child playing a hide-and-seek game where daddy disappears and then is found, to the accompaniment of delighted screams. Analysts would see this "game" as the child reworking love and loss until they are more tolerable. Similarly, adults who end up with the same evil boss or lover over and over again may be recreating an emotionally difficult situation in an attempt to master it.

Intrapsychic Conflicts

In addition to the drives that fuel our lives, Freud went on to propose that the psyche could be divided into three parts, the *id, ego*, and *superego*. The id is present at birth and is the seat of the instincts. It is unconscious, and it is impulsively driven by the *pleasure principle*. In contrast, the ego and the superego are both unconscious and conscious. The superego is where self-criticism and judgmental capacities develop, as children internalize the restrictions and judgments adults place on them. The ego mediates between the id and the superego, attempting to reconcile raw desire with socially appropriate behavior. The ego develops slowly and operates by the *reality principle*. One goal of psychoanalysis is to strengthen the ego so that it directs the personality more of the time, keeping the punitive aspects of the ego and the potentially destructive aspects of the id in check so that appropriate, vitalizing choices can be made. Psychological symptoms and self-defeating patterns are the result of internal struggles in which a person attempts to reconcile battles between basic aggressive and sexual instincts (id) versus the conscience and moral beliefs (superego). Even though this "structural theory" is rarely applied as it was originally conceived, it supplies a valuable metaphor for looking at the struggles that people have between their raw aggressive/sexual instincts and their conscience.

FOR A CLASS ACTIVITY

In groups of three, each person should take on the role of the id (raw impulses), superego (moral conscience), or the ego (reasoning, logical self). Situate yourselves with the id facing the superego and the ego sitting in the middle like a referee. Now begin a conversation (more likely an argument) in which the id wants to do something wicked or socially inappropriate and the superego tries to cajole and scold the id into restraint. Before things get totally out of hand, the ego's job is to mediate this struggle, getting the two sides to agree to a reasonable compromise.

According to psychoanalytic theory, this sort of debate among the three intrapsychic parts of the self occurs internally all the time. The therapist's job is to strengthen the ego as much as possible so it can do a more effective job of helping the client live productively and happily.

Most modern analysts don't think that the personality literally has an id, ego, and superego. Freud's original structural theory about these aspects of the psyche, and the conflicts between them, is now the focus of only a handful of psychodynamic practitioners. Most are expanding Freud's ideas to explore how therapists can help these aspects of client's psyches get along, even when they are not fully developed (Druck, 2018). However, many analysts from a variety of approaches still focus on conscious and unconscious conflict among desires to be controlling, dependent, aggressive, or sexual (Carveth, 2018); or on relieving feelings of guilt, shame, anxiety, and jealousy (Wurmser, 2015a). Treatment is deemed successful when the analysand (the patient or client) can bring more things to awareness and thus resolve these conflicts, examine their less adaptive solutions, and choose better ones.

Psychosexual Stages

Freud observed that children between 3 and 5 years old often develop a more intense bond with their opposite sex parent. Freud borrowed from classical literature and termed this the Oedipal stage after Sophocles's play *Oedipus Rex,* in which an exiled son returns home and unknowingly murders a man who is his father and marries a woman who turns out to be his mother. He later went on the propose that development of the personality proceeded as physical development occurred, with particular zones of the body being invested with libidinal energy at each stage (see table 4.1). Personality traits in adulthood derived from childhood experiences of under- or over-gratification of the primary psychosexual need at that age.

As with several of Freud's other ideas, modern research has not confirmed this proposition; as such, the developmental stages are not the main focus of modern psychoanalytic theory. However, analysts continue to look for recurring themes and patterns in a person's life, and they expect that, usually, these themes and patterns are related to early experiences with attachment figures that occurred at particular developmental periods. The hope is that by seeing how the past is echoed in current difficulties, patients can free themselves to live more fully in the present.

TABLE 4.1. Freud's Stages of Psychosexual Development

Stage	Age*	Erogenous zone/Activity	Fixation results in ...
Oral	0–1	Lips/Sucking	Oral fixation
Anal	2–3	Anus/bladder and bowel control	Compulsivity
Phallic	4–5	Genitals/masturbation	Gender confusion
Latency	6–12	None; energy is sublimated	Repression
Genital	12–Adult	Genitals/Sexuality intimacy	Low or hypersexuality

*Ages are approximate and vary by individual.

Exploring the Past

This is a significant therapeutic emphasis shared by all varieties of psychanalytic (loyal to the basic frame of Freudian analysis), as well as psychodynamic (informed by many Freudian concepts) theories. Current problems are thought to stem from unresolved issues that originally occurred in early childhood. Freud focused on such things as the impact of breastfeeding, toilet training, and early sexual feelings, but it is far more useful to expand this idea to include the influence of any intensely pleasurable, traumatic, or otherwise significant events. For example, instead of focusing on exactly when or how harshly someone was toilet trained, contemporary practitioners listen for ways in which their client might have been shamed when they enjoyed pleasant sensations in their body or expressed a desire for physical comfort or closeness (Lichtenberg, Lachmann, & Fosshage, 2016).

Other traumas can be seen as disruptions to our sense of security with our early attachment figures who are, after all, our first loves. These early traumas may have been *repressed* (buried), but it is generally thought that they continue to influence our internal templates for all our relationships. These templates set us up to expect to be safe and happy, insignificant and ignored, or painfully abandoned by others. It is an interesting exercise to look at our acquaintances in close relationships and see how their behavior is related in some way to what they witnessed in their parents or experienced as a child. We probably all have friends who repeatedly get into relationships with partners who are abusive or distant, even though this causes them great distress. From this perspective, it is just early history repeating itself!

Resistance

People are usually not crazy about the idea of delving deeply into buried secrets and painful memories. Psychoanalytic theory predicts that there will be a certain amount of resistance to such probes, however subtle, that are intended to bring unconscious material to the surface. A certain amount of client reluctance is, therefore, expected and anticipated. Another useful concept from this theory states that when you encounter ambivalence on the part of clients who say they want to change but sabotage their own efforts, it can be a sign that progress is being made.

When practicing this theory, you anticipate and expect that your clients will become resistant during those times when you are getting close to painful, repressed material. This is considered a normal part of the growth process and is expected to be part of the treatment. In fact, practitioners would get suspicious if clients were being a bit too enthusiastic and cooperative.

Whether you subscribe to this idea or not, it is of immeasurable help to remind yourself when you encounter client resistance and reluctance that clients are just doing the best job they can to protect themselves from perceived threats. Here, you are meddling in their lives, stirring up painful stuff, pressing and pushing them in areas they would rather not venture. It is like you are pulling on old scabs—and it hurts. A lot.

Defense Mechanisms

When threatened, people try to defend themselves with a variety of strategies, including withdrawal and counterattacks. As a neurologist, Freud noticed this same sort of process operating within the body when a system would mobilize defenses to deal with a perceived threat. It seemed reasonable to imagine that the same sort of thing happens psychologically during those times when individuals believe they are under attack, sometimes even beyond their awareness.

Defense mechanisms function to reduce inner tension and anxiety, but they may not always be effective. It is, thus, one of the therapist's roles to help clients identify their favored defenses and understand their impact on present behavior. This is tricky, because defenses exist for a reason—to protect unconscious vulnerabilities. In fact, almost all behavior that, at first, may appear counterproductive and self-defeating serves some purpose, even if it has side effects. In more recent times this is called "secondary gains" or "payoffs," that is, certain benefits that protect someone from things that might be even more destabilizing. For example, consider why someone might repeatedly engage in angry outbursts that consistently get him in trouble. Ask yourself, why would someone go into fits of rage that push others away and may even end with him in trouble with the law? It turns out that he "enjoys" payoffs as a result.

FOR REFLECTION

Before we continue with this example further, consider for a moment some of the reasons why this individual may continue to engage in angry behavior that gets him in trouble and seems to only be a problem for him, blocking the things he says he wants most in life—intimate friendships and a life partner. What "payoffs" might be helpful to him by remaining stuck in this pattern? How is his anger acting as a defense, even if it has some annoying side effects?

In spite of his complaints and protestations that he hates the way his anger gets him in trouble with others, it turns out that this behavior serves him well in some regard. First, he usually gets his way since he has trained others to fear his outbursts; people tend to defer to him because they don't want to trigger him. Second, he gets to feel powerful, a feeling that is important to him because he is actually quite insecure. Third, anger is the way he learned to show passion. As a male growing up in a family with traditional gender roles, this is the way a man is supposed to express feelings of frustration or dissatisfaction—lashing out at others. Finally, anger allows him to destroy things on his own terms. When he scares others away, he can blame them for being weak. It is the way he tests others to determine if they are worthy to be members of his inner circle.

So it is with many such dysfunctional behaviors (shame, guilt, worry, anxiety): They act as defensive and protective reactions that allow the person to function (to some degree). Otherwise, there would be a lot of discomfort, commitment, and hard work involved in learning something new and facing the unknown. This also helps explain, to some extent, why people remain stuck in untenable or even abusive situations—they fear the alternative may be even worse and so find ways to keep themselves stuck, even at an unconscious level. It is for this reason that we attempt to draw out the client's hidden and disguised motives very gradually and sensitively.

Even therapists who do not think of themselves as psychodynamic find themselves using the language of defenses, because many of the ego defenses have become part of everyday language. You have heard before, for example, things such as "You are in denial," "You're just projecting your stuff on to me," "Stop intellectualizing," or "He became so freaked out he just regressed." In each of these instances, what is being described is a way that a person is combating a situation that is experienced as overwhelming, and so attempts are made to hide.

FOR A GROUP ACTIVITY

Working together, supply examples for each of the following common defense mechanisms. Share your best examples.

RATIONALIZATION:	Justifying a situation by making up rational reasons to explain irrational behavior
REPRESSION:	Censoring painful experiences by excluding them from conscious awareness
PROJECTION:	Perceiving that others have those characteristics or behaviors that you find unacceptable in yourself
REACTION FORMATION:	Acting the opposite way from the way the unconscious is nudging you
DENIAL:	Pretending that something undesirable is not really happening
SUBLIMATION:	Converting unacceptable or forbidden impulses into socially acceptable behavior
REGRESSION:	A retreat to an earlier stage of development because of fear

FOR REFLECTION OR DISCUSSION

Which are your own "go-to" defense mechanisms?

Dreams

According to Freud, dreams were seen as the "royal road to the unconscious," the most useful means by which to decode what a person longs for or fears the most. In the traditional psychoanalytic format, complex symbols and metaphors were uncovered and interpreted as the means to discover hidden impulses and repressed material. Within contemporary psychoanalytic practice, dreams are still seen as the mind's way of structuring experience to its own liking, but the work that is done with this awareness is a far more flexible and more intuitive process (Blechner, 2018). When clients bring their dreams to us in sessions, rather than being the ones responsible for interpreting what they mean, as some absolute truth, we instead turn the question around and ask, "What does that dream say to you? What meaning do you attach to it that seems most significant to you?"

Along with many of Freud's original ideas, his notion of dreams as repressed wish fulfillment has not stood the test of time. Many other theories, and neurological research, now offer other explanations for the meaning of dreams, including the idea that they actually have no meaning at all—except to what we create in our own minds out of random fragments that result from residual neurons firing while we sleep. That is not to say that dream interpretation cannot play an important role in therapy, just that the possible interpretations are now open to greater possibilities.

FOR HOMEWORK

Whenever a client brings a dream into session, it is often useful to explore possible meanings. Before you can hope to help others make sense of their dreams, it would be useful for you to have some practice examining your own inner experiences.

Keep a notebook and nightlight by your bed. Since you tend to forget your dreams unless you immediately write them down, make a promise to yourself that you will write down all your dreams for a week. Before you go to bed each night, tell yourself that you will remember your dreams. Each time you wake up in the middle of one (which is the only time you will actually remember them) scribble down some notes about the gist of what happened. In the morning, review your notes and draw some hypotheses about what the dream means to you.

Catharsis

"I've never really told anyone about this before, but I ... This is kind of difficult for me. ... Uh, well, it's just that I've felt so much shame about it for so many years. I just want to tell someone about it ... tell *you* about it. I think I'd feel better if just, you know, if someone knew about it. And then maybe you could help me forgive myself."

Catharsis is the experience we all have when we share something that is bothering us to someone we trust, especially someone we sense (or hope) will not interrupt or critically judge us. It represents the release of pent-up emotional energy that occurs through clients telling their stories in a more open and honest way. You have experienced the power of catharsis many times in your own life. Perhaps you were talking to a friend or family member about something very upsetting and afterward you noticed how much better you felt. This confidante may have done nothing else but listen to you, allow you to leach out all your frustration, but that was quite enough.

Almost all therapeutic approaches make some use of this process by allowing people to dump a lot of their stored-up frustrations and complaints—to a point. It is generally not a good idea to let this go on without some intervention or rechanneling because clients can end up feeling sorry for themselves or engaging in "poor me" victim roles. Even the most action oriented or brief therapeutic approaches still make time for the client to share what is most bothersome, and do so in a way that this process is initially fairly unstructured and reveals much of the emotion that is attached to the critical features.

It may strike you that it is not nearly enough to just sit there and listen to someone pour his or her heart out, but this is so often exactly what some people need to do (at least in the beginning). It is so rare that most people have anyone in their life who will really listen to them and make a sincere effort to understand without judgment. Or course, it is usually necessary to go far beyond the initial storytelling to make a significant difference in the client's life.

Corrective Emotional Experience

Rather than merely talking about feelings, contemporary therapists seek to help clients alter their self-perceptions and behavior in light of their therapeutic experiences and, it is hoped, new insights. Of course, this is easier said than done. Holmes (2009) illustrates this by sharing what one of his clients said in response to Freud's rule that you should say whatever comes to mind, however embarrassing or shameful: "If I could do that I wouldn't need to be here in the first place" (p. ix).

Once there is some degree of emotional arousal, often directed toward the therapist in the form of transference, attempts will be made to work this through in more constructive ways. In other words, within the security of the therapeutic relationship, the client can fully experience emotions and express them without being abandoned, shamed, ignored, or punished, but rather being seen, heard, and valued. This experience of safety becomes a model for how clients might experience themselves with others in the outside world. They grow in their ability to tolerate and explore feelings because the therapist subtly cajoles them into fully experiencing the intensity—in safety—and thus creates a chance for the intense feeling to change into something that offers relief.

An approach that shares some of these assumptions described in this section, but also utilizes features from other theoretical traditions, is emotionally focused therapy (EFT), which holds that you can't leave a place you've never been, so fully experiencing a disruptive emotion is the place to start

(Greenberg, 2017). We will be discussing EFT in much greater detail in a later chapter. Suffice it to say for now that a client is encouraged to re-experience a memory or thought, and its associated emotion, rather than avoiding it. The therapist and client stay with the emotion in all its nuances until it is fully felt and accepted; thus, the emotion is transformed into something constructive rather than festering away somewhere deep inside.

TREATMENT PROCEDURES

The psychoanalytic style of therapy is a relatively long-term relationship that is designed to help people explore their unconscious issues that are at the core of current problems. Through the use of interpretation, dream analysis, free association, transference, and other methods that access repressed material, the practitioner helps clients understand the source of their troubles and apply what they learn to their daily lives. There are several strategies that are used to bring about this process, many of which are embedded in the special kind of relationship that is established.

Hardly anyone practices traditional psychoanalysis any longer, and certainly nobody who is taking this particular class. There is just too much pressure in today's climate to operate briefly and to accommodate vast differences in the cultural context of people's experiences. After all, who has time (and money) to commit to showing up for sessions three times each week for five years? With that said, the model has been adapted and abbreviated in recent times in such a way that that following features have been retained. Many of them are included as part of any generic, eclectic approach (Shedler, 2010).

1. Focus on affect and expression of emotion
2. Exploration of attempts to avoid distressing thoughts and feelings
3. Identification of recurring themes and patterns
4. Discussion of past experiences, their meaning, and impact
5. Focus on interpersonal relations
6. Focus on the therapeutic relationship
7. Exploration of fantasy life and what it reveals

We will also describe, in greater detail, some of the clinical strategies and techniques that have emerged from psychoanalytic theory, many of which are now considered mainstream and used by therapists in a variety of settings.

Evenly Hovering Attention

Freud was the first to advocate a type of helping alliance in which the therapist would appear cool, calm, and collected no matter what unfolded or was revealed in the session. Consistent with his scientific training, practitioners were schooled in the importance of objectivity and neutrality in their chair-side manner. It was hoped that the more neutrally you present yourself, the more pure would be the client's *projections* (subjective perceptions) about who he or she imagines you are. Thus, clients are encouraged to create fantasies and feelings about their therapists, providing material for exploration and insight—a process practitioners call *working through*.

As you might imagine, there is a very delicate balance to reach in which, on the one hand, you present yourself as neutrally as possible so as to not contaminate the transference that must naturally develop. On the other hand, you don't want to appear so withholding and aloof that you are perceived as disapproving or even punitive. Psychoanalytic practitioners, while appearing somewhat neutral and objective, present themselves as empathic, caring, nonjudgmental, with a kind of "evenly hovering attention," similar to what a good parent provides (Stern, 2018). Remember that many people who attend counseling or therapy may have already experienced lots of rejection in their lives from parents or adults who were overdirecting, neglectful, or worse, so finding this delicate balance of warm neutrality and nonreactivity is a key element for therapists.

FOR A PRACTICE ACTIVITY

Practice "evenly hovering attention" in helping relationships with a partner. One of you takes on the role of a client, thinking of a very provocative, sensitive, perhaps shocking imaginary issue you could talk about such as being an abuser, drug dealer, or perhaps someone in a witness protection program who committed a violent crime. Imagine that you are feeling very reluctant about your life because of fears of being judged.

The other person will be the therapist. Your job is to listen with neutrality, detachment, and evenly hovering attention. Present yourself as interested, nonjudgmental, and noncritical, encouraging the person to speak about his or her experience. For now, it doesn't matter which skills you use because this is only an exercise in practicing an interested but unflappable therapeutic stance.

Afterward, talk to one another about what the experience was like. Give feedback to one another. If time permits, switch roles and try another round.

Transference

Freud originally conceived of transference as a projection of unconscious desires onto the therapist. Through the analysis of this fantasy, it was believed that repressed memories and unresolved conflicts of childhood could be resolved, especially those involving parental figures.

Whether you subscribe to psychoanalytic thinking or not, it's rather obvious that therapeutic relationships have elements that are based on both reality and fantasy. You see people as they really are, as well as how you imagine them to be. You impose onto others the images of others who have resembled them, often responding to them based on these prior associations. Sometimes you even project attributes that are created by your own past experiences rather than people's actual behavior. This is especially true with authority figures, one association that clients often make with respect to a therapist.

FOR PERSONAL REFLECTION

Think of a time recently in which you projected onto someone feelings that were transferred from another relationship. For example, can you recall an incident where you had a strong emotional reaction, either positive or negative, to someone you had just encountered, and when as you look back on it, you had little "data" for doing so?

One especially fertile place to look for such a process is related to authority figures. Notice, for example, the ways you perceive your instructor that are based less on his or her behavior and more on your images of what he or she is like. Whom does your instructor remind you of? What are ways your interactions with your instructor are similar to other relationships you have experienced before?

Typically, transferences involve the repetition of some previous relationship pattern, one that is inappropriate and distorts reality. For instance, when you look at your instructor for this course, you react to him or her not only as he or she appears in reality (if you could watch an objective video) but also as you imagine him or her to be. The feelings that you have toward this person, whether admiration, disappointment, frustration, or strong attraction, are not just based on what he or she did or said, but also how you interpreted and experienced those interactions as filtered through your distorted perceptions. These reactions are strongly influenced not only by what actually occurred but also some of the prior experiences you've had with other authority figures who have served in a similar role. Sometimes you may feel judged or criticized by your instructor less because of his or her actions than by your prior associations with other teachers who have reminded you of this person or situation.

Whereas Freud and traditional psychoanalysts believed that almost all the feelings one has toward a therapist are projections, fantasies, and distortions and are a manifestation of past struggles, Kohut (1977) reconceived transference as something else altogether: a real alliance in which the client creates a new parental relationship rather than merely reliving an old one. Modern therapists build on this assumption and believe that most of the reactions to the therapist are genuine and reflect what is actually occurring between two people involved in a very intimate, intense relationship (Racker, 2018). The relationship between client and therapist becomes a source of conflict and ambivalence, especially considering it is designed to be a blank slate on which people may project their fantasies about unresolved authority figures. Once clients gain insight into their distortions, they are able to work through the conflict first with the therapist and later by resolving issues related to other relationships in the past and present.

In a nutshell, it may be helpful to work with your clients' transference issues in the following way:

1. Observe how unconscious and unfulfilled needs are played out in sessions.
2. Notice the ways in which the therapist is idealized by the client as a need for more constructive "parenting."
3. Use positive transference as leverage without bringing the client's attention to this process.
4. Once a solid relationship has been established, the therapist can invite attention to the client's transference and explore it and its meaning for the client's other relationships.

FOR PERSONAL REFLECTION

Bring to mind the image of someone you don't like very much, someone who really gets underneath your skin. This may be a person who once betrayed you, someone who rejected you, or someone who has been repeatedly abusive toward you.

Now imagine that a new client comes in to see you who bears a striking resemblance to your nemesis, either in appearance or mannerisms. How do you suppose you would feel working with this individual who reminds you of another person whom you despise? Do you think there is any way possible that your strong feelings would not affect your relationship with this client?

Situations such as this (called countertransference) are why psychoanalytic theory considers it so crucial for you to work through all your own unresolved issues before you attempt to help others. Otherwise, your unconscious desires, repressed memories, and unresolved issues can infect the work you try to do with others.

Countertransference

The client isn't the only one who projects and distorts the relationship. Therapists, as well, have strong feelings toward their clients—both positive and negative—that have little to do with that person. Our buttons sometimes get pushed by people who remind us of others we have encountered in our lives (Racker, 2018). We respond to them not as they really are, but as we imagine them to be. Some of the most easily identifiable signs that countertransference may be going on include the following:

- The arousal of guilt from unresolved personal struggles that parallel those impulses and emotions of the client
- Impaired empathy in which you find it difficult to feel caring and respectful toward the client
- Inaccurate interpretations of the client's feelings due to your identification and projection
- Feelings of being generally blocked, helpless, and frustrated with a particular client
- Evidence of boredom or impatience in your inner world during work with a client
- Unusual memory lapses regarding the details of a case
- Mutual acting out in which the client begins living out your values and you begin acting out the client's pathology
- A tendency to speak about a client in derogatory terms
- An awareness that you are working harder than the client

I (Jeffrey) remember one instance in which I was seeing an elementary school principal as a client. Because I had been a rather precocious child who frequently found myself in trouble with the principal, I did not have the best of feelings toward this woman who reminded me of my former nemesis. Although ordinarily I am quite flexible about the ways I schedule sessions, doing my best to arrange appointments in a way that is most convenient for clients, with this woman I was more than a little unyielding. I might normally say something such as, "When would you like to reschedule?" but with the principal, I said instead, "I'll see you next Thursday at 3:00."

"But I can't make it then," she replied with astonishment. "You know I can't get away from school until 3:30 when the last children have left."

"Well then," I said with a scolding tone that gave me more pleasure than I'd like to admit, "if your therapy is really important to you, you'll find a way to be here, won't you?"

I am certainly not proud of the way I handled this case but it is a good example of how my own personal feelings got in the way of my compassion.

The worst part is that I really wasn't seeing this woman the way she was because I had projected onto her the image of other authority figures from my own past.

FOR A FIELD STUDY

Talk to experienced therapists about instances in which they have had strong countertransference reactions toward particular clients. This is a difficult, risky area to discuss because it represents a loss of control and poor judgment on the part of the therapist, so be prepared from some resistance unless you have a trusting relationship with the professional.

Through training, supervision, and increased self-awareness, therapists attempt to closely monitor and check those personal reactions that are triggered by clients or the things they share. This is especially true with respect to so-called "difficult" or resistant clients, or when impasses occur in a conflicted therapeutic relationship. After all, interpersonal difficulties almost always involve both participants who are triggering one another. This is one of the most challenging aspects of the job, one that is facilitated by considering several important questions that are designed to be most helpful:

1. What am I doing to create or exacerbate the problems?
2. What personal issues of mine are being triggered?
3. Who does the patient remind me of?
4. How am I acting out my impatience with this client's progress?
5. What expectations am I demanding of this client that he or she is unwilling or unable to meet?
6. What needs of mine are not being met?

You will notice that all these questions prompt the therapist to consider his or her own contributions to the issues, rather than just blaming the client for the problems between them. It is interesting to consider that not everyone agrees who the most challenging people to work with are. Some therapists love working with borderline personality disorders, eating disorders, substance abuse, impulse disorders, the kinds of diagnoses with the worst prognoses and that many others find most frustrating. So often, what we prefer, and what we most avoid, reflect our own unresolved issues.

VOICES FROM THE FIELD

Welcome to an exploration of the beauty of your life story. I am a psychotherapist: more specifically, a psychologist and a psychoanalyst. I have seen hundreds and hundreds of patients over the course of my 40-plus year career. Every one of them has had a story to tell, a story that despite its often gut-wrenching pain is indeed beautiful, both in its uniqueness and its complexity. It is a story that the person may never have dared to tell before finding the safety of my office, perhaps feeling too inconsequential or guilty or ashamed.

Keeping silent and shut down over the years, the person often develops symptoms such as depression, anxiety, or obsessions, or becomes involved in various addictive activities, or in one dissatisfying relationship after another. These are not chance happenings. They occur because the person is driven to repeat past experiences in the present. They occur because the person has not previously been listened to or heard. They occur because the person has not been given the time or space to explore his or her own mind within the safety and comfort of a therapeutic relationship.

—Linda Sherby, PhD, ABPP
Boca Raton, FL

PSYCHOANALYTIC INNOVATORS

In the last part of the 20th century, there was a strong movement among psychoanalytic practitioners to move away from Freud's emphasis on instinctual drives and psychosexual stages of development and focus instead on the ways that primary relationships are internalized as templates for future intimate relations. Termed *object relations* or *ego psychology*, several different theorists concentrated their treatment efforts on the basic bonds between infant and parent(s) and continue to influence practice today.

Whereas traditional Freudian psychoanalytic therapy, as it was originally conceived by Freud, is now virtually obsolete, self-psychology, object relations therapy, and recent innovations based on them are alive and flourishing, particularly in the area of treating personality disorders. Theses psychodynamic approaches have evolved in such a way that they reflect the needs of contemporary practice. Applications of these theories, as well as some modern version of them, will be described further in the next sections.

Object Relations Theory

Melanie Klein was an Austrian analyst who migrated to Britain after World War I. Early in her career, she applied psychoanalysis to children (including, allegedly, her own son and daughter). Her ideas attracted the attention of many British physicians who worked with children but got her into conflict with more traditional Freudian analysis—namely, that infants and toddlers are not so much moved to gratify sexual and aggressive drives but were motivated to connect with other "objects" (as in the phrase, "the object of my affection").

Donald Winnicott (1958) was a British pediatrician and analyst whom she inspired. Winnicott was John Bowlby's contemporary (you may recall Bowlby's developmental theory of attachment), and they both came to prominence in post–World War II Britain as they sought to serve the great tide of orphans and traumatized children who needed treatment at that time. Winnicott is famous for his idea about the "transitional object" used by children as comfort in stressful situations or at bedtime. Similarly, he conceived of therapy as a "holding environment" that provides a safe, secure, dependable relationship in which clients can work through early but residual relational conflicts.

Typical of the way so many other revisionists took a central idea of Freud's and ran with it, Heinz Kohut was intrigued with one of Freud's papers on narcissism, which is the condition of excessive self-involvement. Kohut was a Viennese medical doctor who fled to the U.S. to escape the Nazis and eventually became a famous lecturer and member of the Chicago Institute for Psychoanalysis. He rejected Freud's ideas about the internal drives and ego states, focusing instead on "self-states." Although Freud and current diagnostic manuals treat narcissism as a pathological state marked by obsession with one's own needs, Kohut's theory stressed that self-focused development can be healthy if it leads to productive activities and balanced self-esteem. Kohut also emphasized the role of empathy in the therapeutic alliance, believing that one of the most important ingredients is helping people—even narcissists—to feel understood (Kohut, 1984; 1997). Rather than only interpreting events of the past as a road to understand current problems, Kohut recommended a treatment in which here-and-now behaviors are identified and explored. Defenses are identified as they play themselves out in sessions. Rather than sparking further resistance, if handled sensitively, such interpretations can lead to greater ego strength and resilience.

Just as in traditional psychoanalytic practice, contemporary object relations therapists see the past as a strong influence on behavior in the present. However, rather than remaining aloof and completely detached, they often create a more natural, empathic, and supportive relationship that fosters a degree of attachment without complete dependence. The goal is to provide a secure environment with clear boundaries. This type of relationship encourages clients to explore the nature of their relationships with others, as well as with the therapist in sessions (Carveth, 2018).

Self-Psychology Theory

According to this theory, it is excessive self-centeredness and narcissism that lead to many personal problems. When you get stuck in the stage of egocentrism and grandiosity typical of a 4-year-old, you are likely to feel awfully disappointed with others not living up to your expectations. Kohut, for example, specialized in working with severe personality disorders by structuring an empathic relationship with clear boundaries. Self-psychologists often call this type of relationship a "holding environment" because you are metaphorically holding someone with caring but consistent, stable force. Because you are likely to be tested a lot with these types of cases, it is crucial that you have in place clear rules and boundaries for handling inevitable acting out.

Otto Kernberg (1984; 2012) applied concepts of self-psychology to understanding personality disorders, including one severe type known as borderline personality disorder. Unlike what it sounds, someone caught between the boundaries of being sane and insane, this pattern is characterized by intense, contradictory interpersonal patterns. Such individuals tend to be manipulative and extremely difficult to deal with. It would be the consensus of most therapists that this is among the most challenging cases of all because such individuals are unpredictable and often do their best to get underneath others' skins as a means of self-protection. In fact, one of the major determinants as to whether a client is bestowed with this toxic label occurs when the client appears so annoying, manipulative, and irritating that the therapist can't get him or her out of mind.

Kernberg and his colleagues have recently sought to integrate the contributions of other therapeutic systems into a more contemporary and responsive version of psychoanalytic treatment that brings in elements of empathy, the here and now, affective experience, and a more genuine relationship in the treatment of personality disorders (Caligor, Yeomans, Clarkin, & Kernberg, 2018). As you might guess, other theoretical approaches we present in this text are not equipped to impact personality change (which is logical, as from certain perspectives, there is no such thing as a "personality").

Interpersonal Psychoanalysis and Interpersonal Psychotherapy

This relatively new approach springs from the original notions of Karen Horney and Harry Stack Sullivan, analysts who drew attention to how an individual's dynamics develop and are most meaningfully viewed in the context of relationships with other people. Horney was a German psychoanalyst who later emigrated to the United States. She questioned Freud's theory of sexuality, as well as its instinct orientation. She acknowledged that penis envy might occur for some women, but thought that men, in parallel fashion, envied women's ability to bear children—hence, "womb envy."

As one of the first female psychiatrists, she decided that female behavior was a neglected issue and wrote a series of important papers in which she sketched out her ideas about how much of women's behavior that analysts depicted as "neurotic" actually fit within cultural expectations of rigid gender roles (Horney, 1945). She also developed a theory of the "coping strategies" that individuals develop in relationships. The first strategy, "moving with," is seen as healthy; the other three as neurotic:

1. "Moving with"—Individuals with this style use communication and negotiation to agree, disagree, compromise, and build solutions.
2. "Moving toward"—These individuals tend to give others what they want at the expense of themselves. They might say, "If I give in, I won't get hurt."
3. "Moving against"—These individuals seek to control or exploit others. They might say, "If I beat them to the punch, I won't get hurt."
4. "Moving away"—These individuals distance themselves and try not to care. They might say, "If I don't let anyone get close to me, I won't get hurt."

FOR PERSONAL REFLECTION

We all like to think of ourselves as well adjusted rather than neurotic, but being under stress can push us to use interpersonal styles that are less adaptive. In your lesser moments (in conflicts with your family, for example), which of the three neurotic coping strategies that Horney described do you tend to fall into? Do you think this might have implications for countertransference tendencies you might have when working with difficult clients?

Harry Stack Sullivan also had strong influence on American psychoanalysis. He developed his ideas while studying schizophrenia and what we would now call severe borderline personality disorder. He, like Horney, challenged Freud's psychosexual theory and developed a lifespan theory of personality development that featured relational capacities. Additionally, he emphasized how society and culture influence personality development and psychopathology. He coined the term "problems in living" to try to get away from words implying that his patients were mentally ill.

Building on Sullivan's (and to some extent, Horney's ideas), interpersonal psychotherapy (IPT) emphasizes how interactional problems (rather than intrapsychic problems) contribute to individual problems. Interpersonal therapy was initially developed in the 1970s as a placebo (yes, a placebo!) to be used in clinical trials' testing other therapeutic approaches, but it was found to have positive effects, particularly for people with depression. It is now a brief approach—(12–16 sessions)—and structured as a manual-based treatment. This approach has gained in popularity because of its success in research studies with many hard-to-treat problems (e.g., severe depression, post-natal depression, bulimia, and bipolar disorders (Weissman, Markowitz, & Klerman, 2017). It has also been adapted for use in resource-poor countries and is recognized by the World Health Organization as a first-line treatment for depression.

FOR PERSONAL REFLECTION and A CLASS ACTIVITY

The management of boundaries plays an important part in ego psychology and self-psychology. Because these theories have been applied often to cases of severe personality disorder, it is especially important to provide a predictable, solid relationship to set appropriate limits that clients might not be able to maintain on their own.

Think of times you have been involved in teaching or helping relationships in which someone set firm boundaries about what you could and could not do. You understood that these rules existed for your own safety and welfare rather than as part of some arbitrary bureaucracy or the helper's convenience. How did this structure help you?

In small groups, identify the boundaries that have been established in your class. These include all rules, both explicit and implicit, that are designed to further goals, maintain safety, and keep things running smoothly. Talk about the ways these boundaries are enforced.

CONTEMPORARY DEVELOPMENTS

Obviously, the world today is very different from 19th-century Victorian Vienna that spawned Freud's original ideas. Furthermore, advances in neurology, psychology, and related social sciences have demonstrated that although some of Freud's theories have withstood the scrutiny of empirical investigation (e.g., unconscious conflict), others have not (e.g., dreams as repressed wishes, Oedipal complex, death instinct). Yet many of the essential assumptions and techniques of psychoanalysis have stood the test of time.

Some of Freud's original disciples such as Alfred Adler, Franz Alexander, and Otto Rank began making revisions in the basic psychoanalytic model almost from their first involvement in the movement. They realized that if this novel psychological approach was going to help those who needed it the most, then somehow it would need to be abbreviated in such a way that symptoms could be relieved in a matter of months rather than years and would need to be more obviously applicable to people's foremost concerns.

Relational Psychoanalysis

Relational psychoanalysis is an area that is currently receiving much research and attention. It came about as therapists sought to integrate ideas from the object relations school of thought with interpersonal psychoanalysis. Followers of this point of view argue that humans' primary drive is toward *intimacy* and therefore any urges and desires are shaped by, and must be understood within, the context of a relationship. When clients repeat historical patterns by behaving in ways that were established long ago in the family of origin, this is called *enactment*. For example, if a client says in anger, "I knew you'd be running late for my appointment today—I'm less important than your other clients," this most likely resounds with echoes from the past.

The holding environment that Kohut and the self-psychologists emphasized is seen as key in this approach. As therapists provide consistent and calm attention, they help clients break out of the repetitive patterns of relating to others that maintain dysfunctional templates and practice new ways of relating that are far more useful.

Attachment-based therapy is a similar relational approach based on ideas developed by John Bowlby and others who followed in his footsteps. The idea was to bring Freud's concepts about the crucial impact of a child's earliest relationships in line with modern ideas about biologically based behavior (Fonagy, 2018). Most attachment-based therapeutic interventions target infants, young children, and foster children who, due to the disturbances in caregiver behavior, are at risk for developing an attachment disorder. The interventions involve consistently providing "a secure base" in therapy and teaching the caregiver the skills and inclination for doing so as well. Within a "circle of security," the child can learn to trust self and others, thus freeing up energy for exploration, learning, and so forth.

Because the attachment styles one forms in early life can replicate themselves in later relationships, adults may also benefit from reworking their attachment style to be more secure. Brown and Elliot (2016) have developed a manual for how to treat adults with dismissing, anxious-preoccupied, and disorganized or fearful attachment styles. This focused work involves the therapist being the secure base and gradually reshaping the client's inner template for the kinds of relationships they are attracted to, form, and enact, in healthier directions.

Brief Psychodynamic Psychotherapy

As is true in general, long- and short-term practitioners embrace different values in their work (Levenson, 2017). In traditional psychoanalytic treatment, the therapist attempts to deal with underlying characterological changes and expects to be around throughout the whole process of transformation. Therapy is viewed as the most important part of a person's life, and the participant is expected to make a major investment of time, money, and commitment. In any short-term treatment, including brief psychodynamic models, the emphasis is not on a cure but rather on relief of presenting symptoms. In addition, there is considerable reality-based attention to time constraints and limited financial resources.

Most contemporary psychodynamic practitioners have abandoned many of Freud's original tenets, such as use of the couch or seeing instincts as the primary source of motivation, while retaining the emphasis on grappling with the past to become more free and well adjusted. It makes sense, of course, that any theory originally devised over 100 years ago during a different era would need considerable revision and adaptation to fit our current needs. Most dramatically, the changing therapeutic landscape of managed care and an increasingly diverse and less privileged client population have forced practitioners to shorten their treatment methods.

In fact, a version of *brief* (several months instead of several years) psychodynamic therapy has been developed to give clients maximal benefit from the key techniques of psychoanalysis, adapted for modern problems and treatment conditions, in a limited time (Levenson, 2017). Adaptations are made that explore past history in a more limited way while still helping clients increase their awareness of defenses and entrenched patterns. Likewise, personal reactions in the relationship are acknowledged, but because of time limitations, do not become a major focus of treatment. Like in most other forms of therapy, there is an emphasis on applying and practicing new learning to the outside world. Finally, the number of sessions is often negotiated ahead of time with continuous reminders of the prearranged date for closure.

Although there are as many different theories of psychodynamic treatment as there are traditional approaches to psychoanalysis, most of them follow similar principles in their work.

1. Treatment has been abbreviated from the mandatory four times a week for five years to structures that are more realistic and cost effective (weekly sessions for several months).
2. As with any form of brief therapy, clients are carefully screened and selected to make certain they are good candidates for abbreviated treatment. This includes those with

    a. adjustment reactions (depression and anxiety that are the result of life events),

b. problems in everyday living (relationships, work, and family problems), and

c. milder forms of personality disorder.

3. Level of motivation is a key consideration, assessed by determining the client's degree of honesty, openness, psychological mindedness, realistic expectations, and willingness to make reasonable sacrifices.

4. Sessions are devoted not only to coming to terms with the past, but also to looking at present behavior and concerns. This might sound like a rather obvious approach but actually represents a recent innovation.

5. Treatment goals are defined in more specific, limited ways. Rather than seeking to reshape a person's whole personality, the brief dynamic therapist focuses on identified, negotiated goals related to presenting complaints. You would usually stick with one theme or set of issues—maladaptive relationships, ineffective coping styles, unresolved parental issues, unsatisfying work—rather than trying to cover the whole spectrum of a person's life.

6. Attention is directed more toward ego functioning than instinctual drives. This means that clients are helped to look at their characteristic ego defense mechanisms (e.g., denial, rationalization, sublimation) and decide if, or when, they are helpful—or not.

7. Practitioners use a variety of interventions from many other approaches as needed. This is now standard practice for followers of any therapeutic model.

8. Most psychodynamic clinicians make similar adaptations when borrowing behavioral, cognitive, systemic, or other strategies for specific presenting problems. Experience and empirical research have shown that insight alone often isn't enough, especially for those with impulse disorders, addictions, and other behavioral disorders. Thus, practitioners are far more inclined to be confrontive and direct instead of waiting patiently for clients to figure out things on their own.

9. It is no longer enough to rely purely on case studies, personal experience, and the collected works of Freud to plan interventions and seek guidance for treatment plans. For example, a number of empirical outcome studies have been undertaken to demonstrate the effectiveness of the key ingredients of short-term psychodynamic therapy when compared to other approaches (e.g., Steinert, Munder, Rabung, Hoyer, & Leichsenring, 2017).

Just as in regular versions of psychoanalysis, the relationship is critical but in an altered form that emphasizes a more present-oriented, authentic alliance in which the therapist becomes more of a teacher/consultant rather than a parent figure. This approach does not much resemble the method first developed by Freud over 100 years ago, but then not much in the way any profession currently operates is the same as it was in the last century.

FOR A FIELD STUDY

Interview several people who have participated in psychoanalytic therapy to find out about their experiences. Ask them to comment on what they found most useful about the sessions. As they look back on the therapy, what stands out as having been the most enduring result?

STRENGTHS AND LIMITATIONS

Whereas there once was a time when almost all practicing therapists expressed allegiance to psychoanalytic theory, this approach is now restricted to mostly those in private practice, those doing relatively long-term personality reconstruction work, and those in urban areas with a fairly affluent client population. Obviously, because psychoanalytic therapy has been traditionally very time consuming and expensive, it has been most well suited to those who have the time, inclination, and capacity for insight-oriented work.

There has been over a century of criticisms leveled at Freud and his disciples—that the theory is too complex, that its concepts have not been empirically validated, that it is sexist and culturally biased, that it ignores the pragmatic realities of the disadvantaged and poor, that it overemphasizes the influence of the past to the exclusion of the present, and so on. There are literally hundreds, perhaps thousands, of books written that attack the model with passionate vehemence. Yet the theory endures and has dedicated practitioners around the world.

Until recently, psychoanalytic and psychodynamic therapy were evaluated scientifically somewhat less often than other therapies, in part because conducting a systematic, long-term evaluation of any treatment or approach is very expensive. The theory also included, especially in its early years, concepts that were very difficult to conceptualize, operationalize, and measure such as instincts, transference, and personality change. However, in recent years a number of meta-analyses (a rigorous method for summarizing and synthesizing the findings across several independent studies) have found intriguing results. For example, individuals involved in both short-term (less than 40 hours) and long-term (more than 1 year or 50 sessions) psychodynamic therapy experienced significant change from pre-treatment to post-treatment compared to individuals in control groups. This is good news for adherents to this theory, but here is even better news: In many studies, the benefits of psychodynamic therapy actually increase with time after therapy has stopped (Shedler, 2010). Additionally, consistent with the intentions of its original proponents, psychodynamic therapy has proven to be efficacious for treating depression, anxiety, panic, somatoform disorders, eating disorders, substance use disorders, personality disorders, and even violence and aggression (Leichsenring, et al., 2015; Leichsenring & Steinert, 2017; Taubner, Fonagy, Bateman, & Rabung, 2017). And it appears that intrapsychic change may actually occur (Bateman, Target, & Fonagy, 2018).

Psychoanalytic and psychodynamic therapists are also licensed psychologists, counselors, psychiatrists, and social workers; as such, they are mandated by their professions to practice in a way consistent with established standards of care that are based on current ethics, cultural competence, and empirical research. As a result, psychoanalysts and psychodynamic therapists have been influenced strongly by developments outside their own discipline and have sought to integrate these innovations with their own training. Committed therapists with psychodynamic roots continue to aspire to help people find the best within themselves: courage, resilience, gratitude, generosity, and forgiveness (Ahktar, 2014).

Despite the limitations of psychoanalytic theory, it formed the foundation for all forms of therapy. It was the first systematic model and the one most widely practiced. Furthermore, many of its essential ideas have been so integrated into the public consciousness and therapeutic lore that it is very difficult not to think psychodynamically when looking at personal problems.

FOR PERSONAL APPLICATION

Thinking psychodynamically means that when someone is encountering difficulties, you might ask yourself and the client several relevant questions such as the following:

1. What is the relation of what you are experiencing now to what you have encountered in the past?
2. Which experiences in your early life have most shaped who you are today?

3. What motives and forces beyond your awareness might be affecting your judgment?
4. What fantasies and dreams have you had that might be related to your presenting problem?
5. How have your feelings for me, as your therapist, reflected the kind of relationships you have experienced with others?

VOICES FROM THE PAST: SIGMUND FREUD

Katharina

I made an excursion into the Hohe Tauern so that for a while I might forget medicine and more particularly the neuroses. I had almost succeeded in this when one day I turned aside from the main road to climb a mountain which lay somewhat apart and which was renowned for its views and for its well-run refuge hut. I reached the top after a strenuous climb and, feeling refreshed and rested, was sitting deep in contemplation of the charm of the distant prospect. I was so lost in thought that at first I did not connect it with myself when these words reached my ears: "Are you a doctor, sir?" But the question was addressed to me, and by the rather sulky-looking girl of perhaps

FIGURE 4.1. Sigmund Freud

eighteen who had served my meal and had been spoken to by the landlady as "Katharina." To judge by her dress and bearing, she could not be a servant, but must no doubt be a daughter or relative of the landlady's.

Coming to myself I replied "Yes, I'm a doctor: but how did you know that?" "You wrote your name in the Visitors' Book, sir. And I thought if you had a few moments to spare. … The truth is, sir, my nerves are bad. I went to see a doctor in L— about them and he gave me something for them; but I'm not well yet."

So there I was with the neuroses once again—for nothing else could very well be the matter with this strong, well-built girl with her unhappy look. I was interested to find that neuroses could flourish in this way at a height of over 6000 feet; I questioned her further therefore. I report the conversation that followed between us just as it is impressed on my memory and I have not altered the patient's dialect.

"Well, what is it you suffer from?"

"I get so out of breath. Not always. But sometimes it catches me so that I think I shall suffocate."

This did not, at first sight, sound like a nervous symptom. But soon it occurred to me that probably it was only a description that stood for an anxiety attack: she was choosing shortness of breath out of the complex sensations arising from anxiety and laying undue stress on that single factor.

"Sit down here. What is it like when you get 'out of breath'?"

"It comes over me all at once. First of all, it's like something pressing on my eyes. My head gets so heavy, there's a dreadful buzzing, and I feel so giddy that I almost fall over. Then there's something crushing my chest so that I can't get my breath."

"And you don't notice anything in your throat?"

"My throat's squeezed together as though I were going to choke."

"Does anything else happen in your head?"

"Yes, there's a hammering, enough to burst it."

"And don't you feel at all frightened while this is going on?"

"I always think I'm going to die. I'm brave as a rule and go about everywhere by myself—into the cellar and all over the mountain. But on a day when that happens I don't dare go anywhere; I think all the time someone's standing behind me and going to catch hold of me all at once."

So it was in fact an anxiety attack, and introduced by the signs of hysterical "aura"—or, more correctly, it was a hysterical attack the content of which was anxiety. Might there not probably be some other content as well?

"When you have an attack do you think of something? And always the same thing? Or do you see something in front of you?"

"Yes. I always see an awful face that looks at me in a dreadful way, so that I'm frightened."

Perhaps this might offer a quick means of getting to the heart of the matter.

"Do you recognize the fact? I mean, is it a face that you've really seen some time?"

"No."

"Do you know what your attacks come from?"

"No."

"When did you first have them?"

"Two years ago, while I was still living on the other mountain with my aunt. (She used to run a refuge hut there, and we moved here eighteen months ago.) But they keep on happening."

Was I to make an attempt at an analysis? I could not venture to transplant hypnosis to these altitudes, but perhaps I might succeed with a simple talk. I should have to try a lucky guess. I had found often enough that in girls, anxiety was a consequence of the horror by which a virginal mind is overcome when it is faced for the first time with the world of sexuality.

So I said: "If you don't know, I'll tell you how *I* think you got your attacks. At that time, two years ago, you must have seen or heard something that very much embarrassed you, and that you'd much rather not have seen."

"Heavens, yes!" she replied, "that was when I caught my uncle with the girl, with Franziska, my cousin."

"What's this story about a girl? Won't you tell me all about it?"

"You can say *anything* to a doctor, I suppose. Well, at that time, you know, my uncle—the husband of the aunt you've seen here—kept the inn on the —kogel. Now they're divorced, and it's my fault they were divorced, because it was through me that it came out that he was carrying on with Franziska."

"And how did you discover it?"

"This way. One day two years ago some gentlemen had climbed the mountain and asked for something to eat. My aunt wasn't home, and Franziska, who always did the cooking, was nowhere to be found. And my uncle was not to be found either. We looked everywhere, and at last Alois, the little boy, my cousin, said: 'Why, Franziska must be in Father's room!' And we both laughed; but we weren't thinking anything bad. Then we went to my uncle's room but found it locked. That seemed strange to me. Then Alois said: 'There's a window in the passage where you can look into the room.' We went into the passage; but Alois wouldn't go to the window and said he was afraid. So I said: 'You silly boy! I'll go. I'm not a bit afraid.' And I had nothing bad in my mind. I looked in. The room was rather dark, but I saw my uncle and Franziska; he was laying on her."

"Well?"

"I came away from the window once, and leant up against the wall and couldn't get my breath—just what happens to me since. Everything went blank, my eyelids were forced together and there was a hammering and buzzing in my head."

"Did you tell your aunt that very same day?"

"Oh no, I said nothing."

"Then why were you so frightened when you found them together? Did you understand it? Did you know what was going on?"

"Oh no. I didn't understand anything at that time. I was only sixteen. I don't know what I was frightened about."

"Fraulein Katharina, if you could remember now what was happening in you at that time, when you had your first attack, what you thought about it—it would help you."

"Yes, if I could. But I was so frightened that I've forgotten everything."

(Translated into the terminology of our "Preliminary Communication" this means: "The affect itself created a hypnoid state, whose products were then cut off from associative connection with the ego-consciousness.")

"Tell me, Fraulein. Can it be that the head that you always see when you lose your breath is Franziska's head, as you saw it then?"

"Oh no, she didn't look so awful. Besides, it's a man's head."

"Or perhaps your uncle's?"

"I didn't see his face as clearly as that. It was too dark in the room. And why should he have been making such a dreadful face just then?"

"You're quite right."

(The road suddenly seemed blocked. Perhaps something might turn up in the rest of her story.)

"And what happened then?"

"Well, those two must have heard a noise, because they came out soon afterwards. I felt very bad the whole time. I always kept thinking about it. Then two days later is was a Sunday and there was a great deal to do and I worked all day long. And on the Monday morning I felt giddy again and was sick, and I stopped in bed and was sick without stopping for three days."

We [Breuer and I] had often compared symptomatology of hysteria with a pictographic script which had become intelligible after the discovery of a few bilingual inscriptions. In that alphabet being sick means disgust. So I said "If you were sick three days later, I believe that means that when you looked into the room you felt disgusted."

"Yes, I'm sure I felt disgusted," she said reflectively, "but disgusted at what?"

"Perhaps you saw something naked? What sort of state were they in?"

"It was too dark to see anything; besides they both of them had their clothes on. Oh, if only I knew what it was I felt disgusted at!"

I had no idea either. But I told her to go on and tell me whatever occurred to her, in the confident expectation that she would think of precisely what I needed to explain the case.

Well, she went on to describe how at last she reported her discovery to her aunt, who found that she was changed and suspected her of concealing some secret. ... After this, however, to my astonishment she dropped these threads and began to tell me two sets of older stories, which went back two or three years earlier than the traumatic moment.

... She went on to tell me of yet other experiences of somewhat later date; how she had once again had to defend herself against him in an inn when he was completely drunk and similar stories. In answer to a question as to whether on these occasions she had felt anything resembling her later loss of breath, she answered with decision that she had every time felt the pressure on her eyes and chest, but with nothing like the strength that had characterized the scene of discovery.

... At the end of these two sets of memories she came to a stop. She was like someone transformed. The sulky, unhappy face had grown lively, her eyes were bright, she was lightened and exalted. Meanwhile the understanding of her case had become clear to me. ...

I hope this girl, whose sexual sensibility had been injured at such an early age, derived some benefit from our conversation. I have not seen her since.

Reference: Freud, S. & Breuer, J. (1895). (J. Strachey & A. Strachey, Trans.). In J. Strachey, A. Strachey, and A. Richards (Eds.), *Pelican Freud library* (Vol. 3) (pp. 190–201). London UK, Penguin.

SUGGESTED READINGS

Ahktar, S. (2014). *Good stuff: Courage, resilience, gratitude, generosity, forgiveness, and sacrifice.* Plymouth, UK: Jason Aronson.

Ahktar, S. (2018a). *Sources of suffering: Fear, greed, guilt, deception, betrayal, revenge.* New York, NY: Routledge.

Ahktar, S. (2018b). *Mind, culture, and global unrest: Psychoanalytic reflections.* New York, NY: Routledge.

Blechner, M. J. (2018). *The mindbrain and dreams: An exploration of dreaming, thinking, and artistic creation.* New York, NY: Routledge.

Brown, D. P., & Elliot, D. S. (2016). *Attachment disturbances in adults: Treatment for comprehensive repair.* New York, NY: Norton.

DeYoung, P. A. (2015). *Relational psychotherapy: A primer* (2nd ed.). New York, NY: Routledge.

Fonagy, P. (2018). *Attachment theory and psychoanalysis.* New York, NY: Routledge.

Freud, S. (1900). *Interpretation of dreams.* London, UK: Hogarth Press.

Horney, K. (1945). *Our inner conflicts.* Oxford, UK: Norton.

Jung, C. (1955). *Modern man in search of a soul.* New York, NY: Harcourt Brace.

Jung, C. (1963). *Memories, dreams, reflections.* New York, NY: Pantheon.

Levenson, H. (2017). *Brief dynamic therapy* (2nd ed.) Washington, DC: American Psychological Association.

IMAGE CREDITS

CHAPTER 5

What Is Learned Can Be Unlearned: Behavioral Approaches

LEARNING OBJECTIVES

After reading this chapter, you should be able to do the following:

1. Describe history of behaviorism through key discoveries of classical conditioning and operant conditioning.
2. Identify several influences that led to behaviorism emerging as a theory of psychotherapy in the mid-20th century.
3. Provide examples of how therapists can use principles of systematic desensitization, reciprocal inhibition, stimulus generalization, and stimulus discrimination with clients.
4. Identify basic principles and therapeutic techniques of behavioral therapy.
5. List steps of behavioral goal setting, contingency contracting, and the assessment of progress.
6. Describe how the techniques of relaxation training and sensate focus are implemented.
7. Identify studies offering evidence supporting the effectiveness of contemporary behavioral approaches with specific types of clients.
8. List key contributions and potential limitations of behavioral approaches.

You probably remember something about Ivan Pavlov and his animals salivating to the sound of dinner bells, John Watson and his phobia-conditioned rats, and B. F. Skinner's prowess in teaching pigeons to play ping-pong or mice to run mazes. What, you might ask, does any of this have to do with helping people? Well, behavioral theories of intervention were developed as a direct outgrowth of experimental studies of how animals learn behavior, as well as how they are programmed to act in particular ways. If we understand the ways that behavior is reinforced, we can design treatment programs to increase the frequency of fully functioning behaviors and discourage those that are self-defeating.

As just one example of this, consider the extent to which many people are so addicted to their mobile devices. Some studies have found that adolescents may check their phones as often as 300 times a day, mostly for self-defense in case someone posted something about them that requires a response or denial. There is other evidence that the average person physically touches their phone over 2,000 times a day, rearranging it, checking its location. You see a group of people sitting at a dinner table at an expensive restaurant and each one of them is sending a message to someone else not present, or perhaps photographing themselves to show the world. Every time a phone bings, rings, or vibrates, it distracts us, in some ways eroding the level of intimacy and engagement with others. So, the question that comes to mind is why this behavior is so pervasive, so seductive, so dominant in our lives? Or, more to the point we are investigating in this chapter, why is the behavior so resistant to extinction? Why do we feel powerless to resist the temptation to check mobile devices every few minutes?

You may recall that in operant conditioning the reinforcement schedule that is most powerful and difficult to alter is a variable interval schedule. This occurs when the rat is pressing the button, hoping for a reward in the form a food pellet—except the poor creature is never quite certain when that reward is going to happen. It's not as if every time he presses the button the result is predictable and dependable; instead, it feels like the consequences are fairly random, which of course they are.

Now consider what happens with our attachments to our phones. We may check hundreds of times in a row without receiving any meaningful messages or significant news, perhaps only spam, annoying requests, and bothersome telemarketers. But maybe, just maybe, one of these times there really might be something fun or interesting waiting for us. And *that* is one of the powerful mechanisms that underlie this behavior. It illustrates how behavioral theory helps us to understand and predict behavior, as well as suggest ways to break self-defeating patterns.

HISTORY OF THE BEHAVIORISM MOVEMENT

As with any of the other theoretical families that are presented in each chapter, there is almost as much diversity within the behaviorist school as there is between it and other models. Even at the very beginning of its inception as a therapeutic approach, there was great heterogeneity in the diverse paths taken, from that of systematic desensitization (Joseph Wolpe), applied behavior analysis (B. F. Skinner), social influence (Albert Bandura), and later the cognitive behavior modification therapies (Donald Meichenbaum). Nevertheless, behavior therapists have always favored an objective, empirical approach to predicting and managing behavior, one that favors bringing about change by controlling the external environment as much as possible.

Ivan Pavlov and Classical Conditioning

Pavlov was a Russian physiologist interested in the digestive processes of dogs, so it seems particularly ironic that he ended up launching the behavioral movement that was to have such a profound impact on psychology and education. Yet, if you know anything about the ways great discoveries were made, you know they often they resulted from accidents and serendipitous encounters. Columbus thought he had arrived in India only to find that poor navigation and misguided beliefs landed him on a completely unexpected continent. Everything from x-rays and many drugs to Post-it notes were similarly discovered by sheer accident. So perhaps it isn't surprising that the study of digestion would lead to behavior therapy.

Like any good scientist, Ivan Pavlov was a keen observer. During his investigations into the physiology of metabolic processes in the early 1900s, he noticed that his subjects began salivating before he even presented them with their dinner. Just the sound of food being prepared was enough to spark a strong anticipatory emotional response. In other words, the dogs became conditioned to respond in a particular way just at the sight of food or the sounds associated with its delivery.

Pavlov began pairing the presentation of food with other cues, such as a flashing light or a ringing bell, simply to prove that he could condition the dogs to salivate in response to almost any neutral stimulus. He was, thus, able to demonstrate quite convincingly how animals and humans learn to like, or even fear, certain relatively innocuous occurrences in the environment through the process we now call classical conditioning. Depending on your prior experiences, and whether they were rewarding or aversive, you may develop strongly conditioned preferences or aversions toward things you once encountered.

FOR PERSONAL REFLECTION

What are some of your greatest fears, phobias, and neuroses? Assuming that you were not born with particular aversions to these things, how were these attitudes conditioned in you?

John Watson and Learned Neuroses

Following Pavlov's work, John Watson, an American psychologist, was credited as being the founding parent of behaviorism. He conceived of the new science of psychology, launched a few years earlier by his contemporary William James, as a purely objective enterprise, one that is directed toward predicting and controlling behavior. Watson rejected psychoanalysis, the prevailing treatment approach at the time. In his famous credo, Watson (1924) crowed: "Give me a dozen healthy infants, well-formed, and my own specified world to bring them up in and I'll guarantee to take any one at random and train him to become any type of specialist I might select—doctor, lawyer, artist, merchant, chief—and yes, even beggar-man and thief, regardless of his talents, penchants, tendencies, abilities, vocations, and race of his ancestors" (p. 104).

Well, Watson certainly didn't lack any confidence in himself! Yet he did have evidence from his animal studies that it was indeed possible to control behavior. Once he began experimenting with humans, he discovered that he could both create phobic reactions as well as take them away by using principles of behavior modification. In his classic case of "Little Albert," Watson demonstrated that he was able to condition an 11-month-old infant to develop a fear of a white rat and eventually to generalize that fear to anything that resembled the hated object (piece of cotton, mitten, Santa Claus beard). The implications of this study were profound for it showed how neurosis and psychological symptoms might develop as a result of conditioning processes. Once it was understood how maladaptive behaviors are elicited and reinforced, similar methods could be used to countercondition the symptoms. Unfortunately, Little Albert's mother yanked him out of the experiment before Watson had a chance to undo the psychological damage. (Fortunately, the ethics for research on developing new theories has dramatically improved participants' experience!)

B. F. Skinner and Operant Conditioning

If Watson was the specialist in classical conditioning, employing the method first discovered by Ivan Pavlov to elicit certain responses by presenting particular stimuli, then B. F. Skinner became the master of instrumental or operant conditioning in which stimuli were used to increase or decrease target behaviors. This later became known as behavior modification.

Skinner called operant conditioning "operant" because organisms go around "operating" in the world, doing whatever they do, and in the process, they encounter events that they seek to repeat (*reinforcing stimuli*). As a result, whatever behavior they were doing just before the reinforcer occurred— the operant—will increase. Skinner made this discovery early in his career by observing that the rate at which rats and pigeons pressed a bar in his now-famous "Skinner Box" depended not on any preceding stimulus (like Watson and Pavlov had shown) but on what happened next (specifically, food pellets). Then, because he was running out of food, Skinner accidentally discovered that he didn't have to give the animal a reinforcer every time to maintain the operant. This discovery kicked off years of experiments on schedules of reinforcement and the like, about which Skinner wrote his first book, *The Behavior of Organisms* (1938).

Skinner envisioned a utopian world in which people would be reinforced systematically for good deeds that benefit society through shaping and maintaining their behavior with behavioral principles; he described how it could be done in his book, *Walden Two* (Skinner, 1948). Following the philosophy once articulated by British philosopher John Locke, Skinner believed that people are indeed born as "blank slates" on which experience writes its impressions. As you may recall, he set out to support this thesis by demonstrating all the ways that pigeons, rats, and people could be conditioned to behave in certain ways according to various schedules of reinforcement. With several colleagues (Lindley, Skinner, & Solomon, 1953), he was also the first to use the term "behavior therapy" as a means of treating hospitalized schizophrenics.

FOR DISCUSSION

The excerpt in "Voices From the Past" at the end of this chapter (see pages 117–119) was published in 1945 in the *Ladies Home Journal*. If you had picked up that issue from the newsstand and had never heard of B. F. Skinner, what would you have thought of the article? What do you know about the times that would have made Skinner's approach to dealing with a baby in the house plausible or attractive? Does his idea have any appeal to you, at least in part? Why or why not?

The First Behavior Therapies

The disciples of Watson and Skinner concentrated mostly on exploring the ways that humans and animals learn, spawning a whole set of new theories to explain memory, knowledge and skill acquisition, as well as why certain behaviors don't persist. It was a South African psychiatrist, Joseph Wolpe, and an English psychologist, Hans Eysenck, who began applying behavioral principles to the practice of therapy.

At this particular time in the middle of the 20th century, psychoanalysis was supreme, practically the only legitimate form of therapy. A sizeable number of disgruntled ex-analysts were in the process of setting up their own schools of thought, but at that point in time the main option available was long-term, insight-oriented excavations into the unconscious.

Wolpe (1958) first began experimenting with cats, demonstrating that they could be "taught" to develop anxiety neuroses by shocking them and then curing them of their symptoms by using counterconditioning methods. He was the first brief therapist, demonstrating that he could rid animals and people of their symptoms in just a few sessions rather than the usual number of years that were required in psychoanalysis.

Wolpe also developed a method that is now called *systematic desensitization*, a kind of counterconditioning that uses relaxation strategies to help clients suffering from anxieties and phobias to learn alternative ways to respond to threatening stimuli. This works because of the process he identified as *reciprocal inhibition*, in which a novel stimulus results in a decrease of a habitual response. For example, people who have developed a fear of flying use this principle when they listen to music to distract themselves from their usual anxious responses to the sensations of the plane taking off.

Wolpe's work on the conditioned stimulus led him to elaborate other concepts that are still important today. *Stimulus generalization* is what is hoped for when a behavior therapist conditions a child to speak in response to a social cue (thus overcoming selective mutism), and then trains the child's parent and teacher to present the same social cue, with, it is hoped, the same response from the child. *Stimulus discrimination* is conditioning that fine-tunes a behavior so that it occurs in relation to a very specific response—in this case you would want the child speaking in response to only certain types of social cues (Wolpe & Plaud, 1997).

All kinds of behavior can be conditioned (learned). An innovative study done on stimulus generalization and discrimination demonstrated how pigeons were taught to distinguish paintings by particular artists (Watanabe, Sakamoto, & Wakita, 1995). When shown paintings by Picasso, a pigeon was able to obtain food by pecking; when shown a Monet, pecking had no effect. After a while, the pigeons would peck when they were shown Picasso paintings they had never seen before (evidence of stimulus generalization, not to mention potential as art critics), but not Monet paintings (evidence of stimulus discrimination). This is pretty impressive, but there's more—the pigeons even learned to discriminate between cubist (Picasso's style) and impressionist (Monet's style) paintings. If you are wondering what pigeon learning has to do with your future clients, consider this: In a follow-up study, Watanabe (2001) trained college students and pigeons to do essentially the same thing with Van Gogh and Chagall paintings. Later he showed that he could teach pigeons to discriminate between "good" and "bad" paintings by children, claiming that by using color and pattern cues, pigeons can learn the concept of "beauty" as defined by humans (Watanabe, 2010). Just think of the possibilities this suggests for how human behavior can be conditioned!

If Wolpe was the supreme innovative behavioral clinician, then Eysenck (1952) was the scientific genius who first applied empirical methods to measure the objective effects of therapy as it was practiced at the time (i.e., "psycho-analytic and eclectic psychotherapeutic methods"). The bad news was that he found that neurotic people didn't improve as a result of these treatments any more quickly than they would have if they had received no treatment at all. The good news, well ... there wasn't a lot of good news. But he did bring a lot of attention to the objective measurement of therapeutic outcomes, which is one of the foundations of the behavioral approach.

A decade later, Albert Bandura (1969, 1977), spurred on by the challenge to develop reliable intervention methods that could be verifiably measured, developed a handbook of behavioral principles that used as their core neither the operant theory of Skinner, nor the classical theory of Watson and Pavlov, but rather the concept of modeling or social learning. Bandura believed that people can learn and be reinforced not only directly, but also through observational learning. His idea of social learning theory proposes that behaviors can be learned by individuals who model the behavior of others who get rewarded, even without being rewarded themselves. (Every teacher has seen this in action—when one kid does something and gets a laugh from the class, a number of class clown wannabes immediately try the same thing.) He also noticed that among humans, self-efficacy, the belief that one can perform a task or behavior, is strongly related to whether they take it on, persist, and succeed. He thus loosened up behavioral theory considerably, adding to its methodology an appreciation for cognitive, verbal, and observational features in the change process.

FOR HOMEWORK

In looking at the process of modeling, Bandura noted that influencing others emanates from a sense of personal power. People pay attention to others whom they perceive as powerful. There are many different kinds of personal power that give you the ability to command attention in others' eyes. There is the obvious physical power—that is, an imposing physical presence. There is also the kind of power that comes from being seen as an expert, a source of nurturance, an icon of prestige, or a sex object.

Advertising companies understand this phenomenon all too well, design-ing their commercials in such a way that they display one or more of these modeling processes. Thus, the spokespeople for products tend to be celebrities (prestige), dressed in white lab coats (expertise), sexually alluring (models), or physically commanding (athletes). They know you are far more likely to be influenced by such a commercial, or enjoy a music video or computer game, if the dominant figures radiate one or more varieties of power.

Look at the advertisements on television, internet, or in magazines to find samples of the various kinds of modeling power that are intended to influence consumers' buying habits. In particular, what types of social models are used to sell to the group you plan to work with—children, young adults, elderly people, men, women, or particular social or ethnic groups? (Can you compete?)

There were several influences that led behaviorism to become a second force to counter the dominance of psychoanalytic theory during the middle of the 20th century:

1. Rational philosophy during the 18th-century Age of Enlightenment and British empirical philosophers set the stage. John Locke, in particular, was among the first to talk about humans as being born as "blank slates" written on by experience.

2. Wilhelm Wundt was the first experimental psychologist. All psychology students memorize that in 1879 Wundt established the first psychological laboratory in Leipzig. This gave a scientific foundation to the field.

3. Ivan Pavlov's laboratory studies at the turn of the 20th century demonstrated the ways that organisms learn behavior through classical conditioning.

4. John Watson demonstrated experimentally the ways that classical conditioning is applied to individuals' learning—and unlearning—dysfunctional behavior.

5. B. F. Skinner and other learning theorists demonstrated operant conditioning in which behaviors are reinforced or extinguished by certain stimuli.

6. Learning principles were applied to address a number of human problems, such as the use of reward and punishment systems to encourage or discourage particular behaviors.

7. Scientific and empirical methods were applied to psychology, social work, medicine, and education.

FOR A CLASS ACTIVITY

One easy way to remember the differences between the two learning modes is that classical conditioning involves stimulus-response learning (taking out your appointment book signals that a session is over), whereas operant conditioning involves response-stimulus learning (the client reports on successful home-work and receives a big smile—a rewarding stimulus—from the therapist).

In small groups, talk about other ways that these two forms of conditioning might operate in therapeutic relationships. In other words, what examples can you think of in which particular therapist behaviors elicit desired responses in clients and when therapists might reinforce or extinguish client behavior?

BASIC PRINCIPLES AND TECHNIQUES

As behavioral theory was subsequently applied to therapeutic settings, a general consensus emerged as to certain principles that behavior therapists generally agree on (Martin & Pear, 2014):

- Genetics play a role, but individual differences are derived primarily from different experiences.
- Behavior is learned and acquired largely through modeling, conditioning, and reinforcement.
- Behavior has a purpose, one that is often important to identify before it can be altered.
- Behaviors must be viewed in the context in which they occur.
- Therapy should be based on the scientific method and be systematic, empirical, and experimental.
- Goals should be stated in behavioral, specific, and measurable terms, with progress assessed regularly.
- The focus of treatment should be on the present. Even if behaviors are long-standing, they are maintained by factors in the current environment.
- A client's environment can be manipulated to increase appropriate behaviors and decrease harmful behaviors.
- Education—promoting new learning and transfer of learning—is an important aspect of behavior therapy.
- Clients must take an active part in their treatment to successfully change their behaviors.

- The treatment plan is formulated collaboratively by both client and clinician.
- Clients have primary responsibility for defining their goals and completing homework tasks.

Within this framework, how does the behaviorally oriented practitioner go about conditioning, reinforcing, and educating the client to change? Like many of the other theories that have been around for a while, many behavioral concepts and techniques have been co-opted by other therapeutic systems and in educational settings.

Reinforcing and Discouraging Certain Target Behaviors

One major application of behavioral theory is the systematic use of reinforcement (rewards and punishments) to increase or decrease target behaviors. On the most subtle level, therapists use smiles and frowns to indicate their relative approval of what is going on. Other verbalizations can be more direct as illustrated in the conversation that follows.

CLIENT:	It was so much harder than I thought. I had no idea. ...
THERAPIST:	But the important thing is that you did it! I know how difficult that was for you.
CLIENT:	Yeah, I guess you're right about that.
THERAPIST:	[Smiles and nods her head, offering encouragement]
CLIENT:	It was one of the hardest things I've ever tried.
THERAPIST:	You can sure say that again.
CLIENT:	But I still think that maybe I shouldn't move so fast, maybe I should wait a while before I go any further.
THERAPIST:	[Shakes her head, frowning slightly] I can certainly understand how you would feel hesitant, but I'm not sure I agree with you.
CLIENT:	Well, maybe it's not as bad as I think it is.
THERAPIST:	Absolutely. You'd be surprised how strong you can be. [Widens her eyes.]

On one level, it appears as if the therapist is just being supportive (and she is). She is also being quite systematic in using both nonverbal and verbal reinforcement strategies to encourage optimistic statements and discouraging those that are filled with doubt. Because the therapist's approval is so important to the client, subtle cues lead the course of the interaction in directions the therapist believes are most helpful.

Shaping Behavior Incrementally

Learning does not usually occur in one single dose of reinforcement, but rather develops in successive approximation toward the ultimate goal. You don't start out waiting for the right behavior to occur and then attempt to reward it or you may end up waiting a very long time. Instead, you pick a series of little goals, each one leading to the next stage, eventually ending up at the final objective. Like a hunk of clay, the intention is to shape its form through a series of small, incremental movements.

Imagine, for example, a child is approaching kindergarten age but who has, much to his parents' chagrin, resisted every attempt at toilet training. What can be done? Until he acquires the requisite behavior, the school will not accept him! Using shaping principles, the therapist would work with the parents to set up a successive approximation plan that rewards small steps along the way. So, first, the child is rewarded for going into the bathroom at the appropriate time. Next, just touching the toilet while nature calls will earn the reward. Then, sitting on the toilet just for fun will be reinforced. Eventually—success!—followed by receiving a much-coveted reward. But as you can see, for this to be successful, the therapist will likely be involved in shaping the parents' behavior as much as the child's.

Therapists of every variety use shaping techniques in sessions, usually without even thinking about it. Let's say, for instance, that you have a client who persists in communicating in a rather annoying, counterproductive manner. He rambles constantly, talking to fill up space. You have wondered if this style is intended to avoid real intimacy and keep people from getting too close, but regardless of its purpose, it makes working with him very difficult. Furthermore, you suspect that his dysfunctional interpersonal style is responsible for many of his other problems that occur at work and with his few friends.

You have tried waiting for an instance when he abandons his talkativeness in favor of brevity so you can reward this behavior, but you have not yet recognized a single opportunity to intervene. From the moment he walks in the door until the time he leaves, he talks nonstop. You could confront him, of course, but the behaviorist recognizes clearly the disadvantages of any intervention that might be perceived as punishment. It is far preferable to use positive reinforcement whenever possible.

Because you can't reward the target behavior that is your final objective, your job instead would be to shape his behavior in desired directions through a series of little steps. When the client pauses to catch his breath during a particularly long-winded story, you immediately jump in and tell him how lovely it is to enjoy a companionable moment of serenity with him. A little later, when he is momentarily distracted by a sound outside the room, you use that opportunity to tell him how much you like the way he speaks with his eyes as well as his mouth. You even find a rare occurrence when he manages to tell a relatively brief story (completely irrelevant to the work in therapy, of course) and you jump all over that by thanking him for being so concise and how much easier it is to hear and understand him when he speaks in shorter periods.

In each of these examples, you are using your own approval as leverage to shape the client in a particular direction. Although Carl Rogers and other humanists have called this unduly manipulative, Skinner once responded in a debate that he thinks all teachers and therapists subtly shape the behavior of others by selectively rewarding some behaviors over others. When Rogers hears an expression of feeling, he immediately lights up and reflects what he understands, yet if the client intellectualizes, Rogers would be inclined to ignore that response. This is called extinction and is designed to discourage those behaviors that are not thought to be useful.

Measurement of Progress and Outcomes

Behaviorists are very big on measuring outcomes as objectively as possible; it is part of their historical legacy that is still alive in the context of empirical validation of treatments and assessing outcomes. They want to know from clients exactly what they are going to do, how often they are going to do it, and what will happen if they don't do what they say (as in reality therapy, consequences are very important). Ideally, behaviors are a lot easier to measure if they are observable actions. This is consistent with behavior therapy's preference for dealing with actions that can be seen rather than internal processes. So, clients (or teachers or parents of child clients) might be asked to record every instance of a behavior that is targeted for change early in treatment, several times during treatment, and at the end. Not only does this activity conform to the scientific principles of observation and measurement, but it clearly demonstrates to interested parties that the smoking or the head banging or the angry tantrums (for example) are, in fact, decreasing. This evidence in itself is reinforcing for the therapist and the client!

The emphasis on measuring outcomes is one of the enduring influences that behaviorism has had on our field, establishing the practice of therapy as both a science and an art. To some extent, all practitioners are now required to evaluate the impact of their interventions and demonstrate that their methods are indeed effective.

It's Action That Counts

Although it is no longer the only approach that concentrates on what the client is doing rather than thinking, sensing, or feeling, behavior therapy was certainly the first theory to promote changes through action methods. The behaviorist doesn't dwell long on what people are feeling inside, but rather moves things along toward what needs to be done.

Unlike its main competition at the time, psychoanalysis, behavior therapy concentrates on the present rather than on the past. Likewise, insight is minimized with the rationale that understanding why you are so messed up doesn't necessarily change anything in your life. If you have known people who have been in therapy for years, without any apparent, visible changes in their behavior, perhaps you are sympathetic to this argument.

To summarize the main points, behavior therapy remains in the present rather than the past. It minimizes the role of insight in the change process, instead focusing on specific actions that can be taken. It plays down the importance of relationship and affective variables, preferring to create a therapeutic connection that is businesslike, collaborative, and problem oriented. Rather than investigating underlying causes of behavior or unconscious motives, the behavior therapist sticks with presenting complaints and observable symptoms. You would have a lot of company if you thought this might be a gross simplification of the human experience.

VOICES FROM THE FIELD

I started my own practice in behavior analysis because I saw that I could relieve suffering very effectively among clients (and clients' caregivers) who had not been able to obtain results any other way. I have seen some very impressive "turn-arounds" that reinforce my commitment to this theory. Let me give you some examples.

Zachary was a 3-year-old boy diagnosed with Autism when he began behavior analysis therapy. Prior to beginning therapy, he only spoke about three to five words and would not engage in social interactions with others; he also lacked the ability to identify objects, his feelings, or the feelings of others. When trying to escape a task or when presented with something new, he engaged in tantrums and head banging. At present, Zachary (now age 7) is on the honor roll in a general education class; he engages in social interactions with others and he goes for months without a tantrum or self-injurious behavior.

Victor is an 11-year-old boy diagnosed with Autism who began behavior analysis therapy at the age of 10. Prior to beginning therapy, he had no friends at school and did not participate in activities due to a lack of social skills. He is now one of the most popular boys in his class! He walks up to his peers and asks them questions. In addition, the students in his class have been taught how to interact with him (for example, not accepting one-word answers from him). With these successes under his belt, Victor has been able to advance faster and move on to other tasks.

Carolina is a 24-year-old young woman diagnosed with mild mental retardation. She has a history of verbal aggression, property destruction, promiscuous behavior, tantrums, elopement, non-compliance, self-injurious behavior and physical aggression, leading to multiple occasions of involuntary detention for mental health evaluation. Since the onset of therapy with me one year ago, Carolina has gone as many as 2 months without any incidents and she has only been involuntarily detained twice (as opposed to a few times a month).

A big part of my practice is educating people on how behavior works, so they can eventually create change without my assistance. Behavior analysis is a great skill to apply to your everyday life; it's also a great skill that can foster your tolerance of others who behave in a less than favorable manner. This theory teaches that we behave the way we do because of our history of reinforcement or punishment from our environment, so if I misbehave and receive reinforcement for it, common sense logic says that I will be more likely to misbehave in the future. Behavior analysis goes well with my logical way of thinking and need for results that are measurable. It has also helped me understand myself and why I do the things that I do, and it has helped me understand why others behave the way that they do. Most of all, it's taught me that the only way to change how someone behaves with me is to change how I behave with them.

—Yanivis Machado-Gonzalez, BCBA, LMHC
The Shaping Academy for Behavioral Development

BEHAVIORAL TECHNIQUES

The behavioral approach is loaded with practical, concrete strategies that you can use in sessions regardless of your favored theoretical orientation. Many of these techniques are so universal that they are employed by most therapists when the situation calls for it.

FOR A HOMEWORK ASSIGNMENT

Find a setting in your community that operates a behaviorally oriented treatment program to manage daily life. This might be found in a local psychiatric hospital, a group home for adolescents or the elderly, a classroom environment, or perhaps a correctional facility.

Spend some time observing the way this behaviorally oriented program is managed. Note the special kinds of reinforcers that are used to increase and decrease target behaviors. If possible, talk to members of the staff, as well as the clients, about how they experience the system.

Remember that not every client presents the sort of problem that lends itself to specific treatment objectives and objective measurement of outcomes. If someone comes to see you and wants to stop some annoying behavior, learn to become more assertive, or work on some particular goal, the behavioral approach is ideal for those circumstances. At other times, clients won't even know what is bothering them, or they don't feel ready so much to change behavior as they just want to be listened to and heard. Or perhaps clients want to understand some aspect of their lives a little better. They may eventually be ready to make the kinds of changes that lend themselves to behavioral intervention, but remember that like any of the models, behavioral techniques are ideally suited to some circumstances but not to others.

Goal Setting

This a very nifty, useful method that helps clients translate their concerns into specific therapeutic tasks. There was a funny movie about therapy made several years ago called *What About Bob?* (unfortunately, there are lots of movies that make fun of therapists) in which Richard Dreyfuss employed a strategy with his clients called "baby steps." The method was ridiculously simple but no less valid: Changes are often best brought about when people are encouraged to take small, successive steps in the direction they wish to go.

A behavioral approach to counseling incorporates into its procedures the expectation that clients will complete homework assignments in between each session. If you think about it, the actual therapy represents less than 1% of the person's waking time during the week. Even if the person came for sessions three times per week, that would still be just a drop in the bucket compared to all the rest of the time that the person spends engaging in the same dysfunctional behaviors. So, therapists in general, and behavioral practitioners in particular, are always looking for ways to help people apply what they are learning in their real lives where things matter the most.

It is one of the most frustrating parts of this job that some people will come in and talk your ear off and yet they don't actually do anything in the world to change their patterns. They come in week after week, report on how wonderful they feel, perform like circus animals jumping through all your hoops, but they still engage in the same self-destructive behavior. This isn't their fault, of course. Transfer of learning, or generalization of learning, from one situation to another is the most difficult challenge of change processes. You've got to help people to start applying new changes in their lives outside of sessions, where it matters most. The best goals are those that meet the following criteria.

Mutually developed goals. One mistake that beginners make is in assigning or prescribing homework assignments to their clients. This is a recipe for disappointment because people tend to not feel committed to goals that they didn't come up with themselves. Imagine that your client returns the next session and says to you: "Gee, I'm sorry. But I wasn't able to do that assignment we talked about. I was just too busy." Then the client looks you directly in the eyes as if daring you to say something.

If, however, the goals are mutually constructed, then you have the leverage to say to the client:

THERAPIST:	Okay, I guess what you said last week wasn't so important to you after all.
CLIENT:	Well, that's not true. It is important.
THERAPIST:	This is your life we're talking about, not mine. You were the one who came up with this homework assignment, and then you decided not to do it after all. That's fine with me. You will do it when it finally matters more to you than anything else that you allow to get in the way.

Developing mutual goals involves negotiating with the client a therapeutic task that is consistent with the work you've been doing and encourages one baby step in the right direction. You typically end the session with a statement such as this: "So, let's summarize what you understand we did today and what you've agreed you will do before we see each other next time. I heard you say that you very badly want to change the pattern of trying to get approval from your boss. To make progress in that area, you've said that you will limit yourself to visiting her office once per day instead of the usual two or three times."

Specific goals. Consistent with behavioral principles, it is important to declare goals that are concrete, observable, and measurable. Ideally, you want to help the client to come up with a homework assignment in which it is clear exactly what will be done, how many times this will take place, where and with whom the action will occur, and what the consequences will be for doing (or not doing) the assignment.

Realistic goals. During your negotiations with clients over what they will do in between sessions, it is extremely important that the assignment is reasonable. Contrary to what you might imagine, clients tend to want to do too much. They declare homework assignments that are way beyond what is probably manageable. Because it is so important to build in success experiences, you want to make sure that the goals are realistic.

Imagine you are working with someone who wants to begin an exercise program for a number of good reasons. This isn't only about physical health and lifestyle issues, but also is related to the person's work on self-image and practice of self-control. The dialogue sounds like this:

CLIENT: So, what I'm going to do this week is go to the health club I just joined and work out every day for an hour. [This is very good in meeting the criterion of specificity, but not in being realistic.]

THERAPIST: Let me get this straight. In the previous week, and every week before that, you haven't worked out a single time. And now you are saying you are going to do it every day for an hour?

CLIENT: Do you think that's too much? [Because mutuality is important in these negotiations, the therapist doesn't want to take too strong a role in telling the client what to do. Instead, efforts are more indirect.]

THERAPIST: Well, what do you think? I certainly don't doubt your commitment. And you probably will visit the club most days just like you want to, but maybe it would be more realistic to start out a little more modestly. So, improving on "zero," let's pick a number of times that you can absolutely commit to, for starters.

The therapist already has in mind a goal that she thinks is realistic, say, three times per week for half an hour, but she will take the slower route to negotiate a goal that is definitely manageable, with no excuses possible. It may turn out that this client does work out every day as he intends, but the declared goal should be modest to make certain it can be achieved.

Relevant goals. In the zeal to translate discussion into some sort of action, beginning therapists often make the mistake of reducing a very complex issue to a goal that is specific but hardly pertinent to the main themes. Resist the urge to push clients to work on goals prematurely, or to bite off the most irrelevant part of the problem just because it lends itself to a homework assignment.

A client has been struggling with feelings of hopelessness and despair. He feels worthless and incompetent—in school, with his friends, and at home. During the conversation, he casually mentioned that he hasn't been completing all his school assignments. Because the therapist feels so helpless and sad for her client and wants to do something constructive immediately, she jumps on the school assignments as the place to concentrate their attention. This turns out to be very conducive to a specific therapeutic task that can be completed, but lost in the dust were all the other important feelings that were just beginning to be explored. This client was just discouraged from talking about his feelings, something with which he is already extremely uncomfortable, so that they could work in territory that both find easier going. He may not be truly motivated to make a change in his homework behavior, so the therapist may be setting them both up for failure if she persists in this focus without a shared understanding about why this goal is relevant.

FOR AN ACTIVITY or HOMEWORK ASSIGNMENT

Work with a partner to help him or her negotiate a specific goal that can be accomplished within a reasonable period of time. Start out by using your active listening skills and a few open-ended questions to find out what the problem is. It would probably be advisable to start out with something relatively minor.

Negotiate with your partner to devise a goal that meets the criteria that have been discussed. One way to remember them is to use the pneumonic device SMART in which each of the letters signals one of the things to keep in mind:

1. **Specific.** What exactly do you want to accomplish?
2. **Measurable.** How will you identify success, in increases, decreases, or attainments?
3. **Attainable.** To what extent is this a realistic goal at this time?
4. **Relevant.** Is this goal directly connected to the presenting issues and appropriate, given the timing?
5. **Time bound.** When are the deadlines and target points to accomplish what was declared?

After you are done, your partner should have written down exactly what he or she is going to do, how often, and under which circumstances. You should then make plans to talk again within a specified period of time so there is some accountability.

One final criterion to keep in mind when helping clients work toward goals is to make sure they are ethical. What if, for instance, someone wants help to become more exploitative of others? Or what if a drug dealer feels guilty because of his chosen profession and wants your assistance to reduce this annoying side effect? Or what if someone comes to you requesting help with an activity that is immoral or illegal?

As you have no doubt learned in other courses, the practice of therapy is fraught with moral dilemmas and ethical conflicts. You will want to discuss thoroughly with your clients the consequences of their choices and decisions about which goals they want to accomplish.

Relaxation Training

This is another generic strategy that has become mainstream in the field. You are most likely already familiar with it, in which a person is taught to relax various muscles systematically as an attempt to control inhibiting stress or anxiety. The instructions resemble a kind of hypnotic trance induction method in which the client is invited to get as comfortable as possible and to close his or her eyes.

You begin with breathing, asking the person to concentrate completely on the process of drawing in and exhaling a breath.

> *With your eyes closed, listen to the sound of my voice and allow it to help you relax. Notice that with each breath you take you can feel your chest rising, and falling, and rising. [Time the cadence of your voice to the actual rising and falling of the client's chest.]*
>
> *Each time you exhale, I want you to just think the word "relax"; say the word "relax" to yourself. As you do so, with each breath you take, you will find yourself becoming more and more calm, more and more relaxed. Just spend a minute enjoying how good it feels to breathe deeply and think the word relax. Just follow your breath as it originates deep inside your chest, gathering together all the toxic air in your body and bloodstream, and then as your chest contracts you can feel all the used air exhale out through your mouth and your nose. As you exhale, you think the word "relax." Then you breathe deeply and slowly taking in fresh oxygen, nourishing your body and your mind. Just let your breathing help you to relax.*

After a few minutes of teaching the person how to use deep breathing as a relaxation exercise, directions are now used to help the person to go to a much deeper state of serenity. This is often done through imagery in which a particular scene is created on the beach, floating on a cloud, or walking through a quiet meadow. You can even ask the client to go to the place in which he or she feels most safe.

Next, deep muscle relaxation is often introduced. The client is asked to imagine that each muscle in the body is stretching itself, all the tension draining away.

> *Beginning with your feet, I want you to picture each of the tiny, little muscles in your feet beginning to relax. From the tips of your toes, up your instep, around your ankles, at your heel, you can feel each of the muscles stretching out like rubber bands. Imagine as you lie there, so relaxed, concentrating on your breathing, thinking the word relax as you exhale, that your feet are becoming light as feathers, almost able to float of their own accord. And now you can feel this warm sensation of relaxation and stretching begin to move into your calves and lower legs.*

The client is continually directed to concentrate on breathing, thinking the word relax, and to imagine each and every muscle in the body—from the legs, to the abdomen, to the chest, down the legs, into the hands and fingers, tip into the shoulders and back, into the neck, the face, and all the tiny little muscles around the eyes and nose and mouth, moving into the scalp. This whole process might take half an hour the first time. Throughout the exercise you are watching carefully for the least sign of tension and, if detected, you back up a little and keep working until the person is ready to move on. Most people find this experience to be incredibly refreshing and relaxing.

Depending how deeply you want to take the person, or how much tension he or she is carrying, you can include further imagery.

> *You lie there completely relaxed, with every muscle in your body stretched out and drained away of tension. I'd like you to picture an escalator that is going down, down, down. I'd like you to step onto the escalator and, as it takes you lower, I want you to feel yourself become even more deeply relaxed. You are continuing to move down, and with each descent of a floor, you can feel yourself become more profoundly relaxed, almost as if you could float away.*

If this resembles some sort of hypnotic procedure, that is because it is. Relaxation methods are favored induction methods to put people into

FOR HOMEWORK or A CLASS ACTIVITY

Working with a partner, practice using an abbreviated form of relaxation training. Start out by asking the person to close his or her eyes and concentrate on breathing for a minute or two. Each time the person exhales, repeat the word "relax," inviting your partner to repeat this with each subsequent breath.

For this exercise, you will concentrate solely on one region of the body—the chest. Ask the person to visualize that all the muscles in the chest are loosening, stretching, and expanding, making it progressively easier to breathe. Encourage your partner to take deep, cleansing breaths, each one bringing a greater sense of serenity and relaxation.

Suggest that your partner imagine himself or herself resting in a special or favorite place that feels especially safe and relaxing. This could be lying on a beach, sitting in a favorite chair, or swinging in a hammock—wherever the person associates a place of peace and quiet.

Remind your partner to keep concentrating on breathing deeply and calmly, thinking the word "relax" on each exhale and picturing himself or herself resting in that special place.

After a few minutes of this process, ask your partner to talk about what the experience was like, as well as to give you feedback on what worked best and least effectively. If time and the situation permit, reverse roles so that each of you has a chance to practice.

hyper-suggestible states. There is no magic to this; you are simply helping the person let go of conditioned tension responses.

The beauty of this method is that, once learned, the client can use it whenever he or she is confronted with stressful situations. By thinking the word "*relax*" and taking a few deep breaths the person can bring back the same feelings of self-control and serenity.

The relaxation method is a relatively simple procedure to learn, although as with any therapeutic strategy, supervision and feedback are required from more experienced practitioners. There are several different scripts that you can learn, each one adapted to a specific type of presenting concern. There are a number of useful resources that you can consult, either scripts available online or in manuals (e.g., White, 2018).

Sensate Focus Exercises

In the field of sex therapy, various behavioral homework assignments are combined with other forms of therapy to help couples make steady progress eliminating sexual dysfunctions (Wincze & Weisberg, 2015). Most such problems, from orgasmic difficulties in women to erectile problems in men, are caused in part by inhibiting thought processes. How can one possibly have an orgasm if you are constantly thinking to yourself, "I wonder if I'll come this time?" How can one maintain an erection if you are continuously thinking, "I wonder if it will stay hard or whether I'll lose it again?" It is, thus, a kind of performance anxiety that creates or exacerbates most such sexual problems.

To combat such self-defeating thinking, and to build in a series of successful experiences, therapists often use a series of progressive homework assignments for couples. Essentially, all sexual dysfunctions are conceived as a systemic rather than individual problems (more on that theory in Chapter 8). What this means is that although it may appear that the man or the woman has the sexual problem, it is actually the result of interactive dynamics between them. A man who has premature ejaculation may be expressing anger unconsciously to his partner, "Ha, ha, ha. I got off and you didn't." A woman who doesn't have orgasms with her partner may be saying, "You aren't good enough to excite me." Quite often, individual sexual problems are signs of some other relationship difficulty that must also be addressed. But sometimes focusing simply on behavior provides a shortcut that can lead to other changes.

The sensate focus exercises, while developed more than 50 years ago by William Masters and Susan Johnson (1970), are one of the most powerful methods for addressing sexual dysfunction. By focusing on touching and the sensations it brings, sensate focus uses behavioral strategies to reduce "spectatoring" to remove internal pressure and to create positive, successful, loving experiences for the couple (Weiner & Avery-Clark, 2017). The exercises begin with each partner directed to pleasure the other one through a full body massage, but without touching one another's genitals. This removes all pressure to perform. Later, in the case of a premature ejaculator, he might be directed to try brief penetration, focusing on only the sensations, and then to immediately withdraw. In the example of erectile dysfunction (that is not organically based), he might be specifically ordered to focus on the pleasant sensations that occur just before an erection but not having an erection (this is also called a paradoxical directive and will be discussed in Chapter 10). With a woman experiencing orgasmic difficulties, her partner may be directed to touch and please her in ways that have nothing to do with eliciting sexual arousal.

FOR PERSONAL APPLICATION

This might very well be the most fun exercise in the book. Tell your spouse, lover, or partner that you have a homework assignment for school. (If you don't have a partner, your first job is to find one.)

Turn off the phone and create complete privacy with no interruptions.
Take a bath or shower together.
Take turns spending a total of 30 uninterrupted minutes pleasuring your partner (without leading to sex or orgasm) while he or she remains relatively still and passive. Have your partner verbalize what he or she enjoys most.

This assignment is often a variation of the first step in behaviorally based sex therapy in which couples are taught to reduce performance anxiety associated with lovemaking.

Very slowly and progressively, partners are given other assignments that involve behavioral principles of reinforcement and changing the automatic stimulus-response patterns ("My partner has that look; I'm getting nervous, so quick! I'll take out the trash!") by using *stimulus control procedures* to change the relationship between touch and anxiety/avoidance. Such therapeutic strategies are incredibly effective, by the way, demonstrating cure rates well into the 90% range (if there is no underlying physical problem involved such as side effects from blood pressure medication or a neurological disease).

Contingency Contracting
This is another excellent structure that you already know about and use in your life intuitively. As it was originally conceived, the idea was to control

better the reinforcers of target behaviors. After goals are specified and a plan of action is constructed, the final step includes identifying the agreed-on consequences. When you declare to yourself that you will allow yourself a dessert if you are able to stay within your scheduled diet for the day, you are using this strategy. If you tell a reluctant client that she can stop coming to sessions if she manages to stay out of trouble for two weeks, you are also employing contingency contracting.

Recall that behavior can be increased in two ways, according to the behaviorist:

- *Positive reinforcement.* This is also known as rewarding people when they do something desirable. Common examples include smiles, verbal encouragement ("Great job!"), and prizes (candy or "screen time" can a particularly potent rewards for kids).
- *Negative reinforcement.* This is another kind of reward in which you remove something that the person finds undesirable. For example, you might take away some dreaded chore once the person does what has been agreed on.

There are also two ways to decrease the frequency of behavior:

- *Punishment.* This involves applying some stimulus that the person finds noxious or undesirable. When someone doesn't do what he or she is supposed to, the person is punished by doing extra chores. Keep in mind that punishments (and rewards) are perceived differently. Some kids actually enjoy negative attention and other individuals find what you consider to be a punishment to actually be enjoyable in a perverse way. Also remember that punishment has its side effects in that it often produces defensiveness, anger, or withdrawal.
- *Reinforcing incompatible behavior.* Another way to decrease the frequency of certain behaviors is to reinforce other behaviors that are incompatible with it. This is the strategy behind relaxation training, for example, because you can't be anxious when you are also feeling calm.

Depending on the situation, the individual, and the desired goal (to increase or decrease behavior), you would design a personalized contract that includes the following components:

1. Which behaviors do you wish to change and in what direction?
   I want to increase the amount of time I spend with my family members and decrease the time I spend at work.

2. What is your plan of action?

   I agree to spend a minimum of 30 uninterrupted minutes with my husband five out of seven nights. I plan to spend at least 2 hours on the weekend with my two children doing just what they want to do. Furthermore, I will not bring work home with me more than three nights per week instead of the five nights that I have been currently doing so.

3. What might get in the way?

   Regarding the first goal with my husband, he might not always cooperate because he also has his own commitments. As for the second goal with my children, it has been easy in the past for me to let myself get sidetracked when the phone rings. The third goal is the most challenging of all because I can't control my workload; my boss may assign me tasks that have to be completed within a deadline.

4. How do you propose to overcome these obstacles?

   First, I will kidnap my husband if necessary, even if we have to get out of the house to go for a walk so we make sure we take the time to debrief one another. If he still won't cooperate on a regular basis, I will follow through on our getting marital counseling to address the issues. The same goes for my children: I will take them and leave the house to do something together so we aren't interrupted or distracted. As for the situation at work, I intend to have a conversation with my boss and explain the new limits under which I will be working. I realize he will try to circumvent and sabotage my efforts, but it is completely within my power to enforce what I say I will do.

5. What are the contingencies that will be put in place?

   Well, much of this new behavior is self-rewarding and intrinsically pleasurable. But I know myself well enough that I need some incentives. If I manage to do what I say I'll do with my husband and children for 3 weeks in a row, then I will schedule a family trip to Disneyland to celebrate. If I don't complete these family goals, I will cook dinner and clean up an extra night each week for a period of 4 weeks. With respect to my work goal, my reward will be to have my children cook dinner an extra night each week because they will enjoy more of my company. If I don't follow through on this plan, then my punishment will be to not spend any money on clothes or luxury items until such time that I can maintain this new pattern for 3 weeks in a row.

In constructing contracts, either for yourself or clients, it is generally a good idea to work on one behavioral goal at a time. When developing a reward system, keep in mind that it is better if they can be delivered immediately and if they may be applied frequently to small, successive steps toward the ultimate goal (Miltenberger, 2015).

Often, contracts such as this might be signed and witnessed as a powerful form of accountability. People are far more likely to do what they say they want to do when they have made public commitments about their intentions. Try putting the contract on the refrigerator where everyone in your household can see it and you must face it every day, and then try to weasel out of your agreement.

Behavioral Intervention Plans

Counselors who work in schools, or who work primarily with children, use a slightly different form of contingency contracting typically called a Behavior Intervention Plan (BIP; Johnson, 2018) or a Behavior Support Plan (BSP; Crone, Hawken, & Horner, 2015). These plans include the same elements as contracts, but usually involve getting adults together on behalf of a child to decide how to systematically and consistently modify the home and school environment so the child's undesirable behaviors are extinguished while adaptive behaviors become more frequent. In a school setting, Behavior Intervention Plans are developed when a student has become a disruption to the learning process in the classroom and needs to interact more appropriately and safely others. A BIP or BSP includes specific statements about the following:

1. The behavior targeted for change
2. The short and long-term behavior goals
3. How the behaviors and progress will be measured
4. Who will do what, such as the roles of teachers, instructional assistants, and parents
5. Details about positive and negative reinforcement that will be used
6. How and when the plan's implementation will be monitored and evaluated for effectiveness

Let's look at how this works. I (Marilyn) once worked with a second-grade boy (let's call him Stephan) who was becoming very unpopular with the other kids in his class. He pretended to be a lion at recess, creeping up on others and roaring at them in order to get their attention. Not surprisingly, this usually worked; they ran away screaming and were complaining to their parents about him, which wasn't making the principal happy. He was being raised as an only child by his grandmother and grandfather in a rural area where it wasn't easy to arrange "play dates," so he hadn't had much peer experience to teach him what works and what doesn't when making friends.

I met with Stephan's grandparents, his teacher, and the teacher's aide who monitored outdoor recess. We targeted several specific goals: (1) eliminating his roaring behavior as the short-term objective, and (b) increasing several specific friendship skills (including offering to help, giving and receiving compliments, ignoring someone who is annoying you, and starting and maintaining a conversation) as the long-term goals. We decided that the teacher's aide would log all roaring incidents and make a chart of how many times they occurred each week. I agreed to be responsible for teaching the friendship skills to Stephan, one each week, through role playing during individual sessions. I also met with the class once a week for a month, providing a general "friendship skills" intervention focused on each of the skills in turn. I taught the children to notice when others performed a specific skill and to reward them. They practiced replying to a peer offering help by saying, "Thank you! I liked your offer to help me," or "I don't need help right now, but thank you for offering to help me." By doing this, I engaged Stephan's peers to reinforce him (as well as others) with attention for a prosocial skill and to stop reinforcing his annoying roaring habit. I set the teacher up with a chart that would help her record Stephan's instances of performing the skill of the week. I supported the grandparents in arranging for Stephan to meet another child for a fun activity each week and complimenting him afterwards on his specific instances of using his new friendship skills. We all agreed that we would meet back together in a month, compare our frequency charts, and modify the plan as needed.

When we met one month later, Stephan had not roared in two weeks. He had enthusiastically implemented each friendship skill I had taught him, as recorded by his teacher. His teacher shared the general impression that he was much more accepted; she had observed him being invited to work with other children during group assignments several times. The principal was happy that she had had no more complaints about his behavior from other parents. Stephan's grandparents, who had learned how to support his peer relationships, were relieved that he was making friends.

CONTEMPORARY DEVELOPMENTS

Behavior therapy was the first treatment method designed to be short term, symptom oriented, and concerned with reaching specific, identified goals. No wonder, then, in today's climate of managed care that this approach is so popular among insurance administrators who like its emphasis on accountability, precise measurement of outcomes, and efficiency. It is cost effective from the standpoint that if it is going to work with a given case, there will be observable results in a relatively short period of time.

There are now over a dozen different journals devoted to the practice of this brand of therapy. Consistent with its heritage, the focus of much of the research is on empirically validating specific methods with particular client problems such as obesity and health behaviors. A quick sampling of any recent issue of the *Journal of Applied Behavior Analysis* will capture articles on a breadth of behavioral theory applications on topics such as social skills deficits in an adolescent with pervasive developmental disorder, effectiveness of video-based training on staff implementation of a problem-solving model with adult inpatient clients, the functional analysis and treatment of rumination with a timed flavor spray, bully prevention through positive behavior support, and teaching abduction prevention skills to parents and children.

Behavioral principles and techniques can be especially useful for addressing parent–child problems and are often taught in group parenting classes. The Oregon Social Learning Center, for example, teaches parents how to stop rewarding their child or adolescent's bad behavior such as voicing a demand more and more loudly until the parent finally gives in to make the noise stop, thus expertly using negative reinforcement to make sure the parent's "giving in" behavior continues (Patterson, Chamberlain, & Reid, 2016). Parent–Child Interaction Therapy (PICT), developed by Sheila Eyberg and her colleagues (McNeil & Hembree-Kigin, 2011), is a treatment for conduct-disordered young children that teaches parents how to encourage prosocial behavior and decrease negative behavior. Family Behavior Therapy (FBT) was developed to address an adult's drug abuse and other behaviors that tend to co-occur in clusters of related problems and aims to change the behavior of the client as well as others in the family (Dishion, Forgatch, Chamberlain, & Pelham, 2016). It can also be applied to many parent–child situations that families find perplexing, such as children ignoring parents' requests or bedtime problems. Essentially, family behavior therapists teach the family to focus on behavior and see it as something that is learned and can change, but must be shaped and rewarded (Falloon, 2015).

Quite a number of technological advances have also made it possible to deliver reinforcers through remote devices or to communicate with therapists via the Internet. Individual record keeping and evaluating outcomes are becoming much easier with the use of portable devices, which are being used by more and more people to track all kinds of behaviors (Abedtash & Holden, 2017). These innovations make it possible for people to keep much more accurate records of their progress, as well as to make adjustments as needed. This is good, because as you might expect, progress monitoring on a device is more likely to lead to goal attainment, particularly when outcomes are reported or made public and when information is physically recorded in the app (for example, each 5-minute session of mindful breathing). The most contemporary development of all in this approach is the way that its practice has been incorporated and synthesized into so many other methods. Despite misrepresentations and misuse, interest in learning and behavior theory has grown steadily. Over the past 60 years, applied behavior analysis (ABA) has become recognized as the treatment of choice for behavior problems associated with mental retardation, autism spectrum disorders, brain injury, and other disorders. ABA specialists focus on the "ABCs" (antecedents, behaviors, and consequences) to understand and then change problematic behaviors), often by simply changing the environment that reinforces the problem (Kearney, 2015).

Behavioral medicine has also come on the scene and represents an inter-disciplinary approach to the prevention, diagnosis and treatment of health behavior problems, and rehabilitation and promotion of health. Behavior therapists are more and more frequently called on in medical settings to help clients make changes that will help them overcome health problems such as obesity or heart disease or comply with difficult regimens such as those required for diabetes. Health care professionals now see behavioral interventions as cost-effective ways to help people make changes (like getting on that exercise bike or conditioning themselves to get to sleep on time) that will boost their health and quality of life.

Strengths and Limitations

Obviously, human beings are made up of far more than observable behaviors. We are thinking beings and also feeling beings. Although in recent years behavior therapy has been all but swallowed up by the cognitive-behavioral approach, there is still a suspicion of anything that is too non-empirical, nonobjective, and illogical. As such, this is a relatively mechanistic approach.

Behavior therapy downplays the importance of insight in the change process and also minimizes the importance of the therapeutic relationship. That is not to say that contemporary behavior therapists don't spend time working on their alliances with clients, just as they also explore issues related to self-understanding, but the theory has not emphasized these factors much. This is changing rapidly as behavior therapy moves from its own first wave (applying behavioral principles to clinical targets) and second wave (including cognitive or verbal behavior and social/emotional behavior as targets) to the new third wave (characterized by openness to other clinical traditions, a focus on contextual change, an emphasis on function over form, and the construction of flexible and effective repertoires) (Hayes, 2016). These newer behavioral therapies, including acceptance and commitment therapy (ACT) and dialectical behavior therapy (DBT), will be described in a later chapter. However, for some clients, pursuing insight is just a distraction; focusing on behavior is what's realistic and manageable.

The stance of the therapist in this approach is that of an expert who designs strategies in collaboration with the client. There is, thus, a danger of manipulation and abuse of power when the inequality of roles is emphasized. Again, in practice, behavior therapists may operate very differently from this style, but the original theory implies that it is the professional's job to figure out what the problem is, design a treatment strategy, implement that program, and then measure the outcome. This has contributed much to the status of the field, especially with regard to developing empirically validated treatments for specific disorders.

VOICES FROM THE PAST: B. F. SKINNER

In that brave new world which science is preparing for the housewife of the future, the young mother has apparently been forgotten. Almost nothing has been done to ease her lot by simplifying and improving the care of babies.

When we decided to have another child, my wife and I felt that it was time to apply a little laborsaving invention and design to the problems of the nursery. We began by going over the disheartening schedule

FIGURE 5.1. B. F. Skinner

of the young mother, step by step. We asked only one question: Is this practice important for the physical and psychological health of the baby? When it was not, we marked it for elimination. Then the "gadgeteering" began.

The result was an inexpensive apparatus in which our baby daughter has now been living for 11 months. Her remarkable good health and happiness and my wife's welcome leisure have exceeded our most optimistic predictions, and we are convinced that a new deal for both mother and baby is at hand.

We tackled first the problem of warmth. The useful solution is to wrap the baby in half-a-dozen layers of cloth—shirt-nightdress, sheet, blankets. This is never completely successful. The baby is likely to be found steaming in its own fluids or lying cold and uncovered. Schemes to prevent uncovering may be dangerous, and in fact they have sometimes even proved fatal. Clothing and bedding also interfere with normal exercise and growth and keep the baby from taking comfortable postures or changing posture during sleep. They also encourage rashes and sores. Nothing can be said for the system on the score of convenience, because frequent changes and launderings are necessary.

Why not, we thought, dispense with clothing altogether—except for the diaper, which serves another purpose—and warm the space in which the baby lives? This should be a simple technical problem in the modern home.

Our solution is a closed compartment about as spacious as a standard crib. The walls are well insulated, and one side, which can be raised like a window, is a large pane of safety glass. The heading is electrical, and special precautions have been taken to insure accurate control.

After a little experimentation we found that our baby, when first home from the hospital, was completely comfortable and relaxed without benefit of clothing at about 86 degrees F. As she grew older, it was possible to lower the temperature by easy stages. Now, at 11 months, we are operating at about 78 degrees, with a relative humidity of 50%.

When awake, she exercises almost constantly and often with surprising violence. Her leg, stomach, and back muscles are especially active and have become strong and hard. It is necessary to watch this performance for only a few minutes to realize how severely restrained the average baby is, and how much energy must be diverted into the only remaining channel—crying.

Remember that these advantages for the baby do not mean additional labor or attention on the part of the mother. On the contrary, there is an almost unbelievable saving in time and effort. For one thing, there's no bed to be made or changed. The "mattress' is a tightly stretched canvass, which is kept dry by warm air. A single bottom sheet operates like a roller towel. It is stored on a spool outside the compartment at one end and passes into a wire hamper at the other. It is 10 yards long and lasts a week. A clean section can be locked into place in a few seconds. The time which is usually spent in changing clothes is also saved. This is especially important in the early months. When we take the baby up for feeding or play, she is wrapped in a small blanket or simple nightdress. Occasionally she is dressed up "for fun" or for her play period. But that is all. The wrapping blanket, roller sheet, and the usual diapers are the only laundry actually required.

We have also enjoyed the advantages of a fixed daily routine. Child specialists are still not agreed as to whether the mother should watch the baby or the clock, but no one denies that a strict schedule saves time, for the mother can plan her day in advance and find time for relaxation or freedom for other activities. The trouble is that a routine acceptable to the baby often conflicts with the schedule of the household. Our compartment helps out here in two easy. Even in crowded living quarters it can be kept free of unwanted lights and sounds. The insulated walls muffle all ordinary noises, and a curtain can be drawn over the window. The result is that, in the space taken by a standard crib, the baby has in effect a separate room. We are never concerned lest the doorbell, telephone, piano, or children at play wake the baby, and we can therefore let her set up any routine she likes.

Before the baby was born, when we were still building the apparatus, some of the friends and acquaintances who had heard about what we proposed to do were rather shocked. Mechanical dishwashers, garbage disposers, air cleaners, and other laborsaving devices were all very fine, but a mechanical baby tender—that was carrying science too far! However, all the specifics which were raised against the plan have faded away in the bright light of our results. A very brief acquaintance with the scheme in operation is enough to resolve all doubts. Some of the toughest skeptics have become our most enthusiastic supporters.

It is not, of course, the favorable conditions to which people object, but the fact that in our compartment they are "artificial." All of them occur naturally in one favorable environment or another, where the same objection should apply but is never raised. It is quite in the spirit of the "world of the future" to make favorable conditions available everywhere through simple mechanical means.

Source: B. F. Skinner, "Baby in a Box," *Ladies' Home Journal*, vol. 62, pp. 30-31, 135-136, 138. Copyright © 1945 by The B. F. Skinner Foundation. Reprinted with permission.

SUGGESTED READINGS

Crone, D. E., Hawken, S. L., & Horner, R. H. (2015). *Building positive behavior support systems in schools.* New York, NY: Guilford.

Johnson, C. (2018). *Implementing effective behavior intervention plans: 8 steps to success.* New York, NY: Routledge.

Kearney, A., (2015). *Understanding applied behavior analysis: An introduction to ABA for parents, teachers, and other professionals* (2nd ed.). Philadelphia, PA: Jessica Kingsley Publishers.

Martin, G., & Pear, J. (2014). *Behavior modification: What it is and how to do it* (10th ed.). Upper Saddle River, NJ: Pearson.

Mazur, J. E. (2016). *Learning & behavior* (8th ed.). New York, NY: Routledge.

Skinner, B. F. (1948). *Walden two.* New York, NY: Macmillan.

Watson, D. L., & Tharp, R. G. (2013). *Self-directed behavior: Self-modification for personal adjustment* (10th ed.). Belmont, CA: Wadsworth.

Weiner, L., & Avery-Clark, C. (2017). *Sensate focus in sex therapy: The illustrated manual.* New York, NY: Routledge.

IMAGE CREDITS

CHAPTER 6

The Primacy of Personal Experience: Humanistic Approaches

LEARNING OBJECTIVES

After reading this chapter, you should be able to do the following:

1. Contrast the shared beliefs and assumptions underlying humanistic approaches with those of psychoanalysis and behaviorism.
2. Describe the distinguishing features of humanistic therapists' approach to healing relationships.
3. Articulate the impact of the notion of self-actualization proposed by Abraham Maslow on post-World War II American psychology.
4. Identify several influences of existential philosophy on the development of existential therapy.
5. List key tenets of existential therapy such as self-awareness, responsibility, freedom, and angst.
6. Describe the existential therapist's stance and role in treatment.
7. Evaluate contemporary innovations, strengths, and limitations of existential therapy.
8. Articulate the basic assumptions and core conditions of person-centered therapy proposed by Carl Rogers, including congruence, unconditional positive regard, and empathy.
9. Provide examples of person-centered techniques such as reflection and immediacy.
10. Evaluate Rogers's tenets regarding the therapeutic process expressed in his writing.
11. Describe contemporary revisions to address potential limitations of person-centered therapy.
12. Articulate the basic assumptions of Gestalt therapy.
13. Provide examples of how specific Gestalt techniques are implemented.
14. Evaluate the strengths and potential limitations of Gestalt therapy for clients with particular needs and preferences.
15. Describe the evidence supporting contemporary applications of humanistic therapy such as emotion-focused therapy for clients with particular problems.

The term, "humanistic" has come to mean many things throughout the ages. During the Renaissance it was used to describe secular rather than religious scholars who studied the ancient cultures of Greece and Rome. As a philosophy it came to mean an approach to making sense of the world and human actions in terms of their capacity for thinking and action that was for the betterment of the world. It represented a moral and ethical stance that was both optimistic and hopeful about the world and its inhabitants. To a certain extent, it emphasized rational thought, tempered by compassion.

The family of humanistic therapies is a diverse group of approaches that branched off in different ways from the central premise that emphasizes growth and self-actualization. Although the theories may share a set of basic assumptions about human nature, they go about their work in very different ways. Some humanistic theories (existential) are rather intellectually dense and philosophical in nature, whereas others focus on unexpressed feelings (person-centered) or primary experience (Gestalt). What makes them all humanistic in orientation is a strong belief in the power of people to heal themselves, especially in the context of a genuine, authentic relationship. The humanistic practitioner seeks to create an alliance with clients that is warm, caring, genuine, respectful, and engaging. The therapist is not only allowed to be authentic and real in the relationship, but also is encouraged to be so. Humanistic approaches emphasize the importance of shared connections between all people, regardless of their backgrounds and life experiences, and the healing power of these connections.

SOME SHARED BELIEFS

At the time that humanism came into prominence the two major forces in the field, behaviorism and psychoanalysis, were fighting for dominance. Each argued that the best way to do therapy was either to concentrate on presenting symptoms or underlying causes. Although psychoanalytic practitioners did advocate that the therapeutic relationship was the core of healing, they stressed a kind of alliance that was fairly antiseptic in that the therapist's personhood was to be kept in the background. Furthermore, consistent with Freud's thinking, most analysts believed that humans were essentially driven by their instinctual drives: sexuality and aggression. The object of therapy was to help people to control their basic nature. Behaviorists, on the other hand, had wholeheartedly adopted the scientific method and thus limited their focus to how behaviors that could be observed, measured, and counted could be shaped and were not interested in the unanswerable (and irrelevant) question of how to live a good life.

By contrast, humanism viewed people as essentially good and growth oriented. If they experienced problems or engaged in destructive acts, it was because they had wandered away from their basic nature. Given a fertile environment characterized by an accepting, respectful, and caring relationship, people could be helped to regain their emotional and spiritual footing.

Basic Assumptions

There are several characteristics of a humanistic approach, regardless of which brand is practiced (House, Kaslisch, & Maidman, 2018; Schneider & Krug, 2017):

The primacy of experience. Rather than quantifying or measuring behavior, the humanist seeks to understand personal experience in its essence. Every individual is unique. Human experience is irreducible to simply needs and drives. Subjective inner states should be honored and respected.

Growth orientation. People have the tendency to grow and actualize their potential. Increased self-awareness and self-acceptance will help people in their journey toward greater fulfillment and productivity.

Free choice. Rather than being deterministic, humanists believe that people can become almost whatever they choose.

Responsibility for self and others. Following the lead of Carl Rogers, one of the founders of the humanistic movement, practitioners feel a responsibility not only to engage in more caring, civil, and respectful interactions with others, but also to advocate on behalf of social justice concerns.

You can see that these assumptions are quite different from those presented in the previous chapters. If psychodynamic theory has been described as deterministic and instinct driven, and behaviorism is observation and measurement driven, then the humanistic approaches focus much more on the choices that people make and the freedom they have to determine their own futures. Of course, with that freedom comes awesome personal responsibility.

The Healing Relationship

It is through the relationship with a helper (therapist, counselor, teacher, coach, parent) that people are able to sort out their troubles and regain their composure. This special type of relationship includes a kind of non-possessive love, care, and respect. Clark Moustakas, a strong proponent of humanistic therapies, described the therapist's role as composed of three characteristic facets:

1. *Being in.* Empathy means crawling inside someone else's skin so that you can feel what he or she is experiencing. All of your ability to read what another is feeling, to respond sensitively, and to mirror what you hear and see is based on the accuracy of your "felt sense." To experience pure empathy, you must leave your own self-centeredness and enter into the being of another. Needless to say, this is a very challenging journey.

2. *Being for.* Helping relationships are hardly neutral ones in the sense that you have complete allegiance to your clients. You may not support the destructive things they do and the irritating behaviors that get in the way, but you never waver in your acceptance and respect for them as people. When times are tough, you are the one person they can count on for support and encouragement.

3. *Being with.* As an individual, distinct person, you have your own perceptions, beliefs, and feelings that are separate from those of your clients. Even when you are involved in the empathic activity of "being in," you are still apart, fully aware of your own internal reactions and perceptions. The authentic sharing of selves in therapy is a reciprocal process in which both participants are profoundly influenced by the interaction. Just as the client is affected by the encounter, so too is the therapist impacted dramatically. The humanistic relationship is, thus, an authentic engagement. "Being with," writes Moustakas (1986), "certainly means listening and hearing the other's feelings, thoughts, objectives, but it also means offering my own perceptions and views" (p. 102).

FOR A CLASS ACTIVITY

Form small groups of about six participants. Each of you talks to one another about a time in your life in which you were having a difficult time and a strong relationship with a helper (teacher, coach, counselor, neighbor, etc.) made all the difference. Rather than focusing on what this helper did that was most valuable, focus instead on the kind of relationship that developed.

After each of you has had a chance to share something personal, then discuss what it feels like to be in a group together talking about your experiences. What is added when such experiences are shared?

FOR PERSONAL APPLICATION

One of the most useful concepts that you can use to improve the quality, intimacy, and satisfaction of all your relationships is to practice empathic listening. This means focusing your full and complete attention on the other person and resisting all distractions, both internal and external. It involves putting yourself in a place of perfect openness so that you can enter the other person's world without judgment or criticism. You simply make yourself present for the other person, doing your absolute best to listen carefully and respond compassionately.

We warn you: This is very hard to do. It is so natural to divide your attention, let your thoughts wander, and become critical and judgmental of what another person is saying or doing, or to think about the advice you'd like to give. Empathic listening, however, requires you to suspend your own needs in the process of entering another person's world.

Report back to class how this practice went, what problems you encountered, and what you noticed was different about your conversations.

BACKGROUND AND HISTORY

Humanism emerged as much as a cultural artifact as a scientific revolution. It was a product of the 1950s, a time of eternal optimism, faith in the human spirit, material affluence, and a search for personal meaning.

It was Abraham Maslow, perhaps more than any other thinker, who converted the widespread cheerfulness and optimism of post-WWII America into a psychology of positive mental health. Remember that at this time the only alternatives available were largely mechanistic (behaviorism) or deterministic (psychoanalysis). Then Maslow's (1954) voice was heard, advocating that psychology should not just focus on the emotionally dysfunctional and mentally ill but also on those who are most fully functioning. He decided to identify the individuals who were exceptionally "self-actualized," contemporaries such as Eleanor Roosevelt and Albert Schweitzer, and use them as models for human potential. He also believed it was possible to study scientifically not only observable behavior but also internal experience.

FOR PERSONAL REFLECTION or **A CLASS ACTIVITY**

Among his findings, Abraham Maslow discovered that self-actualized people have a high frequency of peak experiences—magical moments of insight, creativity, spiritual transcendence, intimacy, or harmony. Think about the peak experiences of your life, those moments of sublime ecstasy in which you transcended ordinary reality. These could have been religious, creative, intellectual, emotional, or physical experiences.

Try to recall the texture of what took place—how you felt, saw, heard, and experienced reality in a distinctly different way. Recapture the power of those moments and how they changed forever your perceptions and lived experience.

Select one such event from the past year. Talk to classmates about what happened and what it meant to you.

Although Maslow started the ball rolling (with a little help from some friends), others worked independently of his efforts, making their own discoveries about the best in human nature. These included names you might have heard before, such as Carl Rogers (the developer of client-centered therapy), Rollo May (the first American existential therapist), Erich Fromm (popular writer of books on love and personal meaning), Clark Moustakas (author of books on the meaning of loneliness), James Bugental and Alvin Mahrer (both psychologists who developed humanistic approaches to therapy), and many others. We are not throwing all these names at you because we think you should commit them to memory, but merely to highlight that dozens of people were involved in promoting the humanistic movement, each of them with a unique viewpoint.

EXISTENTIAL THEORY

Rather than a coherent psychological theory, this is really a philosophical approach to helping people that examines issues of personal meaning. This model is much less about therapeutic techniques and more about offering a perspective on the human condition to guide helping efforts (van Deurzen & Arnold-Baker, 2018). Rather than offering an integrated helping model or specific techniques, it instead presents a way of thinking about (and experiencing) what it means to be a reflective and fully alive human being. As such, this philosophy can be incorporated into many other therapeutic approaches that emphasize finding and creating meaning.

Background and History

Existential theory has its heritage in the philosophical writings of European theologians and philosophers, who make for some very difficult bedtime reading. Unless you have a strong background in this discipline, it is likely that tackling the original sources of Soren Kierkegaard (1813–1855), Frederich Nietzsche (1844–1900), Martin Heidegger (1889–1976), Jean-Paul Sartre (1905–1980), Martin Buber (1878–1965), and Karl Jaspers (1883–1969) will be quite a challenge. To give you the "one-minute existentialist" version of their ideas, they were basically concerned with the meaning of human existence. Some took the approach that God provided the foundation for finding meaning in life (Jaspers, Buber), whereas others (Sartre) believed that in the absence of God it is up to each individual to find his or her own reason for living. This overwhelming sense of freedom is also a kind of prison in that we must accept responsibility for the choices we make.

The existential themes are the stuff of movies and novels. Indeed, some of the most thought-provoking stories you have ever heard or read probably deal with the search for meaning in life, with issues of freedom and responsibility, and with the dread of annihilation. Many of the world's greatest writers (Franz Kafka, Fyodor Dostoyevsky, Albert Camus) have presented provocative themes in which human characters struggle with existential issues and their consequent moral choices. In fact, the term *existentialism* was first coined by writer and philosopher Jean-Paul Sartre to describe the state of despair expressed by characters in his novels.

FOR PERSONAL REFLECTION

Existentialists are fond of being provocative by encouraging people to wrestle with life's ultimate questions. One of the most disturbing of all subjects is our own mortality. According to this approach, it is the prospect of our own impending death that forces us to confront the urgency of living each moment to its fullest.

When philosopher Bertrand Russell, well into his 90s, was once asked about what he would like for a gift, he said with great passion that he would like to get on his knees on the busiest street corner in London and beg passersby to give him the precious moments of their lives that they waste. This was clearly a person who was in the throes of facing his own existential mortality.

Consider your own path. Regardless of what you think happens after you die, whether you go to heaven, purgatory, nirvana, whether you believe yourself destined for reincarnation, or simply food for worms, your time on this planet is certainly limited. With each tick of your heart, the precious moments of your life are forever being used up. How many such heartbeats do you think you have left before this extraordinary muscle stops forever? A million? A billion? Not so many really, especially when you consider how long you're going to be dead.

When you ponder your own impending demise, what does that bring to the surface? Knowing that your time is limited, realizing that the precious seconds of your life are ticking away (already 100 more just since you started reading this reflective exercise), how do you wish to spend your life? Do you really want to waste time feeling depressed or bored or lonely?

How might you engage more completely with your life? If you knew you only had a few weeks left to live and every day you are granted is a precious gift, what choices would you make as to how you would spend your time differently?

Victor Frankl and Logotherapy

A far more personal approach to the subject of human existence was also undertaken in Europe, but rather than in academic settings or philosophical societies, new ideas were spawned in the concentration camps of Auschwitz. Within the span of just a few years, psychiatrist Victor Frankl ended up being "transferred" from head of the most prestigious department in Austria to being interned in the death camps of Germany. As he watched his family and friends perish, Frankl mused about why some of the inmates managed to survive while others seemed to give up. He postulated that those who found some underlying meaning to their suffering, even if it was simply to last long enough to tell the world about what was happening, were able to cope in ways that others could not. The will to live seemed to emanate from a strong conviction that there was some reason or purpose for the challenges put in their path.

In his book, *Man's Search for Meaning*, now regarded by many as one of the most important works of the 20th century, Frankl (1962) set forth his ideas about existential theory that were to form the foundation for a system of helping that he called logotherapy. Foreshadowing quite a number of schools that would emphasize the value of one's attitude even in the most horrible conditions, Frankl (1962) presented his credo of survival:

> *We who lived in concentration camps can remember the men who walked through the huts comforting others, giving away their last piece of bread. They may have been few in number, but they offer sufficient proof that everything can be taken from a man but one thing: the last of the human freedoms—to choose one's attitude in any given set of circumstances, to choose one's own way. (p. 104)*

You can probably see why Frankl's ideas about human freedom and making choices about whatever life hands you have resonated for multitudes of people across many cultures. The implications of his message are profound: regardless of the circumstances in which we find ourselves, in spite of the trials and tribulations we must face, it is the choices we make about our attitudes and actions that determine our ultimate reactions. This means that as therapists, one of our main jobs is to help people examine their personal choices in life to find their own personal meaning.

Existential Principles

Existential philosophy—and hence, psychotherapy—assumes that inner conflict (usually experienced as anxiety) is due to the individual's confrontation with the givens of existence. These givens, as noted by Yalom (2009), include the inevitability of death, freedom and its resulting responsibility, existential aloneness, and meaninglessness. These four givens or ultimate concerns are the facts of human life with which each person must come to terms. To be an existential therapist means that you highlight the following issues in your sessions (Schneider & Krug, 2017; Yalom, 1998, 2009):

1. *Self-awareness.* There is only the present. Nothing else exists except the now. To the extent that you are living in the past or future, you are dead, not fully alive.

2. *Isolation.* Each of us is born alone and will die alone. Everything else is illusion. We will spend our lives seeking intimacy and trying to connect to others, but ultimately, we must confront our own essential aloneness.

3. *Personal meaning.* It is up to each individual to find a purpose for living. This is not a one-time proposition but an on-going struggle to continuously redefine our lives in light of new experiences.

4. *Freedom.* Each of us is confronted with choices every day. Freedom may be the foundation of democracy, but it also presents some awful choices. Freedom is terrifying; most people want a whole lot less of it. They fear making bad decisions. They want others to make decisions for them.

5. *Angst.* This is another word for anxiety, but in German it means a more general, free-floating kind of dread. The consequences of dealing with existential issues or of trying to hide from them is that we must all live with angst. It is always there, just below the surface. You can try to ignore it, medicate it, or distract yourself as much as possible, but angst will remain your lifelong companion. It involves an acceptance of a certain amount of discomfort, but not so much that life is disrupted.

6. *Responsibility.* We are responsible for our lives—for the choices we make or do not make. We are also responsible for our own freedom. Many people live in a type of prison of their own creation, trapped by their own refusal to be responsible for their lives.

7. *Death.* This is the biggie. This is the one you would like to run from the most. Death is what kills us, but ultimately it is also what makes us most alive.

To be an existentialist means that you think a lot about life's ultimate issues. Regardless of the issues your clients present and the problems they face, you see at their core the fundamental themes of what it means to be alive. You incorporate discussions about these themes as part of any intervention you attempt. No extra charge.

FOR A FIELD STUDY

Interview or talk to several other people about what gives their lives greatest meaning. What is it that most drives them to get out of bed in the morning, to make sacrifices, to work hard? What are they searching for most in life?

Get in the habit of talking to as many people as possible about existential themes. Spend considerable time yourself writing in your journal and reflecting privately about the meaning attached to your own existence.

Existential Therapy

It was not until Rollo May adapted existential ideas for contemporary therapeutic practice in North America (May, 1983) that this approach really began to exert a significant influence as a therapy. Other practitioners such as James Bugental, Clark Moustakas, Alvin Mahrer, and Irvin Yalom also played an influential role in developing systems of therapy that used existential ideas as their core.

Should you decide that you want to be an existentialist or practice existential therapy, we warn you that you have your work cut out for you. There is no easy path if you walk this way. Existential philosophy is dense, complex, and difficult to master. Furthermore, there is precious little guidance for the practitioner because the emphasis is not on technique but on therapist stance. You can *be* an existentialist, but you cannot *do* it with a step-by-step recipe. This, of course, gives you even more freedom to use whatever methods you want as long as they are embedded in an underlying existential way of life and practice.

Contemporary developments in existential theory and practice have made the approach far more pragmatic and flexible than other models. Although this brand of therapy still recognizes the value of long-term work as the best means to improve people's quality of life and promote profound change, it has also been adapted to briefer systems of intervention.

A number of contemporary therapists use existential therapy as their mainstay, while integrating other ideas and techniques as needed—a type of integrative practice about which we will say much more later. Existentialism provides a flexible theoretical framework to organize helping efforts, regardless of the treatment method employed. This kind of existential-integrative approach permits a therapist and client to co-invent unique ways of working together that can change from moment to moment, depending on what is needed (Barnett & Madison, 2012).

If you are the type who needs concreteness, who thrives on action plans and likes specificity, then you will likely feel very frustrated with this approach. Then again, maybe that is *exactly* what you need most. There is an idea (supported by existentialists) that the most direct path to growth is not the way that is most convenient, comfortable, and familiar to you, but rather the journey that stretches you and presents reasonable obstacles to be overcome. In addition, you must equip yourself with the means to help a variety of different clients who present a host of different issues and problems, each one requiring an individually designed and negotiated therapeutic approach—and some of them will be grappling with existential issues.

FOR REFLECTION

Who are the clients that you can imagine would be most suitable for an existential approach? What sorts of issues might they bring to sessions? What conditions would need to be met for this theory to be optimally useful?

Consider, for instance, whether you are dealing with a long-standing intractable problem or a crisis situation. What is the client's capacity for insight in terms of intellectual functioning and tolerance for ambiguity, patience, and motivation? How much time are you likely to have to get the work done? What is it that your client wants most from the sessions?

A Different Sort of Relationship

A large component of existential work, or all therapy for that matter, is the relationship you develop with your clients (Kottler & Balkin, 2017). Without such a strong alliance, it is difficult to earn trust, respect, and influence, much less be forgiven for inevitable mistakes. Although this approach was originally an offshoot of psychoanalysis (in Europe it was even called existential analysis), a fundamental change was implemented in which the connection with clients became a more authentic, here-and-now engagement. Rather than using therapist neutrality and client transference as the leverage by which to promote exploration and insight, existential therapy uses as its core the genuine, human connection that clients and therapists feel toward one another. Clients might talk about the past, but the therapist will be listening for connections with the present, including the present counseling relationship, to highlight in feedback to the client. This shift is reflected quite well in the deeply respectful "I–Thou" (as opposed to an "I–It") relationship highlighted in Martin Buber's existential philosophy (Buber, 1996). It is the immediacy and "realness" of the therapeutic encounter that is essential in the work.

Keeping in mind the importance of boundaries, the dangers of dual relationships, and the potential for exploiting clients through inappropriate boundary violations, an existential relationship is highly professional but also quite personal. The therapist presents himself or herself as a real person. The goal is make an authentic connection to clients in such a way that they feel they are treated as persons rather than as objects of treatment (van Deurzen & Arnold-Baker, 2018). In addition, clients look to you for examples of how to be authentically engaged in life, so the "person of the therapist" is very visible in this approach.

This type of relationship is not unidirectional, because the therapist must not only help the client to increase self-awareness, but also must do this as well. You'll recall that the psychoanalytic practitioner seeks to monitor personal reactions in order to deal with transference issues. The existentialist also does, but for quite a different reason: Rather than guarding against personal reactions that might pollute the relationship, the goal is instead to use these feelings. In fact, many of the most prominent theorists in our field, regardless of their theoretical orientations, consider that one of the greatest gifts of this work is the opportunity to learn from our clients and be influenced by them in our personal lives and professional development (Kottler & Balkin, 2017).

In practice, this means that when you are with clients (note again the emphasis on *with*), there are two parallel processes going on in the relationship. On the one hand, you are closely following the client's experience, using your heart, head, and soul to really get a sense of his or her world. At the same time, you are following what is going on inside of you, noting your very personal reactions to what is taking place. You might not always share your own process because therapist self-disclosure is probably the single most abused skill, but you would monitor closely and carefully how each of you in this relationship is responding and reacting to what is happening.

Whereas other systems of therapy emphasize objectivity in the relationship, the existential practitioner seeks to be "a participant 'in' the relationship rather than the detached observer who stands 'outside' the client's psychic world and comments upon or interprets it" (Spinelli, 2015, p. 12). As you no doubt can imagine, this sort of commitment requires a high degree of personal involvement.

The Therapeutic Process

Although existential therapy is extremely flexible, some practitioners have set forth a general overview of the process involved in helping people. In describing what occurs in every session he conducts, Mahrer (2004) described four general sequential steps:

1. *Being in the moment.* This means focusing totally and completely on the here and now, as well as teaching the client to do the same. Both participants in the process note internal feelings, identify those affective states, give them names, and then access the feelings at the deepest levels. Imagine, for example, during an intense interaction with someone, anyone for that matter, and stopping to ask one another what the experience *feels* like during that instant. This often leads to breakthroughs in awareness and level of engagement.

2. *Integrating the felt experience into primary relationships.* This means making connections between what is felt to more fulfilling relationships with others. The relationship comes into play again because it is through the therapeutic encounter that clients are able to apply what they have learned to other relationships. Hopefully, the trust and intimacy become generalized to other contexts.

3. *Making connections to the past.* Although things start out in the present with self-awareness and presenting complaints, these are linked to experiences that have occurred previously. The client is invited to relive early life scenes and re-experience what was felt. This is one major difference from psychoanalysis in that clients are not merely encouraged to talk about past events but to experience them emotionally all over again, working them through in ways that were not possible previously.

4. *Integrating what was learned.* This means becoming a new person in the present. The work is not just about talk but also about *applying* what was discussed to create a different, and more authentic, way of being in the world.

FOR PERSONAL APPLICATION

Try being in the moment. First, prepare yourself to embrace whatever comes into your mind and heart as you read these instructions. Start with the very first thing that comes to mind. Anything! It does not matter.

Be aware of how you are censoring and limiting yourself. Just let yourself go. Do not be concerned with what is important.

What are you feeling that is rather prominent in your life right now? This can be a good feeling or a bad one. Let yourself feel this emotion right now. Do not block yourself but let it flow.

As you experience this feeling, what are you aware of in your body? What sensations are present? What images come to mind? Just attend to whatever is happening.

Whatever has come to you, use it in some way. Make some connections between what you just experienced and what you have lived before. Make yourself receptive to whatever emerged. Ask yourself what you just learned.

If possible, talk to a friend, classmate, or family member about what you experienced. Let the experience deepen the intimacy between you and another.

Some Recent Developments

Existential therapy is increasingly being adapted to serve in a variety of contexts. From the description in this chapter, you might have pictured the only plausible client as an adult who is bright, verbal and relatively psychologically intact. But the basic relational stance can be applied in other settings, and every client can be assumed to have the freedom to choose his or her response to life. There are now resources available for using an existential approach to work with substance-abusing teens, adult men with career issues (Bell, 2018), clients affected by poverty (Evans, Kluck, Hill, Crumley, & Turchan, 2017) and natural disasters (Scott & Weems, 2013), cancer survivors (Masterson, Rosenfeld, & Breitbart, 2018), and the person who is imminently facing death (Yalom, 2009).

A growing theme in existentially oriented treatment—probably brought on by the unique opportunities and anxieties of this century—involves supporting clients' finding or restoring a sense of meaning in life. You'll recognize meaning as a core existential theme developed by earlier existential philosophers; it is increasingly seen as a core component of mental health and wellbeing, with the absence of it leading to disintegration and despair. There's just so much coming at us that we need to make sense of these days, and many existential techniques are handy for therapists in helping clients for whom this is the core issue (Hill, 2018; Russo-Netzer, Schulenberg, & Batthyany, 2016).

As one example of this applied to one of the major crises of our times, millions of refugees around the world are being displaced and forced to leave their home countries and are subjected to torture, rape, loss of identity and culture, and ongoing trauma. Yet it is primarily the ways we make meaning from experiences that determine their ultimate effect. Such meaning making is the job of most forms of therapy, regardless of what they are called and the circumstances in which they take place.

Daod (2018) describes how when working with refugees first escaping their homeland how important it is to help them to find or create meaning in their suffering and to stop thinking of themselves as helpless victims. He mentions one example of a little Syrian boy who first landed on a raft in Greece, absolutely overwhelmed and confused by everything that was going on. While standing on the beach the boy looked up and saw a helicopter overhead and asked Daod what it was doing. Daod explained to the terrified boy that the helicopter was taking pictures of him because he was such a hero to have escaped his country and made it all the way to safety in a new home. This was a critical moment for the boy in terms of finding meaning in all the suffering he had encountered in much the same way that Victor Frankl developed his own ideas in the concentration camp.

VOICES FROM THE FIELD: LOUIS HOFFMAN, PHD

Why become an existential psychotherapist?

As an existential therapist, I've frequently heard colleagues and students comment, "I've always liked existential theory, but I don't know what to do with it in the therapy room." Students considering taking a course on existential therapy ask questions such as, "Am I going to be able to understand this theory?" "Are we going to have to read Kierkegaard and Sartre?" and "Will this class be relevant to what I do in therapy?"

Existential psychotherapy seems to draw both intrigue and hesitation from students and professionals in the mental health field. This is not a surprise from a therapy approach embracing paradox and priding itself in being largely technique-less. However, the fear of existentialism is largely due to a lack of understanding. Existential therapy is less threatening than it first appears, but also much more exciting and powerful than is often realized.

Being an existential therapist is an extremely exciting career. The experience of working with suffering people to help them find healing, new insight, and authentic relationship in itself is rewarding. An added benefit is the colleagues you will meet. It is a wonderful group of people that is drawn toward existential therapy and we are always happy to welcome new colleagues.

Some Strengths and Limitations

We have mentioned previously that the philosophies behind the existential approach are intellectual, complex, and cerebral, although in practice the concepts are applied to practical circumstances and emphasize direct experience. Person-centered and gestalt theories, which share existential therapy's humanistic assumptions, are even more focused on the here and now. This is often quite useful because people in crisis, those who are experiencing acute trauma, those with severe diagnoses (such as schizophrenia), or those with limited interest in insight, might not be good candidates for an existential approach.

Although much of the foundational theory comes from Western philosophers, there is quite a lot in the approach that is compatible with many worldviews and with Eastern philosophies that look at ways of being (Yang, 2017). Nevertheless, one would have to be especially vigilant in adapting this approach to members of different cultural groups. Issues of responsibility and freedom are interpreted very differently based on one's gender, race, socioeconomic status, sexual orientation, and in any other context in which someone is a member of an oppressed or marginalized group. It is one thing for older, White, male philosophers and theorists from the previous century to talk about the importance of personal responsibility and taking charge of one's own sense of freedom, and quite another to be a client who is treated by others in the community, or nation, as if he or she is unwanted and worthless. The whole idea of freedom may be a core idea of empowerment, but such a therapeutic task must be understood and embedded in the particular life story and cultural background of each client.

PERSON-CENTERED THEORY

In the 1920s, at the time that Carl Rogers was training as a psychologist, he was offered essentially two approaches to his craft—one as a behaviorist, the other as a psychoanalyst. Yet neither theory provided the sort of warmth and human contact that he believed people crave in their lives—or that worked with his clients. Rogers envisioned a kind of helping relationship quite unlike the rather sterile, objective, detached encounters preferred by his contemporary practitioners. Like many other theorists, he was crafting an approach that best reflected what *he* would want most in a helping relationship. Given that Rogers never really felt understood during his lifetime, it is no wonder that he developed a theory that so emphasized helping people feel understood.

In his autobiography, Rogers (1980) writes about several individuals who influenced the development of his ideas: John Dewey and his philosophy of educating the whole person, Otto Rank's (a disciple of Freud) relationship-oriented therapy, theologian Martin Buber's notions about intimate relationships, Soren Kierkegaard's philosophy on the meaning of life, and the Chinese Buddhist thinking of Lao-tse. Before Rogers became a psychologist, he was first and foremost a divinity student. Then there was the practical streak in him that drove him to learn from his students and clients, creating a way of relating to people that would enhance their feelings of being understood.

Like so many other theoreticians who would come before and after him, Rogers was a voracious reader and synthesizer who was able to pull together many diverse ideas into a coherent stream of thought. (Freud did much the same thing in his own early development, reading philosophy, literature, and archaeology as the main sources of his work.) Prior to developing his client-centered style of treatment, he had written a manual on personality assessment (Rogers, 1931) and another on working with difficult children (Rogers, 1939). In both cases, he showed an early proclivity for describing practical things that could be done during the diagnostic and treatment process.

Rogers was also influential in a number of other ways that are often forgotten (Kirschenbaum, 2008). He was the first researcher and therapist to record and transcribe his sessions, using 78 RPM records that had to be changed every 7 minutes. He won an Academy Award for Best Documentary Film. He was nominated for a Nobel Peace Prize for his work on behalf of ending armed conflicts in South Africa, Northern Ireland, Nicaragua, and elsewhere. His theory was also the single most popular approach to therapy for a half century.

Basic Assumptions

It was during his tenure at Ohio State University during World War II, and later at the University of Chicago and University of Rochester, that Rogers formulated his model of therapy that had several distinct features that were considered radical for the time:

1. Building on the work of Theodore Reik and Otto Rank, both students of Freud, Rogers sought to incorporate the concept of listening with the "third ear" and responding to people with empathy, compassion, and caring. The therapist gives full and complete attention to the client, concentrating on the internal experience of self, and then reflects to the client what was heard and understood.

2. Applying his training as a social scientist and empiricist, Rogers (1957) attempted to research systematically the core conditions of helping, which he labeled *congruence, unconditional positive regard,* and *empathic understanding.* These variables, which he believed were the necessary and sufficient conditions for change to take place, were later tested empirically by several of his followers (Carkhuff & Berenson, 1967; Truax & Carkhuff, 1967). Modern versions of these core therapist characteristics are still considered significant today (e.g., von Glahn, 2018).

FOR A HOMEWORK ASSIGNMENT

Watch a video of Carl Rogers doing therapy with a client. There are many such recordings available by a number of publishers or that you can find on-line. Rather than concentrating on the limited skills and interventions he uses (mostly active listening), observe the way he builds a relationship with his client, valuing trust and authenticity above all else.

You will notice that Rogers doesn't appear to be using many complex or fancy techniques during his session but rather just concentrates on remaining fully present with his client, opening space for the person to explore more deeply core feelings.

Consider what it would be like for you to experience this sort of interaction with Rogers or someone who practices this approach.

3. Rogers developed a structure for conducting interviews and facilitating counseling sessions that relied on the therapeutic relationship as the means to encourage greater self-acceptance. You have certainly heard of "active listening" or "reflecting feelings," techniques that emerged from the client-centered style and that are now considered generic skills that are part of all training programs in counseling or therapy.

4. Rogers was never content to restrict his interventions to the traditional individual session format. From the very beginning, he was interested in facilitating growth in groups and classrooms. The whole encounter group movement of the '60s was encouraged, in part, by Rogers's contributions to the concept of a safe, trusting, supportive community that made it possible for participants to express their most authentic selves.

VOICES FROM THE PAST: CARL ROGERS

The following is from a speech he gave to the senior graduating class of Brandeis University, November 5, 1955.

I have been informed that what I am expected to do in speaking to this group is to assume that my topic is "This is Me." I feel various reactions to such an invitation, but one that I would like to

FIGURE 6.1. Carl Rogers

mention is that I feel honored and flattered that my group wants, in a personal sense, to know who I am. I can assure you it is a unique and challenging sort of invitation, and I shall try to give to this honest question an honest answer as I can.

So, who am I? I am a psychologist whose primary interest, for many years, has been in psychotherapy. What does that mean? I don't intend to bore you with a long account of my work, but I would like to take a few paragraphs from the preface to *Client-Centered Therapy*, to indicate in a subjective way what it means to me. I was trying to give the reader some feeling for the subject matter of the volume, and I wrote as follows. "What is this book about? Let me try to give an answer which may, to some degree, convey the living experience that this book is intended to be.

"This book is about the suffering and the hope, the anxiety and the satisfaction, with which each therapist's counseling room is filled. It is about the uniqueness of the relationship each therapist forms with each client, and equally about the common elements which we discover in all these relationships. This book is about the highly personal experiences of each one of us. It is about a client in my office who sits there by the corner of the desk, struggling to be himself, yet deathly afraid of being himself—striving to see his experience as it is, wanting to be that experience, and yet deeply fearful of the prospect. This book is about me, as I sit there with that client, facing him, participating in that struggle as deeply and sensitively as I am able. It is about me as I try to perceive his experience, and the meaning and the feeling and the taste and the flavor that it has for him. It is about me as I bemoan my very human fallibility in understanding that client, and the occasional failures to see life as it appears to him, failures which fall like heavy objects across the intricate, delicate web of growth which is taking place. It is about me as I rejoice at the privilege of being a midwife to a new personality—so I stand by with awe at the emergence of a self, a person, as I see a birth process in which I have had an important and facilitating part. It is about both the client and me as we regard with wonder the potent and orderly forces which are evident in this whole experience, forces which seem deeply rooted in the universe as a whole. The book is, I believe, about life, as life vividly reveals itself in the therapeutic process—with its blind power and its tremendous capacity for destruction, but with its overbalancing thrust toward growth, if the opportunity for growth is provided."

Perhaps that will give you some picture of what I do and the way I feel about it.

Core Conditions

Throughout his career, Rogers talked a lot about the role of therapists and teachers in creating conditions that are optimal for producing change. He did not really believe that you could teach anyone anything worth learning; the job of a helper is to facilitate change by structuring a climate that makes it possible. This atmosphere emphasizes the core ingredients of trust, caring, and empathy in the relationship (Rogers & Russell, 2002). These ideas would apply equally to any mentoring or teaching relationship, whether as a coach, parent, or book author. Consider that if you didn't feel some level of trust and regard from us, if you felt we were condescending or disrespectful to some of your values and beliefs, you would hardly be open to what we have to offer you.

FOR A GROUP ACTIVITY

In small groups, talk to each other about what you would consider the optimal conditions for promoting positive growth and change. This discussion should include features that would be universally present in good therapy relationships, the classroom, parenting, coaching, and even in your class right now.

Look to your own experiences in which you have made the most significant and lasting changes. What variables were present in the setting or circumstances that made your growth possible?

Rogers identified several factors that he considered necessary and sufficient for change to take place. We need to point out, however, that although these core conditions are often useful and sometimes necessary, they are hardly enough for some people to get off dead center and maintain their momentum over time.

Contact. The relationship between a helper and client, whether that involves a teaching, coaching, parenting, or therapeutic encounter, must involve some sort of psychological contact in which the participants are open to one another and subject to mutual influence.

Authenticity. Rogers believed that it was critical for a helper to be real with a client, that is, to be genuine, congruent, and transparent. This sort of modeling makes it possible for the client to follow the therapist or teacher's lead and risk revealing himself or herself as well.

Unconditional positive regard. There are times, of course, when it is very difficult to accept what certain people do, especially when their behavior is self-defeating, destructive, abuse, or hurtful toward others. There is a difference, however, between not accepting people's actions and not accepting their core being. Rogers felt it was critical to communicate consistently that clients are accepted unconditionally even if certain behaviors are not.

Empathy. Rogers defined empathy as the ability to crawl inside someone else's skin and feel what he or she is feeling. It is a process of knowing another deeply, resonating with his or her experience, without judgment or evaluation. Needless to say, this is *very* difficult to do.

Okay. It's time for a test.

A new client walks in to see you. You take a deep breath, clear your mind of all distractions, and put away the work and your mobile device so you can give this person your full attention. You remind yourself about the importance of staying focused and clear. You put away all judgmental thoughts so you can be fully present with this other person. Once your mental checklist is completed, you nod your head for the client to begin.

With minimal preliminaries, the man tells you that he has a habit of becoming sexually involved with several farm animals. He feels a little guilty about this because he does not wish to cause harm to the calves or sheep that he prefers, but he would rather not stop this behavior because he finds relationships with human women far too threatening.

You remember not to scream, laugh, or otherwise show shock and disgust on your face, directing him in the most casual voice to tell you what he wants you to do to help him.

"I don't know," he tells you. "Maybe just tell me that I'm not screwed up or anything because of what I do."

Let us put aside what you might actually *say* to this client, whether you would offer him reassurance or tell him you think he is very disturbed. Our question for you is what you would *feel* inside toward him. Granted, you have only just met him and hardly had the chance to develop any sort of alliance. Nevertheless, Rogers's core conditions demand that no matter what a person does, or how he or she behaves, everyone deserves to be respected and valued as a human being. You might very well consider this behavior to be maladaptive and self-destructive (not to mention abusive toward animals), but the true test is whether you can engage this person—and others like him who present behavior that you may personally find quite distasteful—with genuine caring and respect.

This man was actually Jeffrey's very first client, in his very first session during an internship. He had been concentrating so hard on being empathic and nonjudgmental during the interview that he really did not even notice that his behavior seemed the least bizarre until after he left. It was only on reading his notes, and picturing himself presenting the case to his colleagues, that he realized how bizarre this case was.

Jeffrey believes that what he did to help the client most (and he did help him within a relatively short period of time) was to listen to him and be with him without judging him as a person. Jeffrey did eventually confront the man about his cow and sheep courting rituals and gently suggested that he might want to consider members of his own species, but he was open to hearing Jeffrey because he felt that he was respected. It would be difficult to underestimate the power of such unconditional regard, even when the behavior itself is so far out of bounds.

Features of a Client-Centered Session

As is so often the case, when one innovator comes up with a good idea, others adapt it for their own purposes. While at the time it seemed downright radical to construct an interview based on humanistic principles, today almost every practitioner makes use of the core message behind healing relationships based on respect and caring.

It is somewhat rare these days for professionals to practice a pure form of person-centered therapy. There have been too many changes in the cultural landscape, research base, and professional demands since the '60s and '70s when humanistic approaches were most popular. Nevertheless, many of the features described here still have value in our times of managed care and brief therapy, even if they must be adapted accordingly.

Full and complete presence. Regardless of the way you practice, it is important to give clients the best part of yourself. Often they are used to being neglected, ignored, or devalued, so you owe them the commitment to be as fully present and attentive as possible.

Openness and unconditional regard. There has been considerable debate about whether unconditional regard toward clients is possible, much less desirable. We prefer to think about the concept with respect to people's essence rather than their behavior. Quite often clients do annoying, obnoxious, self-destructive things that we find difficult to accept unconditionally. But you can unconditionally accept a client, as a person, and still *conditionally* accept his or her behavior.

Authenticity, genuineness, transparency, and warmth. These are all different ways of saying that you present yourself as a real, authentic person in the relationship. You provide the sort of support, trust, and caring that make it possible for clients to take risks and face themselves in new ways.

Immediacy. This is one of our absolute favorite interventions that involves being as present as possible with a client. Instead of talking *about* something, it is far more dramatic to bring it into focus by pointing out ways that the very behavior is unfolding before your eyes.

THERAPIST:	You've been talking for some time about the difficulties you have getting close to people. I was wondering how that applies to our relationship.
CLIENT:	Excuse me?
THERAPIST:	I think you know what I'm saying.
CLIENT:	I'm not sure.
THERAPIST:	Okay, right this moment I'm trying to get closer to you, to talk about our relationship, and you act like you don't know what I'm talking about as a way to push me away.

CLIENT:	I still don't know what you mean.
THERAPIST:	Look at how you are sitting right now. You've pulled your chair back and you are leaning as far away as you can. Your arms are crossed and I can feel you visibly pull away, as if what we are talking about is so frightening that you need to put some distance between yourself and me. This is exactly what you were talking about that occurs in many of your other relationships.
CLIENT:	[Shrugs and looks down]
THERAPIST:	What you are you aware of right now?

The immediacy brings the discussion into the ultimate present moment. Instead of merely talking about an issue, it is being played out in the session.

Empathy and active listening. This concept is now so universal that it is hardly worth mentioning. Yet the importance of empathy and the application of active listening skills (reflection of feeling) are one of the major contributions of this theory to mainstream practice.

You will have numerous opportunities in other courses to practice the core helping skills of active listening that are now considered so generic they are no longer exclusively identified with client-centered therapy. The skills of listening, reflecting content (restating), and reflecting feelings are among the simplest of interventions but also the most difficult to master. In the following example notice how the helper tries to take the student to a deeper level:

STUDENT:	I just don't see the point of learning all this stuff. And the idea of giving us a test on the material sounds ludicrous.
INSTRUCTOR:	You're pretty frustrated and overwhelmed with the sheer volume of ideas that you have to learn. [Notice the way the helper did not give in to the temptation to explain or defend. The focus is kept on the student's feelings.]
STUDENT:	Well, you gotta admit, you give us all these new theories at once. You say you're trying to teach us to work cooperatively and to develop compassion and empathy, but you're really teaching us to memorize a bunch of facts that have little meaning. I mean, how are we supposed to apply all this stuff?
INSTRUCTOR:	You're really having some doubts about how you're going to do on the first exam. You're scared that you might not do very well. [Among all the many messages conveyed in the student's communication, the instructor chose to focus on the fear of failure. There are many other things that could have been said instead.]

STUDENT: No. That's not it at all! The point I'm trying to make is that you're just asking too much of us.

INSTRUCTOR: You're feeling annoyed, even angry with me, because I've misunderstood you. Your main concern isn't so much how you will do on the test but rather that you're not learning as much as you would like to.

The beauty of this approach is that this last intervention, which is not a particularly accurate reflection of what the student is thinking and feeling, nevertheless encourages further exploration together. The instructor is still resisting the urge to be defensive and is trying hard to fully understand what the student is experiencing and trying to reflect back what has been heard.

When you first learn these skills, you will practice initially repeating verbatim what the other person says (parroting). Once you can do that consistently, you will move on to restatements in which you reflect the content of what was communicated ("You find the workload and structure of this course to be unreasonable"). After you can do this fairly well, you will then add to your repertoire reflections of feeling that take considerably greater sensitivity and deftness because you must go as deeply as you can to find the true essence of what the person is experiencing. In the preceding example, for instance, it may very well be that the problem has little to do with the class itself and may be more related to other pressures the student is feeling in life. Or the feelings of anger and frustration may be legitimate responses to the instructor's behavior. In any case, the client-centered approach uses empathy to get to the heart of the matter.

FOR PERSONAL APPLICATION

You can never get enough experience practicing active listening skills. The method involves (a) listening as closely and carefully as you can to what another person is communicating, (b) using both verbal and non-verbal means to communicate interest, respect, and caring, (c) decoding the underlying meaning of what is being said by asking yourself what the person is feeling deep inside, and (d) reflecting to the person what you hear, see, sense, and feel.

Active listening skills work equally well to deepen relationships with family and friends as they do with clients. Keep in mind, however, that until you make these skills part of your natural repertoire, they will not only feel awkward to you, but also your loved ones may ask you to stop trying that "counseling stuff" on them. Over time, you will notice how much more intimate and open your conversations become as you become more fluent and proficient in reflecting others' felt experiences.

Focus on affect and feelings. In contrast to the other theories that were most prominent at the time (behavioral, psychoanalytic, existential), Rogers concentrated on the importance of accessing and expressing feelings. Whereas almost all therapists use active listening skills, client-centered practitioners focus as much as they can on the unexpressed feelings in the communication. This approach is evident in the following interaction led by a school counselor:

CLIENT:	It could be that my parents won't be home later when I get done with school.
COUNSELOR:	You don't sound sure about that and you're a little anxious because you don't know what to expect.
CLIENT:	It's no big deal. I'm used to being on my own a lot of the time.
COUNSELOR:	You do strike me as very capable of taking care of yourself, especially for someone so young, but I also hear some hesitation in your voice. Being alone isn't something that you greatly look forward to.
CLIENT:	Well, sometimes I get a little scared. There was this one time. …
COUNSELOR:	You don't want to be a burden on your parents because you know they've already got a lot to take care of. But still, you wish you could spend some more time with them. You miss them.
CLIENT:	Yeah.

In this brief dialogue, you can appreciate how quickly you can move a client from superficial conversation to a deeper-level exploration of underlying feelings. When this skill of reflecting feelings is combined with other skills you will learn, many of which are borrowed from other theories, you have a powerful repertoire of interventions to deal with anything that might arise.

FOR PERSONAL APPLICATION

Sit down with someone who is important in your life—a partner, family member, friend, coworker, or classmate. Spend some time talking to one another about your feelings toward one another. Avoid the temptation to say what you think, what you imagine, or what you know, and instead say what you feel. This is a difficult task, one that you may feel some resistance to complete.

We both have tried on more than a few occasions to get this sort of discussion going at a party or social gathering when everyone is talking about superficial, predictable things. As you probably imagine, about half the time we are ignored and the other half indulgently humored. It is fun, though, and stimulating to get together with friends or loved ones and break through the usual conversational routines by talking on a much deeper level.

Contemporary Revisions

Even after more than a half century, theoreticians and practitioners are still advancing Rogers's basic ideas and his approach remains one of the most popular around the world. An entire journal, *Person-Centered and Experiential Psychotherapies*, is devoted to testing the rather abstract ideas that Rogers and other humanists originally proposed. One such example involves operationally defining and measuring the actualizing tendency that is so often mentioned in the literature (von Glahn, 2018).

As we've mentioned, many client-centered premises have been integrated into most other approaches to therapy. The contemporary demands for evidence-based treatment planning, for instance, have been stylized according to a more person-centered approach (Adams & Grieder, 2014). Indeed, much of what all therapists do in their work is related far more to who they are than what they do (Kottler, 2017b). This means that whereas the helping skills you learn are certainly important, so too is your natural way of being in sessions, presenting yourself as a model of someone who can demonstrate in your own life what you teach to your clients.

However, even as most therapeutic approaches have incorporated aspects of person-centered principles, there are still therapists who are dedicated to following in the footsteps of Rogers by continuously examining, revising, and applying updated principles of person-centered therapy as a viable, stand-alone option. In this refined approach, clients and therapists work collaboratively and more actively than Rogers suggested in order to make progress on the troubling life issues that brought them into therapy.

The following updated roadmap is based on suggestions by Cain (2010) and others who are informed by the continued testing of Rogers's ideas (Adams & Greider, 2014; Cooper, O'Hara, Schmidt, & Bohart, 2013). You'll notice that some of these conditions relate to the client, and some to the therapist:

- Clients must want to alleviate a problem or attain something new.
- Clients should expect that therapy will be helpful.
- The client and the therapist are accepting and affirming of each other.
- The therapist is fully present and actively engaged.
- The therapist supports the client in setting the direction and the goals of therapy.
- Both work collaboratively to find the means to achieve the goals.
- The therapist "gets" the client's subjective reality and conveys empathy.
- The therapist highlights potent emotional experiences to help the client learn.
- The therapist monitors the quality of the relationship and repairs any strains.
- The client believes that the therapist attends to what matters most for the client's own growth.

While these conditions may constitute the best therapy for some clients, you'll find that they are very powerful for many others.

Some Strengths and Limitations

Client-centered approach continues to enjoy widespread popularity, and many practitioners use it as a base into which they integrate other approaches. However, it has limitations like all the rest. For one thing, in this era of symptom-oriented, brief treatments, Rogers can seem almost quaint in his naivete. As we mentioned earlier, he was flat-out wrong in thinking that the therapeutic relationship is a necessary and *sufficient* condition for change to occur—decades of research have shown it may be for some, but it is not for all. It may be a highly fertile environment from which to promote changes, but with some clients it is hardly enough to make a difference. In fact, several other successful therapeutic approaches since Rogers's time have been developed that downplay the relationship altogether, including behavioral approaches. And then there are certain clients who could care less about the relationship at all; they just want a quick fix, some clear advice, or a far more business-like consultation that keeps things formal and highly structured.

As you begin doing therapy, you will discover that some clients do not seem to want empathy, or they care much more about how their significant others think about them rather than being grateful for your unconditional positive regard. Sometimes, the time-honored technique of reflection is not experienced as helpful by the client; it is just so non-normative within the culture of the client that it feels bothersome, or worse, disingenuous. For example, when I (Marilyn) was in graduate school, I practiced my newfound skills on family members, as we all do. One time this practice did not have the effect I intended. My grandmother-in-law had just moved into an extended care facility because she was becoming dangerously forgetful and had left her gas stove on all night. My family brought her to our home frequently, though, and on one of these trips Grandma was complaining about how tasteless the food was at her new place. "Sounds like you really don't like the meals there," I reflected with the best of intentions. She just glared at me: "Honey, that's what I just said." I have since found that other senior citizens and others from particular subcultures look at you quizzically if you stay too long with non-directive, empathic skills. A modern-day person-centered therapist would counter by saying that the therapist must adapt to the client's experience of being wholly supported, whatever that takes, rather than being a one-note empathic samba (Adams & Greider, 2014).

Finally, the theory may seem to value feelings over other domains of experience. While this is just what some clients need, other individuals and some cultural groups find it extremely intrusive and inappropriate to talk about deep feelings with a nonfamily member. Furthermore, some people do not need to get a handle on their feelings as much as they would profit from controlling their behavior or managing their thoughts.

GESTALT THEORY

No other theory was carved more closely from the personality of its inventor than Gestalt therapy. In fact, in its early days, the approach was known as the "Fritz style," referring to Fritz Perls. Like several other theories (e.g., rational emotive behavior therapy), this close association between the approach and its charismatic leader is a mixed blessing. Gestalt therapy became known as an aggressive, combative, anti-intellectual approach largely because Perls thrived on controversy and provocation. Yet many of the subsequent innovators (Polster & Polster, 2000; Ullman & Wheeler, 2009) and contemporary developers (Cole & Reese, 2018; Kolmannskog, 2018) demonstrated a sensitivity that would make the practice of this theory almost unrecognizable to Perls.

Early Background

Like so many other intellectual refugees from Nazi Germany, Perls eventually made his way to America where to set up a psychoanalytic practice in New York. Following the lead of Wilhelm Reich, another disciple of Freud, Perls was as concerned with the body as the mind. This proved especially convenient for him because language barriers made it difficult for him to communicate effectively in his new, adopted language. Clearly, he needed a working method that relied less on talk and more on action. This would become his distinctive hallmark.

You may recall from a psychology class that in the early years of studying how learning occurs, some theorists borrowed ideas that were percolating among German physicists. At the time, scientists were attempting to study the tiny particles of nature by breaking everything down to its most basic molecular elements. Another approach was taken by scientists who believed that true understanding of the physical world can only occur by looking at the whole rather than reducing something down into component parts.

This same Gestalt approach was applied to humans as well. Several German scientists, such as Kurt Lewin and Wolfgang Kohler, concentrated their attention on learning processes that were described as a form of insight in which the person (or animal) solves problems by looking at the whole. It is a kind of "eureka" phenomenon that contrasts with the other theories (such as behaviorism), which believed that learning occurs incrementally through successive reinforcement.

FOR PERSONAL REFLECTION or **A CLASS ACTIVITY**

Think about a time recently in which you experienced insight as a gestalt, meaning that you had a single moment of revelation or inspiration rather than (apparently) a slow, gradual process of learning. Although, in fact, there may well have been a series of accumulative events that led you to this transformative moment, the integration of everything occurred swiftly, decisively, and without warning.

Tell your own stories to one another about a transformative experience that occurred as a sudden moment of insight. As you look back on the event, what do you think most contributed to this learning?

In one classic Gestalt experiment that you might remember, monkeys were presented with bananas that were just out of reach. To get the food, they had to figure out a way to use a stick as a tool or a box as stepladder, thus solving the problem. Rather than resolving this dilemma through trial and error, it appeared that the monkeys learned through insight—an "aha" moment in which they realized what needed to be done.

Likewise, Perls used the concept of Gestalt to describe the irreducible nature of human growth. He believed that people became disconnected from their essential selves—fragmented—and that the process of therapy was one of helping them to reintegrate themselves into a whole.

Collaborating with his wife, Laura Perls, and Paul Goodman, an American who was conversant in both existential and Taoist philosophy, Fritz Perls began writing about his ideas that appeared extremely novel at the time. Like so many other ex-psychoanalysts, he was fervent in his desire to break with the ideas of Freud, from whom he became estranged after a brief encounter that he felt was disrespectful. He never forgave what he considered Freud's humiliation of him and did everything he could to refashion a theory that was as far from the master as possible. If psychoanalysis was formal, fate driven, and biologically based, then Perls would develop an approach that was whimsical, playful, and based completely in the present rather than the past.

A Theory of Being and Doing

Just as important as Perls's publications were the workshops he began running at the Esalen Institute in California, an influential center devoted to personal growth that still flourishes today. The rules in these seminars were few but rigidly enforced: (a) participants must stay in the here and now, (b) no talking about people who were not in the room, (c) focus must remain on personal awareness—the nervous tapping of one's finger or the tremor in one's voice, and (d) emphasis was placed on personal responsibility.

In the Gestalt approach, there is an emphasis on both heightening awareness and then acting on what is experienced. It seeks to integrate all aspects of the body, mind, and spirit. People are helped to stay in the moment and focus only in the present to become more fully alive.

FOR PERSONAL REFLECTION

One name for activities that remain completely in the present is flow. Based on his research with surgeons, athletes, musicians, rock climbers, and others, Csikszentmihalyi discovered that people are able to operate at peak performance and with maximum engagement when they are able to lose themselves in an experience with effortless action. It is as if the person and the activity flow together as one (Csikszentmihalyi, 2014).

Locate a cracker, the most humble of all foods. (If none is available, any food item will work.) Put the cracker in front of you and spend a few minutes studying it intensely. Notice the different color gradations, the speckles of salt, the tiny holes, the geometric shapes and perfect symmetry. Notice as well the imperfections and unique qualities of this single item that appears at first to be like all others of its kind.

Pay attention to what is happening inside of you as you study the cracker. Notice increased salivation in your mouth, any body sensations, as well as where your thoughts drift. Gently bring your mind back to a complete focus on the cracker.

Now, slowly, very slowly, reach for the cracker and hold it between your fingers. Note how it feels, its lightness and texture. In exaggerated slow motion, bring the cracker to your lips (take at least 30 seconds just to bring it to your mouth). Notice the way it feels in your hand, your arm, and any other part of body.

Bring the cracker to your nose first. Smell it. Take a deep breath.

Touch it to your lips. Gently. In slow motion.

Now, take a tiny, little bite of the cracker and slowly taste it.

Take several minutes and savor the cracker, eating it as slowly as you can. Through each stage of the process take your time feeling, smelling, and tasting the cracker with your whole being.

When you are done, consider what you became aware of.

According to this theory, you cannot *do* Gestalt therapy; you must *be* a Gestalt therapist. You will notice this sounds familiar—this is the same stance that existentialists take. This means that you must demonstrate a high degree of authenticity, creativity, sensitivity, and realness—not just in your work but in your being.

Gestalt Techniques

Although in theory the therapist's stance is more important than actions, this approach is known mostly for its varied and creative techniques that are used by practitioners of all orientations, some of them considered classic interventions. Essentially, Gestalt techniques are offered to the client in the form of "experiments" that have the goal of increasing the client's awareness of different parts of the self. The therapist and client then process and integrate what was learned, with the goal of moving forward.

The here and now. According to Gestalt theory, everything important happens in the present, and efforts are made to keep clients in the moment. They are constantly asked what they are aware of and what they are experiencing, as we might do of you: "This moment, as you read these very words, what are you aware you are experiencing in your body? What sensations to you feel? What thoughts have been ricocheting inside your head? Look around the room. What do you notice that you previously missed? Now, back inside of you: As you continue to read the rest of the page, notice what has changed."

Unfinished business. Fritz Perls's approach to therapy clearly had roots in psychoanalysis. Just as he talked about the polarities that people experience (reminiscent of id and superego), he also believed that things from the past continue to haunt us in the present. However, rather than focusing on the unconscious or repressed memories, Perls honed in on unexpressed feelings such as resentments: "During unguarded moments, when you are tired or vulnerable, what does your mind drift back to that still feels unfinished or unresolved? This could be a single conversation that was left hanging, a task that you never completed, or a relationship from the past that is still bothering you."

Channels of resistance. Like Freud, Gestalt therapists subscribe to the notion that certain behaviors get in the way of growth. Rather than calling them defense mechanisms, Perls described several means by which people try to block themselves from having complete contact with themselves and others. "What are some ways that you are aware that *you* do that?"

Choice of language. There are certain words and phrases that are verboten in Gestalt therapy. Clients are not permitted to overgeneralize by using the term *you* to refer to others, or *it* to refer to some statement. If a client were to say, "It was a difficult situation," he or she would be redirected to say, "I had a difficult time with the situation." Ownership is critical.

The empty chair. This technique is especially valuable for helping clients resolve inner conflicts, especially when they are not fully aware what is holding them back. The therapist uses a form of role-playing and assigns different "parts" of the client (for example, past self and future self) or others in the client's life (for example, the client's long-lost father) to visit the session (in imagination) and walks the client through sitting in and speaking from chairs. This technique often opens pent-up emotions, but often helps clients release them and move on with their life.

FOR AN ACTIVITY

Work with a partner to increase your skill using Gestalt present moment interventions. This is a particularly difficult assignment because of the way it requires you to do some things that are not usually part of ordinary interactions (unfortunately).

Sit opposite your partner, facing him or her fully. Spend one minute (time it with a watch or you will quit early) staring into one another's eyes. As you do so, become aware of what you feel inside you and notice in your partner.

Talk to each other about what that was like for you.

Resume eye contact. Take turns completing the stem sentence: "One thing that I am aware of. ..." Complete at least five successive rounds. Afterward, process the experience.

Some Strengths and Limitations

While some of the particular techniques of Gestalt therapy, such as talking to an empty chair that you pretend to be occupied by someone with whom you have issues, there is a much more elaborate theory of working that is best learned by experiencing it. (No surprise here!). This means going to workshops or institutes or finding a Gestalt therapist with whom you can work.

In Gestalt therapy, the emphasis on the client and the therapist making genuine contact by focusing on their immediate experience can make this work quite lively (see Sheldon, 2014, for awareness practices that you can use yourself as well as with clients). The contact occurs through "dialogue," but in the Gestalt sense that something done or lived rather than talked about. Dialogue can involve dancing, singing, poetry, movement, or any modality that expresses and moves the energy between the therapist and the client(s), so non-verbal experience is given importance. Not surprisingly, Gestalt therapy has been adapted for working with children, who usually communicate best through play or art, and for treating trauma. It can be especially powerful when done in a group setting (Cole & Reese, 2017). However creative and expressive, though, the interaction must always fall within the bounds of ethics and the appropriateness of the therapeutic task (Wheeler & Axelson, 2015).

Not surprisingly, Gestalt therapists have been challenged to come up with research that supports their ideas and they are committed to doing so (Roubal, 2016). By the nature of its assumptions about the most important aspects of human experience, the theory does not lend itself well to quantitative measurement, though case studies and qualitative designs have illustrated how gestalt therapy can be useful for clients with long histories of treatment, personality disorders, and multiple diagnoses (Dominitz, 2017). Indeed, greater contact with the "here and now" and practicing with I–other boundaries may be just the kind of in-depth treatment for clients whose issues are not touched in briefer and more logic-oriented therapies, such as clients with eating disorders (Seubert, 2018).

CONTEMPORARY EXTENSIONS OF HUMANISTIC THEORY

Just as psychoanalytic theory entered the 21st century with a pragmatic flavor that is more responsive to the demands of contemporary life and the managed care movement, so too has humanism continued to evolve. Although humanistic practitioners remain loyal to the basic tenets of the philosophy that stress free choice, personal responsibility, and authentic engagement, new theoretical innovations also emphasize briefer methods that combine features from other approaches, provide greater gender and cultural sensitivity, employ both qualitative and quantitative research methods, and provide far greater flexibility in methods. In addition, humanism has embraced some of the postmodern theories such as constructivism—or rather, constructivist approaches have updated humanism. As you learn in a later chapter, constructivist thinking shares some of the beliefs of humanism in terms of looking at a person's inner perceptions, but stresses the cultural rather than individual context for this experience.

Applying the Skills of Humanism

We noted earlier that humanistic theory was empirically tested during the '60s and '70s when Robert Carkhuff and several colleagues (Carkhuff & Berenson, 1967; Truax & Carkhuff, 1967) attempted to examine the core conditions that Rogers first identified. Among other things, they discovered support for the importance of empathy in the helping process in which therapists who were accepting, open, and accurately reflecting the client's experience were seen as most effective. Carkhuff attempted to measure these core conditions, with limited success, but also was instrumental in specifying the therapeutic skills that are involved in the empathic process.

When Thomas Gordon (1975, 1986, 1987) devised a structured training program for teaching these core helping skills to parents, teachers, and leaders, humanistic theory became translated into behavioral skills. Ironically, the core values of the philosophy became somewhat lost.

One example of the useful helping behaviors derived from Rogers's theory by Thomas Gordon, and still popular today in settings such as organizational consultation and parent education, is the idea that problems come in two basic varieties: those that "belong" to the client and those that may appear to be of that nature but really belong to the teacher, counselor, or leader. For instance, consider the following examples that apply to classroom situations:

- A child is carving his initials in the desk.
- A child is talking to several friends while the teacher is talking.
- A child is upset because he or she got a poor grade on an assignment.
- A child doesn't understand a lesson.

In the first two examples, it is really the teacher who has the problem rather than the student. The big mistake that teachers make is trying to solve their own problems by missing this important point. "Excuse me, mister," the teacher says to the kid who is having a wonderful time carving up the desk. "Do you have a problem?" The child, of course, is thinking to himself that the only problem he really has is the teacher who will not let him finish the job.

Whether applied to the classroom or to counseling or business situations, the helper is first taught to distinguish between who "owns" the problem. When it is the teacher, then the best intervention is called an "I" message, as in "I have a problem with what you are doing." When the child owns the problem, then the most suitable intervention is active listening, which you would recognize as reflecting content and feelings, skills that are easily recognizable in Rogers's style.

In the following example, a parent uses both skills during an interaction with her child:

PARENT:	I wanted to talk to you because I have a problem with the way you have been acting lately . . . yelling at me and slamming your door when I say "no" to something you want.
CHILD:	[Defiantly] So?
PARENT:	I realize that this is not so much your problem as it is mine. I am the one who does not like what you have been doing and you are perfectly fine with the way things are.
CHILD:	[Nods her head cautiously and suspiciously]
PARENT:	So, I wonder if you could help me with my problem.
CHILD:	[Shrugs]
PARENT:	It's just that I have been having a hard time lately; my feelings have been hurt a lot and I've been upset and sad. But I noticed that hasn't been easy for you, either.
CHILD:	Well, you gotta admit, it's not fair that I have so many rules.
PARENT:	This has been so frustrating for you, feeling like I don't trust you.

FOR REFLECTION

In the following example, identify who "owns" the problem—you or the client.

YOU:	How can I help you this morning?
CLIENT:	Help me? You haven't done crap for me since we started these sessions!

Based on this assessment, would you use an "I" message or active listening? Frame the way you would respond.

Notice the subtle shift that just took place in which the parent started off owning the problem, using "I" messages to state clearly that she was the one who needed help. Once the child was engaged in the conversation and agreed tacitly to participate in the process of problem-solving, the parent used active listening skills to reflect her feelings. Now they are both involved in a mutual problem-solving process that will not only take care of the parent's problem but also explore the child's feelings at a deeper level.

Carl Rogers and other humanists never intended that their theories would become translated into such specific action skills, but many generations of counselors, teachers, and parents have been trained in these methods to enhance their professional and personal relationships.

Focusing

Eugene Gendlin, a psychiatrist and one of Rogers's students and colleagues, had a special interest in applying client-centered theory to more severely disturbed populations. Like his mentor, Gendlin wrote about his patients with schizophrenia with a special sensitivity, avoiding the use of medical terms and instead trying to describe the human experience. Like so many creative thinkers in the field, Gendlin later went his own way, developing a theory that drew on his knowledge of existential philosophy and emphasized accessing primary experience (Gendlin, 1981, 1996).

We're sure you recognize that it is possible to "know" things without yet being able to put them into words. Focusing-oriented psychotherapy uses person-centered techniques and Gestalt-type techniques to highlight and help clients become fully aware of their felt, bodily sense of things. As you can imagine, this is helpful for clients needing to become aware on non-verbal aspects of various disturbances or integrate previous traumatic experiences. Focusing can help clients to get a "felt sense" of what they truly want or a "felt shift" involving new insights about a situation. In fact, clients can be taught to use focusing techniques on themselves, not just in the therapy room. It is even possible, Gendlin taught, to let your body interpret your dreams (Gendlin, 1986).

Focusing-oriented psychotherapy has a worldwide cadre of innovative therapists who go strive to go "beyond the talking cure" (Madison, 2014a, 2014b). We'll say more about similar body-oriented approaches in a later chapter, but the point we'd like to leave you with here is that the "person" in person-centered therapy includes more than things a client can easily articulate. Focusing techniques can help the client and therapist become aware of these.

Pre-therapy

One of the contemporary innovations in the humanistic movement has been to combine ideas from several different approaches. Prouty (1994; Prouty, Werde, & Portner, 2002), for example, combined Carl Rogers's original theory with the experiential approach of Eugene Gendlin to use with severely disturbed clients and those with profound cognitive impairment, calling his person-centered/ experiential approach "pre-therapy." The emphasis throughout this method is on establishing *contact* with a client through direct experience and awareness.

Like so many theorists we have studied, Prouty created his approach out of painful feelings and experiences with his cognitively impaired and mentally ill brother. After encountering Gendlin and Rogers, Prouty found he had a talent for establishing "psychological contact" (Rogers's first necessary condition for client growth) with individuals whom others couldn't reach. He elaborated his ideas about how to do this, using focusing techniques as a way to be together with contact-impaired clients who could only utter non-language sounds, communicate in limited ways, or who refuse to engage.

Prouty did this by breaking down the notion of contact into sub-types, which gives a therapist more options joining with a client by directing their awareness. *Reality contact* is awareness of people, places, things, and events. *Affective contact* is awareness of distinct moods, feelings, and emotions. *Communicative contact* is what happens when individuals use symbols (like language) to convey aspects of their reality and their affect. In pre-therapy, where communicative contact is limited, the therapist attunes to and reflects things in the present experience of the client (including aspects of their present reality and affect) to establish a sense of *empathic mutuality*. Not surprisingly, this approach has caught the attention of those who serve individuals with dementia, autism spectrum disorders, intellectual disabilities, and severe psychosis—individuals who are at a "difficult edge," needing support but unable to engage in ordinary talk therapy (Sommerbeck, 2014). Not surprisingly, Prouty's ideas have a growing following around the world.

FOR PERSONAL REFLECTION

Here is a pre-therapy technique for you to try that uses focusing to explore reality contact: Focus on your earliest awareness of waking up this morning. What was the first sensation and feeling that captured your attention? What did it feel like in your bed?

What are you aware of right now? Look and listen around you. Notice where you are. Now go inside and concentrate on what you are experiencing in your body. What thoughts are reverberating inside your head? What are the feelings and sensations that are most present for you?

An exercise such as this takes practice because it's difficult to focus on the present moment. But for some, this is more possible than it is to recollect and recount what happened in the last week.

Emotion-Focused Therapy

Les Greenberg, like his predecessors mentioned earlier, tested aspects of humanistic theory applied to the therapeutic process in an extended program of research. One key finding was that emotional arousal by itself is not particularly helpful unless clients are helped to resolve the internal struggle by processing, reflecting, and making sense of their strong emotions in therapy (Greenberg, 2002). This was in marked contrast to the philosophy of the humanistic encounter group movement from many years ago when participants were encouraged, if not pressured, to express all their feelings as honestly as possible. Many people ended up as casualties in such groups because of the unbridled and irresponsible actions of group members who would lash out at others under the guise of being therapeutic (Kearns, 2007; Yalom, 2005). In other words, whereas it was once believed that expressing feelings, emoting, and otherwise giving vent to pent-up emotions were intrinsically therapeutic, this is not always the case unless people are helped to complete the cycle in constructive ways. As you have no doubt noticed in yourself and others, giving release to strong feelings such as anger can also lead to more potent emotional explosions.

Emotion-focused therapy (EFT), conceived by Sue Johnson and Les Greenberg, is designed to help clients do just that: It helps clients process and make sense of their strong emotions and then use them productively. Johnson and Greenberg began as couples' therapists, watching hours of video sessions in an attempt to identify what led to positive change. They drew on Rogers's humanistic and Perls's experiential ideas about productively processing their clients' emotional experiences (which, as you might imagine, are prevalent in couples therapy), eventually publishing a study establishing emotionally focused couples therapy as an evidence-based treatment (Johnson & Greenberg, 1985). Soon after, Greenberg decided to further develop his ideas by concentrating on individuals, integrating ideas from Gendlin and others, calling it a *process-experiential approach* (Greenberg, Rice, & Elliot, 1993). In the meantime, Johnson continued to develop emotionally focused couples therapy (EFCT), integrating ideas from attachment theory alongside systemic and humanistic principles.

Over the years, Greenberg has elaborated EFT's conceptual base by integrating ideas from cognitive, constructivist, and narrative therapies (Greenberg, 2017). EFT practitioners conceive of every diagnosis as having an emotional problem at its core: It's not that the emotions themselves are the problem, but the fact that clients often work so hard to avoid them or ignore them until they explode. A key tenet of EFT is that one has to have a feeling in order to change it, so sessions focus on supporting clients in feeling their emotions—authentically and deeply—and EFT practitioners have honed experiential techniques to do just that. I (Marilyn) have shown many of my classes video demonstrations of Dr. Greenberg working with a client, and I've often seen my students (as well as the client) blinking back the tears!

Once clients feel and identify an emotion, they can accept, regulate, explore, transform, use, and narratively make sense of it. They learn to tolerate some emotions and use others to fuel their progress toward goals. EFT is especially good with clients who have two common problems that drive people to therapy: anxiety (Watson & Greenberg, 2017) and depression (Dillon, Timulak, & Greenberg, 2018). We want to offer one caveat, however: Unlike the techniques of focusing, EFT is not an approach that can be casually applied. Fortunately, however, therapists who are devoted to EFT and EFCT have developed a host of training opportunities and supervision tools (e.g., Brubacher, 2018; Greenberg & Goldman, 2018; Greenberg & Tomescu, 2017; Johnson, 2019).

Back to the Personal Dimensions of the Therapist

Another thread of contemporary humanism has not abandoned its original conception, even with the current emphasis on empirical validation of concepts and translating theory into specific skills: the importance of the personal characteristics of the therapist. Humanistic theorists tend to write about the *person of the therapist* as much as his or her skills demonstrated in sessions (Kottler, 2017a, 2017b, 2018; Kottler & Carlson, 2015). This means that in addition to the interventions you select, the techniques you employ, and the theory you follow, who you are as a person also has a significant impact on the client. It is not surprising, then, that attention as to how best to prepare therapists to make active and purposeful use of themselves, in and out of the session, has grown. In fact, a comprehensive training and supervision approach to developing the person of the therapist has been developed and tested (Aponte & Ingram, 2018; Aponte & Kissil, 2016).

One of the most intriguing challenges of humanistic psychology is for its advocates to practice what they preach. Nothing is more frustrating than to hear stories about "crazy shrinks" or supposedly humanistic educators and therapists who cannot apply in their own lives the same principles they espouse and teach to their clients and students. You have certainly been exposed in your life to leaders or teachers who could not—or would not—practice in their own lives what they advocated for others. This hypocrisy resulted in a loss of respect you felt toward them and eroded your trust in their competence. It's hard to take someone all that seriously when they can't do what they tell others.

One of the gifts of choosing therapy as a profession is that we have such a clear mandate to continue to work on ourselves, not just with regard to professional skills, but also personal growth. In that sense, we become inspirational models for our clients.

The facets of humanistic psychology that have always appealed to us most are the attention given not only to the relationship between people, but also the emphasis on the humane values of caring, compassion, authenticity, unconditional regard, respect, and honesty. Many humanistic practitioners have been encouraged to apply in their personal lives the knowledge and skills they learned for the benefit of their clients. It is certainly a major benefit of our profession that everything learned about therapy can make us more effective human beings, more loving and caring toward others, more skilled at communicating our needs and responding to others, more expert at reaching personal goals, and more highly evolved in our moral, spiritual, emotional, and intellectual development.

CONCERNS AND CRITICISM OF HUMANISTIC APPROACHES

Humanism has been criticized, quite legitimately, as being excessively self-oriented. There is all this talk about *self*-actualization, *self*-expression, *self*-awareness, *self*-fulfillment, leading to *self*-centeredness and narcissism, especially during times when political and corporate leaders exhibit such extreme self-promotion and self-interest. Autonomy and independence are valued over cooperation and interdependence that are so much a part of other cultures (Latino, African, Asian, indigenous). Of course, Maslow, Perls, Rogers, and others died before the multicultural movement was launched, before humanistic psychology's focus on a person's lived experience morphed into other more responsive movements. Perhaps today, self-actualization would be redefined in terms of social responsibility, relationship competencies, and cultural sensitivity rather than its original emphasis on personal freedom and self-expression.

Another concern has to do with how the therapist's genuineness gets brought into the relationship with the client. We have alluded to this throughout the chapter, but it bears mentioning again. Sadly, more than one therapist has gotten confused on this issue, and more than one client has been abused in the name of therapist genuineness and authenticity. Seasoned humanistic therapists would see these instances as tragic misunderstandings of the heart of the approach, but beginning therapists would be well advised to be especially careful about acting in the client's best interest while being "real."

The benefits of being a humanistic therapist, as positive as they might be, do not come without personal costs that are often burdensome. These personal costs are reflected in many ways, including signs and symptoms of therapist impairment. Which part of the human is therapist and which part is humanist? How can the roles be integrated? What is the effect of their interaction on quality of life? How can the therapist stay well while entering deeply into the world of so many tormented souls? These are questions that are yet largely unanswered with the exception of legal and ethical guidelines that tend to present the therapist as a "thing" rather than a living, breathing, changing being. Exploring these struggles will help therapists of all theoretical orientations to understand themselves better, as well as to become more effective models of humane values and humanistic behavior.

SUGGESTED READINGS

Cole, P., & Reese, D. (2017). *New directions in Gestalt group therapy.* New York, NY: Routledge.

Frankl, V. E. (1992). *Man's search for meaning* (4th ed.). Boston, MA: Beacon Press.

Greenberg, L. (2015). *Emotion-focused therapy: Coaching clients to work through their feelings* (2nd ed.). Washington, DC: American Psychological Association.

Hill, C. E. (2018). *Meaning in life: A therapist's guide.* Washington, DC: American Psychological Association.

House, R., Kaslisch, D., & Maidman, J. (Eds.) (2018). *Humanistic psychology: Current trends and future prospects.* New York, NY: Routledge.

Kirschenbaum, H. (2008). *The life and work of Carl Rogers.* Alexandria, VA: American Counseling Association.

Kolmannskog, V. (2018). *The empty chair: Tales from gestalt therapy.* New York, NY: Routledge.

Kottler, J. A., & Balkin, R. (2017). *Relationships in counseling and the counselor's life.* Alexandria, VA: American Counseling Association.

Kottler, J. A., & Carlson, J. (2015). *On Being a Master Therapist: Practicing What We Preach.* New York: Wiley.

Madison, G. (2014). *Theory and practice of focusing-oriented psychotherapy: Beyond the talking cure.* Philadelphia, PA: Jessica Kingsley.

Schneider, K. J., & Krug, O. T. (2017). *Existential-humanist therapy.* Washington, DC: American Psychological Association.

Sheldon, C. (2014). *Gestalt as a way of life: Awareness practices.* Bellingham, WA: CreateSpace.

van Deurzen, E., & Arnold-Baker, A. (2018). *Existential therapy: Distinctive features.* New York, NY: Routledge.

Yalom, I. D. (2009). *Staring at the sun: Overcoming the terror of death.* San Francisco, CA: Jossey Bass.

IMAGE CREDITS

CHAPTER 7

Thoughts Before Feelings: Cognitive Approaches

LEARNING OBJECTIVES

After reading this chapter, you should be able to do the following:

1. Describe the basic assumptions of cognitive therapies regarding how problems originate in distorted schemas and patterns of thought.
2. Provide examples of cognitive distortions and how they can be countered or refuted.
3. Differentiate between cognitive therapies and cognitive behavior therapy in their use of techniques to promote therapeutic change.
4. Describe the basic ideas and processes of cognitive therapy, comparing the approaches of Albert Ellis and Aaron Beck.
5. Describe the background and basic concepts of Adler's individual psychology and his approach to therapy.
6. Define key Adlerian concepts such as basic mistakes, inferiority and superiority complexes, sibling constellations, lifestyle issues, courage, and social interest.
7. Describe steps of the Adlerian treatment process, including the lifestyle assessment, interpreting early recollections, exploring mistakes and core fears, and developing strengths.
8. Describe the background, basic ideas, and processes of reality therapy.
9. Articulate how you would use the steps of the WDEP model to assist a client with a specific concern.
10. Evaluate the evidence supporting each of the cognitive therapies, their strengths, and their potential limitations.

This chapter represents a marriage of convenience. At first glance, the various approaches to cognitive, cognitive-behavioral, rational emotive, and Adlerian therapy might not seem to fit in the same chapter. Alfred Adler, as an original disciple of Freud, could technically be considered to have a neopsychoanalytic approach. Since it was also the first systemic model because of Adler's interest in underlying family structure, it could have been placed there as well. Reality therapy, also included here, is a kind of brief therapy and can be seen as a particular type of behavioral approach. But all these therapies place a strong emphasis on the importance of one's thoughts and beliefs as a major influence on one's choice of actions. For this reason, we see them as "chapter-mates" even if they might look quite different in practice.

All these approaches, as well as their modern variations, are enjoying popularity because of their adaptability to brief intervention, their emphasis on goal attainment, and their flexible, pragmatic strategies. Cognitive therapies have also been subjected to the most empirical research support in terms of their outcomes and are thus frequently included in many large studies. They lend themselves to application in a wide variety of settings, making them especially useful for school counselors on the one hand, or medical staff on the other. Each has a fairly structured step-by-step process, which makes them easier to learn than other models that are more general or philosophical. Each one also stresses the importance of accepting responsibility for one's thoughts and choices. Apart from these similarities, the models also have some distinctly different features.

AARON BECK AND COGNITIVE THERAPY

Psychiatrist Aaron Beck developed cognitive therapy as a way to treat depression by asking his patients to examine their dysfunctional thinking that often leads to their problems. His approach examined the self-defeating thought patterns that operate inside people's heads to keep them from changing maladaptive behavior. "If the patient is inclined to stay in bed and to neglect her family and work," Beck (1997) wrote as an example, "her observations of these behaviors and somatic symptoms are then 'translated' by her information processing into: 'I am lazy; I am an irresponsible person; I deserve to be punished' and a vicious cycle is established" (pp. 57–58).

Thus, Beck argued that to promote deeper, lasting changes, the therapist must go beyond the client's irrational thinking to reach the underlying belief structure. Unless this secondary change takes place, then the symptomatic relief may become only temporary and relapse will be inevitable (Beck, 2018). Beck has tested and refined his ideas for decades to incorporate new scientific findings about the mind and calls his most recent and comprehensive version the *generic cognitive model* (Beck & Haigh, 2014).

FOR REFLECTION

Before we discuss some of the beliefs and thought patterns that are considered to be irrational, illogical, or not grounded in reality, what are some examples of those that *you* consider to be most maladaptive?

As an example to get you started thinking in this way, consider that someone says to himself, or out loud, "This sort of thing always happens to me."

What strikes you as inaccurate about this statement?

Now, consider for a few moments other proclamations that people make that represent exaggerations and distortions that lead to feelings of helplessness, frustration, or discouragement.

Dysfunctional Styles of Thinking

In his early work, Beck was interested in the ways that his patients developed thinking patterns that predisposed them to depression. He found that in many cases they had overly pessimistic thoughts, such as "I have to protect myself, I'm better off isolated from other people.... There's no point in trying anything, because I would only fail" (Beck, 2018, p. 8). He deduced that early childhood experiences and interactions shaped *schemas*, the underlying beliefs and assumptions that people carry around inside them, and these in turn influenced their everyday thinking patterns. These cognitive schemas can be either positive ("I am good at overcoming adversity") or maladaptive ("I'll never get anywhere in life"). They may also be influenced by (a) how much emotion is tied up in them, (b) how long they have been operating inside someone's head, (c) who was involved during their first inception, (d) how significant that person was, (e) how detailed and well developed they are, and (f) how they dictate behavior (Leahy, 2017). Schemas are, thus, the bedrock for "automatic thoughts" that pop into one's head as truth. As you might imagine, changing a negative thought is easier that changing a schema that continues to generate negative thoughts and interpretations of all of live events—but it is a place to start.

According to cognitive theory, there are a number of consistent patterns of thought distortions that are evident in people's schemas, as well as in their everyday behavior. Examples of this include the following:

1. *Overgeneralization* in which someone makes an erroneous assumption that a single case necessarily means that something is always true. "Because this guy won't go out with me, I'll never find anyone to love me."

2. *Personalization* involves exaggerating the extent that events in the world apply to oneself. "Every time I plan a party, it always rains."

3. *Dichotomous thinking* means dividing things into extreme all-or-nothing categories. "Either I get the job and achieve greatness, or I lose the opportunity and become destined for mediocrity."

4. *Mind reading* represents a kind of arbitrary inference in which a person assumes that he or she knows what others are thinking. These conclusions are generally not supported by objective facts. "I can tell the instructor doesn't like me because he ignored the question I asked in class."

You can see a pattern emerging here, one in which there are cognitive errors, such as denial, exaggeration, or some other form of illogical process. There are many others such as catastrophizing (always expecting the worst), negative filters (looking for problems), and blaming others by default. In any of the cognitive approaches, it is crucial for the therapist to teach clients how to recognize automatic thoughts and label these distorted patterns—and then substitute more realistic, flexible, and accurate thinking instead.

FOR A CLASS ACTIVITY

Working with a partner or in small groups, list the prominent schemas in your thinking. This includes the most common cognitive scripts that guide your life, the things you tell yourself about who you are, what you can and cannot do, and what the world is like. Examples might include schemas such as "I'm not good at math," "I have bad luck," "I am the sort of person who does well in groups," and "A moral person is someone who always tells the truth no matter what."

After you have created a list of those schemas that are most influential in your life, talk about ways they are helpful as well as counterproductive. You might also ponder when and why you built each schema.

FOR LATER REFLECTION

Pick one of the schemas you developed earlier. Experiment with an alternative statement that seems more empowering, one that could emerge as a new schema. Use a chart like the one in the example that follows to come up with advantages and disadvantages of each statement.

After doing the exercise, what changes might you make in your thinking?

FIGURE 7.1. Schema analysis.

Schema Analysis

	Advantages	Disadvantages
Belief: my income determines my worth		
Short-term	I keep looking for a better job	I beat myself up after every paycheck
Long-term	more money in the bank	I neglect things and people I love
Belief: income is important but doesn't determine my worth		
Short-term	I relax a little and am happier	I could stay stuck where I am
Long-term	I enjoy what I have and who I am	no fancy cars or trips

Beck was also most helpful in identifying specific belief patterns for each of several major personality disorders, rather entrenched styles of interaction that are often impervious to change. He and several others described those that are most prevalent for each diagnosis (Beck, Davis, & Freeman, 2015). Some of these will be familiar to you since you see evidence of them in public figures, friends, acquaintances, classmates, and family members.

NARCISSISTIC: "I am special and deserve more than anyone else."

BORDERLINE: "Everyone will eventually abandon me so I should ruin things on my own terms."

DEPENDENT: "I am helpless and need others to take care of me."

AVOIDANT: "It's senseless for me to try anything new because I will get hurt."

PARANOID: "Everyone is out to get me and ruin my life."

ANTISOCIAL: "It's everyone out for themselves, so if I don't take advantage of others they will get the best of me."

Beck and his collaborators (Farb, et al., 2018) have developed ways to address a number of these persistent patterns. This requires great skill and a durable therapeutic alliance because individuals who have personality disorders do not typically see their thinking as a problem in the first place.

Yet the persistent, patient, and skilled cognitive therapist can, over time, help such individuals develop ways of directing their thinking in more functional ways, thereby reducing distressing emotions and behaviors that consistently get them in trouble.

FOR HOMEWORK

Begin to sensitize yourself to the ways that people express themselves with language that indicates dysfunctional thinking. One of the keys to the cognitive approach is being able to recognize when someone is distorting reality, exaggerating his or her predicament, or otherwise engaging in self-defeating thought patterns. The main clues you will have to identify such overgeneralizations, dichotomous thinking, and mind reading are the ways that people talk to themselves, as well as speak out loud.

We wouldn't recommend that you continuously point out to people when they speak in the language of external control or helplessness (they will quickly become annoyed rather than grateful), but train yourself to notice evidence of this behavior. The more you practice such critical scrutiny, the more skilled you will become doing so in sessions with your clients.

Principles of Cognitive Therapy

There are a number of similarities between Beck's approach and others that follow, but it also stands out as being the one cognitive approach that is most empirically based and stresses collaboration in the relationship. These are some of the major premises of this approach:

1. Emotions result from cognitive processes. In other words, thinking precedes feeling.
2. Therapy is brief, focused, and time limited. It deals with presenting problems and identified symptoms.
3. It employs a solid therapeutic relationship as a means to achieve desired goals. Although practitioners value the importance of this alliance they don't dwell on it. The therapist and client work together as a team.
4. Therapy is conceived as psychoeducational and uses the Socratic method of inquiry and dialogue. Clients are challenged to explore the origins and usefulness of their underlying beliefs.
5. Homework is valued as an especially important part of treatment. Clients are expected to translate talk into specific action they will take in between sessions.

FOR PERSONAL REFLECTION

All the cognitive therapies are especially sensitive to language because the way people talk is the best clue as to how they think internally. The idea is that if you can change the way people express themselves out loud, you can also alter their cognitive processes. Compare, for example, the difference between the following:

"I *must* leave now because I *have* to take care of another *obligation*."

versus

"I *choose* to leave now because I *want* to take care of another *commitment*."

This distinction is more than being a little nit-picky about a few words. In the first case, the person feels trapped, while in the second instance, the action is identical but the internal perception of it is quite different.

In the statements that follow, there are examples that reveal illogical or irrational thinking. Change each statement to an alternative that is more em-powering. We've started you off with a few so that you can complete the rest.

IRRATIONAL STATEMENT; ALTERNATIVE STATEMENT
"I should ..."; "I want to ..."
"You make me upset ..."; "I feel upset when ..."
"I must ..."
"It's awful that ..."
"It's so unfair that ..."
"I can't ..."
"Everybody feels ..."
"This always happens ..."
"I never get ..."

If you can get in the habit of speaking out loud with carefully chosen words that imply self-control and rational expression, you can change the way you think. According to cognitive theories, it is this internal dialogue that deter-mines how you feel based on your personal interpretation of events.

Applications to Specific Problems

One of the real strengths of Beck's cognitive therapy is its application to common psychological complaints such as depression, anxiety, and obsessive-compulsive disorder. Much research has been done to evaluate cognitive therapy as a way to address depression, particularly as it compares to drug therapy. Most often, cognitive therapy has been found to be equal, if not superior, to medication. It would appear that the most effective treatment of all for biologically based depression (as opposed to reactive depression) is a combination of cognitive therapy with the appropriate choice and dosage of anti-depressant medication (Dobson & Dobson, 2018).

Other followers of this theory (including Judith Beck, his daughter) have been quite diligent in evaluating the effectiveness of this approach with specific presenting problems such as chronic pain, bipolar disorder, generalized anxiety disorder, phobias, obsessive-compulsive disorder, and sleep disorders (Dobson & Dobson, 2018). Others have found that it is helpful for those suffering from chronic pain (Thorn, 2017). Still others have been helpful in providing practitioners with a variety of cognitive techniques for use children and adolescents (Friedberg & McClure, 2015).

Some Limitations

Cognitive therapy has fared well as it has been exported and used around the world, both in terms of its popularity with therapists and its outcomes with clients. However, as you would expect with any theory that emphasizes one domain of human experience (thinking) over all others (feeling, being, sensing), there is sometimes difficulty applying it to individuals of particular cultural backgrounds and life experiences. The cognitive therapist must take special care, while building the relationship, to understand the client's view of the world and preferred ways of learning. The whole notion of logic and rationality as primary values is, for instance, most typical of modern Western cultures. Among certain members of cultural groups, such as those of indigenous peoples, a cognitive approach will need to be adapted to fit cherished beliefs and perspectives. This has been successfully done, for example, with Māori clients in New Zealand, when the therapist took time to understand culture-specific processes for engagement, spirituality, metaphor as an important teaching tool, and the importance of family involvement (Bennett, Flett, & Babbage, 2014). Yet it also makes sense to approach *every* client with the stance that we will need to be educated about their way of understanding the world and how they prefer to take in new information.

FOR AN ACTIVITY

Get together with classmates or a partner and imagine that you are depressed. Really get into this state of mind by recalling a time in your life (which hopefully isn't going on right now) in which you felt perfectly miserable and hopeless. Picture that you have low energy and difficulty with your sleep habits. You are feeling discouraged and incredibly helpless. You feel utterly worthless.

Adopting this mode of being, make a list together of all the thoughts you are experiencing that are part of your depression. Identify as many dysfunctional thoughts as you can.

Once you are done, talk about the ways these ideas are based on distortions, exaggerations, overgeneralizations, and mislabeled beliefs. Now, think about what might you tell yourself instead. Practice trying on these new, more realistic beliefs about yourself and notice how you feel differently.

COGNITIVE BEHAVIORAL THERAPY (CBT)

There has been much confusion and uncertainty about the similarities and differences between "cognitive therapy" and "cognitive behavior therapy (CBT)." In one sense they are both the same thing, simply representing an evolution of labels, or different branding by their advocates. The backgrounds of the theorists, whether steeped in behavioral or cognitive concepts, originally determined their preferred label, although that has become largely meaningless today.

From a strictly behavioral perspective, *thoughts* are not observable and so are not a worthy focus that can be counted or subjected to a functional analysis of what is rewarding and maintaining a behavior. But a few decades ago, some clinicians proposed that maybe thoughts are just a form of mental behavior. At the very least, particular beliefs certainly seemed to be closely related to behavior. Eventually most practitioners and writers began to integrate techniques from both approaches.

Here's an example to illustrate this idea. Suppose a father brings in his 9-year-old daughter to see you because she is refusing to go to school. After establishing a strong therapeutic relationship with them and gathering basic information about how the school refusal actually plays out at home, you ask each of them what they believe this behavior means. Whatever treatment plan you develop would likely include both cognitive components that hone in on their internal processing of this problem, as well as specific aspects of behavior. From your cognitive therapy arsenal, you might identify with them the thoughts the girl has about going to school (or leaving home) and then uncover basic schemas that are getting in the way. During this exploration, the girls says things like, "Nobody likes me because I have red hair," "I always get sick at school and embarrass myself," and "Dad gets sad when I leave him alone." Then you'd challenge these schemas and automatic negative thoughts and help the child replace them with more accurate and helpful thoughts.

Once these thinking patterns are explored and challenged, you might next rely on some interventions to deal with the specific behavior. This could include systematic desensitization, relaxation training, modeling, and shaping behavior through differential reinforcement, contingency contracting, and so on. You may also ask her to rate and measure her reluctance on a daily basis and explore, together, what's going on when it is higher or lower. You could suggest doing "experiments" about what it takes to keep the intensity of fear lower. And you'd certainly track and reward even her attempts to go to school, expecting eventual success, while having her notice and correct her sabotaging thoughts all along the way until her new, helpful ones become automatic.

You can see how CBT is similar to CT, but with the additional use of behavioral techniques to help effect change (including behavioral change). Essentially, here are the main features of CBT:

- The therapist and client work together as a team, but clients are the expert on themselves; the therapist is the expert on the theory and techniques.
- Therapy is goal oriented and targets the resolution of a specific problem. The goal is approached in a step-by-step way so that progress toward the goal is regularly made and tracked.
- Therapy is usually short term. Clients do homework outside session, practice skills they learned during sessions, and report on results.
- The therapist helps the client discover the capability of choosing positive, helpful thoughts and behaviors for oneself.

Strengths and Limitations

Like CT, CBT has been adapted to many disorders, clients of all ages, and settings around the world. It has been implemented in individual, couple, family, and group settings (Farmer, & Chapman, 2016). As we noted earlier, the evidence supporting it continues to accrue, in part because CBT techniques and assumptions fit so well with the modern scientific paradigm that determines what gets studied and how (Weisz & Kazdin, 2017). Books and workshops on CBT techniques are widely available; some have linked video illustrations on how to do the key techniques such as cognitive rehearsal (e.g., Wright, Brown, Thase, & Remiriz Basco, 2017). Clients are even encouraged to do CBT on themselves (for example, see Gillihan, 2016, 2018).

Unfortunately, CBT has become somewhat of a "catch all" approach, at least in the way it is mentioned in community settings. Sometimes counselors and therapists who aren't sure of their theoretical approach find it safest to tell the world that they do CBT because the label is so familiar and widely accepted. Yet all therapy that purports to be CBT is not necessarily aligned with this efficient and parsimonious theoretical model. Clinicians who practice it casually often do not see the results described in the research studies that use well-developed treatment protocols. Clinicians who employ some of the techniques and worksheets may also not take the time to understand the client's culture or view of the problem, leading to premature treatment dropout.

It's also important to know that sometimes clients need a dose of supportive, person-centered therapy before they are ready to look at their limiting beliefs and self-talk. I (Marilyn) once had a client who had flunked out of her first year of law school because she had a panic attack during the end-of-year final exam. She came to see me, saying she wanted to use the summer to gear up to restart law school in the fall, but she was very anxious about the prospect of a reoccurrence of panic symptoms that felt so suffocating and terrifying. I could see that she put a lot of extraordinary pressure on herself so I was prepared to launch CBT to work on her perfectionist beliefs. I asked her to monitor what she was saying to herself and report that to me in the following session.

When we sat down to work the next week, she said, "I have a question. Can we just talk?" She was telling me that she first needed support while exploring her life in general. We did look at her beliefs later, and she (being a lawyer in training) was pretty good at disputing her own irrational and illogical thinking. She got through her first-year exams (the second time) with flying colors and later went on to pass the Bar using the same strategies we had developed in therapy. This client taught me that some who consult us primarily need a strong, longer-term therapeutic relationship to relieve their symptoms, and one that is less directive, rather than a brief, goal-focused approach—at least at first.

ALBERT ELLIS AND RATIONAL EMOTIVE BEHAVIOR THERAPY (REBT)

The name of this theory is a bit complicated because Ellis liked to think that it is so comprehensive that it embraces every facet of human experience. At one time or another he labeled it cognitive therapy, humanistic therapy, constructivist therapy, brief therapy, behavior therapy, and finally as rational emotive behavior therapy (Ellis, 1996, 2001); the title kept expanding to be more inclusive (and more fashionable, as times changed). Although it is sometimes lumped together with CT and CBT, we treat it separately as a unique contribution since it was developed simultaneously with Beck's work.

With good reason, people sometimes have difficulty separating Ellis from his theory. He presented himself as a thoroughly authentic, down-to-earth, honest, and crusty fellow. He also swore a lot, which put off some members of his audiences. He was unapologetic in attacking religious rigidity as a form of cognitive disturbance. And he was a bit full of himself as many prominent people can be. In speaking about other theoreticians at a conference at which he was presenting, he expressed with his usual mischief and irreverence that he didn't much care about what others thought of him. With humor and a twinkling smile, he gestured toward his co-presenters and announced, "They hate my telling them that I am—of course!—right and that they are—indubitably!—wrong. In my youth, I would have stupidly bothered myself about that, would have shown a dire need for their approval, and would have told them that they were great guys or gals and scholars. … What, me honest and impolite? Never!" (Ellis, 1997, p. 69). He carried on like this at workshops and with his clients and supervisees until he died in 2007.

When I (Jeffrey) was first beginning my career, I arrived late at one of his workshops. The room was packed and the only vacant chairs were in the first row. Unbeknownst to me, these spaces were reserved for those who had volunteered to serve as demonstration clients on stage during his performance. And it was a performance indeed. In the first few minutes he announced that if anyone in the audience might be offended by his foul language, including the nuns in attendance sitting in the back row, they might as well leave now. If that's how things began, then the way the first session ended was with me on stage working with Ellis on an unresolved issue in my life. While I found the brief encounter to be interesting, to say the least, I can't say I was cured of my suffering as much as amused by how provocative and direct he could be with someone he's just met.

We count ourselves among those who got a tremendous kick out of Ellis's confrontational nature, which is evident in his many books and recordings. We enjoyed his sense of humor, his playfulness, and his willingness to push the limits of what he could get away with. Yet, he unnecessarily alienated folks who were turned off to his ideas because he came across so strongly. He was not always the best salesman for his own ideas whereas others (e.g., Bernard & Dryden, 2018) have been more persuasive, at least with different audiences he could not reach.

Background of REBT

There are two aspects of Ellis's background that deserve mention in understanding his approach. The first is that he grew up as an awkward, shy, insecure, self-described "social phobic"—not surprising, because he was grossly neglected as a child. The second was that he read as much philosophy as he could from adolescence onward, searching for ideas that might bolster his inner strength and give him courage to overcome his fears. Specifically, he devoted himself to reading about what makes people happy and most satisfied with their lives.

As a form of self-therapy, Ellis began reading the works of ancient philosophers such as Confucius, Epicurus, Epictetus, as well as rational thinkers such as Spinoza, Kant, and Santayana. He immediately seized on the idea that he could cure himself of his own excessive worries if he tried to think more encouraging thoughts. For instance, when he received rejections by girls and magazine editors (an endless source of misery in his adolescence and early adulthood), he learned to tell himself that he wasn't a lousy person or writer just because someone didn't select him or his work.

FOR PERSONAL APPLICATION

Talk about ways that you keep yourself on "probation." You consider yourself worthy only to the extent that you act in accordance with your highest, perfectionistic standards. If you should make mistakes, mess up, or in any way act less than perfectly, you judge not only your behavior but also who you are as a person.

What would it mean, for example, if you received a grade on your next assignment, test, or paper that is less than you expect? What would you tell yourself about what this would mean?

From these humble beginnings, Ellis began his training as a psychologist, and later as a psychoanalyst, studying the works of Karen Horney, Alfred Adler and Harry Stack Sullivan. Once in practice, he became frustrated that his patients were not getting better faster and searched for new ideas to become more efficient. From his reading of psychology and philosophy, as well as the great novelists, Ellis settled on the idea that happiness comes from two main sources: (a) unconditional self-acceptance irrespective of any specific performances, and (b) a high frustration tolerance to deal with disappointments. Once he combined these basic ideas with the importance of cognition in determining people's perceptions and subsequent emotional responses, Ellis had the makings of a new system of therapy.

Basic Ideas

Originally, Ellis (1962) described a dozen distinct irrational beliefs that he later distilled into a few basic themes. As was mentioned earlier in the discussion of Beck's cognitive therapy, one of the keys to using this approach is being able to recognize readily the most common thoughts that get in people's way.

The five "biggies" that you should be most familiar with are described next. Each of these is summarized in Table 7.1 alongside Beck's nominations for most dysfunctional beliefs. In each case, we have also supplied an example of how the idea might be challenged.

1. *"Life isn't fair (and it ought to be)."* What is it that strikes you about this that is irrational? Well, clearly life is not fair. If it were, you wouldn't have to lock your doors and everyone would treat you just as you feel you deserve. In truth, people live by different rules than you do. It is one thing to wish that other people were more like you and that life would give you just what you deserve; it is another thing to expect it.

2. *"It's awful."* Things may be disappointing, frustrating, annoying, but almost never terrible. "Awful" represents the worst possible thing that could ever happen, usually a gross exaggeration of the situation. If something is merely disappointing, or only a setback, then it doesn't become a major catastrophe, just a minor challenge. When people are "awfulizing," they are making themselves upset by distorting or exaggerating what is occurring.

3. *"I can't stand it."* In truth, you can stand almost anything except death. It may sometimes feel as though life is difficult, but it is always something you can handle once you keep things in perspective. Remember, for example, those times when you have had to go to the bathroom very badly? It didn't seem like you could make it to the nearest toilet, but somehow you were able to tolerate the pain. The same holds true with emotional suffering. It may not seem as though you can stand it, but once you stop whining and feeling sorry for yourself, you can almost always bring things back under control.

4. *"I must get what I want."* It is one thing to want something, quite another to demand that you get it. Ellis calls this "musturbating," a form of self-abuse in which people use "shoulds" and "musts" to communicate their belief that they are special and deserving of whatever they think they need most.

5. *"I'm incompetent."* People often make absolute judgments about who they are based on a sample of their behavior. It is irrational to label oneself as shy, stupid, or incompetent just because one (or more) times you acted that way.

TABLE 7.1. Comparison between Beck and Ellis's Dysfunctional Beliefs

Beck's Cognitive Therapy	Ellis's Rational Emotive Therapy
Overgeneralization	Absolute judgments
Personalization	Musturbating and shoulding
Dichotomous thinking	Awfulizing
Mind reading	Life isn't fair

FOR PERSONAL REFLECTION and HOMEWORK

In his original list, Ellis identified 13 irrational beliefs that help keep us miserable. For each one of them, think about what it is about this internal statement that is not based in reality or logic. In other words, why is each of these thoughts irrational?

- "Everyone must love and appreciate me all the time."
- "I must be competent in everything that I do in order to feel okay about myself."
- "Some people who are different from me are bad and should be punished."
- "It is terrible when I don't get what I want."
- "Other people and events cause me to be unhappy and I have little control over this situation."
- "If I keep dwelling on something awful, maybe I can prevent it from happening."
- "It is easier to avoid difficulties in life rather than having to face them."
- "I need someone stronger than I am in order to take care of me."
- "What has happened in the past determines how I must be in the future."
- "I should become upset over other people's problems."
- "There is a perfect solution to every problem and it's possible for me to figure out what it might be."

Some of these statements might not immediately strike you as irrational or illogical. Circle the ones that seem like reasonable assumptions to you and then read some of the REBT literature to find out what it is about them that distorts or exaggerates reality. You might want to start with the excerpt from Ellis's book, *A New Guide to Rational Living,* at the end of this chapter.

The ABC Theory

One of the most useful ideas from this theory, and one that is quite easily taught to clients, is its model of emotions that helps explain the process by which people become emotionally disturbed, as well as the means by which to dispute those irrational beliefs. In this ABC theory (D and E were added later), the usual scenario unfolds as follows.

A—The *a*ctivating event. A particular situation or precipitating event is believed to cause the emotional suffering. In this first step, you simply describe what it is that bothers you and the situation that you believe is causing the problem. Let's imagine, for instance, that you receive a grade on a class assignment that is less than what you hoped.

B—The irrational *belief*. According to this theory, it isn't the situation that causes your emotional pain as much as it is whatever you are telling yourself inside your head. If, for example, you were thinking to yourself, "Oh, well, so what if the grade isn't what I wanted? I'll do better next time," then you would hardly be upset. But if, on the other hand, you were thinking the following thoughts, you'd be very distraught:

- "I can't believe I blew this assignment *completely*. I'm such an idiot!"
- "This means I'll *never* be a good therapist."
- "This is the *worst* thing that ever happened to me. I'll *never* recover from this."
- "It isn't *fair* that the teacher graded the assignment the way she did."
- "I *should* have been treated differently than this."

If you note the italicized words, you'll see clues as to the parts of these internal statements that are illogical or irrational. One good way to determine whether a thought fits this criterion is whether it is based in reality. You should also look for the following:

- Exaggerations ("This is the worst thing that ever happened to me.")
- Dogmatic demands ("I must get what I want.")
- Self-evaluations ("I am worthless because I performed less than satisfactorily.")

C—The emotional *consequence*. This is the result of the irrational thinking, the emotional symptoms that result from the internal beliefs. Distinctions are made between unhealthy emotional responses and those that are reasonable given the circumstances. There is a big difference, for example, between sadness and depression, or annoyance and rage.

In this case, the student who was telling himself the foregoing thoughts would most likely feel upset. As a therapeutic procedure, the client is often asked to rate on a 1–10 scale just how upset he or she feels. It is at this point that you might choose to borrow reflective listening skills from the humanistic approach to draw out and reflect the client's feelings.

The following ratings provide a baseline for measuring progress after the cognitive interventions.

Depressed	5
Anxious	8
Frustrated	9
Discouraged	9
Angry	6
Confused	7

D—*Disputing the irrational beliefs.* Going back to the irrational beliefs, the actual therapy takes the form of challenging the thoughts that exaggerate or distort the situation. This complete process, summarized in Table 7.2, continues by asking a series of questions:

- Where is the evidence that this is true?
- Who says that this must be the case?
- Does the response seem logical and reasonable, given the situation?
- If a witness or video camera were observing this scene, would this person or device record things exactly as you report them?

TABLE 7.2. Steps in the REBT Process

1. Start with the **activating event** by asking the client what is most bothersome.
2. Identify the irrational **beliefs** that are the real culprits in producing negative emotions.
3. Plot the emotional **consequences** that are experienced, rating them in their levels of intensity.
4. **Dispute** these irrational beliefs by challenging assumptions and encouraging clearer reasoning.
5. **Assess** the effects of the interventions. If necessary, repeat the process.

In the preceding example, the distraught student might be asked to explore questions such as the following:

- "Who says that this assignment must represent a fair and accurate assessment of what you learned?"
- "Who says that your grade should be fair?"
- "Where is the evidence that because you got a grade lower than you expected this means you are hopeless as a potential therapist?"
- "So what if you got a grade you don't like? What are you telling yourself that really means?"
- "Did you really blow the assignment completely, or rather did you merely perform less well than you had hoped?"

E—New emotional *effect.* If the cognitive interventions have been successful, there will be a different emotional outcome. Sometimes the goal isn't to eliminate completely all emotional distress. Who, after all, is going to feel nothing at all after a disappointment or upsetting situation? But it is reasonable to expect that you can reduce significantly the magnitude of the emotional arousal, basing it more in reality.

In our example, the student rates his feelings again but this time with numbers that are more than half what they were previously. Now he is telling himself the following:

> *Well, it is a little disappointing that I didn't do as well as I had hoped. And I do think that the assignment was rather unclear and inconsistently graded. But that is the way things sometimes go in this imperfect world. Just because I didn't perform perfectly doesn't mean I won't do better on the next assignment. Even if I don't improve, these tasks in class don't even reflect how well I will do in the field. But they do provide useful feedback that I can use to improve my knowledge and skills. So, this is hardly a terrible disaster, merely a very minor setback.*

Obviously, if this is what you chose (and it is a choice) to say to yourself, you would feel very differently about this situation than if you ranted and raved internally, blaming the instructor, yourself, and the conspiracy of the universe to make your life miserable.

FOR PERSONAL APPLICATION

Among all the theories in the text, we have found REBT to be among the most easily personalized in daily life. In fact, there is not a day that goes by that we might not challenge some exaggerated thinking when we are aware of feeling unduly upset about something. Somebody cuts you off in traffic. You get disappointing news. You burn the chicken on the grill. You feel slighted by someone's actions. These and a dozen others each day provide the opportunity to examine what we are saying to ourselves about these events.

Think of something going on in your life right now that you are upset about. Starting with the activating event (what you believe created the discomfort), proceed through the steps previously covered in which you identify your irrational beliefs, describe the emotional consequences, and then dispute those thoughts and assumptions that are exaggerated, distorted, or not based in reality. Finally, notice the new emotion that you feel after going through all this.

Specific Disputing Strategies

There are two parts where beginners often get stuck applying the REBT method we just reviewed. Identifying irrational beliefs takes a fair bit of reading in which you familiarize yourself with the patterns that are most common. Once you do, you'll hear little bells ringing in your head any time you hear someone say "should," or "must," or "fair." Likewise, when you hear someone say something such as "He really made me mad," or "That really hurt me," you'll automatically make the conversion in your head to "You made yourself mad over what he said" and "You really hurt yourself when you chose to think that this action was all about you."

These examples lead into the most difficult part of the therapeutic process in which you dispute the client's irrational beliefs. The trick, however, is to do so in a way that you shake old ideas loose without alienating the person in the process. There are two such rhetorical styles for teaching alternative ways of thinking. These are used in most forms of CT and CBT as well, so it is worthwhile to devote some time to learning them.

In the *didactic method*, you adopt a tutoring sort of style, explaining the logical method and generating alternative ways of thinking.

> *You have been talking at length about what a lousy student you are, but I hear this self-assessment is based almost totally on your grades in this one class. You have also mentioned dozens of other classes in which you did quite well. I'm confused by this discrepancy. It seems as though you are overgeneralizing from one situation to make a total evaluation of your performance as a student in every other setting. Another way of thinking about this same scenario is to remind yourself that you are a fallible human being who doesn't always function at the optimal level.*

In the *Socratic method*, a more questioning, challenging approach is used to dispute a client's irrational beliefs.

> *Where does it follow that because you got what you think is a low grade—and I don't necessarily agree with that—that this means you are stupid? Where is the evidence to support that conclusion? I'd like to see those data, because frankly, it's all in your imagination.*
>
> *I wonder what you could tell yourself instead about this situation, keeping your attention purely on what is reasonable and rational in these circumstances. Let's assume for a moment that you did "totally blow the class," a gross exaggeration in its own right; so what does this say about you? Where is the evidence that this means you are stupid and that this is the "worst possible thing that could have ever happened"?*

You can see in both disputing strategies (and in others called logical, philosophical, empirical, and functional disputing), that it takes skill and practice to become proficient at these methods. In one example, Ellis and Dryden (2007) describe how they took one basic irrational belief of a depressed client—"I absolutely must do well and be approved of by others"—and were able to identify dozens of derivative irrational beliefs such as the following:

- **Awfulizing:** "It's absolutely terrible when someone criticizes me or disagrees with me."
- **Overpersonalizing:** "When she says she is too busy to do something with me, it really means she doesn't like me."
- **Perfectionism:** "I can't believe I made such silly mistakes. It's not like me to do that."
- **Disqualifying:** "She did give me a good assignment to do, but that's only because nobody else was around who could do it."

Apart from the specifics of these disputing strategies, notice the general style of the interventions. Your job is to (a) listen carefully to what the person says, (b) decode the underlying thinking that is represented in the verbalizations, (c) identify the core irrational beliefs implicit in the statements, and (d) challenge the validity of assumptions that are clearly the result of distortions and exaggerations. In addition, the use of humor helps to reduce the extent to which people take themselves, and their problems, too seriously (Ellis & Dryden, 2007).

If that seems like quite a lot to do, the good news is that this is one of those therapeutic approaches that works equally well with yourself as it does with your clients. The better you get at recognizing and correcting your own irrational beliefs, the more skilled you will be to do so with those you wish to help.

FOR A CLASS ACTIVITY

Get together in groups of three, with one person agreeing to work on a current problem that lends itself to disputing irrational beliefs. Ideally, this would be an issue that is not terribly serious but one that matters to that person. With two of the partners acting as team helpers, take your "client" through the following steps:

1. With what are you struggling? Collect background information on the nature of the difficulty, specifically identifying the precipitating event (A) and the emotional consequences (C).
2. What are you feeling? List at least a half dozen different feelings, because rarely is there only one reaction.

3. Rate each feeling on a 1–10 scale according to how upsetting it is. A 10 represents an extreme reaction, whereas a 1 is minimal and a 5 about moderate.
4. What are you telling yourself about this situation that is making you upset? Help your partner label each of the irrational beliefs that are the source of the difficulty. Look especially for the following themes: should's, must's, absolute judgments, demands, exaggerations, and over-personalizations.
5. Where is the evidence to support these beliefs? Dispute the irrational self-statements.

Some Strengths and Limitations

Rational emotive behavior therapy shares many of the strengths and weaknesses of Beck's theory presented earlier. Its concepts and methods easily fit within modern requirements of documented treatment planning (Fulkerson, 2015), and it has been included in clinical trials that bear evidence for its success (compared to control groups) for short-term symptom reduction associated with many psychological problems and diagnoses (Dobson & Dobson, 2018). For example, Ellis and Bernard (2005) have adapted and applied it to childhood disorders. It is also easily adapted to group and psychoeducational settings (Ellis & Ellis, 2011). It is noteworthy that it was used as the basis of the U.S. Army's first soldier and family cognitive resiliency training classes for those involved in Operation Iraqi Freedom (Jarrett, 2013). Interestingly, it is also receiving increased attention as an intervention that can be used to enhance the athletic performance, motivation, and psychological well-being of competitive athletes (Turner & Davis, 2018; Wood, Barker, Turner, & Sheffield, 2018). Recent proponents have aligned it with the positive psychology movement, claiming that using REBT methods can be a tool for achieving more lifelong happiness and less emotional misery, which may in turn lead you being more caring and accepting of others and the world in general (Ellis, 2019).

REBT is a more confrontive approach than many others, one that requires the therapist to actively challenge the client's irrational beliefs. After all, people don't usually give up their cherished assumptions easily, especially when they get a lot of mileage out of remaining stuck. Yet challenge and confrontation are just what some of us need to get out of our cognitive ruts. However, such directness, unless done very sensitively, it can be unhelpful for some clients, especially those dealing with unresolved trauma.

Cultural background is another important consideration. On the one hand, challenging someone directly is very rude in many collectivist traditions. On the other hand, an active, directive, therapist who gets to work quickly, for a limited number of sessions, fits well for many cultural groups (even some of the same ones that avoid confrontation). The *Journal of Rational-Emotive and Cognitive-Behavior Therapy* is replete with examples of how REBT has been successfully adapted and implemented with clients from diverse cultures around the world. The bottom line is that the therapist must work out a way of offering the main ideas from REBT so they are welcomed by the client. It is extremely important with this approach, perhaps more so than with most, that you do not just follow a formula but personalize the theory and techniques in such a way that they fit with your unique style. Of course, for you to do this effectively, you will first need considerable practice in applying the methods to yourself.

ADLERIAN THERAPY

Let's be clear from the outset: Many fans of Adlerian therapy would be confused why this theory is included in a chapter within cognitive models, or why it doesn't deserve a chapter of its own considering its historical influence and uniquely integrative perspective. Alfred Adler can be viewed as a chameleon in that he appears to change form depending on the background against which he stands. We don't mean that this camouflage was deliberate on his part; quite the contrary: He did his best to communicate in a manner that was as clear and cogent as possible. But practically every other theory now claims him as a grandparent. He could have easily been placed in the chapter on psychoanalytic theory, action-oriented therapy, constructivist therapy, or integrative approaches.

Adler's theory of individual psychology is remarkable in that it was developed a century ago and yet still enjoys popularity and a dedicated following of therapists. In summarizing Adler's important contributions that have influenced current practice, many would now strike you as rather obvious because they have formed the basis of so many other theories. Because he was so much more pragmatic and flexible than Freud, Adler was able to reach a different constituency by introducing the following ideas:

1. The importance of thinking processes on feelings (he was the first cognitive therapist)
2. The impact of early family experiences and birth order on present behavior (he was among the first family therapists)

3. The value of constructing specific plans of action (he was the first to emphasize action strategies to follow insights)
4. The importance of an egalitarian, collaborative counseling relationship (moving far afield from the stance of psychoanalysts, who were seen as authority figures)
5. An assessment of "style of life" and social behavior as they affect personality development and mental health (arguing for the importance of contribution through social action)

Perhaps you can appreciate why Adler is so difficult to pin down in a theoretical category. Nevertheless, Adler and his contemporary followers hold that *you are what you think* (Carlson & Englar-Carlson, 2017), so we have included him in this chapter.

Background

Adler named his theory to reflect his cherished convictions. *Individual* psychology references a translation from the German word "individuum" or "that which cannot be divided." He selected this term to reflect what he saw as the unity and self-consistency of the person in thought, feeling and action, in direct contrast to Freud, who divided the person into "parts" (id, ego, superego). Quite a number of modern writers (see Carlson & Englar-Carlson, 2017 and Oberst & Stewart, 2014) have adapted the original theory to a variety of other applications and settings, each of which brings the original ideas into a fresh package.

Whereas Freud was (overly) concerned with biological factors and psychosexual development that influence a person's behavior, Adler (1931) took a far more holistic perspective. Freud may have been a fatalist (some would say a pessimist), but Adler viewed people as essentially goal directed with the capacity for being creative and responsible for their own choices.

Adler introduced one of the first structures for conducting an intake interview, the standard clinical assessment method used to collect background information, form a diagnosis, and create a treatment plan. He approached this task by conducting a thorough exploration of a person's lifestyle or style of life (meaning their unique, unconscious, habitual way of responding to life, thought to be formed by influences within and beyond the family early in life), and an especially a detailed family history, occupational record, history of love relationships, and social competencies.

Adler was himself a sickly child, subject to frequent bouts of a respiratory disorder, a vitamin deficiency, pneumonia, and even several near fatal accidents. No doubt these early experiences with feeling helpless led him to think a lot about a person's internal sense of inferiority or superiority. (He was the one to coin the term *inferiority complex*.) This would help explain how Adler ended up compensating for his own early health problems by becoming a physician himself.

Adler had great faith in the human capacity for overcoming disabilities. This belief served him well, not only in breaking away from Freud's charismatic influence, but also in supplying him with the confidence and resilience he would need to sustain his work in the face of mounting criticism, both in his native Austria and abroad. Once he first opened a medical practice specializing in nervous diseases, Adler focused on some rather unique client groups: circus performers, tailors, and other working-class people. He also became quite involved in the social rights movements of his day, advocating for better working conditions for the poor, school reform, sex education, and he was a vocal leader in equal rights for women; he later asserted that such involvement was crucial for mental hygiene (which mental health was called at the time). In so many ways, he was far ahead of his time.

Like Freud and Fritz Perls, both nonreligious Jews, Adler escaped his homeland just prior to the outbreak of Nazi domination and immigrated to America (Freud left a bit later for England). Using New York as a base for his clinical and lecturing activities, Adler spent the latter part of his life promoting his theory, eventually recruiting others (Ansbacher & Ansbacher, 1956; Dreikurs, 1967) to carry on his work.

Rudolph Dreikurs founded the first Adler Institute in North America as a way to introduce his ideas to professionals who were, at the time, enamored with traditional psychoanalytic thinking. Needless to say, it was tough going because Adler was often branded as a traitor to the master's original teachings. Adler did indeed directly contradict the orthodoxy of Freudian theory, although he was quite consistent in crediting his mentor with promoting the role of early childhood experiences, bringing attention to the meaning of dreams, and suggesting that symptoms served some useful purpose.

Basic Concepts

Like Freud's original concepts, many of Adler's ideas have become part of everyday language. He talked about *inferiority or superiority complexes* as part of the primary style in which a person presents himself or herself to the world and moves toward life goals. He was the first to bring up *lifestyle issues* as the background from which people make life decisions. He foreshadowed family systems thinkers by asking clients to examine the *sibling constellations* and patterns in early home relationships. His innovative, experimental orientation in sessions, (using techniques such as "*acting as if* ") led him to try therapeutic techniques that resemble what later developed into Gestalt therapy. He looked at the origins of dysfunctional thinking that led to what he called *basic mistakes.* He asserted that mental health exhibits itself with true interest in the plight of those less fortunate, and *the courage to take purposeful action* to better oneself and others. In many ways, Adler's concepts are still a great fit with our contemporary views of holistic health and wellbeing.

Social Interest and Mutual Respect

Adler was very big on the concept he called *Gemeinschaftsgefuhl,* or "social interest" in English, though some of the passion implied in the German word is lost in translation. He was among the first psychotherapy theorists to take a strong stand for advocacy and social interest, believing that our responsibility and professional role extends beyond our own clinical practice. Adler's conviction was that a feeling of commitment to one's community and acting with a sense of belonging toward the betterment of all is a key aspect of mental health. He believed that when people are treated with respect and dignity, they will develop social interest and find the courage to strive on the useful side of life. Adler foreshadowed the civil rights movement when he wrote, "The ironclad logic of social living is equality" (Adler, 1959, p. 40).

Birth Order

You most likely take it for granted that birth order affects the ways a person might develop, but Adler was among the first to observe that sibling position might be a critical variable to consider. Clearly, an eldest child does not grow up in the same family, nor have the same parents, as would younger brothers and sisters. During the earliest stages of a family, parents are insecure and unskilled. They lavish attention on a first-born child, sometimes spoiling him or her rotten. By the time subsequent offspring arrive on the scene, parents have calmed down a bit. This results in middle or youngest children developing in ways that could be very different from their elder sibling.

FOR PERSONAL APPLICATION

Make a chart of your position in the structure of your family, noting the ages of each sibling and the relative space separating each of you. Consider how your birth order has affected the ways you have developed as a person. What would most likely be different if you had been born earlier or later in your family's history?

The Helping Process

According to an Adlerian approach, therapy proceeds along a series of progressive stages that will strike you as quite logical.

Establish a collaborative relationship. This is an empathic, supportive relationship but one that is based on democratic principles and essential equality. The therapist uses all the regular skills favored by any other professional at this stage, using well-timed questions and reflections of feeling and content, to build a solid alliance. Like most other approaches you have studied, it is now considered standard operating procedure to use empathy and support to establish a sense of trust. If that does not happen first, subsequent therapeutic efforts are likely to be less than successful.

Lifestyle assessment. A thorough history is explored, including family background, belief system, cultural heritage, personal goals, and other facets of being human. Basic questions are directed toward the person's early family constellation ("What was it like for you growing up?"), social relationships ("To whom are you closest?" and "What is most satisfying to you about your friendships?"), work life ("How do you feel about your job?"), sexuality ("How satisfying are your intimate relationships with a partner?"), and sense of self ("How do you feel about who you are?"). In addition, like any other form of treatment, clients are asked standard questions:

1. "What would you like help with?"
2. "What are you expecting or hoping that I might do for you?"
3. "How would you like things to be different after our sessions are over?"
4. "What have you already tried in your efforts to take care of your concerns?"
5. "What support is available to you during this difficult time?"
6. "What are some of the strengths and assets you bring to our relationship?"

These are the sorts of questions that you would bring up in a session with a new client regardless of your theoretical orientation. They help you to efficiently and quickly gather background information, assess preliminary expectations, and find out what the client has already tried before. However, an Adlerian therapist might spend an entire session (or more) on these questions because they provide rich information related to changes the client needs to make, whereas others might whiz through them in 10 minutes to get to other matters.

FOR A CLASS ACTIVITY

Practice doing an intake interview with a partner. Using the six questions as a guide, take about 10 minutes each to conduct the initial phase of a first session. When acting in the role of a client, it does not matter whether you present yourself as you really are or role-play someone else. In reality, even when you pretend to be another person, you are still being a part of yourself.

During the interview, take brief notes on what you learned, but do not let your writing distract you from maintaining good attending and listening behavior. Concentrate only on asking these open-ended questions and inserting a few encouraging probes, perhaps reflecting feelings and content as appropriate. When the 10 minutes are over, regardless of how far down the list you have gotten, summarize what you have heard your partner say.

Give each other feedback on what you liked best and least about the interview. If an observer is present to serve in that role, then invite him or her to debrief you.

Interpreting early recollections. A type of family constellation questionnaire is often used to gather relevant information on family experiences. The goal at this stage is to assess which early events were most influential on current patterns. This inquiry would begin by asking the names, ages, and occupations of parents, as well as the sibling positions. The client would also be asked to supply the most dominant personality characteristics of each family member.

A number of other questions would be introduced:

"Who was your mother's favorite child?"
"Who was your father's favorite?"
"What did your parents expect and want for each of their children?"
"Which parent did you resemble more?"
"To which sibling were you closest?"
"What were conflicts about in your family?"

Other questions would be used to explore earliest recollections:

"What is your earliest memory?"
"Describe your first sexual experience."
"Which incident in school stands out as being most significant to you?"

Each of these questions will provide additional clues to the therapist about the client's inner world, sense of self, basic approach to life, and what may need to change.

FOR A FIELD STUDY

Ask several people you know to tell you about their earliest memory. Direct them to tell you the story of what happened and how they felt about it. Make sure they do not get lost in the details but concentrate instead on their personal reactions to the event. Discover what stands out as being most significant to them about this early recollection. (You might want to experiment with the detailed suggestions on how to do this in a workbook offered by Mosak, Schneider, & Mosak, 2012).

To rehearse this field study, it would first be a good idea for you to complete the exercise yourself in a journal. After you have written out the narrative and identified the central themes, give the recollection a name at the top.

For example, my (Jeffrey's) earliest memory is carrying my brother home from the hospital on my lap in the back of the car. I remember being terrified by the responsibility of having this living, squirming thing in my arms and being afraid that I might drop him or hurt him. I would, thus, give this story the title of "Fearful of Responsibility." Possible conclusions I might have drawn from this experience? Avoiding responsibility altogether, striving to control (for feeling "out of control"), striving to become competent, knowledgeable, and highly skilled, or even "super" responsible.

Exploring mistakes. Find out what the person believes he or she has done wrong in life. Identify thought disturbances and core fears that get in the way. Because Adlerian therapy is classified as a type of cognitive therapy, practitioners explore with clients the self-defeating thinking patterns that contribute to their distorted perceptions, which might include the following:

- *Overgeneralizations.* "Because I didn't do well on this exam I have no aptitude at all for this subject."
- *False goals.* "It is my job in life to make everyone happy."
- *Misperceptions.* "I never get any decent breaks."
- *Denial of worth.* "I'm shy. I don't deserve the promotion."
- *Faulty values.* "You have to do whatever it takes to get ahead, even if that means taking advantage of others."

You will recognize that many of these dysfunctional beliefs are also found in the cognitive theories previously described. Each of the approaches might have slightly different names for the thinking patterns, but they all address basically the same themes. One area in which Adlerian theory has been especially helpful is identifying and addressing core fears.

Core Fears

An Adlerian lens can be used to examine the most common fears presented by clients. Those that have been identified most often include the following areas (Carlson & Englar-Carlson, 2017; Sweeney, 2015):

Fear of being imperfect. One of our deepest, darkest secrets that many of us hold is that we are a fraud. We may even gravitate to helping others as a way to reassure ourselves that we are not nearly as defective as we really feel inside. To make matters worse, as therapists we are not often allowed to show our vulnerabilities and failures. Our clients and the public demand that we appear poised, confident, in control, and perfectly healthy in every way. This only contributes to the unrealistic expectations for ourselves that we cannot possibly meet.

Fear of being vulnerable. The more you reveal yourself authentically and honestly, the more likely that others will discover you to be inept and unprepared. We spend our lives pretending to know and understand far more than we really do. On the other hand, when we risk greater intimacy, we are more vulnerable to painful rejection.

Fear of disapproval. Everyone wants to be loved and appreciated by everyone else almost all the time. That may not be possible, but it is still part of the eternal search. The more you risk showing yourself as a real person, disclosing your true and authentic self, the more you put yourself at risk for deep hurt when others disapprove of you—or simply don't like you.

Fear of responsibility. We have each made lots of mistakes in our lives, giving us lots of reasons for regret. If only you could do things differently. If only you could make up for past errors in judgment. If you could start over again.

So, how can a person cease and desist from being ruled by their fears? With courage. According to Adler (1959), courage should not be confused with recklessness or foolhardiness; rather, it involves the strength to overcome a fear that should be overcome. Courage is derived from the French word *coeur*, and literally means to "take heart." Courage means being willing to take on hardships and dangers, while also being determined to endure fears if they are for a good cause (Sweeney, 2015).

Moving from insight about distorted perceptions and fears to action, the client is encouraged to make new choices that are consistent with desired goals. The first step in this phase is to identify clearly what it is that the client wants most. These goals must be realistic and reasonable. For example, a client who wants to become a good speaker but is trembling at the thought of making a presentation for work might be coached to act "as if" public speaking was great fun while practicing in front of a mirror. Later, this could be tried with a small group of friends (perhaps getting one of them to play a laugh track on their phone to bolster confidence and keep it fun). The rationale is that when clients begin to act differently, they begin to feel differently and see themselves differently—and so do others.

FOR PERSONAL APPLICATION and A CLASS ACTIVITY

Which of the core fears hit you particularly hard? As you review each of them, consider recent, specific times in your life in which you have struggled with these issues.

Get together in small groups of classmates—or if you are particularly daring—with family or friends. Talk to one another about your most deeply held fears, especially those that you rarely allow yourself to explore.

A Plan of Action

Almost any of the contemporary problem-solving methods might be used next in an Adlerian approach (Sweeney, 2015). Essentially, you would progress through the following steps:

- What are some possible ways that you could meet your goals? Among the alternatives, which one would you like to try first? Which one do you think is the best option?
- What plan of action could you follow that will get you going in the desired direction?
- What do you think about the results of your effort? To what extent has your plan produced the desired outcome?
- What would you like to do next that will get you even closer to your goal?
- What has been getting in your way and compromising your efforts to be more effective?

Because the Adlerian approach is both insight- and action-oriented in addition to addressing core beliefs, the therapist will not be shy in helping clients convert their self-declared goals into specific homework assignments or tasks that can be completed between sessions. Throughout every step in the process, a collaborative, supportive relationship would be used as leverage to keep the client motivated and making progress.

Strength and Flexibility

Lest you think Adlerian theory is primarily for adults in individual therapy, let us assure you that some of its favorite fans are avid parent educators (for example, Popkin, 2014). Adlerian ideas map especially well onto school contexts, as Adler often worked with the parents and teachers of children he was treating (Dinkmeyer, Carlson, & Michel, 2016; Nelson, Lott, & Glenn, 2013). They have also been applied to working with teens, and an Adlerian version of play therapy with younger children has been developed (Kottman & Meaney-Whalen, 2016). Adler was one of the first major theorists to practice group therapy because he saw individual problems as essentially social, and group work continues to be an important modality for his therapy (Sonstegard & Bitter, 2004). Fulfilling the long-standing claim that Adler was the first family therapist, his ideas have now been integrated in a system of family therapy (Sherman & Dinkmeyer, 2014).

The North American Society of Adlerian Psychology (NASAP) is a thriving group that supports professionals from many fields who use Adlerian ideas and publishes *The Journal of Individual Psychology*. There are more than 50 organizations and institutes that provide training in the psychological and philosophical tenets of individual psychology. Clearly, Adler's approach to therapy has stood the test of time.

Some Limitations

Although it might seem that Adler tried to include a little something for everyone in his approach, it is more his followers who have found ways to do so. You can find within this theory a little bit of everything that you will recognize from other approaches. One reason for this, of course, is so many other therapists have borrowed and adapted Adler's ideas for their own purposes. Another reason for this is that Adler was himself integrative in his attempt to create a theory of therapy that addressed the multiple domains of the whole person, existing within the past, present, and future. You could get the distinct impression from studying this model that it seems to wander all over the place, from attention to the past to a focus on the present, from a cognitive to a behavioral to an affective approach. We see this as is quite a good thing, actually, because the Adlerian theory gives you an overall framework wherein you also might integrate a host of other methods that appeal to you or seem potentially useful to your clients.

VOICES FROM THE FIELD

Doing "To" vs. Doing "With"

Today, with concerns about the effects of child abuse and domestic violence, as a society we are moving away from punishment, especially physical punishment, to discipline and motivate proper behavior and have instead replaced it with the practice of rewards, believing it is more "kind" to the child. Let's take a closer look at the use of rewards to see if you agree.

Suppose your spouse or partner came to you and said, "Honey, I have this great idea! Every night that you cook dinner for the family I am going to give you a sticker to put on a chart, and at the end of the month, if your chart is all filled up, I will give you a nice reward! What would you like it to be?" What would you be feeling? What would you be thinking? What would you be deciding about your spouse or partner? Or about yourself? Would you be learning the responsibility of cooking dinner for the family?

A common reaction to this scenario is to reject the idea and/or person because of feeling, among other things, demeaned, disgusted or confused, or saying they would cook the dinner anyway because it needs to be done. Some like the idea of "getting something." Some think, "That's a long time. I don't know if I could do it."

The above situation is what our children may be thinking, consciously or subconsciously, when we use rewards. It is appealing to "get something" for completing a task or chore, and because of this appeal, we can say that "rewards do work" to motivate, at least in the short term. However, what if the child no longer wants the reward, or wants a bigger reward?

The effect of rewards is usually time limited. The reason for this is that there are "hidden costs" to both the child and the adult who offers rewards. What are these costs? There is a little understood dynamic that occurs with the use of rewards. Rewards establish a superior/inferior relationship, creating a "double bind" for the child. Since the reward is appealing to the child, by accepting the plan the child agrees to be placed in an inferior position, relinquishing (prostituting) her dignity and self-respect. If she does not agree to the plan, thereby retaining her dignity and self-respect, she misses out on something she would enjoy and risks disappointing the adult or making the situation worse for herself by the adult. She cannot "win" in either scenario. The child loses respect for both the adult and herself. This is why rewards fail in the long run: no one can stand to be in the one-down position without compensating in some other way, usually through misbehavior or wanting a greater reward to make it more worthwhile, etc. And all this occurs subconsciously, making it difficult for children (or adults) to sort out what is actually going on.

The above dynamic can be described as a manipulation in which the child and the adult agree both to be manipulated and to manipulate as they each negotiate to get what they want. The "reward" is actually for the adult, because the child thinks, "If you give me what I want, I will 'reward' you with what you want." It is a dynamic that invites self-interest vs. genuine contribution, cooperation and problem solving to meet the needs of the situation: the keys to social interest and socially useful belonging and behavior. Another concern is the message conveyed by the reward about the task or chore. By making the reward the focus, the task or chore is cheapened, de-valued or degraded. It robs children of the opportunity to feel capable and responsible for the contribution they can make by doing something important and useful, and takes away from the intrinsic value of the task itself. Both punishments and rewards are done by adults to children. When we "do to" others, we are the ones taking responsibility vs. the other person also being involved in solving the problem collaboratively as equals.

Adler and Dreikurs emphasized the importance of feeling genuine belonging (connection) and significance (capability and worth through contribution) achieved through having choices, opportunities to contribute, by feeling recognized, by recovering from mistakes with dignity intact, and by being shown respect. Punishments and rewards violate these. Finding solutions together "with" the child encourages and empowers her to develop problem-solving skills, invites accountability with dignity, and ultimately builds relationships of mutual respect, the foundation of social interest needed for the betterment of the world.

—Lois Ingber, LCSW, Certified Positive Discipline Lead Trainer
Founder, Adlerian Consulting
lois@adlerianconsulting.com

REALITY THERAPY

Reality therapy is another approach that emphasizes an individual's thoughts, but it has a very different flavor from the approaches just reviewed. Reality therapy, also known as choice theory, has a straightforward, common-sense feeling to it, and it is big on personal responsibility. Everything in this approach is about addressing four main questions:

1. What do you want?
2. What are you doing (or not doing) to get what you say you want?
3. What are the consequences of the choices that you have been making?
4. What would you like to do instead?

When William Glasser first began exploring the nature of personal responsibility for one's problems, he was a practicing psychoanalyst, just like Albert Ellis and many of the other writers mentioned in this book. Just as Ellis got sick of listening to people whining all the time about how miserable their lives were, Glasser became impatient and frustrated listening to patients in the veteran's hospital blame others for their plight. He tried his best to help them to accept responsibility for their own problems by interrupting their endless ruminations and asking them instead to look at what they were doing and what results this behavior was producing (Glasser, 1965).

Next, he moved on to another tough problem of irresponsibility: addictions. Glasser believed that some type of addiction in humans is inevitable given our propensity for instant gratification, but he felt that positive addictions such as noncompetitive exercise and meditation could be reasonably substituted for negative addictions such as drugs or alcohol (Glasser, 1976).

After moving into the area of juvenile delinquency, Glasser found another difficult population with which to experiment by helping lawbreaking teenagers to be more responsible for their actions. He then applied his ideas to educational settings and decided that schools would be far better off if they focused on a success rather than a failure orientation (Glasser, 1990).

Aspects of this approach are clearly existential (emphasis on freedom and responsibility), behavioral (focus on specific outcomes and consequences), client centered (importance of an accepting, nurturing environment), as well as cognitive (clarification of internal reasoning processes). What is singularly unique, however, are the specific underlying assumptions of the approach, as well as the structured therapeutic program that is followed.

Underlying Assumptions

Several main ideas form the background for reality therapy that have been summarized by Wubbolding (2017).

- People are driven to satisfy their universal needs for safety, comfort, freedom, belongingness, power, and fun.
- We are also highly motivated to fulfill our personal desires, which are unique to each person.
- We become frustrated when what us are getting out of life is less than what us want or perceive they need.
- We behave in such a way to meet our needs and wants, making intentional choices that have particular consequences.

"Is That Working for You?"

Similar to strategic and solution-focused therapists you will read about later, Glasser was fond of asking people if what they were doing was working for them. (You will recognize this technique as it has been freely adopted by famous TV and radio therapists!) He noticed the phenomenon that people keep repeating the same self-defeating behaviors over and over again even though they were not producing desired results. It is, thus, extremely helpful to ask clients, or rather challenge them, to consider if what they are doing, the choices they are making, are likely to get them what they say they want and need most.

No Excuses

People are often unhappy because they are trying to control others in an effort satisfy their basic needs. From a reality therapy perspective, happy or angry emotions are important because they are signals that something must change, but changing our own thinking or changing our actions is the only way to get more of what we want from life. Essentially, clients need to take to heart the famous poster slogan, "If it is to be, it's up to me," and take responsibility for creating what they want.

In other words, commitment and follow-through are critical for accomplishing one's expressed goals. At the most ambivalent level, if people are asked how badly they want something, or how hard they are prepared to work for it, they might shrug and say, "I don't know." At the next minimal level, someone might offer instead, "Sure, I want it, but I don't want to work that hard for it. I'd prefer it just fall into my lap." A little more energy might be invested if the person thinks or says, "Okay, I'll try it and see how this works out." Quite often people are inclined to make lots of excuses for why they did not manage to do what they say is so important. In this approach, clients are not permitted to blame others, nor are they allowed to use any excuse for not following through on declared goals. Either you want to do it or not; the proof is in the outcome. Excuses and blaming others just gets in the way of progress.

FOR PERSONAL REFLECTION

In this excuse-making exercise, make a list of all the reasons you can think of why people would not have been able to accomplish objectives that they claimed were important to them. Imagine, for example, that you declared that you wanted to devote a significant amount of energy and time into learning the material in this book and class. When pushed to put your actions behind your words, you agreed that you would spend a minimum of an hour, four times per week, to reading about theories that interest you. (Okay, this was an ambitious goal.)

Now picture that you might have a number of excellent reasons (remember, you are smart, so any excuses you come up with would be good ones) for why you were not able to accomplish what you said you wanted to do. Consider the following excuses as possibilities:

- "I didn't have time."
- "I meant to do it but got distracted."
- "I couldn't help it."
- "Something came up I couldn't control."
- "I'll try to do better next time."
- "Procrastinating runs in my family."
- "I've always been this way."
- "It was just bad luck."

Now imagine that the very next time you amended your declared assignment, you committed yourself to the notion that there could be no legitimate excuse for not doing what you say you want to do.

The Therapeutic Process

Reality therapy has become a favored approach in schools, not only because Glasser (1969, 1990) wrote about applications for this setting, but also because the approach is rather simple to learn. He believed that if you could design educational institutions in such a way that they radiated a warm, accepting, supportive climate and at the same time you absolutely required people to be responsible for their choices and behavior, you could remove much of the punitive atmosphere that students find so pervasive. This would contribute to what he described as a "success identity" rather than the usual sense of failure that problem children experience.

There are basically four sequential steps to his "WDEP" helping process (also summarized in Table 7.3).

1. Ask the client what he or she wants. Explore the person's personal desires, goals, and wants.
2. Figure out what the person is already doing.
3. Evaluate the results of this action. Is it working?
4. What is a new plan that can be constructed that is more likely to produce desired results? The best such plans are highly realistic, specific, and completely within your own power to control (so there are no possible excuses).

TABLE 7.3. Steps of Reality Therapy in the WDEP Model

W—Explore bask **wants**.

D—Find out what you are **d**oing.

E—Evaluate whether it is working.

P—Formulate a new **p**lan.

Clearly, a strong relationship between the therapist and client that includes non-judgmental support is crucial to keep the client working on such hard questions. As clients devise new plans, some of them may fail abysmally, but the therapist and client simply get to work on a more feasible plan. Learning from mistakes is seen as part of the process.

FOR PERSONAL APPLICATION

Apply reality therapy's process to your own life by asking yourself the following questions:

1. What is it that you want?
2. What are you doing to get what you want?
3. How well is this working?
4. What excuses are you using to explain why the consequences are not as desirable as you would prefer?
5. What could plan you do instead?
6. How committed are you to making this change?

Strengths and Limitations

Like the proponents of every other approach, reality therapists enthusiastically believe that this theory works with almost everyone almost all the time; there are some aspects of its philosophy that you might find to be culturally and gender biased. Notions such as freedom, personal responsibility, and control are distinctly Western ideals. In other parts of the world and among indigenous peoples, values such as cooperation, interdependence, and shared responsibility are considered far more important than the North American emphasis on rugged individualism. However, some have actively adapted reality therapy and choice theory to other cultures, including an African-centered approach (Mickel, 2013).

Reality therapy/choice theory continues to inspire pragmatic innovations in interventions for people who are sometimes seen as challenging. For example, reality therapy was recently found to be helpful for older persons who struggle to make choices that fulfill their needs but also align with their dreams and wants (Sauerheber, Graham, Britzman, & Jenkins, 2016) and with women inmates (Grills, et al., 2015). With respect to the other end of the lifespan, a version of reality play therapy has been developed and has shown very promising results (Davis, Pereira, & Dixon, 2015). Essentially, reality therapy is straightforward yet flexible enough to be adapted to many settings, so therapists around the world continue to contribute to its evolution (Wubbolding, 2017). This pragmatic approach is likely to appeal to practitioners for some time to come, and its techniques are widely used in integrative approaches, as you will see in a later chapter.

FOR HOMEWORK

Taking action or putting ideas into practice is an integral part of reality therapy. As in a few other approaches, there is a strong belief that what you do outside sessions is far more important than what you do in sessions. There are people who can talk and talk, complain and whine, and state all their preferences and good intentions but never actually *do* anything to change their predicaments.

1. Focus on some aspect of your current behavior that needs work.
2. If your client was engaging in such self-defeating behavior, what would you say?
3. What excuses do you consistently use to avoid taking greater responsibility?
4. What is a realistic plan you have for getting your needs met more effectively?
5. What will you do when things do not work out as planned or when you feel discouraged?

In Conclusion

Because the leaders of modern cognitive theories drew ideas from Freud and Adler, and later interacted with one another on a regular basis and read one another's material, there is little doubt that many of the approaches in this chapter converged. Beck, Glasser, and Ellis sat on panel discussions together, listening to one another's ideas, debating their differences, and sometimes coming to consensus about shared points of commonality. Just as the cognitive therapists have been strongly influenced lately by constructivist paradigms, systems theorists have been integrating cognitive principles into their work. During actual sessions, it is becoming increasingly difficult to identify which approach a practitioner might be using because so many models may come into play.

VOICE FROM THE PAST: ALBERT ELLIS

This excerpt is from pages ix–x of his book, How to Stubbornly Refuse to Make Yourself Miserable about Anything *(Citadel Press, 2006).*

The three basic Rational Coping Philosophies that REBT stresses are these:

Unconditional Self-Acceptance (USA) instead of *Conditional Self Esteem (CSE)*. You rate and evaluate your thoughts, feelings, and actions in relation to

FIGURE 7.2. Albert Ellis

your main Goals of remaining alive and reasonably happy to see whether they aid these Goals. When they aid them, you rate that as "good" or "effective," and when they sabotage your Goals you rate that as "bad" or "ineffective." But you always—yes, always—accept and respect yourself, your personhood, your being, *whether or not* you perform well and *whether or not* other people approve of you and your behaviors.

Unconditional Other-Acceptance (UOA). You rate what other people think, feel, and do—in accordance with your own general social standards—as "good" or "bad." But you never rate *them*, their *personhood*, their being. You accept and respect them—but *not* some of their traits and doings—just because, like you, they are alive and human. You have helpful *compassion* for all humans—and perhaps for all sentient creatures.

Unconditional Life-Acceptance (ULA). You rate the conditions of your life and your community as "good" or "bad"—in accordance with your and your community's moral Goals. But you never rate life itself or conditions themselves as "good or "bad"; and, as Reinhold Niebuhr said, you try to change the dislikable conditions you can change, have the serenity to accept those you cannot change, and have the wisdom to know the difference.

REBT does not say that these three major philosophic acceptances will make you incredibly happy. They won't. … But your emotional-thinking-behaving problems will most probably be reduced—and so will your disturbed feelings about your thoughts, emotions, and actions.

What to do to cope with your own, other people's, and the world's problems? Make yourself fully *aware* of your own needless shoulds, oughts, and musts in addition to your desires and preferences. See your own (and others') irrationalities as clearly as you can. Dispute them realistically, logically, and pragmatically. Dispute them thinkingly *and* emotionally *and* behaviorally … Arrive at basic Rational Coping Philosophies, as noted above. Continue, continue, continue!

SUGGESTED READINGS

Beck, A. T., Davis, D. D. & Freeman, A. (2015). *Cognitive therapy of personality disorders* (3rd ed.). New York, NY: Guilford.

Bernard, M. E., & Dryden, W. (2018). *Theory, research, and practice of REBT.* New York, NY: Springer.

Carlson, J., & Englar-Carlson, M. (2017). *Adlerian psychotherapy.* Washington, DC: American Psychological Association.

Ellis, A., & Ellis, D. J. (2011). *Rational emotive behavior therapy.* Washington, DC: American Psychological Association.

Glasser, W. (2013). *Take charge of your life: How to get what you need with choice theory psychology.* Bloomington, IN: iUniverse.

Kottman, T., & Meany-Walen, K. (2016). *Partners in play: An Adlerian approach to play therapy.* Alexandria, VA: American Counseling Association.

Leahy, R. L. (2017). *Cognitive therapy and techniques: A practitioner's guide* (2nd ed.). New York, NY: Guilford.

Mosak, H. H., Schneider, L. E., & Mosak, L. E. (2012). *Life style: A workbook.* Chicago, IL: Alfred Adler Institute.

Neenan, M., & Dryden, W. (2015). *Cognitive therapy: 100 key points and techniques* (2nd ed.). New York, NY: Routledge.

Wright, J. H., Brown, G. K., Thase, M. E., & Remiriz Basco, M. (2017). *Learning cognitive-behavioral therapy: An illustrated guide.* Washington, DC: American Psychological Association.

Wubbolding, R. E. (2017). *Reality therapy and self-evaluation: The key to client change.* Alexandria, VA: American Counseling Association.

Wubbolding, R., & Brickell (2017). *Counselling with reality therapy* (2nd ed). New York, NY: Routledge.

IMAGE CREDITS

Fig. 7.1: Illustration by Liesl McCormick.

Fig. 7.2: PsychotherapyNet, "Albert Ellis on REBT Video," https://www.youtube.com/watch?v=QAwYVlkagMk. Copyright © 2013 by Psychotherapy.net.

CHAPTER 8

All in the Family: Systemic Approaches

LEARNING OBJECTIVES

After reading this chapter, you should be able to do the following:

1. Explain how notions of circular causality versus linear causality impact the understanding of relational processes.
2. Describe the contributions from several fields to the emergence of systemic thinking.
3. List key principles of systemic thinking used in family therapy.
4. Identify relational rules governing a family's interaction patterns that can be observed.
5. Describe specific theoretical influences on the practice of family therapy such as structural family therapy, humanistic/experiential family therapy, Bowenian family therapy, and multicultural family therapy.
6. Discuss common beliefs and assumptions that typify family systems therapy.
7. Review the key tasks that a systems therapist attends to when working with families.

Traditionally, all theories of counseling and psychotherapy were conceptualized within the context of a single individual's life. There may have been some attention to larger cultural or family influences within a client's life, but most of the focus was centered on individual development, maladjustment, symptomatic patterns, and responsiveness to particular interventions in sessions. It has only been in the last several decades that far more broad, alternative models were developed to better account for the ways that any person's problems represent issues and forces within larger systems. The whole idea of looking at a problem as an isolated phenomenon now seems rather quaint. We could make a case that today almost all approaches to helping must take into account the family and culture in which the person resides. In a sense, all therapeutic models are systemic from the perspective that they recognize and utilize the inter-dynamics of an individual in the larger world.

However, there are theories of counseling that were developed specifically with families in mind. And it will probably come as no surprise to you that there are as many different theories of family therapy as there are those designed for individual or group settings. That means, of course, another barrage of names and terms with which to familiarize yourself. The good news is that approaches to family therapy have more in common than they have differences; family practitioners tend to be much more cohesive as a group than do their colleagues in other specialty areas.

THINKING IN CIRCLES RATHER THAN IN STRAIGHT LINES

Representing a departure from the historically traditional approaches to helping, systemic theory sees human interactions as resulting from *circular* rather than *linear* influence. In other words, the usual way of understanding situations is that

1. the husband did something that *aggravated* his wife;
2. the teacher expected too much from the student, which *caused* him to overreach his capacity; or
3. the boss yelled at her subordinate, which *made him* feel inadequate.

Notice in all three of these examples, the verbs that describe what happened—"did something," "expected too much," and "yelled"—imply that the actions of one person *caused* the behavior of another. In truth, human interactions are a *lot* more complex.

If you think in circular interactions rather than straight lines of cause-effect relationships, then the dynamics of what takes place between people become a matter of continued reciprocal influence. This kind of thinking, in which behavior is examined in terms of mutual effects and underlying hidden forces, is an important part of all the theories mentioned in this chapter.

FOR PERSONAL REFLECTION or A GROUP ACTIVITY

Take each of the three examples and convert them into scenarios that represent mutual effects and influences over one another. Instead of imagining that the husband aggravated the wife, picture instead that when the husband came home from work and plopped his feet up on the table, the wife took this as a personal affront. Although he had hoped for, and expected, a warm greeting from his wife, she appeared cold and withdrawn. Before you blame her as the cause for their conflict, consider that she had been harboring some residual hurt from their lovemaking the previous night when the husband had made a comment that caused her to feel unattractive. Just before his remark, however, she had appeared unresponsive to something he had been doing to arouse her, making him feel inadequate. And then. ...

Well, you get the point: It is virtually impossible to trace back who is at fault or the cause of the problem because each participant in the process is both the cause and the effect of the other's actions.

Make up situations to explain how the other two examples might have resulted from circular dynamics.

THE EMERGENCE OF SYSTEMIC THINKING

There are several different disciplines that have contributed to the systems approach, making it the most integrative of all the frameworks. Many of the contributions not only come from traditional social sciences, but also from biology, physics, and mathematics. Even within the helping professions, contributions from all the specialties, including psychology, psychiatry, social work, sociology, organizational behavior, counseling, medicine and nursing, have all been instrumental in creating the family therapy approaches. This spirit of discovery that springs from transdisciplinary integration is seen in the work of early family therapists. It is also something we may see increasingly in the future. Here, we give you a quick tour of some of the key ideas that influenced the emergence of the systemic thinking that is so much a part of family therapy.

Natural Science

Lewis Thomas is a cellular biologist who specialized in studying ant and termite colonies, as well as writing a series of essays on the mysteries of science. In particular, he made observations about the ways cells are organized according to the same design as the larger planet (Thomas, 1974). In his musings about the ways that cells are structured, Thomas noticed that each of a cell's various parts—mitochondria, nucleolus, chromatin, endoplasmic reticulum—has a striking similarity to the components of a planetary body such as Earth. Thomas wondered if our planet is not just a cell in a larger organism and whether we are not just bits of floating protoplasm. In his classic book, *Lives of a Cell*, he wrote these words that seem particularly prescient now that we are all so connected by the Internet, Twitter, and blogs: "We pass thoughts around, from mind to mind, so compulsively and with such speed that the brains of mankind often appear, functionally, to be undergoing fusion" (Thomas, 1974, p. 98). You now hear this interconnectedness as "hive mind," which characterize how groups of people sometimes interact and influence each other through social media.

Such musings led Thomas to make comparisons between the ways that termites and ants communicate with one another, as if they are not separate beings but all part of one neurological system operating as a single, purposeful entity. These apparently whimsical hypotheses are all part of a general philosophy that led scientists to look beyond their own narrow disciplines to the underlying structures of physical forces. This is the same motive that drove Albert Einstein to devote his life to searching for general laws to account for physical forces. It is also part of the ways that scientists in almost all disciplines are now crossing traditional boundaries to borrow metaphors that help explain complex phenomena.

Mathematics

Of all fields of study, you would think that higher-order mathematics would be the most linear of all. Numbers line up so purely and logically in straight lines in which *A* leads to *B*, which leads to *C*. Everything you ever learned about geometry, algebra, and calculus only confirms the belief that the universe is orderly and linear.

It took a mathematician, Norbert Wiener (1948), to observe that not everything in the physical world does indeed proceed in a linear manner. Take the regulation of a thermostat, for instance, the favorite metaphor to explain a term we will say more about, *circular causality*. The heater is set at a particular temperature. When it receives information that the warmth has dropped below a threshold level, it kicks in to reestablish a stable environment. This happens in your body all the time without your awareness—if you get too hot, you sweat until you cool off; if your blood sugar drops too low, you find something to munch on until you get satiety signals from your stomach and your brain. Your body seeks to stay in a stable condition (homeostasis). This same kind of feedback mechanism also operates in the biological world of organisms (equilibrium) and helps explain what happens in families as well. Any nonverbal gesture, expression, or action within the family acts as both a cause of others' behavior, eliciting responses, and also the effect or result, from others' behavior. There are continuous, self-regulating feedback loops, which Wiener called "cybernetics," from the root Greek term that describes the person who steers a boat.

With the power of modern computing, it has become possible to generate mathematical models that capture multiple feedback loops to show how people in relationships influence each other "dynamically." It is even possible to predict the success or failure of the relationships based on particular parameters that can be introduced into a mathematical model (Gottman & Peluso, 2018). Perhaps this computing possibility will one day put dating services (and therapists) out of business! Or perhaps, as is their intent, these models will help therapists refine their focus on empirically determined aspects of the relationship that make the most critical difference.

Physics

Quantum physicists (see Capra, 1975; Zukav, 1979) discovered two important ideas in their work that sharply contrasted with the traditional ideas of Sir Isaac Newton. The first is that everything is connected to everything else; you can't study one little aspect of the world without including all the interconnected parts and the underlying patterns. Second, you can't study an object without influencing and becoming part of the phenomenon you are investigating (Becker, 2018).

Again, there are rather clear parallels between quantum physics and the work of therapists. The systems approach also believes that you can't look at anyone's behavior without considering all the interconnected parts. Likewise, once you enter the system to study what is going on, you also become a part of the family.

Systems Theory

There was a great scientific revolution in which some theoreticians such as Karl von Bertalanffy attempted to think beyond their parochial disciplines and unify all knowledge, especially with regard to all living systems. In his book, *Organismic Psychology and Systems Theory* (1968), Bertalanffy argued that when studying any sort of living organisms such as humans it was necessary to look at the bigger picture rather than just individual actions. Bertalanffy is still regarded as the developer of general systems theory, the theoretical foundation for many family therapies (Becvar & Becvar, 2018). Once you expand your window of observation, it becomes far more apparent that the behavior of any single individual is affected by the actions of others within that system. The functioning of the whole is, thus, far more important than the individual parts.

Psychoanalysis

It was Alfred Adler (1931) who first expanded Freud's theory to include family dynamics in the understanding of a problem. Nathan Ackerman (1937/1958), another psychoanalyst and one of the earliest proponents of family therapy, also drew attention to the power of families to shape the directions taken by individuals. He founded a family therapy training institute in New York and co-founded the very first family therapy journal, *Family Process*. Murray Bowen was another psychoanalyst who, in the 1940s, began combining ideas from psychoanalysis and systems theories by developing new language to describe complex family interaction patterns (which we will discuss later in this chapter). Just as with almost every other theory you have studied, the first generation of family therapy practitioners were mostly psychoanalysts who sought to integrate modern ideas and to formulate ways of doing therapy that were more useful and accessible, or at least better suited to their working style and personalities.

Anthropology

Gregory Bateson (1979) studied families with schizophrenic members as the context for those hospitalized patients who ended up "crazy" as a way out of an untenable situation. With an interest in both cybernetics and anthropology (he was also married to and influenced by Margaret Mead), Bateson noticed that communication patterns represented the ways that systems functioned. He observed that individuals' very subtle nonverbal and verbal cues acted as both causes and effects of others' behavior. Furthermore, he noticed that behavior caused particular reactions in circular, rather than a linear, way. *Linear causality* is, thus, based on the idea that one event or action elicits a particular response. In *circular causality*, however, influence moves in multiple directions at the same time. And sometimes, when problems are really entrenched, it can be a *vicious* circle!

Bateson gathered together a group of researchers to study the communication patterns of families with schizophrenic children (Bateson, Jackson, Haley, & Weakland, 1956). Composed of a cultural anthropologist (Gregory Bateson), communications theorist (Jay Haley), chemical engineer (John Weakland), and psychiatrist (Don Jackson), this eclectic group of scholars tried to decode the complex patterns of interaction that take place in families with a schizophrenic member. They noticed, for example, some intriguing mixed messages embedded in the communications between a parent and child with psychosis. Labeled as a *double bind*, the following scenario unfolds:

1. A mother warmly greets her hospitalized son: "Oh, honey, I've missed you so much! Come give me a hug!"
2. The son approaches as directed.
3. The mother squeals in indignation after being touched: "Not so hard! You'll mess up my hair."
4. The son backs away and starts to withdraw.
5. The mother punishes: "Now what's wrong? Why must you always act so crazy? Don't you love me?"

Under such circumstances, it was theorized that developing schizophrenic traits is a logical escape from an untenable situation. Putting aside genetic and biochemical predispositions to psychotic disorders that we now understand are so influential, this theory had wide application to many other areas.

SOME PRINCIPLES OF SYSTEMIC THINKING

We have no intention of confusing you further by adding another dozen theories to your already bulging list. After all, there are whole other texts devoted to this subject (see Becvar & Becvar, 2018; Goldenberg, Stanton, & Goldenberg, 2017; and Minuchin, Reiter, & Borda, 2014). Nevertheless, it would be helpful for you to become minimally familiar with the basic concepts that are universal among most of the approaches.

Circular Causality

As already discussed, the basic idea is that you think in circles instead of in lines. Instead of assuming that one person is the cause of a conflict, look at the way conflict occurs in the context of others who are pushing one another's buttons. This means that conflicts are always the result of several parties and almost never the result of one scapegoat.

Here's another example of the circular causality process: Unhappy and disengaged from her husband, a mother becomes overinvolved in her relationship with her young adult son, who still lives at home. In her obsessive devotion to her son, the mother neglects her younger daughter. The teenaged girl begins to act out for attention, while the son becomes less and less independent, staying close to home because he feels his mother needs him. The mother believes that the family problems stem from the absent father. The father resents this and becomes angry, withdrawing further from his wife, and sides with his daughter. This influences … Well, you get the point. Rather than a simple cause-effect situation, each member of the family becomes the instigator for the others' behavior. It is virtually impossible to assign blame or even identify who is the real problem. Furthermore, it is not useful to do so.

FOR A GROUP ACTIVITY

Working in pairs, take a few of the following cases of linear causality and make up scenarios to explain the more complex interactions that might be taking place as part of a circular causality phenomenon.

1. "My instructor is a real jerk. She terrorizes us with her unrealistic demands and ridiculously difficult assignments. We complain, but then she piles on more!"
2. "My father abandoned us emotionally. He was just never around because he didn't care about us. That's why I have such trouble today sustaining relationships with men."

3. "I did well in the competition mostly because of my coaches and the great training I received—they made me what I am!"
4. "I'm just not good at math or any sort of quantitative task because of the way I'm built. I've just never had a head for numbers; nobody in my family does. So, I avoid math classes at all costs!"

Now try coming up with a statement that shifts from linear causality to circular causality. Later, you'll help clients learn to shift their language and their thinking, too. For example, in the first instance, you might say, "The harder your instructor tries to engage you and your classmates, the more you disengage—and then the more she piles it on!"

In a future chapter, you are going to learn about a technique called *reframing* in which problems as presented by clients are redefined in such a way that they may be more easily solved. For example, you would have great difficulty addressing the issues described earlier because of the ways they imply that the solution is to fix the lousy instructor, traumatic past, or bad math genes. Go back and try to reframe these presenting complaints so that they lend themselves far more easily to therapeutic intervention.

In addition, when one person comes in for help, this client might be the one designated as the problem, but therapists should assume that the difficulty is part of interactive struggles. For example, whenever a parent calls for an appointment for a child, we always begin by asking both parents to come in first to provide background information. We tell them that we would like to get their perspective on things before we meet with their child. Although this is true to a certain extent, we've noticed that, more often than not, we don't end up seeing the child at all. It often turns out that the child's problem in school or at home was the excuse that brought attention to other issues in the family. So, as soon as they come in, we start talking to the parents about their child's problems and then shift to what seems to be an innocent question:

"So, tell us a little about yourselves."

They usually look at us quizzically and suspiciously, as if to say, "Why do you want to know about us? We're fine; it's Igor who is driving us crazy."

"It's just that we'd like to get to know you a little better to get some family background that will help us understand your child."

This makes perfect sense to them so we begin talking about their relationship, and before long we often drop the pretense that they are really there to talk about their child when it is apparent that they are the ones with the primary difficulty. Even when it turns out that the child really is the one with the greatest needs, it would still be useful to work on this issue within a family context because the child's behavior is likely affecting others in the household. The child's behavior is also being influenced by others in the family.

Rules of Relationships

Every family (and human system) has rules that guide behavior. Some of these rules are made explicit (e.g., "Take off your shoes when you come into the house") and others are subtle (e.g., "Don't talk to your parents right after they get home from work because they are often in a bad mood"). Some of these rules are very helpful in organizing family behavior, whereas others are extremely toxic and dysfunctional. When rules become so restrictive and rigid that they limit the options available and keep families stuck, then there is often trouble afoot.

As part of the rules that develop in families, a structure evolves that includes various subsystems or coalitions in which some members align with siblings or one parent in opposition to others. It is often easy to see these coalitions establish themselves as soon as a family enters a session for the first time (Simon, 2015).

During most family interviews, you will spend a lot of time studying and identifying the family rules with respect to the following areas:

- *Power.* Who's got it and who doesn't? You may want to realign the structure of the family, empowering members who have been marginalized or scapegoated.
- *History.* What are the family legends, myths, and history that still live within the family? Every family has narratives that were inherited from previous generations. Many themes from one generation play themselves out in subsequent generations. It is common to use a genogram (a pictorial representation) to map out the history of a family, including mention of any ancestors who had particular problems (see McGoldrick, 2016).
- *Coalitions.* Who is most closely aligned with whom? It is helpful to create a family map, which plots out the various subsystems, the levels of engagement or conflict among members, and the relationship of one coalition to others.
- *Hierarchy.* What is the pecking order of those in control? Power isn't only centralized in one alpha member, but everyone in the family has an assigned order in the overall structure.
- *Roles.* Who is assigned to which "jobs"? Members often end up in consistent roles as the "rescuer," the "distracter," the "trouble-maker," or the "helpful one."

FOR A FIELD STUDY

Get together with a classmate, volunteer, or partner to conduct a family assessment. Limit the session to 60 to 90 minutes in which you attempt to gather information about as many of the areas listed here as possible, including family structure, history, hierarchy, power, coalitions, roles, boundaries, communication patterns, and so on. Practice using open-ended questions, reflective listening, and other skills to learn as much as you can.

- *Boundaries.* How easily does the family allow interactions with others? Some boundaries are permeable, permitting influence and interaction from outside the system; others resist any sort of outside interference (making the therapist's job very difficult).
- *Enmeshment.* How overdependent are some members on others? Members sometimes fuse with one another, losing their separate identities in the process. There is a difference between healthy interdependence and overdependence (but keep in mind cultural differences).
- *Culture.* What is the dominant cultural identity of the family and the members? This involves not only ethnicity but the family members' religion, socioeconomic class, career paths, social circles, and other influences.
- *Communication.* How do members relate to one another and what are the rules for these interactions? Note not only the surface interactions but also the meta-rules, or what people are really saying to one another beneath the surface.
- *Life cycle.* At what developmental stage is the family functioning? The tasks of a family with an infant are different than one with a child about to leave home.
- *Metaphors.* What are the symbolic interactions that reveal underlying issues? Communication and interactions often are expressed as metaphors that can be unraveled. A wife can make her husband a dinner of successive appetizers as an expression of her desire for more foreplay in bed.

Obviously, this is quite a lot to attend to in a first family session, especially considering that you already have enough to do just keeping everyone on track and behaving themselves. That is one reason why family therapists like to work in pairs sometimes, so each partner can track different aspects of the session and then compare notes afterward. This also gives you a sense of how much harder conducting a family session might be, which is why it requires additional training and supervision beyond basic practice.

FOR PERSONAL REFLECTION and **A CLASS ACTIVITY**

Family therapists often use drawings or maps (called genograms) to represent the relationships and interconnections that exist in a family system (McGoldrick, 2016). During the initial interview, the therapist might ask a series of questions about historical legacies (family of origin themes), who is aligned most closely to whom (coalitions), who has the power (hierarchy), and sources of conflict (boundaries).

In one family of four, for example, it is determined that the mother enjoys a close relationship with her son and a very dependent (enmeshed) relationship with her younger daughter. The father is in continual conflict with his son and is often estranged from his wife, but he enjoys a solid relationship with his daughter. The maternal grandmother is also involved in the family a lot, resents her son-in-law, and sides constantly with her grandson and daughter against the father. Because family systems are very complicated, this is only a small part of the picture but it could easily be graphically represented in a drawing.

Make two drawings of your own family system, one representing the family you were part of as a child (pick an age that is most easily accessible), and the other depicting your family now. There are many genogram "how-to" instructions (e.g., McGoldrick, 2016) and even genogram software available online.

Get together with others and talk to one another about what you learned as a result of this exercise.

A QUICK REVIEW OF SOME OPTIONS AVAILABLE

Although we promised we wouldn't overwhelm you with excessive names and theories, it might be helpful for you to at least learn about the leaders in the field and the names of their particular theories and approaches (summarized in Table 8.1). Then, when you come across these terms or names in the future, you will at least have some familiarity with them. Additionally, many of these approaches have now been incorporated into what might be called *core family therapy techniques* and are integrated into the approaches of many practicing family therapists.

TABLE 8.1. Summary of Systemic Approaches

Systems Theory	Proponents	Focus Points
Psychoanalytic	Murray Bowen, Nathan Ackerman, James Framo, Christian Gostečnik	Family of origin issues; transgenerational legacies; enmeshed relationships
Humanistic	Carl Whitaker, Virginia Satir	Present experiences; fostering growth and development; authentic relationships
Structural	Salvador Minuchin	Family subsystems, power, and coalitions
Strategic	Milton Erickson, Jay Haley, Cloe Madanes	Interrupting interaction sequences and communication patterns
Multicultural	Derald Sue, Paul Pedersen, Allen Ivey	Cultural worldviews and identity; marginalization and oppression

Psychodynamic Influences and Bowen Family Therapy

We mentioned before that the first family therapists applied psychoanalytic ideas to sessions with multiple family members present. Many were analysts working in hospitals who became frustrated that their patients would relapse when they went back to their "crazy-making" families. Murray Bowen, Nathan Ackerman, and James Framo were among the first to look at multi-generational family patterns as a significant influence on present family problems. In fact, Ivan Boszormenyi-Nagy, another therapist of this persuasion, would only see a client if three generations of the family were present!

Just as you would expect, psychodynamically oriented family therapists look at the way influences from the past, or from multiple generations, shape present family dynamics. Murray Bowen, for example, examined the ways that couples' patterns of inter-relationship, including triangulation (when one person in a pair diffuses tension by drawing in a third person) and emotional cutoff (deciding to feel and act as if a certain family member doesn't exist anymore) are transmitted from previous generations. This was one reason he developed the use of a genogram to plot and trace family history in a systematic way. Bowen felt that anxiety is the driver of these problematic patterns. On the other hand, Bowen saw a "differentiated self"—one that is able to separate feelings and thoughts, instead of reacting to others emotionally—as optimal. The less developed one's self is, the more vulnerable one is to others determining one's functioning and the more one tries to control (either actively or passively) the functioning of others (Bowen, 1974; Kerr, 2019). The individual's family relational patterns developed during childhood and adolescence primarily determine how much self gets develops. Once established, the extent of self-differentiation rarely changes unless a person makes an extended effort to change it—which might include, of course, long-term therapy (Bregman & White, 2011).

In keeping with a trend we noted earlier about therapists sharing ideas and being influenced by others' approaches, some family therapists who trained originally in a systemic model are finding ideas from other approaches increasingly useful. As more and more information has become available about neurobiological aspects of regulating emotions, somatic experiences, and maintaining connections and continuity in interpersonal relationships, some family systems therapists are expanding their approach to include more *relational* concepts. Relational family systems theory incorporates systems ideas with the interpersonal and intrapsychic notions you'll recognize from psychodynamic systems (Gostečnik, 2017). This approach seems to be particularly useful for helping families heal from trauma and abuse occurring during childhood, as it supports individuals in confronting the residual effects of previous relationships within the current family context.

Humanistic/Experiential Approaches

Certainly, you would imagine that there would be applications of this framework to family situations. Individuals such as Carl Whitaker and Virginia Satir developed approaches that emphasized their relationships with family members. They presented themselves as warm, engaging, active, and playful. Carl Whitaker liked to use his personality in service of psychotherapy—he was warm, spontaneous, and had no problem with using self-disclosure and telling stories if his intuition suggested that it would be helpful (Napier & Whitaker, 1978). Virginia Satir was another charismatic leader who taught that healthy families are more emotionally open and expressive—and congruent. She developed the idea, often still taught in treatment settings, that under stress family members tend to fall into other roles that they learned to survive in the family: placating, blaming, being overly reasonable, or being irrelevant and distracting (Satir, 1975).

Both Whitaker and Satir followed the basic humanistic principle of fostering growth through an accepting environment while incorporating gentle humor and stimulating experience. Both were famous for "mixing it up" and getting families active in the sessions. Satir experimented with having members of the family stand up and create living "sculptures" of their typical roles or stances with each other. The idea is that we all adopt familiar habits of relating that can become exaggerated when we are under stress (Chi, 2017). As you can imagine, family sculpting can be quite revealing to everyone in the therapy room. This technique is a great one for intervening when no one wants to talk—or when no one will *stop* talking!

FOR PERSONAL REFLECTION

Both Satir and Bowen believed that the best kind of togetherness between people can happen when both people can also stand on their own two feet; know what they think, feel, want, and need; and share this information with others. Otherwise, people "de-self" to avoid conflict with another person—they don't speak up when differences arise—which requires the other person to use the crystal ball technique to infer what they are thinking.

Think of an incident when this dynamic was at play in one of your important relationships. What was erroneously assumed? What misunderstandings resulted? If each person had directly and honestly spoken up about their thoughts and feelings, what would have happened differently?

Structural Approaches

The ideas contained in this theory developed by Salvador Minuchin and others are now so basic that they have virtually become part of the standard knowledge base of the field. Family therapists often look at the underlying structure of families and seek to initiate adjustments to help members function more effectively. A person's "presenting problem" (the supposed reason they came to talk to you) is being maintained by the social context. It follows that by restructuring and re-contextualizing family systems, therapists can change the way families function, and in doing so, heal and transform individual family members (Minuchin, Reiter, & Borda, 2014). Dr. Minuchin provides an example of this kind of thinking in his book, as you see in the excerpt in "Voices From the Past" next. Note how, from the first moment, the therapist focused on detecting alignments in the system and strengthening ones that need to be strengthened. As he describes, often it is the couple's allegiance to one another that needs to be strengthened.

VOICES FROM THE PAST: SALVADOR MINUCHIN

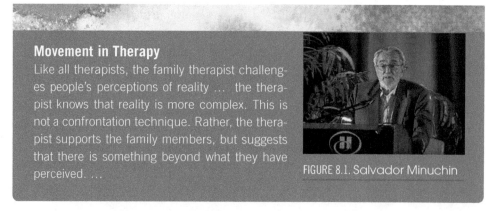

Movement in Therapy
Like all therapists, the family therapist challenges people's perceptions of reality ... the therapist knows that reality is more complex. This is not a confrontation technique. Rather, the therapist supports the family members, but suggests that there is something beyond what they have perceived. ...

FIGURE 8.1. Salvador Minuchin

For example, a wife makes an appointment for therapy because her husband has personal problems and also has great difficulty relating to their two sons. In the first session, the therapist sees the spouses alone. The husband says that he is the member of the family who has the problems. He describes himself as intellectual and logical. Because he is logical, he is sure that he is right; therefore, he tends to be authoritarian.

The therapist interrupts to say that a man who is so concerned with logic and correctness must often be frustrated in life. He criticizes the man for never allowing his wife to perceive the depression he must feel and never allowing her to help him. By this means, the therapist is blocking a well-oiled but dysfunctional relationship in terms of an expanded reality. His observation feels right to the man, who acknowledges his depression, and also fits the woman's never-expressed wish for an opportunity to support her husband. Both spouses experience the therapist's challenging, change-requiring input as familiar and welcome, because it recognizes the woman's felt needs and suggests some alternatives that are available to the man. The therapist then assigns a task based on his "yes, but." Under specified circumstances, when the wife feels her husband is wrong, she is nevertheless to side with him against the children.

The parents bring the children to the next session. The adults have performed the assigned task and feel close. The husband believes that his wife supports him, and she is gratified by the increased sensitivity and decreased authoritarianism he has displayed in response to her support. ...

The father, mother, and son are all repositioned by the therapist's interventions. ... Patients move for three reasons. First, they are challenged in their perception of their reality. Second, they are given alternative possibilities that make sense to them. And third, once they have tried out the alternative transactional patterns, new relationships appear that are self-reinforcing.

Source: Minuchin, 1974

Structural therapists view the family in terms of three components: structure, subsystems, and boundaries. Structure describes the repeated patterns that define family relationships and includes the rules that govern behavior and dictate the roles and functions. The hierarchical structure of the family, to which attention is given early on, is the framework of authority that determines how intra-familial conflict will be mediated—in other words, who makes the rules and who has a say (Colapinto, 2016). We offered you a list of the many kinds of rules that families developed earlier in this chapter. The way these family rules are enforced reveals a structure that ranges from having no flexibility (too rigid) to having too much (chaotic).

Subsystems of families are the coalitions created by the bonding of certain family members. For example, in a healthy family the parents maintain a united front to their children, not allowing them to play them against each other (which children will try with taunts such as, "You're so mean! Dad lets me! You don't love me as much as Dad does!"). The siblings can form a coalition, too, as every parent knows when the chorus of kids in the backseat winds up to chant, "We want ice cream! We want ice cream!" These are generational subsystems; there are other kinds, too, such as those based on gender ("just us girls") or on common interests ("the golfers in the family"). The important thing is that families have different kinds of bonds that come into the foreground at different times, and the parental subsystem is a strong and unifying one.

Structural family therapists also look at the *boundaries* of the subsystems in a family. One useful distinction is "enmeshed" for a family (or a subsystem) that is overly close and "disengaged" for a family in which members are too distant from one another. I (Marilyn) remember an incident when the idea of enmeshment gained new meaning for me. In my training clinic, we had brought a mother and son into the counseling room. We were preparing to observe the pair through our one-way mirror while they completed a parent–child interaction task. While we were just getting started, the mother reached over and began picking her 10-year-old son's nose! We had previously had some differences of opinion in the clinic (probably culturally based) on what constituted enmeshment, but we could all agree on this when we saw it. We were not terribly surprised to learn later that this 10-year-old was still sleeping in his parent's bedroom—and that strengthening the parental subsystem needed to be the first order of business.

Structural family therapy has been applied with great benefit among two types of families that gives psychotherapy its toughest customers: those with eating disorders and those who are poor, marginalized, or otherwise have a hard time accessing mainstream psychotherapy. You would be hard pressed to find a social service agency that hasn't incorporated at least some structural family therapy ideas into standard operating procedures for their family services.

Strategic Approaches

If structural theory examined the underlying patterns of the ways that families organize themselves, then the strategic family therapy approach developed by Jay Haley and Cloe Madanes was concerned with interactional and communication styles and how they could be altered. Because this theory is covered in a later chapter, we will only mention here that this is another model now universally used and incorporated into several approaches. In essence, after identifying the interactional sequence between family members, the goal is then to interrupt this pattern in favor of another means to communicate. The therapist is highly active, directive, and even manipulative, doing whatever it takes to promote changes. Interrupting a pattern requires a wily and creative therapist who can take strategic risks in the session of doing, and prescribing, the unexpected (Keeney, 2010).

Multicultural Family Therapy and Sociocultural Approaches

Although not intended as a *family* systems theory, there is a significant movement in the field to look at the change process on a much larger scale, which takes into consideration the societal forces of marginalization, oppression, and ethnic identity. If psychoanalysis was the first force in the field, behaviorism the second force, and humanism the third force, then multiculturalism has clearly been the fourth force (Jones-Smith, 2018).

Even if you don't find the notion of "forces" as particularly helpful as you make decisions about your future practice, you will certainly be taking into consideration the cultural worldviews and social factors of both you and your client as the context for whatever help is offered. Of course, factors such as ethnicity, gender, and other wider cultural influences and social structures are part of the system to which any given client belongs. But these can be subtly nuanced influences—ones that you will miss if you are looking only at broad categories such as race.

Here's an example: Suppose a family whose race is different from yours (you choose) comes to see you; the parents are worried about the 15-year-old son's Internet addiction. His grades have been dropping and he's been spending more and more time alone in his room. The parents are both highly educated and want their son to be, too—they want him to maintain the social class advantage they've worked hard to attain. The questions are, "How much privacy should a 15-year-old have? Who decides? Can the parents check his computer, or is that violation of basic boundaries? Would it be OK for them to go in, pull the plug, and say, 'That's it for tonight; back to your books!'?" As you imagined this scenario, did racial stereotypes and the need to set them aside come to mind? Most likely they did. But there's more going on here: The way the therapist *and* the family think about the issues of boundaries, family rules, privilege, gender, and parental authority will certainly impact the goals of therapy (McDowell, Knudson-Martin, & Bermudez, 2018), and these will be related to the *many* cultures to which these family members belong (including gaming culture).

FOR HOMEWORK or A CLASS ACTIVITY

Identify the most prominent cultural groups that are likely to be represented in your client population. Brainstorm a list of the most common minority groups in your particular region (for example, particular African American groups, Native American groups, Asian American groups, Latin American groups, or other groups that have been subjected to oppression and discrimination such as gays and lesbians, women, immigrants, or the economically disadvantaged). Among these various populations, select three that you know the least about in terms of basic values, dreams, identity development, and unique issues that may bring individuals from these groups to therapy. Interview several representatives of each of these groups, concentrating on what they would look for most in a good therapist and what negative experiences they have had in the past with helpers.

Get together with others and exchange information about what you learned.

Develop some guiding principles from what you have learned that you can use to guide you in your efforts to be more culturally sensitive and responsive.

From a practical point of view, all therapy has now become multicultural in its application. Regardless of the particular theory you employ in sessions, you must explore and carefully respect the client's cultural background, adapting methods to fit the person's ethnicity, religious beliefs, sexual orientation, gender, and other cultural factors.

A UNIFIED FRONT

Just as you would expect, there are behavioral, Adlerian, cognitive, Gestalt, and other approaches to family and couples therapy. There has also been a trend toward a single "generic" family therapy that blends the best of the accumulated knowledge in the field for use in a variety of contexts (Rivett & Buchmüller, 2017). The theme that stretches across all approaches is the interest in how problems between people are maintained and solved rather than in identifying a single cause attributable to one person (Nichols, 2017). In addition, all models tend to agree on the following:

1. Problems should be understood in the context of their family systems rather than in terms of individual experience alone. Individual problems represent larger family dysfunctions. This means that presenting complaints should be treated in a family rather than an individual context. Most often it is done with members of the nuclear family

present, although some approaches work with the whole extended family or even larger networks that include everyone who is considered important in the person's life. Even those who work with only one person at a time still employ leverage to influence the whole system via this identified person.

2. Change in any one part of the system will affect others who are interconnected.

3. It is more expedient to involve all family members (or as many as you can recruit) in treatment. There are exceptions to this as well. Some practitioners even prefer to conduct one session with everyone present to decide who has the most or least power in the system. Then, the therapist works exclusively with that client to alter the whole family.

4. All therapy is family therapy because even when you work with only one person present, you are still interested in altering the whole system to which the client belongs.

5. Just as the individual goes through a life cycle (toddlerhood, adolescence, etc.), so does a family progress through predictable stages (courtship, beginning family, infant family, etc.).

6. What you experienced in your family of origin while growing up shapes the way your family evolves in the present. Discipline strategies, communication styles, decision-making methods, and even family rituals were all once modeled (for better or worse) in your earliest experiences.

FOR PERSONAL APPLICATION

Look at your current (or last) intimate relationship with a partner, spouse, or lover. Consider the ways you relate to one another, how you make decisions, what you disagree about, how you resolve differences, and what you share as life priorities. Look at some of your daily habits and rituals that have evolved over time.

Now compare your relationship to the ways your parents interacted with one another. Before you protest that things are completely different, try to ignore some of the obvious things on the surface and look more deeply at the underlying structures.

7. Families (and other human systems) organize themselves to maintain stability. We mentioned earlier how this takes place around coalitions,

in which boundaries and hierarchies of power determine who has power and who does not.

8. Family structures exist in a cultural context, reflecting the participants' ethnicity, socioeconomic background, religious preferences, and other social and cultural identities. Two partners in a relationship must negotiate their respective differences, coming to some mutual accommodation. Their offspring represent a blending of the cultural heritage, even as they will be determined to create their own social and cultural identities.

FOR A GROUP ACTIVITY

In small groups, talk to one another about your own social and cultural identities (note, plural) that shape your family life. This includes not only your ethnic background, but also your gender, sexual orientation, socioeconomic class, religion, geographical origins, leisure interests, profession, and family legacies. Also, discuss some of the conversations, disagreements, or conflicts that take place when different backgrounds come into play with your friends or partner.

9. Human behavior is often triangular, meaning that invisible others are often covertly involved in conflicts between two warring parties. When two people are in conflict, look for a missing third party of the triangle who may be meddling, controlling, or otherwise involved in the struggle.

FOR PERSONAL REFLECTION

Think of a time recently when you were involved in an argument or conflict with someone else—a family member, friend, coworker, or classmate. It seemed as if the problem was only between the two of you, but assume for a moment that this disagreement was part of a larger systemic issue. Neither of you operates independently, nor do you function without being part of other behavioral patterns.

Going back to this interpersonal difficulty, think about how you may have been triangulated into a struggle that really involved others.

Back to *your* problem, however: Think of a time when you are fairly certain that conflict occurred in your life because of someone else's stubbornness, attitude, or behavior. Identify, as closely and specifically as you can, exactly what this other person did that caused you so much grief or aggravation.

Now, this next part will really stretch you a bit, so be prepared for some resistance. Pretend that *you* had as much to do with this problem as the other person did. We know you may not believe this yet, so just imagine that this is the case. Picture that this conflict developed not because of what this person did to you, but rather because of what you did to one another. Put fault and blame aside for a moment and concentrate on the circular pattern of influence that developed between you.

In the particular conflict that you are considering, avoid focusing on what the other person did that annoyed or hurt you and instead look at what you each contributed to the problem. Do this without placing blame. Simply make objective observations just as a mediator might do who was asked to step in and sort things out.

Notice how different the struggle looks when you move away from your usual vantage point and instead adopt a more systemic perspective.

10. Families and other systems get stuck in repetitive patterns that restrict their freedom and options to develop more fully functioning ways of interacting with one another and making decisions. In the course of identifying such family patterns, it is then possible to encourage needed adjustments.

FOR PERSONAL REFLECTION and A FIELD STUDY

What were some of the meta-rules in your family? Make a list of some of the unstated laws of your household that were never actually acknowledged overtly. For instance, my brothers and I were told not to fight with one another, but the real rule was just not to fight when our father was around. Next time you get the chance, talk to your siblings to compare notes on the unstated rules in your home.

11. Symptoms that emerge in families are often useful and functional, operating to maintain a state of equilibrium and stability. Often there is a designated client, the family member who "volunteers" to

have the problem to rescue or help others. A child, for example, may develop problems in school as a way to keep his or her parents from arguing with one another over their marital conflicts. A wife will become depressed as a way to punish her husband who needs to feel in control all the time. A grandparent will have recurrent physical maladies as way to keep his or her family together. In each case, these are not conscious or manipulative ploys; rather, individual presenting complaints are examined in the context of what good they are doing—for the individual as well as the family system.

FOR A FIELD STUDY

Sometimes we hang onto our problems because there are benefits to having them—these are referred to as "payoffs." "Payoffs" were often observed by nurses in their patients who didn't improve rapidly after surgery. It was discovered that patients were actually enjoying the benefits of being sick, liking the attention they were getting, and wanting to remain helpless so they could avoid returning to lives that were less than satisfactory.

Interview several people you know (or classmates) who are experiencing some personal difficulty. Start with the assumption that there is something useful about their symptoms, that they are serving some function (or they wouldn't continue).

Most commonly, people might "enjoy" their problems because of the following:

1. In a perverse way, it gives them a sense of power and control ("I am destroying things on my own terms.")
2. They are allowed to avoid responsibility ("It isn't my fault. Do you think I enjoy being in pain like this?")
3. They are able to procrastinate, put off action, and avoid taking risks. ("I prevent you from getting close and distract you from my issues.")

Help your interviewees to identify what benefits or secondary gains they might be getting out of their problems.

Try applying this same method to yourself when you become aware of some annoying symptom. Ask yourself what payoffs you (or your family) might be enjoying as a result of the problem.

Doing Family Therapy

The experience of conducting a family session is a little like running a circus with two, three, or more different acts going on at the same time. We have seen lots of videotapes of famous folks doing sessions and we are here to tell you that they look nothing like our work. We'd prefer to think that's because they hand-picked their best families for demonstration purposes. (Surely, they wouldn't show potential true believers in their system an example in which the family stormed out or started throwing things at one another.) We also think there are certain advantages to doing family work in a training center or university clinic (where they have recording equipment to make these demonstrations) when your colleagues are watching from behind a one-way mirror and can jump in to offer help when it's needed most or when doing co-therapy with them.

In our experience—we've both done a lot of family therapy alone, without the benefit of a co-therapist and a "reflecting team" behind the one-way mirror—it is quite challenging and it often isn't pretty.

There is a certain elegance to an individual session that is only possible because of the control you can exert. Even in group therapy (which is its own exercise in chaos), it is entirely possible to maintain a semblance of order. But families … let's just say that they can be *very* passionate and expressive. Despite your best efforts, they will scream at one another. Little kids will scoot about the room and paint on your walls, and all the while their parents watch indulgently. Sometimes they will agree to lie to you and you will have to use your best detective skills to get to the bottom of something that just doesn't add up. Sometimes combatants must be physically separated from one another to make sure that nobody gets hurt. And it is not uncommon that one or more participants will storm out of the room, slamming the door so hard your favorite picture will fall off the wall.

It doesn't sound as though we like this sort of therapy, does it? Or maybe it seems as though we're trying to scare you off. On the contrary, many believe that the wild and wacky world of family therapy is the future of our field. It is more consistent with the preferences of most cultural groups. It often produces results in far more dramatic and in brief intervals of time. It is also very exciting and stimulating. We like it a lot, and have seen great things happen, even though we come out of each session exhausted.

Notwithstanding this disclosure (which is quite different from how other professionals might feel), here are our general ground rules for those of you who want to jump in and try it:

1. The first thing you have to figure out is with whom you are going to work in the family. Generally, it is best to recruit as many members as possible, but sometimes this isn't practical or desirable. You can even include extended family and friends.
2. You have to join the family to make a difference from within. You must earn the trust of all participants, a tricky proposition when each person is competing for your approval.

3. You have to be careful you don't take sides (or are perceived that way) and walk a fine line so that you are seen as fair and objective.

4. You must maintain control over the session or you will quickly lose any credibility and leverage to initiate changes.

5. You must help members to redefine or reframe the problem so that the focus is not only on one problem member, but also is located within the whole system.

6. You must be highly active and directive to implement interventions.

7. You must look not only at individual dynamics and behavior, but also constantly assess interactive patterns within the context of the family's rules and structure.

8. You have to keep things moving. Especially with children present, you can't spend all your time just talking about things. You've got to do stuff, act out issues, and keep everyone involved and engaged.

9. You must get more than the usual amount of supervision with family cases because things are definitely more complex and volatile—and often address entrenched problems like addictions or family violence. Ideally, you will want to work with a more experienced co-therapist when you are first learning the method.

Stages in the Process

Most approaches to family therapy proceed according to a consistent plan that is similar to what you would do in individual sessions but may also be applied differently (Becvar & Becvar, 2018; Nichols, 2017). You must remember, at all times, that because there are multiple persons in the room, all with their own agendas, all communicating with each other at all times through nonverbal and verbal means, that the process and dynamics of what unfolds are as important as any content that is discussed.

First contact. A lot of information is transmitted during those first minutes of an initial session. Both the therapist and participants form first impressions that shape subsequent sessions so it is very important to be perceived by clients as accessible, knowledgeable, confident, and calm. At the same time that you are busy establishing that first contact with family members and connecting to each person in a way that is intimate and meaningful, you are also observing carefully where they sit in the room, with whom each person interacts the most and least, and what it feels like to be part of this group.

Joining the family. The next stage involves developing relationships with family members to build trust and confidence in your work. Unless you can join the family, you can't intervene in a way that will be very influential. This is a difficult challenge because each family member is hoping you will side with him or her and is watching you very carefully to see whom you favor or agree with. It is almost as if you are the new parent who has been "hired" and everyone is watching you cautiously and suspiciously to see what you will do. In this stage, you use your warmth, authority, and interpersonal skills to build as many connections as you can with participants.

FOR A FIELD STUDY

Interview several clinicians who specialize in family therapy. Find out how they like to work and how they take care of the challenges that have been previously mentioned. How do they maintain control in the room? What do they do if someone confides a secret but forbids them to tell anyone else in the family? How do they handle a family that is so enmeshed that some members are never allowed to express themselves? Find out what they like most and least about family work.

Assessment. This is where you form your diagnostic impressions of the family system, as well as that of each member. You check out coalitions, power hierarchy, communication channels, undercurrents, dysfunctional behavior, all in addition to the individual assessments of each person's strengths and weaknesses. What does it feel like to be part of this family? How do they behave together? How do they solve problems? Who seems to be in charge, and who is really in charge? What goals does each member have for a successful outcome? These are just a few of the questions you might consider.

FOR A CLASS ACTIVITY

Just for fun, do a simulation of a family session. Organize yourselves in groups of six. Three members of your group will get together and decide the roles they will play (mother, father, adolescent, or single parent with two young children, or grandparent, parent, child) and the issues they will present in session.

Two other group members will act as co-therapists. Your job is simply to help the family members talk about why they have come for help. You are not to intervene in any way with this "family" but merely to experience what it's like to work with multiple clients who all have their own agendas. You will need to keep people on track and stop them from interrupting one another. Help each person to be heard and tell his or her version of what is going on. You will also be doing a preliminary assessment.

The sixth group member will be an observer outside the group. Your job will be to take notes on the process of what occurs. Pay attention to the structure and dynamics of the family, the roles each person plays. Note the ways the co-therapists work as a team. Write down impressions you have about the session, being as supportive as you can. When the session is over, your job is to debrief everyone and lead a discussion about what transpired and how each person feels about the experience. Remind the co-therapists that they were not supposed to do a "good" job but merely gain some experience doing a family session in a reasonably safe setting.

Reorientation. Depending on the theory, this stage might be called a number of different things—reframing, reconceptualizing, redefining the problem, reeducating, accentuating the positive—but what you are actually doing is presenting your initial impression of what you believe is going on. This is a really tricky task because if there is significant disagreement with your assessment, you will be fired. Remember also that there are many different opinions in the room, each of which conflicts with the others. You also have to present your image of what is going on in such a way so that you can do something about it. Your first major intervention is redefining or reframing the problem in such a way that it conforms with what you think is most constructive and lends itself to be resolved most easily.

Let's take as an example a family that comes in consisting of a single mother, her own mother, her youngest sister who also lives with her, and her two children, ages 8 and 14. The younger daughter, Kalie, has been identified as the problem: She skips school and hangs out with gang members. When each person is asked what the problem is, they say something such as the following:

MOTHER: I work hard, so I've not been around as much as Kalie needs me. She just needs more supervision and there's nobody around to give it to her.

GRANDMOTHER: Excuse me, dear, but I am in that house more than anyone. What this girl needs is a good whupping. She's just got no discipline. You never taught her nothin' about taking care of her business. You just let her run wild.

TEENAGE SISTER: Well, I'd have to agree with you, Mom. But I also think that I'm sort of to blame as well. Kalie, we've always been close to one another and, ever since you were little, you've seen me out partying all the time. I think you're just trying to be like me.

MOTHER'S YOUNGEST SISTER:	Ya'll just bother Kalie too much. You should leave her alone and not make her do this. She's strong and she can fix this on her own. Besides, she ain't the only one with a problem in this family.
KALIE:	You got that right! Sure, I got a few problems, but so do the rest of ya'll. Mama, you've been bringing that lowlife home. He's just a drunk and he's gonna beat you like all the others. And you, Grandma, you just sit around the house and watch TV all day. You got nothin' to do but worry about others and get in their business.
GRANDMOTHER:	You hush now! You show me some respect.
KALIE:	This lady asked me my opinion so I'm just sayin' …
THERAPIST:	Go on, Kalie, and finish.
KALIE:	I'm tryin' to, if I didn't get interrupted. Nobody else got interrupted. See, that's the thing. They're always on *my* case …

I'm sure you've got a sense of the challenges involved in offering some sort of reorientation of the problem that everyone will accept. You want to move the focus off Kalie and spread the responsibility around to everyone. You want to stop each person from blaming herself or anyone else. And you want to define the situation in a way that you can do something about it. In this example, the therapist would, therefore, wish to make the following points:

- "You are a strong family who really cares about one another." Build on strengths and reinforce positive features.
- "You are all concerned about Kalie and her association with older kids who are getting in trouble. Kalie, you've admitted as well that if you don't start going to school, you're going to have a lot more problems." The presenting problem is acknowledged.
- "I also agree with you, Kalie, that this isn't just about you, that all of you are involved with one another and trying to help one another. For instance, Mom, you mentioned that every time Kalie gets in trouble, it takes your mind off your own troubles. In that way, she's kind of helping you." The focus is widening, taking attention off Kalie, and redefining the problem in a more systemic rather than linear way. This will win Kalie's approval because she doesn't want to be seen as the problem.
- "I'd like to suggest that we start working together, not only by looking at what Kalie has been doing, but how all of you fit into this. That way, we pull together to help Kalie and all of you as well." Notice the use of *we* to emphasize the joined effort.

Structural realignments. It is often necessary in dysfunctional families to make some changes in the ways family members interact with one another. This can have to do with the way decisions are made, the way communication takes place, or the underlying power structure of the family. With the family previously mentioned, you can see immediately in the ways they position themselves that there is some structural work to be done. The grandmother sits on one side with the older child. The mother sits with her sister. And Kalie sits by herself.

FOR PERSONAL REFLECTION

If you were the therapist, how would you ask the family members to reseat themselves in a way that would be more consistent with healthy functioning?

Intervention. The relationships have been established. Assessments and treatment planning have been made. Now it is time to do something therapeutic. In family therapy, perhaps even more than in individual therapy, it is critical to take action. This can involve therapeutic activities in the session as well as homework assignments. Depending on which family theory or technical emphasis is adopted, the intervention can involve an interpretation, a paradoxical directive (you tell the person to do the opposite of what you really want), a family sculpture (having members act out their typical interactions), or an assortment of other strategies. The key here is that you are beginning to help family members communicate with one another in more constructive ways and to initiate changes in the ways they deal with one another.

In Conclusion

Family theories and approaches are distinctly different from those that evolved from models of individual practice, even though they have the same shared professional history. Family therapy is more challenging than individual sessions—and some therapists thrive on this challenge. There is obviously less control, and a certain amount of chaos and conflict is inevitable when space is offered to air one's grievances. Longstanding disagreements and grudges come to the surface. Entrenched patterns, resistant to change, are evident. Whatever problems exist at home are clearly observed during sessions. Things can become quite dramatic at times, sometimes even a bit out of control. It thus takes far more skill and training to manage these experiences in ways that are therapeutic. And yet, family therapy can be remarkably effective for entrenched family problems, such as recovery from child abuse and neglect, teenage conduct problems and substance use, eating disorders, somatic problems, and first episode psychosis (Carr, 2018; Lebow, 2016).

It is clear that family therapy requires more training, more preparation, and more supervision than many other approaches. There are times when family members can't abide by the most basic rules of civilized conduct and the situation is too volatile to conduct family sessions. They are also times when family members are not safe if they are in a room together. No approach—even this powerful approach—is for everyone.

There are licensed family therapists who believe that family therapy is the way to go with every case. There are also clinicians who do family work occasionally, believing that it is best suited for those situations in which the nature of the presenting problem is particularly systemic in origin. For example, when individuals need to separate and individuate from their families, they may benefit from working individually to differentiate themselves from constraining and repetitive family patterns; at a later point, the entire family may be seen. There are other therapists who almost never see couples or families together, believing that you can do your best work seeing one person at a time. Still others have said that all therapy is family therapy, no matter who actually attends the sessions, because when you change one person, you end up influencing the whole system.

It is beyond the scope of this chapter to cover all the facets of systemic theory and their applications. That is one reason you will likely receive specialized training in family therapy, marriage counseling, sex counseling, or organizational development, depending on your career goals and professional interests. You will find it useful to consult additional sources at some later time to familiarize yourself more completely with the theory in this important discipline.

VOICES FROM THE PAST: VIRGINIA SATIR

One basic problem is that our society builds the marital relationship almost completely on love and then imposes demands on it that love alone can never fulfill:
"If you love me, you won't do anything without me."
"If you love me, you'll do what I say."
"If you love me, you'll give me what I want."
"If you love me, you'll know what I want before I ask."
These kinds of practices soon make love into a kind of blackmail that I call the clutch.

FIGURE 8.2. Virginia Satir

More specifically, if I do not feel I count for very much and if you and I have a relationship based only on love, then I can easily depend on your compliments, your attention, your agreement, your money, and so on to make me feel good. If you are not eternally showing me that you live for me, then I feel like nothing. This practice can soon strangle the relationship.

… Another danger is practicing the crystal ball technique. In this one, you assume that because someone loves you or you love someone, each should know ahead of time what the other needs, wants, feels, or thinks, and act accordingly. Not doing so is the same as being unloved or unloving. The fact is that no matter how much you and I may love each other, love doesn't tell me a thing about whether you like spinach or how you like it cooked.

I remember a couple who came to me because they felt very discontented in their marriage of about twenty years. As I talked with them, it became evident that each had tried to second-guess the other using the crystal ball theory: "If we truly love one another, we will always know what the other wants." Since this was their premise, they couldn't very well ask each other questions; that would cast aspersion on their love.

Their guessing had proved all right in a few areas but was now the crux of their being at odds with one another. They were not always guessing right. As we worked together, the couple accepted my invitation and encouragement to talk more openly. When we go to the part where I asked each of them to say openly what he or she resented about the other, the husband cried with a burst of emotion, "I wish you wouldn't always serve me that goddamned spinach!"

After his wife recovered from the shock, she answered, "I loathe spinach, but I thought you liked it. I just wanted to please you." … He then turned to her. "But didn't you notice that I kept eating less and less?" "Oh," she said, "I thought you were reducing."

This episode gave rise to a slogan they used when they realized they were crystal-balling: "Remember the spinach!"

Probably no other couple in the world has had this particular experience, but my guess is nearly all of you have had something similar. Looking back, such an incident seems utterly absurd. And yet it happens again and again.

SUGGESTED READINGS

Becvar, D. S., & Becvar, R. J. (2018). *Systems theory and family therapy: A primer* (3rd ed.). Lanham, MD: Hamilton Books.

Goldenberg, I., Stanton, M. & Goldenberg, H. (2017). *Family therapy: An overview* (9th ed.). Belmont, CA: Wadsworth.

Jones-Smith, E. (2018). *Culturally diverse counseling: theory and practice.* Thousand Oaks, CA: SAGE.

Kerr, M. E. (2019). *Bowen theory's secrets: Revealing the hidden life of families.* New York, NY: Norton.

McGoldrick, M. (2016). *The genogram casebook.* New York, NY: Norton.

Minuchin, S., Reiter, M. D., & Borda, C. (2014). *The craft of family therapy: Challenging certainties.* New York, NY: Routledge.

Napier, A., & Whitaker, C. (1978). *The family crucible: The intense experience of family therapy.* New York, NY: Harper Collins.

Nichols, M. P. (2017). *Family therapy: Concepts and methods* (11th ed.). Boston, MA: Pearson.

Rivett, M., & Buchmüller, J. (2017). *Family therapy skills and techniques in action.* London, UK: Routledge.

Titelman, P. (2015). *Differentiation of self: Bowen family systems theory perspectives.* New York, NY: Routledge.

IMAGE CREDITS

CHAPTER 9

Shift Your Perspective: Constructivist Approaches

LEARNING OBJECTIVES

After reading this chapter, you should be able to do the following:

1. Contrast assumptions underlying postmodern approaches with those of modernist approaches.
2. Identify the key concepts and assumptions of narrative therapy.
3. Apply techniques often used by narrative therapists to an interaction with a hypothetical client.
4. Identify the origin and assumptions of feminist therapy.
5. Review how gender-based societal restrictions and assumptions can negatively impact clients' mental health.
6. Describe the historical roots of feminist therapy.
7. Explain common themes and techniques often used by feminist therapists.
8. Identify distinguishing features and key concepts of relational cultural theory.
9. Describe the origin, major premises, and goals of solution-focused therapy.
10. Apply techniques often used by solution-focused therapists to an interaction with a hypothetical client.
11. Evaluate the evidence supporting each of the postmodern therapies, their strengths, and their potential limitations.

CONSTRUCTIVIST THEORIES

This chapter is somewhat different from those that preceded it because it offers a distinct way of thinking about change processes, rather than a specific program for implementing counseling and therapy. It offers a philosophy that takes into account the unique ways that people view and experience their lives and the wider world, depending on their cultural background, geographical location, gender, and other related variables. It also approaches knowledge and understanding from a highly flexible, fluid, and relative perspective, often challenging embedded cultural scripts that may limit possibilities and options.

Rather than seeing truth as a discoverable entity, constructivism suggests that people's sense of reality and personal identity are pieced together—*constructed*—from their internalized and personally interpreted life experiences. Similar to some of the other approaches you have studied, this means that therapists help clients critically review and challenge their constructed realities, offering the possibility of de-constructing and then reconstructing them differently.

Constructivist therapists work with individuals and families but also examine an even larger context for understanding human behavior: society and its pervasive influences. From a constructivist point of view, we are not only products of our families; we are also strongly shaped and influenced by gender roles, media, cultural identity, dominant language, and the stories we have consumed about who we are and where we come from.

This way of understanding may strike you as so obvious that it barely deserves mention. In many ways, constructivist tenets have been absorbed and integrated into every therapeutic approach, as currently practiced. Nevertheless, we find it useful to highlight these approaches in their own chapter since you'll find the concepts can be incorporated into virtually any other model, whether psychodynamic, existential, cognitive, feminist, and many others.

Constructivist Assumptions

One of the best attempts to explain a "pure" constructivist approach is offered by Anderson (1990) in his highly readable introduction, *Reality Isn't What It Used to Be.* Three baseball umpires are sitting around having a beer after a game, talking about their approaches to their job. "There are balls and there are strikes," says the first one with great authority and confidence, "and I call 'em the way they are." The second umpire frowns and shakes his head, offering his approach: "There are balls and there are strikes and I call 'em the way I see 'em." The third umpire scoffs at both of his colleagues and says, "There are balls and there are strikes, and they ain't nothin' until I call 'em."

The third umpire is what could be called a radical constructivist. He does not acknowledge objective reality except as it is perceived differently by each person. Balls and strikes are creations of each person's imagination, and although we can agree on a general strike zone based on operational criteria, they don't really exist as things. The second umpire, a more moderate constructivist, also views balls and strikes as extensions of his own perceptions. With humility and flexibility, he also acknowledges that others might see them differently. The first umpire, however, believes that things such as strikes and balls actually exist in the world and that everyone would agree what they are.

In a nutshell, the approach taken by constructivist practitioners and scholars is closely aligned with the second and third umpires. It is steeped in a philosophy in which all knowledge is viewed in the context of the language and perceptions of each person. That is an especially helpful stance for therapists to adopt because it keeps us humble, respectful of different experiences, and flexible enough to look at things from multiple viewpoints.

Several writers (such as Winter & Neimeyer, 2014) have summarized the basic principles of constructivist thinking as it would be translated into therapeutic practice. Here are some of the key points:

- Therapists have particular expertise that can be helpful, but they are not necessarily experts about the client's own experience.
- The therapist and the client co-create meaning as they work together.
- The therapist looks for strengths and resources the client can use rather than deficiencies and diagnoses.
- Therapy focuses on a better future for the client.

Narrative Therapy

One popular approach, narrative therapy, owes many of its underlying assumptions to constructivist theory. At first glance, it will not appear much different from other theories you have studied. It seems phenomenological in that it looks at people's inner experience. It is existential in that it searches for personal meaning. It is language sensitive, like the approaches taken by cognitive and Gestalt theories. It is often considered a feminist theory as well, because it looks at the ways that people are "colonized" and marginalized as a function of their gender and ethnicity. Yet it also integrates many of these ideas and makes them more contemporary by including them under the label *postmodern*.

The narrative therapy approach, originally developed during the 1970s and 1980s by Michael White and David Epson in their classic book, *Narrative Means to Therapeutic Ends* (1990), has since been elaborated by others (Denborough, 2014; Moschini, 2018; Winslade & Monk, 2008). These authors talk about a significant shift in the paradigm that therapists use to conceptualize their work. Such a transformation takes the following form:

MOVING AWAY FROM ...	MOVING TOWARD ...
Treatment of disorders	Collaborative conversations
Theoretical superiority	Co-construction of theory
Client inadequacy	Client expertise
Therapists responsible for change	Therapists as guide in conversations
Pursuit of the truth	Respect for client reality
Clients who are wrong or misguided	Clients who do the best they can
Diagnosis and labeling	Curiosity toward understanding
Problems that exist in reality	Problems that exist in language
Objective reality	Subjective perceptions
Reality as internal and private	Reality as public and interpersonal
Therapist knowing	Therapist not knowing

As you can see from this brief summary, narrative therapy takes a very different approach to helping. This can mean some real shifts in the focus of therapy. For example, I (Jeffrey) was taught my whole life (and subsequently taught generations of therapists) that the goal of therapy is to teach clients to accept responsibility for their problems rather than blame external factors outside of their control. Following the assumptions of theories such as reality therapy, Gestalt therapy, and rational emotive behavior therapy, I believed that there was a certain sense of empowerment that comes from taking charge of one's own life, ignoring what is outside of one's control, and focusing on only those things that are within one's power to change. This strategy has worked well in my own life and with my clients. I love saying to people, for instance, "You can't do anything about the past, the weather, your skin color or appearance, or other people's behavior, but you can do a heck of a lot to alter the way you choose to think and respond."

Sounds pretty good, huh?

Then along comes narrative therapy and turns everything upside down. In this approach, rather than teaching people to internalize their problems, the goal is to *externalize* them. This means that instead of saying to yourself, "I choose to be upset about this situation because of the way I am thinking," you would instead distance yourself from the blame. This separates the person from the problem, reduces guilt, counteracts labeling, and assists the client in joining with other family members and friends to defeat the problem (Monk, Winslade, Crocket, & Epston, 1997). The therapist would, thus, ask the client, "How did it happen that these upset feelings managed to first come into your life?"

If you understand the basics of theories already covered, then you can appreciate just how strange and counterintuitive this strategy must appear. Yet, externalizing problems is at the heart of what narrative therapy is all about. Narrative therapists help their clients to feel less stuck in their difficulties, regardless of the situation and setting. For this reason, narrative therapy has been used with great advantage in school settings (Winslade & Monk, 2007) and in family mediation (Winslade & Monk, 2008).

Neimeyer (2009a) describes his unique way of helping clients in the throes of major grief reactions to reconsider and renegotiate how they might view their supposed loss. Rather than seeing the death of a loved one as a "loss," he offers instead the perspective that you don't actually "lose" someone when they die; rather, you simply construct a different sort of relationship with them. They still inhabit your dreams and memories. Their voices still "live" inside you. They still whisper to you and even offer mentoring and guidance during times of trouble. Likewise, you still "speak" to them in your mind and heart. It isn't that they are "lost" or "gone," but rather they live in a different space, one that is still accessible even if it limits physical contact. We find this perspective both freeing and reassuring, representative of the sorts of creative ways that constructivists might think.

VOICES FROM THE FIELD: ROBERT NEIMEYER

In addition to my more formal writing for clinical and academic readers, I also occasionally slow into the sort of reflective writing that requires a less literal engagement with language to speak to issues and feelings that elude more prosaic speech.

The Art of Longing

This poem arose from a conjunction of events—the recent death of my mother-in-law, the last surviving parent on either side of our family, and my driving for hours through a deep Canadian winter to offer a grief workshop. ... The endlessly receding landscape evoked the landscape of memory and our yearning for return. The sensory pull between the strong draw of the past and my forward momentum found expression in the evolving imagery, and hinted at an essential tension in grieving.

> Those of us who have driven
> the long cold road alone
> have watched the thin line
> of trees, frosted white,
> slipping behind
> like memories.
> We know the pull
> of something unseen
> beyond the reach of dry eyes,
> fixed, blinking
> at the distant mist.
> We ride the road
> with our lonely ghosts,
> unwavering in their devotion
> like penitents at the altar
> of our grief.
> This is how we perfect
> the art of longing,
> learn to nurse the hurt,
> refuse the fullness
> of this world.

Robert A. Neimeyer, *The Art of Longing: Selected Poems.* Copyright © 2009 by Booksurge.

For now, we keep driving,
lean into the dimming light,
lean further toward
winter's receding horizon,
and away from arrival.

Source: Neimeyer, 2009b.

Stages in the Narrative Process

Among all the constructivist approaches, narrative therapy is perhaps the most developed in terms of an operating system. They have evolved both a set of therapeutic stages, as well as an extensive catalogue of techniques that help clients to consider alternative, more empowering ways of viewing their difficulties.

Externalizing conversations. The first step is to help the client develop an externalizing conversation in which all the family members are enlisted to join forces against the annoying problem. For example, a young girl is having difficulties with her eating habits, refusing to eat anything except white foods—mashed potatoes, turkey, bread, white chocolate (but no milk!). The therapist approaches the situation by asking the girl, and everyone else in attendance, "When did the white foods start to take over your eating?" By implication, the message is that this is not the girl's fault nor anyone else's fault. Instead, efforts can be directed toward understanding and solving the problem. Another way to do this is to get the client to write a letter to their problem.

Mapping the influence. This clever strategy helps the family explore all the effects and outcomes that result from having the problem (Remember: The identified client is not the only one who "owns" the problem; it belongs to everyone). This conversation helps the client feel heard and understood by everyone else, as well as invites each person to talk about the ways they have been impacted by the situation.

THERAPIST:	I am wondering, Laurie, how the white food restricts your life.
LAURIE:	Well, I can't go to many restaurants. And when I go to a friend's house, I usually have to bring my own food (white bread with mayonnaise and white cheese).
THERAPIST:	Uh huh. How else does it affect your life?

LAURIE: My mom gets mad at me a lot. I guess I understand, but I can't help it.

THERAPIST: I know you can't. That old white food just takes over so that you can't eat anything else.

LAURIE: [Nods her head]

THERAPIST: What about you, Mom? How does the white food control your life as well?

The therapist will continue to track the influences the problem has on each person in the family. At the end of this stage, each person will feel more understood by others and also have a better grasp of the ways that they are all in the same trouble together.

Unique outcome questions. Other theories call this "looking for exceptions." The client is asked to think about those times when she has managed to overcome or ignore the problem. In other words, the participants are encouraged to focus on the times when they were not controlled by the white foods. This logically leads to asking the follow-up question: "How did you manage to fool the white foods into leaving you alone so that you could eat the red gelatin?" This, of course, encourages people to examine the ways they have experienced success and focuses them on what they have done that works.

Unique possibilities. Continuing the style of "curious questioning," clients are asked to consider what things would be like if they no longer had the problem. "If you managed to defeat the white foods and make them cooperate with all the other colored foods, how would your life be different?"

This strategy helps clients visualize a time in the future when the problem is resolved. It is also a subtle way to get clients to suggest their own solutions when they are asked to picture a time when they no longer have the problem and then are asked what they did to make it go away.

Restorying. All these questions and therapeutic conversations are designed to help people change their narratives about who they are and how they got to be where they are. This is similar to cognitive therapies in that the focus is on altering perceptions of events. However, unlike these theories that concentrate mostly on internal dialogue, the narrative approach more broadly examines how reality is interpreted. As far as techniques employed, whereas REBT uses confrontation and challenging strategies ("Just because you have always done it that way doesn't mean you have to continue to do so"), narrative therapy prefers the use of questions ("What did that mean to you?" "How did you manage to resist the temptation?").

Clients are helped to develop an alternative story about their lives. Rather than naming the client's experience, using interpretation and reflective listening, attempts are made to draw out the person's own story, using his or her unique language. Throughout this process, the therapist adopts a stance of curious questioning, a position that encourages the client to create new narratives.

FOR PERSONAL APPLICATION and **A CLASS ACTIVITY**

Write down on a piece of paper (or in your journal) the dominant story of your life. This means the main theme that seems to guide your life, the one that is the greatest source of your self-identity but also that restricts your freedom and options.

Where did this story come from? Who wrote it? How did it come to so dominate your life?

In small groups, share your narrative with classmates. Practice using the stance of curious questioning to draw one another out. For the sake of this exercise, do not rely on skills of interpretation and active listening that you might use with other theories.

The Problem Is the Problem

The narrative approach is somewhat unique, even among the systemic theories covered in this chapter. Each of the models covered in this text, as well as those from other disciplines (science, philosophy, religion, social science), have different ways of looking at the problems that clients present in therapy. Several of the most common assumptions are presented next, each compared with the narrative approach at the end (Winslade & Monk, 2008).

Theory	Basic Assumption
Common sense	The person is the problem.
Religious view	The weak spirit is the problem.
Biological approach	The disease is the problem.
Psychoanalytic theory	The past is the problem.
Behavioral theory	The reinforcement contingencies are the problem.
Sociological approach	The family is the problem.
Anthropological approach	Cultural practices are the problem.
Narrative approach	The problem is the problem.

FOR A GROUP ACTIVITY

Using the contrasting viewpoints chart as a guide, structure a case conference in which each participant presents a different set of assumptions in looking at a case that is presented. Case conferences are usually both a means of quality assurance and supervision for staff. They are usually conducted by the senior clinician or chief administrator. All new cases are presented by those who did the intake interviews, and then everyone shares input about what they think might be going on and how this case might best be treated. In ideal circumstances, there is a lively exchange of ideas and then a consensus is reached about how to proceed with the case in the future. In less than optimal situations, heated arguments, power struggles, posturing, and showboating take place. After all, therapists have very strong opinions about the ways they think therapy should be done. And as you already know, there is not exactly universal agreement on the best way to operate.

For the purposes of this exercise, assume that you are all relatively respectful of one another, even though you have very different viewpoints. One person should be the client and tell his or her story about what is going on in his or her life and with what he or she is struggling. Then each "staff member" will take one of the viewpoints in the chart and present his or her perspective on what he or she thinks the problem is and what needs to be done.

Strengths and Limitations

In the narrative approach, like many other brief therapies, the presenting complaint is treated at face value as the problem to be addressed. There is no assumption that the therapist is the expert in deciding what is wrong, what needs to be fixed, and how this should best be accomplished. This offers a great deal of flexibility for the therapist to tailor the approach to the unique characteristics of clients and the aspects of culture and diversity that they present.

Many narrative therapists are applying narrative therapy in new contexts and to new concerns, including group counseling for stroke survivors (Chow, 2018), children and families (Moschini, 2018; Vetere & Dowling, 2016), those facing end-of-life issues (Goodcase & Love, 2017), and even in sex therapy (Watter, 2019). Narrative family therapy, a family systems variation of narrative therapy (Minuchin, 1998), is increasingly being used in wilderness therapy treatment settings for adolescents. In this (virtually) inpatient setting, the challenge of the wilderness experiences invite the teens to "re-story" their lives (DeMille & Montgomery, 2016). In addition to telling and re-telling their story, sometimes around the nightly campfire, the teens write and receive letters from their family in which both parties reconstruct their version of their past, present, and future together to be more appreciative and hopeful. This technique has the effect of slowing down conversations that have become too heated and allowing narratives to be recreated (Christenson & Miller, 2016).

Most famously, narrative therapy has been found to be very helpful for people who are grieving the loss of someone important in their lives (Neimeyer, 2016). A narrative constructivist approach can be of particular help to those experiencing bereavement and grief reactions to find meaning in their loss (Alves, Neimeyer, Batista, & Gonçalves, 2018). New investigations are exploring how narrative techniques can assist those who have lost a loved one to suicide find meaning in their experience.

We hope you appreciate how different this approach is compared to the others you have studied—and in some ways, more challenging. As a collaborator, the therapist cannot hide behind the role of an expert, and this fact alone can be confusing for clients who have different expectations. Because symptoms and problems are seen as linguistic constructions rather than immutable entities, and diagnoses are seen as potentially harmful labels that reinforce problems, therapists in settings that require documentation of these can find themselves in ethically and philosophically puzzling situations.

FEMINIST APPROACHES

You probably grew up hearing about feminist theory, since it has been evolving for several decades. Over the years, it has broadened and practiced as a therapy (and philosophy) that not only listens to, but *privileges*, the voices and experiences of those defined as "other" by dominant cultures (Conlin, 2017). It views many aspects of gender and power as constructions, rather than features determined by genes, biology, or simply the nature of things. So, as you might surmise, feminist therapy addresses inequities in the experiences of men as well as those of women.

Feminist therapists also acknowledge the wisdom and "know-how" in people who live their lives away from the designated power centers of a culture, rather than imposing the know-how of appointed experts to those who "need help." Applied radically, this perspective can turn everything about therapy as it is commonly practiced today upside down. What is the therapist, you might wonder, if not an expert?

We should also mention that there is not only one feminist therapy but actually dozens of them. There is liberal feminism, radical feminism, feminist postmodernism, feminist family therapy, feminist standpoint theory, feminist psychoanalysis, socialist feminism, and so on. Obviously, a feminist slant can be taken on any therapeutic approach. The common beliefs they all share are the following:

- Personal problems must be understood in light of their political and contextual roots.
- Issues such as freedom, independence, power, and choice have very different meanings in women's lives than in those of men.
- Traits traditionally associated with women have long been pathologized with labels such as *dependent, passive,* and *compliant.*
- Listening and nurturing have been traditionally been undervalued.

Feminist therapy has evolved from being a therapy primarily for women, where it focused on correcting sexist practices of the times into a postmodern, integrative model. The therapist and client together look at how gender, social standing, and power impact the client's difficulties rather than looking at difficulties as diseases or problems that belong exclusively to the client. Instead, feminist therapy looks at how social identity constructions based on gender, sexual orientation, disability, social class and socioeconomic status, race/ethnicity, and nationality are often unjust and therefore lead to distress or perpetuate harm (Enns & Williams, 2012).

In addition to questioning many of the philosophical stances of the Western world, feminist multiculturalists insist on the importance of addressing the practical problems that women (and children and men) of color encounter disproportionally in most societies (Conlin, 2017). These include the following:

- Intimate partner violence
- Sexual exploitation
- The well-being of sexual and gender identity minorities
- Health issues among women (maternal mortality) and marginalized groups (HIV/AIDS)
- Psychological perspectives on older women who have been traditionally ignored
- Disordered eating and body image as they relate to particular ethnicities
- Methodological and statistical issues in research with diverse samples
- Mental health of low-income women, women with disabilities, migrant workers, and immigrants/refugees

After reviewing this list, it is likely apparent that this is an approach to intervention that has social justice and human rights at its core—not just for women, but for all those who have experienced oppression. Increasingly, such a stand has been incorporated into all the helping professions in which we have an obligation and responsibility to support those who have been most ignored or marginalized, as well as to take a proactive stand against forms of racism, ageism, sexism, and the maltreatment of anyone due to their characteristics or beliefs.

FOR A GROUP ACTIVITY

A group of volunteer women (10–12) should form a circle in the middle of the room, surrounded by the rest of the class. Close your eyes and imagine that you were born as boys and grew up as men. Talk to each other as men about what you observe men talk about when they are alone.

Afterward, briefly discuss with one another what that was like for you. Then discuss how your lives would have been different if you were men. Talk about how (possibly) you would have taken different career paths, made different choices, gone in other directions, and how you would have been treated and acted differently.

A group of men should now form a circle in the middle of the room and pretend they are women having a private conversation. After a few minutes of doing so, share what this felt like. Then discuss how your lives might have been different, for better or worse, if you had been born as girls. Talk about different choices you would have likely made and how you might have felt greater freedom in some ways, but restrictions in others.

Afterward, invite the rest of the class to discuss what they observed, how they identified with the process, and what was triggered for them.

Gender and Mental Health

Shifting back from global and societal perspective to an individual perspective, it's clear that there are certainly some gender-based restrictions placed on clients every day. Both men and women are limited by their assigned roles in different ways. For women, the issues are rather obvious with regard to unequal pay, sexual assault, and other forms of oppression, but men as well often find themselves "stuck" in cultural expectations for how they are permitted to behave. One of the key contributions of feminist therapy is to draw attention to how these societal assumptions and gender-based expectations (sometimes more implicit than explicit) can be detrimental to mental health and well-being for those who are boxed in by them. Despite the ideal of gender equality, which most claim to hold dear, girls and boys are still raised differentially in ways that reinforce complementary roles and stereotypes (Jewell & Brown, 2014) but do not necessarily promote optimal mental health. Girls learn at an early age to get their needs met by using gender-based strategies that appeal to emotion, involve being deferential, and play on physical attractiveness. Boys learn to flex their muscles and suppress their tears.

This has important implications for working with clients. For example, think of all the ways that diagnostic impressions and labels can be gender loaded. Men who learned to be the "strong silent type" are accused of emotional restriction and written up for lack of empathic ability. Women who are very emotionally expressive may be called hysterical, and if they do their culturally assigned gender roles well, they may be referred to as seductive, dependent, or passive. Additionally, women are usually designated as the emotional caretakers in relationships, and they often come into sessions on behalf of others in the family. That is one reason such a disproportionate number of women will end up as your clients, not because they are more emotionally unstable than men, but because they are used to being the ones who talk about things while their husbands, fathers, and sons sit at home or hash things out elsewhere.

FOR A GROUP ACTIVITY

On the board (or in your notebook), make two columns, one label "Male," the other "Female." Include under each column all the words and descriptors that you can think of to describe boys and girls. Make the list as exhaustive as you can. To get you started, recall the rhyme of what boys ("puppy dogs' tails") and girls ("sugar and spice and everything nice") are made of.

After you have completed the list, talk about how these cultural expectations shape the sorts of problems that males and females develop in later life.

As should be clear, feminist theory is not just about women, for women, and by women. It is a liberating philosophy that frees men as much as women from their enculturated roles and assigned responsibilities. If the consequence of feminist action is that it results in women acting more like men in terms of power and opportunity, then they will start suffering from stress-related diseases with the same regularity as their male counterparts (and they have). At its best, feminist therapy liberates both men and women from culturally predetermined jobs and roles. For example, more and more often fathers stay home to take care of the kids while mothers choose the high-powered career path, even in cultural groups where this raises some eyebrows. While this frees the family from some societal expectations and constraints, it also has an impact on the career path (and likely the self-esteem) of whomever is staying at home with the children.

One very important point here is that you don't impose your own values or political action on your clients, even as you help them search for alternatives that fit them best. For every woman (or man) who feels trapped by gender and culturally limited opportunities, there are others who feel quite comfortable with their positions and roles. The therapist's role is to help clients examine priorities, privileges, and constraints and create the life that fits for them.

FOR PERSONAL REFLECTION and A FIELD STUDY

Imagine that a new client comes in to see you who has very different ideas about her assigned role in life than you do. Rather than valuing education and a career, she is a stay-at-home mom who is following in her own mother's footsteps. She is extremely deferential toward her husband and even her two teenage sons.

Her presenting problem is that she's depressed. You suspect there is a relationship between her symptoms and her sense of helplessness. Now here is the dilemma: How do you help her deal with her problems without imposing your own values about women's roles?

Find out how other therapists you know restrain their values when clients live very different lives from their own lifestyle choices.

Feminist Therapy

Depending on the client and presenting issues, it is often profitable to spend some time in sessions exploring the influence of assumed gender roles and social power on one's life decisions and choices (Schwartz, 2017). What is frequently discovered is that clients are thinking narrowly and with limited vision because of what they imagine is possible.

- "A strong man is supposed to take care of his family. That's what my grandfather and father always did, even though it killed them both prematurely."
- "I'd never thought about being a doctor. In school girls were told we had a choice of being a nurse, a teacher, or a housewife. Because I had no intention of staying home to raise babies, it seemed like being a nurse was the only way out."

- "I wish my wife would initiate sex more often instead of it always being left up to me. But I guess it's my job to do that. She's just not comfortable with that sort of thing. In fact, she tells me it's the wife's duty to take care of the man but not to enjoy sex herself."
- "I love kids. If I could have my way, I'd much rather stay home and take care of the house and children. But as the oldest daughter in my family, it was expected that I would lead the way career-wise, do something important with my life. I think the most important thing I can do would be to be a mother to my children, but if I tried that, my mother and sisters would feel so betrayed. They'd never forgive me."
- "I am usually the only male at staff meetings. Almost all the therapists are women where I work, and so are the clients, so, I feel like an alien sometimes. They are always making jokes about guys, and I have to go along with it. I'm really not allowed to express certain things or I'll be ridiculed. I actually prefer working with women, but not to the point where I have to feel ashamed for being a man."
- "I feel so ashamed about getting raped at the party. But I guess I asked for it when I had that extra drink."

So many clients have stories such as this in which their freedom and choices feel limited as a result of gender issues. Your job is not only to create a climate in which it is safe to talk about these things, but also to invite an open consideration of the implicit assumptions we have about ourselves, when appropriate.

You might still be wondering what feminist therapy actually looks like, since it is based on a particular viewpoint and set of values. Similar to all constructivist therapies, there is much freedom and variability in what the feminist therapist does in the session, because the main emphasis is on accompanying the client on a journey toward a greater sense of empowerment. Brown (2010) and others, including Velasquez and Velasquez (2017), highlight these commonalities.

1. Context is key; clients' issues are explored while keeping in mind the backdrop of their cultural and social context.
2. Oppression of all types is seen as harmful.
3. A collaborative relationship helps to prevent an imbalance of power between the therapist and the client.
4. Strengths are highlighted and problems are reframed, whereas diagnostic labels are avoided.
5. Diverse perspectives (even ones that counter the views of the therapist) are honored.

6. Social action is valued as an ultimate aim, though this is not imposed on the client.

To accomplish these aims, feminist therapists are likely to use the following techniques in sessions:

- *Power analysis.* Together, the therapist and client examine how being in situations of unequal power has had detrimental impact.
- *Gender role analysis.* The many ways that assumptions about gender roles creep in to our attitudes and behaviors (such as those outlined) are explored for their impact.
- *Reframing.* Therapists offer alternative ways for explaining issues and problems in more positive ways, highlighting client strengths.
- *Therapist self-disclosure.* When appropriate, therapists may briefly share their own experiences as a way to normalize what the client may be experiencing in therapy (for example, how frightening it was to challenge a professor regarding an unfair grade).
- *Social action.* Similar to Adlerian theory, feminist therapists believe that taking action to make life better for oneself or others is empowering and helps to promote a society where equality and mutual respect are the norm.

FOR REFLECTION

If you are still wondering what empowering a client might look like, consider this example of how a therapist working from a feminist perspective helped an adult client with Autism Spectrum Disorder face the painful bullying he had been experiencing by asking the question, "What is a powerful thing you could do right now?" (Brown, 2010). Dr. Brown asserts that this question is really the heart of feminist therapy.

Can you think of some other groups that would benefit from being more aware of the power they have in situations where they have felt powerless, and for whom this question might be helpful and enlightening?

What comes to mind when you ask yourself this question?

Regardless of the theoretical orientation you base your work on, you will certainly be expected to operate in a nonsexist, nonbiased manner so that you don't continue to contribute to the marginalization of women and other groups with less social power than others (including, for example, transgender and gender-variant individuals). What this means for your development, in particular, is that you must become aware of your own gender (and other) biases, regardless of your own background. Furthermore, you must be comfortable in constructing different types of collaborative relationships in therapy, depending on your clients' backgrounds and needs.

RELATIONAL CULTURAL THERAPY

Relational cultural therapy (RCT) is another approach that that has recently gained in prominence; it shares philosophical roots with feminist approaches in that it is relationally and culturally oriented. RCT seeks to reduce individual isolation and to increase connections by fostering *growth-fostering relationships* and *mutual empathy* (Jordan, 2017).

Several decades ago, feminist psychologists began lamenting the fact that mainstream Western psychological theories generally depicted human development as moving from dependence to independence, as you have probably noticed in your developmental psychology textbooks. In contrast, RCT is built on the premise that, throughout the lifespan, human beings grow through connections with others and need connections to flourish or even to stay alive.

According to RCT, isolation is a major source of suffering for people, at both a personal and cultural level. The quality of people's relationships mirrors their mental health; at the same time, relationships are what heal and promote mental health and wellness. Therefore, a primary goal is to create and maintain a mutually growth-fostering relationship in therapy and ultimately in the clients' life outside of therapy. Such relationships offer what is known as the "five good things" (Miller & Stiver, 1997). These include the following:

- A desire to move into more relationships because of how a good relational experience feels
- A sense of zest or energy
- Increased knowledge of oneself and the other person in the relationship
- A desire to take action, both in the growth-fostering relationship and outside of it
- An overall increased sense of worth

Another one of the core tenets of RCT is the central relational paradox (CRP). The CRP assumes that we all have a natural drive toward relationships, and in these relationships we long for acceptance (Miller & Stiver, 1997). However, we come to believe that there are things about us that are unacceptable or unlovable. (Comstock et al., 2008.) Thus, we choose to hide these things and keep them out of our relationships. In the end, the connections we make with others are not as fulfilling and validating as they otherwise might have been because of the parts of ourselves that we keep hidden.

The process of doing RCT involves working with clients to identify and nurture relationships that present opportunities for mutual growth and empathy. First, a strong, connected therapeutic relationship is created because it is a model for these kinds of relationships. In this relationship, a high degree of mutuality is encouraged. In other words, the therapist avoids the position of a neutral authority and instead conveys to clients that they matter. Ideally, both client and therapist celebrate the worth involved in offering mutual empathy to another person through the process of connection (Jordan, 2017).

SOLUTION-FOCUSED THERAPY

Steve DeShazer, originally a classical and jazz musician, and Insoo Kim Berg, who started her professional life in pharmacy and stomach cancer research, each started second careers in social work and sought out more training. This creative pair later married and worked to formally establish and explore real-world applications family systems theory (Berg, 1994; Berg & Kelly, 2005; Berg & Steiner, 2003; de Shazer, 1982, 1985, 1991, 2007), including working with children and families referred by child protective services. They also both helped to found the Solution-Focused Brief Therapy Association, which is still active today.

Like many others breaking away from earlier therapeutic models, these innovators operated very creatively and pragmatically, but with an essential difference: They based their work on constructivist assumptions. This meant that rather than taking on the role of an expert to fix the problem, these solution-focused therapists saw themselves as consultants.

One common misconception about this approach is that therapists offer clients solutions to their problems and get to give lots of problem-solving advice. However, this couldn't be further from the truth. Instead, this approach holds that the client is already an expert on the problem and just needs a little help to redirect efforts in more useful directions. The client constructs the goals for change. The therapist functions as an assistant in the change process, helping the client to plan and implement his or her own change efforts. Clients are held responsible for generating solutions, rather than for having problems. Solutions are constructed by using language that draws attention to the clients' strengths, progress, and solutions.

Major Premises

The theory behind this approach is rather simple: (a) If something isn't broken, don't fix it; (b) if it works, do more of it; (c) if it doesn't work, do something else (Sklare, 2014). There is no attempt to understand how and why the problem developed, only to fix it.

Although the solution-focused approach focused more on specific techniques rather than espousing a grand theory of change, there are several implicit theoretical assumptions in its practice that you will recognize (O'Hanlon, 2010):

1. It is an optimistic view of human beings and their abilities to resolve their own difficulties (similar to a humanistic perspective).
2. It keeps a positive attitude throughout, continuing to concentrate on what is going right rather than what is going wrong (similar to a strengths-based approach).
3. It remains in the present at all times, continuing to look at the presenting problem and its consequences (similar to reality therapy).
4. It sees the client's perception of reality as a constructed rather than an external phenomenon (similar to narrative therapy).
5. It continues to address limited, concrete, specific goals (similar to the behavioral approach).
6. Because change is inevitable and continuous, the best approach is one that capitalizes on gradual shifts and small incremental steps in problem solving (similar to shaping in behavior therapy).
7. Making a small alteration in behavior affects and leads to changes in other parts of the system (similar to any systemic approach).

Staying Flexible

The clinician adopts a very flexible approach to therapeutic work in this approach. Essentially, the following template is followed:

•   If the client completes a straightforward task, give another one.
•   If the client modifies a task, offer an easily changeable task that is ambiguous.
•   If the client doesn't complete homework, don't give more homework.
•   If the client does the opposite of what is asked, give paradoxical directives.

In other words, stay loose and flexible, altering your interventions in response to how clients behave. This may sound logical and reasonable, yet many clinicians stick with their favorite interventions regardless of the outcome. For example, my (Jeffrey's) favorite strategy is to use a skill called immediacy whereby I describe and reflect what is going on in the session as it is happening. This is an extremely powerful, evocative intervention and I love the way it brings attention to the immediate moment. But nothing, even immediacy, works all the time.

For example, suppose I notice that a client is beginning to withdraw just as he is talking about his problems with intimacy in relationships. I (Jeffrey) smile to myself because now I know I've got him red-handed.

"I see that right this moment ... [I pause for dramatic effect] just as you are talking about your difficulty getting close to people ... [I see a sick look on his face, which I ignore because I'm so enjoying this brilliant observation] you are pulling away from me."

In response to this insightful comment, the client visibly withdraws further. He actually leans way back in the chair and wraps his arms around his knees in a protective pose. So, what do I do?

I ignore the cues that are staring me right in the face because, after all, this is my favorite intervention, and I try another use of immediacy. In other words, I try *exactly* the same thing again, which clearly didn't work, because I am committed to this course of action.

"See, even now, just as I pointed out your withdrawal, you pulled away even further. You look curled up inside that chair as if I'm going to attack you."

I'm so proud of this immediacy, again I fail to notice that it is not having the desired effect. So I try again ... and again ... until I realize that we are stuck in a circular process that can only change when I demonstrate sufficient flexibility to back away and experiment with some alternative strategy.

FOR PERSONAL APPLICATION

Think of a time recently in which you were stuck doing something that didn't work very well. This could have been a conversation in which you were trying to get a point across. It could have involved something quite simple such as trying to unlock a door that was stuck. Examine the ways that you remained (overly!) committed to a favorite course of action even though it was not producing the desired effect.

What would it take to get you to be more observant about the effects of any action you choose, changing course when what you are doing is not working?

The hallmark of any self-respecting therapist is flexibility and responding differently to changing circumstances. Because such practitioners don't restrict themselves to one particular ideology, except to use whatever they can find that works, they aren't hampered by purity of application. On the other hand, they may be criticized for operating without much of an organized plan, like mechanics who don't really understand the complex mechanisms and consequences of their tinkering, but amateurishly try different things to see if they will work.

Discovering Patterns and Constructing New Ones

Everything that a person does, says, or doesn't do is a form of communication. Embedded in communications are also deeper-level, metaphorical messages that can be uncovered. These patterns, however, would not be interpreted or brought to the client's attention such as in psychoanalytic treatment. Instead, they are used as templates for interventions.

The therapist seeks to modify the repetitive sequences of behavior, especially those that are dysfunctional. To do this, the therapist must get a complete picture of the problem by asking their clients focused questions (de Shazer & Dolan, 2007; Sklare, 2014):

- When does the problem occur?
- Where does the problem occur?
- What does it look like when the problem is occurring?
- With whom does the problem occur?
- When, where, and with whom does the problem *not* occur?
- What are the effects of the problem on others?
- What behavioral examples of the problem does the client manifest during sessions?
- What is your view of how and why the problem occurs?
- What do you expect and hope will happen when the problem is resolved?
- What have you already done to try to resolve the problem?
- Among those things that you've tried, what has worked and what has not worked?
- How will you know when the problem is resolved? What will be different?

FOR A CLASS ACTIVITY or OUTSIDE ASSIGNMENT

Team up with a partner or find a volunteer who would agree to talk about a problem in his or her life. To make this exercise proceed smoothly, it helps if the problem discussed is one that is fairly specific. Using the problem definition questions as a guide, proceed through the list to get a complete picture of when, where, how, and with whom the symptoms are displayed. Take notes on what you were able to discover.

After you have completed the interview, which should take between half an hour and an hour, debrief one another by summarizing what was learned. Collaborate on identifying the patterns that emerged.

You can easily imagine structuring a whole interview around these core questions. Furthermore, you can probably see how constructive this systematic inquiry would be, for both the therapist and client, to get a handle on exactly what has been going on and suggesting what might need to be done. These questions can also help deconstruct the view of the problem that the client is "married to" at the outset of therapy, replacing problem-focused language with solution-focused language.

The Miracle Question

Sometimes called a skeleton key or crystal ball, this intervention is like a broad-based antibiotic in that it often works with a variety of complaints and situations (de Shazer & Dolan, 2007). Essentially, the device is used during those times when clients feel stuck or at a loss to come up with solutions to their problems. It is also commonly used as an assessment device to determine what the client sees as a satisfactory resolution of the presenting problem.

First, the client is taught a technique called "time travel" in which fantasy is used to go back and forth in time. "Imagine that you are living at a time when you no longer have this problem. Let me know when you have arrived at that point."

Once the client signals that he or she can picture such a scene, the next question follows: "What is different about your life now?"

Obviously, this is an invitation for the client to speak with great enthusiasm about how wonderful life is without the problem. It is likely that the person will mention things such as greater freedom and control, more contentment, and so on.

Okay, now the kicker: "Since you are now so happy and satisfied with having fixed this problem, what did you do to fix it?"

Not always, but quite often, the client will name exactly what needs to be done to make things better. The person solves his or her own problem by going into the future and then looking back at the present. Such a vantage point often frees people to be more proactive and innovative.

We are not saying this will work all the time, or perhaps not even most of the time, but the beauty of this approach is that you have the freedom to try lots of things until you find the right combination. Problem-solving and solution-focused therapists don't talk much about the therapeutic relationship, but the fact of the matter is that if you are able to develop a solid alliance with your clients, you will give yourself lots of latitude to experiment without getting yourself fired.

Scaling

Scaling questions are often used in solution-focused therapy as a way to help clients be specific about a problem and what improvement would look like. The therapist can use them to get the client to rate their problem, their hopefulness, their progress, or anything that might be helpful. The scale used is always from 0 to 10. Here is an example of how it is done:

THERAPIST:	So, Jake, let me see if I can get a better sense of how depressed you've been feeling. On a scale of 0 to 10, with 0 being unable to even get out of bed and 10 being feeling just fine, where would you say you are today?
JAKE:	Hmm … maybe about 4.
THERAPIST:	And where would you need to be in order to go back to work?
JAKE:	Well, I guess about a 7 or 8.
THERAPIST:	Interesting. So, you have a little way to go. What would be different if you were at a 5 instead of a 4?
JAKE:	I guess I'd have enough energy to take Fuzzy to the dog park. Actually, that sounds good … I think I could do that, maybe even today, after our session.
THERAPIST:	Great! It sounds like fun, and Fuzzy would surely enjoy the time with you. How confident are you that you might actually go, on a scale of 0 to 10?
JAKE:	I think a 9. I'm pretty sure I can do that. We'll see!

You get the idea—scaling helps clients be clear with themselves and helps you track their progress, too. In the next session, you'd follow through and celebrate Jake's successes, or come up with even smaller steps if he was unsuccessful. Once he got to a 7 or 8 and went back to work, you'd declare that his progress was "good enough" and suggest that he is ready to graduate from therapy.

Strengths and Limitations

Therapists who use solution-focused therapy are typically aware of its limitations. Sometimes, the name of this approach leads astray those new practitioners who are eager to give clients advice and tell them what to do and think they have found their ideal theoretical home (when nothing could be further than the spirit of this therapy!)

Because it is usually done in just a few sessions, you can't get too attached to seeing how clients change or develop over time. Sometimes clients sense that they need to demonstrate success quickly, and they might not be forthright about lingering issues that trouble them. Often, you are left wondering if the "miracle" endured.

At the same time, solution-focused therapy offers much to the therapist's toolbox. It is generally well received by clients and is adaptable across an array of cultures (Kim, 2013). It is practical and helpful in school settings, where brief resolutions to problems are prized (Sklare, 2014). It has been used to address an array of client concern, including suicidality (Henden, 2017). Many of its techniques are easily adapted for integration into other approaches and have been supported by research as effective (Franklin, Zhang, Froerer, & Johnson, 2017).

SOME FINAL THOUGHTS

You'll recall that at the beginning of this chapter, we mentioned that constructivist tenets are so much a part of current widely held views of how the world works that they have been absorbed and integrated into nearly every counseling approach. Shifting one's perspective has come to be regarded as one of the first things one needs to do when approaching a problem—and this is true in therapy as well as other aspects of life. In terms of approaches for clients, counselors and clients around the world are adapting the theories in this chapter for use with many different client populations and then testing them out in specific research studies, often with good results. Constructivist assumptions mean that these theories are ready-made for adaptation to unique clients and problems around the world.

SUGGESTED READINGS

Brown, L. S. (2010). *Feminist therapy.* Washington, DC: American Psychological Association.

Denborough, D. (2014). *Retelling the stories of our lives: Everyday narrative therapy to draw inspiration and transform experience.* New York, NY: Norton.

de Shazer, D., & Dolan, Y. (2007). *More than miracles: The state of the art of solution-focused brief therapy*. New York, NY: Taylor & Francis.

Jordan, J. V. (2017). *Relational cultural therapy*. Washington, DC: American Psychological Association.

Kim, J. S. (2013). *Solution-focused brief therapy: A multicultural approach to working with minority clients*. Thousand Oaks, CA: Sage.

Madigan, S. (2011). *Narrative therapy*. Washington, DC: American Psychological Association.

Miller, J. B., & Stiver, I. (1997). *The healing connection: How women form relationships in therapy and in life*. Boston, MA: Beacon Press.

Moschini, L. B. (2018). *Art, play, and narrative therapy: Using metaphor to enrich your clinical practice*. New York, NY: Routledge.

Neimeyer, R. A. (2009a). *Constructivist psychotherapy*. New York, NY: Routledge.

Neimeyer, R. A. (Ed.) (2016). *Techniques of grief therapy: Assessment and intervention*. New York, NY: Routledge.

Schwartz, J. (2017). *Counseling women across the lifespan: Empowerment, advocacy, and intervention*. New York, NY: Springer.

Sklare, G. (2014). *Brief counseling that works: A solution-focused approach for school counselors and administrators* (3rd ed.). Thousand Oaks, CA: SAGE.

Vetere, A., & Dowling, E. (Eds.). (2016). *Narrative therapies with children and their families: A practitioner's guide to concepts and approaches*. New York, NY: Taylor & Francis.

Watter, D. N. (2019). *Narrative sex therapy: Using patients' stories to inform practice*. New York, NY: Springer.

White, M. (2011). *Narrative practice: Continuing the conversation*. New York, NY: Norton.

CHAPTER 10

Brief and Action-Oriented Approaches: Just Do It

LEARNING OBJECTIVES

After reading this chapter, you should be able to do the following:

1. Review the historical influences that led practitioners to shorten the length of psychotherapeutic treatment.
2. Contrast the psychotherapeutic treatment goals of insight versus action.
3. Describe the influences of Ericksonian ideas on strategies of psychotherapeutic treatment.
4. List key techniques often used by strategic therapists.
5. Discuss the advantages and limitations of single-session therapy and its best candidates.
6. Review the dimensions of clients' readiness for change.
7. Describe how key practices of therapists using motivational interviewing are applied to clients in various stages of readiness for change.
8. Describe feedback-informed treatment and its relationship to traditional theoretical approaches.
9. Evaluate the evidence supporting brief therapies, their strengths, and their potential limitations.

Any theory that you have already studied most likely has an abbreviated version that is designed for brief intervention. In fact, brief forms of therapy are now so common they have virtually replaced traditional medium or long-term approaches that took months—or even years—to produce results. Challenging economic times, reduced budgets, increased caseloads, and pressure from funding agencies have virtually required therapists to shorten their treatments significantly, getting the client right into action.

Even those approaches that were originally conceived as long-term therapies have since been recast as more efficient models that can make a difference in a matter of weeks rather than years. As the most dramatic example of this, psychoanalytic approaches have traditionally taken years of treatment to be considered effective, whereas now there have been models designed to produce results in a matter of months or even weeks (Hobson, 2016; Levenson, 2017). The same pattern has followed course for other insight-oriented approaches, as well as cognitive, constructivist, and systemic approaches.

At one time it was thought that to do "good" therapy, meaning the kind that deals with underlying issues and long-term gains, the process must necessarily take considerable time, so that a client's insight about problems could emerge and eventually be translated into new ways of being in the world. The idea was that it took many experiences over a matter of years to influence the structure of someone's personality or cognitive schemas, so it could logically take many more experiences over a matter of years for a person to change—become less suspicious, more even-tempered, more trusting, more interested in self and others, and so forth. However, some therapists began reporting dramatic and enduring results within a matter of weeks rather than years. Sometimes, even a single encounter was life altering, leading to clients doing something strikingly different in their lives.

FOR PERSONAL REFLECTION

Think about a time in your life in which your life course was irrevocably changed as a result of a single conversation or encounter. One minute you were merrily going about your normal life, doing the same things you always do, and then—wham!—things no longer seemed the same and you set off on new courses of action.

What was it about this experience that was so impactful, not only in the short run, but over the long haul? What did you do differently as a result of the experience? How was it possible for you to make changes in your life in such a short period of time?

BRIEF THERAPY DEFINED

In today's world, everyone seems to be in a hurry. There is speed dating, speed yoga, and the "three-minute manager," so naturally there would be a demand for brief therapy that is time limited and efficient. It turns out that several decades of development and carefully documented studies have demonstrated that treatment doesn't have be lengthy to be effective. Yet, what is considered "brief" is relative and contextual. To someone in prison, whether metaphorically or physically locked in a cell, each minute can pass with excruciating slowness. Similarly, for some clients, the prospect of waiting months, or even weeks, for relief of symptoms may seem like a life sentence with no hope of parole.

Any number of therapists and counselors may promise to do brief treatment, but their claims may be based on a relative standard that depends on their own perceptions of swiftness. Some therapists who specialize in psychodynamic treatment may see their clients for six months and consider that "brief" compared to the standard Freudian practice of a half dozen years. Other clinicians who work in public agencies with long waiting lists may consider more than five sessions to be beyond their scope of practice.

Brief therapy is defined not so much by the exact number of sessions (ranging from three to 20) but whether the time parameters are established from the outset. In addition, there is usually a specific focus and rather defined treatment goals. Clients are usually screened carefully as to their suitability for limited sessions, usually those who present acute, specific symptoms rather than chronic conditions. Finally, clients must be sufficiently motivated and ready to move forward rather than first work through significant resistance and ambivalence.

Any theoretical approach can be abbreviated according to these preconditions. How quickly you operate depends on where you work, with whom you work, and the demands of the job.

The Theory Behind Brief Therapies

Brief therapists are often highly strategic and problem focused, believing that such resolutions are not only possible, but also within reach in a reasonable amount of time. Obviously, that means there is less time spent talking about how and why the difficulties developed, instead narrowing their efforts toward constructive actions. Instead of delving deeply into the past, explorations are aimed at uncovering the current factors that sustain the problems and prevent change from occurring.

There is no singular step-by-step process for doing brief therapy; instead, there are a number of techniques and strategies that can be tried. There's an underlying belief that therapists can be far more innovative, experimental, and creative in their approach, sometimes doing what is unexpected to disrupt entrenched patterns. This means the client's well-rehearsed story about the problem can be shifted, and whatever other forces are holding the problem in place can be altered, allowing them to dissipate in relatively short order.

Not all the proponents of brief methods are enamored with the value of theory in the first place. Some practitioners find that rigid conceptual frameworks can get in the way of being more pragmatic and flexible. If you remember, however, that a theory is not an exact blueprint but rather a rough guide to follow, you can appreciate that everyone needs such a model to make good decisions about what you believe is going on, what you think needs to be done, and how you might best go about taking care of business. Although some of the brief models examined here tend to downplay theory in lieu of best practices that work, you would be well advised as beginners to do more than merely learn a set of clever interventions and techniques.

Any of the brief or action-oriented approaches presented in this chapter could be useful to you as a guiding framework, or combined with any of the others we reviewed earlier. Of course, you will notice some contradictions among them, as well as some outright opposing forces, but these can be worked through if you keep an open mind and nimble attitude.

FOR A FIELD STUDY

Identify several practitioners who do mostly long-term work, meaning that they see people for longer than a few weeks and sometimes up to several years. You will find these professionals mostly in private practice, but some may work in mental health and community agencies that have a flexible policy or more disturbed client populations. You will also find them more among psychiatrists, psychologists, and social workers than you will among family therapists and counselors, but much depends on their type of job and training.

Despite their preference for doing long-term therapy, it is likely that they are also frequently called on to do brief interventions with clients who can only come for a few sessions. Find out how they adapt their theory and methods to fit the demands of this type of work.

Rather than just speaking hypothetically, ask for specific case examples in which someone came in for only one or two sessions, and this was the plan agreed on from the beginning. How did the clinician reconcile this brief relationship with his or her dominant theory?

In this chapter, we review only those therapeutic models that were originally designed as brief, action-oriented treatments. These time-limited models fall into several main groups: Ericksonian hypnotherapy, strategic therapy, single-session therapy, and the motivational interviewing approach. We should also remind you that there's a version of solution-focused therapy that emphasizes that it is *brief* solution-focused therapy, which we described in the previous chapter. There are also many others we could mention such as problem-solving therapy, behavioral self-control training, and, depth-oriented brief therapy, but what they all have in common is an emphasis on efficiency and symptom reduction within limited time parameters. Each of these frameworks provides the practitioner with a fairly structured plan for what to do during sessions, and this is useful when time is limited. They are certainly not appropriate for every person who walks in, but even if you must (or choose to) do longer-term work, you will still find many of the strategies to be useful.

Each of the action approaches holds in common the following premises:

- Therapy and counseling need not take a long time to be helpful.
- Treatment goals are specific, limited, and realistic.
- The clinician takes a fairly active, directive role in designing and implementing interventions.
- Practitioners adopt flexible, experimental mind-sets that allow them to respond rapidly and decisively to changing circumstances.
- The focus of sessions is on present problems rather than past events.
- Important work takes place outside of sessions during structured homework assignments.
- Most problems are looked at in terms of their larger context.
- Sessions are scheduled flexibly and strategically so as to maximize therapeutic gains.
- Insight, relationship factors, and emotions are typically not the focus; action and changes in behavior are the focus.

Insight Versus Action

This last point highlights a distinction that you may find useful for sorting out any approach to psychotherapy: Does the theory focus more on a deeper understanding of issues, or rather is it concerned primarily with promoting behavior change? Some of the proponents of action-oriented therapy are quite vehement that insight is not only unnecessary, but also possibly counterproductive in that it provides people with excuses for avoiding change: "I can't help it. I had an unhappy childhood caused by my abusive mother and neglectful father."

In a classic article entitled "Insight May Cause Blindness," Watzlawick (1997) drew early attention to this issue and argued that in the modern world, we don't have time to wallow in the reasons for our problems. Furthermore, although once a practicing Jungian analyst, he couldn't think of a single instance in which a client having an insight actually produced any sort of magical change. To bring home this point, he offered the case of a man who compulsively claps his hands every few seconds. When asked why he engages in this behavior, he responds it's to keep the elephants away. It is next pointed out to him that there aren't any elephants in the vicinity, to which he replies: "See, it's working."

Watzlawick (1997) offered four possible ways that this man might be helped:

1. Establish a trusting relationship with the man until he changes his mind about elephants being a problem.
2. Analyze the man's past to discover the unconscious reasons for this symptom.
3. Bring elephants into the session to prove to him that his clapping doesn't keep them away.
4. Break one of his hands so that while encased in a plaster cast, he will be unable to clap.

Surely you will recognize some of the theories you studied in the approaches just listed. Watzlawick was quick to point out that he would never advocate breaking someone's hand to stop a person from clapping, but neither would he do any of the other things. At least the last one, he argued, would probably work. This might strike you as an extreme position to take with regard to the role (or lack thereof) of insight in therapy approaches, but it is typical of some of the models that are designed for one thing and one thing only: efficient removal of a client's symptoms.

FOR A GROUP ACTIVITY

In small groups, organize a debate in which each of you takes one of the following positions:

1. Insight is a necessary condition for *real* change to take place at the deepest possible level. Unless you take care of the underlying problem and understand its origins, symptoms will come up in another form. Those who do not understand history are doomed to repeat the mistakes of the past.
2. Insight is desirable with most clients most of the time but is usually not enough to promote lasting change by itself. There has to be some kind of action component as part of therapy.
3. Insight is, at best, irrelevant, and at worst, a distraction from the real work in therapy. All too often, people use their self-awareness or understanding as a defense to avoid changing. Focus the clients on what they are doing and help them plan to do these things differently.
4. Insight is actually quite dangerous. People already spend too much time thinking about their problems and blaming themselves for what happened and why. The best strategy is to forget about the past and to move on—and do something (nearly anything!) differently.

After each person presents an initial argument for his or her position (maximum two minutes), spend another ten minutes debating one another. A moderator should make sure that everyone gets an equitable share of time and that no one person on the panel is allowed to monopolize the discussion.

Next, devote a few minutes to members of the audience, questioning positions that they find unconvincing or unsupportive.

After the debate is completed, spend time talking to one another about how your own ideas have crystallized or changed as a result of this discussion.

Some Background and Brief History

The first brief therapists were rooted in the approaches we have studied before, but they became intent on finding ways to speed things up. Several of Freud's disciples, notably Otto Rank and Alfred Adler, were impatient with his slow, laborious process of delving into the unconscious and created techniques to help clients learn new ways of being and acting. Subsequently, dozens of analysts from that first generation of protégés experimented with ways that they could shorten the amount of time needed to promote a cure. Many of the most familiar names mentioned in this book, such as Fritz Perls, Albert Ellis, William Glasser, Carl Rogers, and so on, were all committed to getting clients to change more efficiently and devised schools of thought that became influential in their own right.

Brief, action-oriented therapies essentially began with the work of Milton Erickson (1954) and his protégé, Jay Haley (1967, 1973), who interpreted and popularized his methods. Haley had already been working with others who were experimenting with briefer methods for treating schizophrenia (Bateson, Jackson, Haley, & Weakland, 1956) when he came upon Erickson's hypnotic methods. After acting as the biographer for Erickson's strategies, Haley (1976) began developing a brief, problem-solving therapy of his own, as did several of his colleagues (Watzlawick, Weakland, & Fisch, 1974). Eventually teaming up (marrying and later divorcing) with Cloe Madanes (1981), Haley developed a strategic method for working with difficult adolescents and families that used the kinds of *paradoxical* techniques he learned from Erickson.

You might be wondering what a paradox has to do with therapy. Essentially, if you ask people to do something directly (for example, "Stop eating so much!") and they keep engaging in the same behavior, the next line of attack is to try the opposite: Prescribe the same symptoms or behavior that they are already showing ("You don't have enough on your plate—help yourself to some more!"). This paradoxical intervention, actually designed to be disobeyed, often provokes changes in the entrenched dysfunctional patterns.

Jay Haley also spent some time working with another family therapist, Salvador Minuchin, who was a specialist in working with inner-city families in Philadelphia. Whereas Haley had been emphasizing hypnotic methods and paradoxical directives to disrupt the person's self-defeating process, once he collaborated with Minuchin, he began looking at underlying organizational structures (Richeport-Haley & Carlson, 2010; Richeport-Haley & Haley, 2012).

Minuchin and his colleagues were also finding success with a brief method of structural therapy, aimed at altering the hierarchies of power in family relationships. At its simplest level, he might notice that as a family entered the office, they aligned themselves according to their coalitions just by their seating arrangement. A family of four walks in the room, for example. The mother sits between her two children on one couch, while the father sits alone on the other. Minuchin would immediately rearrange this configuration, asking the two parents to sit together, thus realigning the coalitions within the family. Such strategic and structural interventions devised by Haley and Minuchin and others revolutionized the ways that therapy could be done. Rather than merely talking about problems, the clinician intervened to disrupt the underlying organizational structure by taking action in sessions and prescribing new actions outside of sessions (Minuchin & Fishman, 1981).

While these brief action-focused therapies were making their debut, thanks to some "out-of-the-box" therapists, traditional individual theorists such as Albert Ellis, William Glasser, and Carl Rogers also were experiencing success in their methods that were designed for less than a dozen sessions. With contributions from behavioral, cognitive, Gestalt, and other approaches, it was firmly established that solid, lasting changes could indeed be initiated within briefer time periods than could ever have been imagined when the balance between insight and action shifted toward action.

ERICKSONIAN THERAPY

There are few therapists outside of Freud and Rogers who have exerted more dramatic influence on practitioners than Milton Erickson, even though he remains an obscure and mysterious figure. This was a man who rarely wrote anything and had little interest in traveling around promoting his ideas to others. Instead, people made the pilgrimage to visit him to learn his methods, which have been called a form of magic and wizardry. His ways of working inspire contemporary therapists who have to be nimbly effective when there's not much time.

A Typical Erickson Story

Erickson struggled with a physical handicap that confined him to a wheel chair throughout most of his life. As a young man, before beginning medical school, he decided to take some time off to canoe in the wilderness of Canada. The paddling of a boat is no great challenge for a man without functioning legs, especially for one with such highly developed upper body strength, but portaging the canoe, or transporting it over land and across dams, is certainly a major obstacle for someone who can't walk.

Rather than asking for direct help when he encountered a dam, Erickson decided to experiment with indirect ways to solicit assistance. He wondered how successfully he could get people to offer to carry his canoe across obstacles without him having to ask them. He, thus, devised a number of routines that seemed especially effective in getting people to volunteer. From these humble beginnings, Erickson began thinking of ways he could help people with personal problems without approaching the problems directly. Why, he reasoned, was it necessary to deal with resistance and defensiveness if you could bypass all that and just change people at a preconscious level?

Based on the limited writings of Erickson (1954, 1964) in mostly hypnosis journals about a new technique, and later in a series of personal interviews, Jay Haley (1973) sought to chronicle Erickson's therapeutic adventures. There have since been hundreds, perhaps thousands, of stories told about the amazing things that Erickson could do with so-called hopeless cases, but perhaps one representative example involves a catatonic man with schizophrenia who hadn't moved a muscle in many years. He just sat there, immobile, staring off into space from morning until night.

Erickson approached the frozen patient and sat down next to him. Unlike other therapists, he didn't attempt to speak with him or engage him in conversation, which he knew would be fruitless after so many others before him had tried and failed. He just sat with the man for a while, considering that about the only thing he was doing that could be described as a behavior was breathing. Because Erickson could not establish rapport with him—or any kind of connection—by talking to him, he decided to breathe with the patient. He simply matched the pace of his breathing to that of this bricklike human. He timed his inhalations and exhalations to the exact same rhythm of his companion.

After a period of time, Erickson gradually started to slow the rate of *his* breathing and he noticed an amazing thing happen: The catatonic client slowed his breathing, too! Next, Erickson imperceptibly began increasing his rate of breathing and the man matched him as well. Now they were in a sort of collusion, even if the patient wasn't consciously aware of what was going on. They went along that way for some time, with Erickson leading their interaction, and the patient following him.

When after some hours Erickson turned to the patient and asked him if he'd like a cigarette, the patient spoke aloud the first words anyone had heard in a long time. They had begun a dialogue with breathing and then eventually began talking with their voices. This was typical of the creative and unusual ways that Erickson would attempt to make contact with people. Dozens of well-known therapists, from Virginia Satir and Michael Mahoney to Jay Haley, have similar stories to tell of the miracles they have witnessed.

The Antitheorist

The major feature about Erickson is that he was really an anti-theorist; he just didn't believe in theories. He was interested in only results, the ultimate pragmatist. He'd leave it up to others to explain what he did; instead, he would concentrate his efforts on helping people change. That turned out to be a fine state of affairs because others such as Haley (1984), Satir (1978), Bandler and Grinder (1975), and Zeig (1982, 1985, 2010, 2018) would explain and promote his ideas.

Erickson certainly introduced some very novel ideas to the practice of therapy, the most controversial of which was probably an altered therapist's stance. You will recall that most other therapeutic approaches advocate a professional role that is collaborative, open, straightforward, authentic, and transparent. Then Erickson comes along (or rather was discovered operating in the Arizona desert) and he conceived of a new sense of therapist power based on the following ideas:

1. The therapist knows things that the client does not know. As such, the therapist is an expert.
2. There are certain things the therapist knows that the client does not need to know. It isn't necessary to explain what you are doing, or even for the client to understand what is going on.
3. The therapist is entitled to use what he or she knows to influence the client in ways that are believed to be helpful, without necessarily recruiting the client's cooperation and support along the way.
4. Being deceptive or manipulative are ethical and acceptable if they are used for the client's own good.

FOR PERSONAL REFLECTION

Do you believe that it is moral and appropriate to manipulate or trick clients into doing things (for their own good) without their consent? How would you respond to the arguments presented that all therapists engage in such deception whether they admit it or not?

You can see just how radical a vision of therapy can be under this framework. Certainly not all action-oriented therapists, or Ericksonian therapists, subscribe to this idea that it is OK to be deceptive, but almost all of them resort to some form of subtle manipulation to "trick" clients into changing what they do. Furthermore, advocates would argue that even someone such as Rogers was actually being manipulative and *conditionally* accepting when he chose to lead, guide, and direct clients to talk about their feelings in subtle ways while ignoring other aspects of their communication that he didn't see as important.

Fisch, Weakland, and Segal (1982) were most incisive in describing Erickson's contributions to brief therapy by highlighting what he did *not* do in his work. He didn't take detailed histories or delve into the past. He restricted his sessions to prearranged time periods. He didn't encourage people to talk about their feelings, nor did he offer interpretations or bring out client resistance that can take a lot of time.

If this is what he did *not* do in sessions, what he *did* do was the following (Zeig, 2018):

1. Stayed with the present rather than the past
2. Explored thoroughly the presenting problem—when, where, and with whom it occurred
3. Looked for exceptions when the problem did *not* occur
4. Designed arduous tasks for clients to complete that were sometimes worse than the problems themselves
5. Prescribed paradoxical directives to clients that were designed to be disobeyed
6. Ignored the role of insight completely, believing that it was a waste of time, if not dangerous
7. Favored the use of hypnosis to bypass resistance
8. Adapted traditional methods to follow the basic procedure: ask the person to do something he or she is already doing
9. Asked the person to do something voluntarily
10. Used metaphors to approach problems indirectly

As you can readily see, the Ericksonian style of therapy was indeed a radical departure from other theories practiced at the time. Just as with most influential ideas in our field, the best contributions from this approach (such as looking for exceptions) have now been infused into almost all forms of practice.

Contributions, Limitations, and Contraindications

One of Erickson's greatest contributions that has infused many modern therapies reminds us that too often clients are defined by their problems and their psychopathologies. It turns out that sometimes a diagnosis can make a problem more "real" and resistant to change. Instead, Erickson and others shifted the focus to new possibilities rather than problems of the past, relying on his creativity and pragmatism to design unexpected and memorable experiences for clients in sessions. Erickson also firmly believed that no two clients were alike; therefore, it made no sense to develop manuals for treating depression or phobias, for example. Instead, Erickson created individually tailored—and often surprising—solutions for each client.

With unique ideas that have endured, Eriksonian therapy, including his ideas about hypnotherapy, continue to be regularly taught at various institutes and workshops. No, it's not what you imagine—there's no charlatan telling the client to watch a dangling pocket watch. Instead, consistent with basic tenets of brief therapy, it is a subtle and nuanced way of engaging in "problem talk" with clients; it looks more like being inducted into a light trance state (which many of us go in and out of all day long watching commercials or listening to music). The idea is that most clients' struggles have something to do with disowning or dissociating from their problem. But their attempts to control, keep in check, or eliminate it tend to create a stronger connection to it. The hypnotherapist's job, then, is to create a relaxed separation from the problem where clients can embrace and/or lose interest in the problem and let it become boring, irrelevant, or unremarkable—a place from which it is much more easily solved (Flemons, 2012; Leslie, 2014).

It may immediately occur to you, however, that as powerful as these methods might be, there are some problems associated with their application in real-life situations. First of all, when a therapist assumes complete and total responsibility for outcomes and believes that he or she knows what is best for people, there is a greater danger of casualties. We have been to many workshops on this type of treatment (and the ones that follow). We continue to be amazed, even spellbound by the drama and magic of these interventions. We watch demonstrations in videos and on stage, showing the methods in action in which people are transformed before our very eyes. Yet we have also found that when we take the methods back to our own practices, we don't get quite the same results. Of course, one would expect this considering that we have neither the experience nor the support team to back up our efforts. It is one thing to use intrusive, powerful methods when you have a team of observers behind a one-way mirror who can call in suggestions and feedback when you get stuck. It is quite another challenge to operate in solo practice.

Our point is that the more powerful the interventions used, the more careful you must be to use them within the scope of your practice and with the quality and quantity of supervision available. We have also had clients who suffered relapses of problems that were "cured" through these methods, and who came back to counseling in need of developing more insight and positive self-regard.

STRATEGIC THERAPY

There are several brief forms of therapy that have the common distinction of focusing exclusively on specific symptom reduction, relying on a variety of rather innovative, novel, sometimes even paradoxical interventions. They now call themselves by a variety of names. Whether labeled as brief strategic solution-oriented therapy, problem-solving therapy, or brief strategic family therapy, they are all mostly concerned with expanding some of the ideas first introduced by Milton Erickson and his followers.

Eventually working under the auspices of the Mental Research Institute (MRI) in California, Haley and others who were inspired by Erickson began looking at human problems from the perspective of their communication patterns. Premises of this approach were mostly derived from Erickson's work and were combined with the burgeoning field of family systems therapy, as well as the MRI team's own creativity and inventiveness.

In this approach, there was no real interest in theory, but rather in the pragmatics of finding what works with people to provide relief in the here and now. Problems must be examined in terms of what they are expressing and communicating in the context of their larger system. A child who has stomachaches, for instance, may be "speaking" on behalf of others in the family. One of the effects of these symptoms is that it stops bickering parents from arguing with one another long enough to address their child's needs. Problems are thus seen as functional and helpful in some ways.

There are several other assumptions of the approach:

1. There is a much greater likelihood of resolving difficulties if they are defined in a way that says they can be solved.

2. The therapist, as the expert, is clearly the one who is responsible for devising and implementing a plan of action. (You will note this is a marked departure from the more collaborative models you studied earlier.)

3. Small changes lead to big changes. If you can get the client to make a little adjustment in the way things are done, leverage has been created to keep the momentum going. For example, a client who can't seem to lose weight could be ordered to gain one pound, just to prove that weight changes are within one's control.

4. There is no such thing as client resistance in this approach because all people are seen as doing the best they can. (Compare this to other approaches where frustrated therapists label their clients as noncompliant when clients aren't doing what they expect or aren't cooperating in ways they prefer.)

There is a logical, sequential series of stages to strategic problem-solving therapy that begins with collecting data. This is not unlike what happens in any therapeutic approach except that the kinds of information collected are specific and focused. The strategic problem-solving therapist will not delve much into the past, except to find out when the symptoms were most and least disturbing, as well as what has worked and what has not worked before. Instead, the skills that we describe next will be used to create possibilities for change.

Reframing the Problem
Regardless of the theoretical approach you eventually adopt, reframing is one of those concepts that has universal value with almost any client and situation. As you would imagine, clients come into sessions with their own views about what the problem is and what needs to be done to fix it. Often, they've been in treatment before and share a long list of diagnoses they've acquired along the way. Or, they are convinced that someone else is the root of everything wrong. We can say with confidence that attempts to blame a diagnosis or other people for one's problems is not only illogical, distorted, and counterproductive, but also it is almost impossible to make things better if you accept things as they are presented.

"My husband is the problem," a new client will tell you. "He's just lazy and inconsiderate." Even if this were the case that the husband did demonstrate these qualities almost all the time (which is highly unlikely because he would have a different perspective), what could you do to fix the matter? By implication, the way the client is defining the problem, you would dismiss her from treatment, bring in the husband, and then somehow make him less lazy and inconsiderate. It is extremely improbable that you would even get the husband to come in under these terms, much less change his behavior because his wife doesn't like him the way he is.

Instead, what you might do is negotiate with the client, reformulate the problem in a way that is acceptable to her, and also cast it in a form that makes it easier to change. Of course, you can't outright dismiss the client's definition or you will get fired, so you have to be somewhat clever in the ways you reframe it: "It sounds like what you're saying is that you haven't been as effective as you would like in getting your needs met in this relationship."

That is just the starting point for your reframed problem definition. The client prefers to put blame and responsibility on her husband, whereas you would like to work on an issue that is more within your power to change. Because, according to this approach, there is no such thing as resistance but only ineffectiveness on the part of the therapist in selling a particular idea, it is your job to recast things in a more helpful light. Here are some examples:

- When a client talks about the frustration he feels in overcoming some obstacle, that can be reframed as a challenge to be overcome.
- When a client talks about her coworkers who are sabotaging her project, that can be reframed as them trying to help in ways that are different from what she prefers.
- When a client says that he is shy and that's why he doesn't have any friends, you can help him see that he sometimes acts shyly (but not always).

FOR A CLASS ACTIVITY

Whether you ever identify yourself as a strategic problem-solving therapist or not, we can't stress enough how important it is for you to master the skill of reframing. If you can't redefine the presenting problem in a way that you can do something to be helpful, your efforts are likely to be wasted. Often the simple act of offering another perspective on things has a significant impact on the client's perceptions of his or her situation.

Working with a partner, either in class or on your own, brainstorm several different ways that you could reframe the following presenting complaints:

- A child insists that she's getting bad grades because she's stupid.
- A couple who is experiencing sexual difficulties (he is impotent, she has little sexual desire) blame one another for the problems.
- An older man tells you that he has nothing to live for because his children and grandchildren never visit him much anymore.

In each case, you are trying to acknowledge the client's view of things but are also suggesting alternative ways to look at the situation to be more consistent with what you can offer.

Advance Preparation

Because many strategic directives are designed to be challenging, the hardest task is to get clients to comply with the therapeutic tasks. Clients must be motivated and prepared for what they are about to do. Often, subtle or playful approaches help. Following Erickson's lead, therapists might be inclined to say something such as the following:

THERAPIST:	I have a cure for your troubles but I sense you aren't ready for it just yet. [Of course, the client then begs for the solution, but the therapist will not give in.] Perhaps next week, if I think you are ready, I will give you the cure then.
	The following week, the client comes in eager and impatient for the promised cure.
CLIENT:	Okay, okay, so what have you got for me?
THERAPIST:	I still don't think you are quite ready yet. What you will have to do is very distasteful and difficult and I just don't think you are committed to follow through on what I ask you to do.
CLIENT (WHINING):	Oh, but I am, I am. Please, can we do it now?
THERAPIST:	I want you to think about things until next week, decide just how ready you are to do what must be done.

Obviously, by the following week, the client is ready to do almost anything that the therapist asks—even if the tasks are abhorrent. This increases the likelihood of compliance, although it does not guarantee such cooperation.

Directives

Haley (2003) once said, more than a little facetiously, that the object of therapy is to provide experiences that are so onerous or distasteful that clients will cure themselves so they do not have to return again. He was quite serious, actually, when he ordered couples who fought too much to set their alarms at 3:00 a.m. and schedule an argument for no less than 45 minutes. The object of these ordeals—also called paradoxical directives because they are essentially prescribing the symptom—is to cause levels of distress that exceed those caused by the original problem. Of course, for this to work, the clients must be "sold" on the method or they won't do it.

I (Marilyn) saw an example of this when I was a graduate student and was invited to watch "behind the mirror" with my friends who were training as strategic problem-solving therapists. One of the professors was working with a woman who had problems falling asleep and staying asleep. In the first session, instead of giving her suggestions for winding down, drinking a glass of warm milk, darkening her bedroom (which she was ready to refute as "I already tried that!"), he told her that before they could get anywhere he would need her to try to stay up as late as usual but take notes as to what she was doing and thinking about during the last hour before she fell asleep for at least 3 nights. She agreed to do this but came back somewhat ashamed the next week—she hadn't been able to complete the homework because she had fallen asleep.

Accentuate the Positive

Many different systems of therapy have a policy of asking clients not only what is going wrong in their lives but also what is going right. Strategic therapists do this by looking for exceptions to those times when the person is debilitated by the symptoms.

Consider this example: A man complains constantly about the effects of a stroke that has left him paralyzed on one side and with numerous cognitive dysfunctions that impair his memory, perceptions, and reasoning abilities. He feels life is hopeless because he is always a victim of this terrible misfortune.

"*Always* a victim?" the therapist asks him softly.

"Excuse me?" the client answers.

"I asked you if you were *always* miserable as a result of your stroke," the therapist responds, clarifying. "Is there ever a time, even for single minute, when you feel reasonably good? Was there a time today, for instance, when you smiled or laughed at something?"

"Well, yeah, I guess," acknowledges the client. "I had a delicious meal on the way over here. And I saw my grandson …"

The therapist nods. "So, all in all, it has been a fairly pleasant morning for you. You did, for at least a few moments, overcome the symptoms of your stroke and acted as if you are someone capable of being quite content. Tell me, what does your grandson think of you?"

Thoughtfully, the client replies, "Oh, he thinks I'm so cool. He loves helping me out; I think it makes him feel big."

"Ah, so you're providing your grandson a very special experience—not one every kid can have," the therapist observes, noticing the beginnings of a smile on the client's face.

Our point is this: Clients often think that their job is to come into sessions and tell you all the things going wrong in their lives. This includes every complaint imaginable, every injustice, and every single disappointment or setback.

If you let this continue, the conversation will easily be filled up with a litany of such annoyances. The client will use therapy as a dumping ground, which can sometimes be useful but often can make things worse. When you accentuate the positive, you attempt to reposition clients in a place where they are taking a more balanced view toward their lives. There are failures but also successes. There are disappointments but also some progress. Your job is to make that clear.

Remind Clients That Therapy Will End

Since the goal is that the therapist will work themselves out of a job, the client is reminded that treatment will end soon. Some therapists we know do a weekly countdown: "This is our third session; we have three more, so we're about half-way through." While this might seem cold to some, it does encourage clients and therapists to set realistic expectations, get into action right away, and pace themselves so that they get somewhere sooner rather than later.

It also conveys a positive expectation to the client. The implicit idea is that since we don't see our client as needing months or years of therapy, their problem can't be all that intractable! While not promising a cure, the therapist might say, "We can't know for sure where we will be at the end, but there certainly will be new possibilities available at that time. Won't that be interesting!"

Predict a Relapse

Although there are many other strategic interventions, the last one we will mention is quite clever and also has universal application to a wide variety of situations. One of the ways that you can prevent continued relapses is to predict that they will occur so that the client is not unduly alarmed or unprepared.

Just after a client has made significant progress, the therapist might say something like this:

> *"I can see that you are really excited about what you have done and feeling really proud of your accomplishments. I applaud your efforts and think you have made wonderful progress. I must warn you, however, that the effects will not last."*

This gets the client's attention in a big way. A look of worry appears, sometimes even panic.

> *"Just because you experience some setbacks is no big deal, however. Just as I know that you will fall flat on your face, I also know that you have the ability to pick yourself back up—if you choose to do so. The beauty of what you have learned is that you can take a step backward and still not lose sight of where you are headed. You can apply what you have learned again and again."*

This pep talk prepares the client for inevitable backsliding. When you predict a relapse, one of two things will happen. Either you will seem like a magician because what you said would happen did indeed occur, or you will be proven wrong. If the former, the client has been warned and prepared ahead of time. If you are wrong, then there is really nothing lost.

Because the leaders of each theory interact with one another on a regular basis and also read one another's material, there is little doubt that many of the approaches are converging. Just as the cognitive therapists have been strongly influenced lately by constructivist paradigms, reality therapists have been incorporating those ideas, as well as cognitive principles, into their work. During actual sessions, it is becoming increasingly difficult to identify which approach a practitioner might be using because so many of the models may come into play.

Strengths and Limitations

If you have the impression that therapy with a strategic emphasis is much more active and directive than person-centered therapy or the constructivist approaches we reviewed in the last chapter, you would be correct. As such, it is sometimes the best approach for helping clients to make quick change. For example, strategic techniques can help create quick results in sex therapy (Flemons & Green, 2018), and for patients who have had their first heart attack and need to reduce stress (Rakowska, 2015). It can also be very useful when consulting with couples, some of whom may not be ready to commit to family therapy (Rohrbaugh & Shoham, 2015).

Some have criticized strategic therapy for putting techniques first without considering the potential implications of changes the client might make in terms of their broader context (Reiter, 2017). However, it is certainly possible to use strategic tools when working with clients to construct solutions from within a narrative or solution-focused approach (Miller, 2017). In fact, strategic therapy is now most often actually practiced in combination with systemic or constructivist approaches.

Brief strategic family therapy (BFST) is an example of this type of integration. It is an elaboration of strategic therapy that was developed over decades of clinical work with families of teenagers with problem behaviors (including substance use and acting-out behaviors). The BSFT approach was developed by integrating ideas from structural family therapy (Minuchin & Fishman, 1981) with strategic approaches (Haley, 1976; Madanes, 1981) in a limited number of family sessions. The idea is that patterns of family interactions allow or encourage problematic adolescent behavior. When therapists get families to change how they interact, the adolescent's behavior improves (Szapocznik, Duff, Schwartz, Muir, & Brown, 2015). This might be no surprise to you, but the good news is that the changed family interaction patterns tend to last after treatment has ended because multiple family members have changed the way they behave with each other.

Fortunately, strategic methods can usefully be incorporated into many approaches, particularly when you feel the need to change things up and do something the client doesn't expect. For example, brief strategic therapy has also been combined with cognitive behavioral therapy to address clients' problems with binge eating and obesity (Jackson, Pietrabissa, Rossi, Manzoni, & Castelnuovo, 2018), and seems to be more effective than either approach when used alone for accomplishing lasting change.

SINGLE-SESSION THERAPY

What do you think about the possibility of a therapy model that is specifically designed to occur in a single meeting? Before you scoff at the possibility, consider the number of times in your own life that you have been irrevocably and permanently changed as a result of one dramatic incident.

It has usually been the case that when clients don't return after an initial session, they are called dropouts or treatment failures. It is assumed that because the therapist did not meet the client's needs, he or she elected not to return. Working for a large health conglomerate, Talmon (1993) decided to investigate this phenomenon by following up on those who didn't come back after their first session. To his amazement, he discovered that 78% of the 200 ex-clients he interviewed did not return after their one and only session because they already got what they needed! Because this result was so unexpected, and so counter to conventional wisdom, Talmon asked several colleagues to duplicate his study and they not only confirmed his original results but also found that 88% described themselves as "much improved" after their one session.

Talmon began to speculate that if so many people are helped after one session when the therapist had no awareness that such powerful gains were possible, what could be done if therapy was actually planned as a one-shot deal?

Talmon was not the first to observe the power of one therapeutic session. Even Freud once reported a cure after one meeting, as have dozens of other prominent practitioners (Bloom, 1997). Summarizing the research and clinical experience on single-session therapy, both Talmon (1993) and Hoyt (2017) offer several suggestions to keep in mind when doing this type of work.

1. Don't underestimate the power of your own positive expectations: Expect good things and they will happen.

2. Remember that the therapy begins with the first phone call. Talmon, for example, reports telling a client during their first phone conversation, "Between now and our first session, I want you to notice the things that happen to you that you would like to keep happening in the future. In this way, you will help me to find out more about your goal and what you are up to" (Talmon, 1990, p. 19). He points out that with that single statement, he immediately accomplished several things that launched the therapy off to a flying start. First, he emphasized the importance of natural and effortless changes. Second, he focused on what would be possible in the future. Finally, he implied that the client was in charge of his own changes. It's no surprise that therapists of other theoretical persuasions have adopted this technique.

3. Consider calling the client back within 24 hours of the phone call to make the first appointment, not only to prevent "no-shows" and communicate continued interest, but also to plant more therapeutic messages, such as "You've probably already noticed a difference in how you feel just since you took this important step in scheduling a session."

4. Choose candidates for single-session therapy wisely. Obviously, not everyone can benefit from one contact. When time restraints make it impossible for someone to return, when someone has a very specific problem to work on, when someone is in crisis, or when modest goals can be quickly identified, this treatment might be ideal.

5. Decide on who should attend the session.

6. Select an issue or problem with modest goals to target.

7. In your zeal to get through the agenda, don't forget the power of empathy.

8. Use humor. Bringing laughter to an aspect of the problem neutralizes or changes it.

9. Keep track of time and structure the session as needed so the session ends.

10. Work from the client's strengths.

11. Affirm what has already been accomplished.

12. Record the session and give it to the client afterward.

13. Schedule follow-up meeting using the phone or Internet.

Advantages and Special Problems

Single session therapy, while coming to the foreground several decades ago, is receiving a lot of current attention for a number of reasons. There are some practical advantages that make it a good choice, and sometimes the only choice, for making help available. For example, for those in need of humanitarian or disaster relief, a single session may be all that is practical (Akerele & Yuryey, 2017). It is also being tried in Web-based counseling, which you read about in an earlier chapter. For example, single-session Web-based counseling has been made available to people seeking help for problem gambling (Rodda, Lubman, Cheetham, Dowling, & Jackson, 2015). This approach may need some refinement, however, as it seemed that people who used it either wanted advice for solving an immediate crisis or simply wanted to tell their story.

You might rightfully wonder, is single-session therapy effective? After all, most other theories are much more elaborate and insist that clients need time to shift their thinking and work up the courage to try new things. Yet most single-session therapy clients report decreases in their symptoms and impairments, along with the stress they cause, and increase in their understanding their problem and their ability to cope (Hoyt, Bobele, & Slive, 2018). It also lets them access services sooner than being on a waitlist for traditional individual therapy (Ewen, et al., 2018).

It is clear that single-session therapy is not appropriate for all, or even most, people who need help. Generally speaking, it takes time to develop a trusting relationship, gather enough information to do a reasonable assessment, and then to implement solutions. Besides, so often people come in for help in the first place not only to solve problems, but also because they hunger for understanding and attention.

THE BEST CANDIDATES FOR BRIEF, ACTION-ORIENTED THERAPY

As we mentioned earlier, the central issue with respect to brief, action-oriented therapies is when and with whom to use them. Clearly, during times of crisis or when time is limited, there is little choice but to intervene quickly and efficiently, for example when certain things come to light in a suicide assessment (Flemons & Gralnik, 2013). Of course, there are contraindications and best prospects of this type of treatment. You would not, for instance, want to try strategic, action-oriented, brief therapy as your only approach with clients who have any of the following:

- Major thought disorders or psychotic disturbances
- Serious, chronic depression
- Severe emotional and impulsive personality disorders
- Those with underlying, unresolved traumatic issues that are at the heart of their problems

Clients with these conditions would be very tough case in *any* form of therapy. So, who would be the most ideal candidates for time-limited, action-oriented methods? Those with the following:

- High motivation
- Acute, specific problems
- Crisis situations
- Willingness and ability to articulate concerns
- Ability to form a trusting relationship with the therapist
- Ability and willingness to stay on task

Again, the point can be made that these types of clients would do well with most any form of therapy employed and would likely respond rather rapidly to any helping effort. Nevertheless, this chapter helps you to think not only in terms of which approach to use with any given case, but also whether to get down to business right away and help the client take immediate action. Such would be the case with any of the following scenarios:

- A client traveled by bus from across town in a disadvantaged neighborhood. The first statements out of her mouth are how difficult and inconvenient this journey was, how uncomfortable she is leaving her young children at home with limited care, and how reluctant she is to return. Clearly, no matter how successful you are in this first session, it is going to be highly unlikely she can return for more than a few sessions.
- A managed care plan provides for a maximum of only six sessions, after which a review may extend the benefits to four more sessions, tops.
- A person is experiencing an acute problem in an otherwise high functioning life.
- Your own workload is such that your organization does not permit you to see clients for longer than a few months.
- A client comes in with the clear and non-negotiable expectation that treatment will occur rapidly, as in, "OK, let's get to work. I'd prefer that we resolve this matter right away. If necessary, I can come back for another session or maybe two."

Stages of Readiness for Change

Clearly, clients' readiness to change will play into how well brief therapy goes and is a key factor determining its outcome. Some have looked at how people differ on the readiness factor and have developed the transtheoretical stages of change model (DiClemente, 2018; Prochaska & DiClemente, 2005), which is being applied in settings to tailor the type of therapy to the client. It specifies different stages of readiness for change: *Precontemplation* (not thinking about change; not interested) *contemplation* (imagining doing something differently, seeing some possible advantages to changing), *preparation* (getting set up to try something new), *action* (doing something differently; taking small steps toward the goal), and *maintenance* (doing what it takes to keep the new behavior pattern in place; getting back on track after slip-ups). Of course, clients in the *action* stage are much more likely to engage with the therapist, participate enthusiastically, change quickly, and stay in treatment (in other words, they are ideal clients for brief therapy). Clients in the *precontemplation* stage resist taking action, are very tough customers and are at high risk for dropping out of any kind of therapy.

MOTIVATIONAL INTERVIEWING

The therapies we've looked at so far in this chapter depict what can be done with a client who is stuck and wants to change but just can't figure out how. But you probably already know that therapists often are called on to help people who don't particularly want to change! What can be done for the guy whose doctor has told him to exercise or die (but he's a couch potato who hates to exercise), the empty-nest woman who must reduce her drinking or she'll lose her job (but she finds drinking comforting), or the teen who has been court mandated to be drug tested to work his way off parole (but he really hates to give up his before-school joint)? Is there no help for these people?

The good news is that there is a kind of brief therapy designed just for them. Fortunately, these clients often fit in the *contemplation* stage in the model described earlier. They are definitely ambivalent about change and, as you can imagine, at high risk for dropping out of therapy, particularly if they think the therapist is going to try to make them change (Chiappetta, et al., 2018). Fortunately, motivational interviewing (or MI) is therapy that is designed to fan any little spark of interest in change into flames. MI does this by using a client-centered approach to accept, explore, and resolve ambivalence, while also being directive. It is typically four or five sessions, which certainly qualifies it as a brief therapy! Even so, it has been very successful with clients who have substance dependencies or addictions (Miller & Rollnick, 2012), unhealthy habits (Rollnick, Miller, & Butler, 2008), and other mental health problems (Arkowitz, Miller, & Rollnick, 2017).

MI is particularly helpful in tailoring intervention to the client's readiness for change with the different strategies or processes of change that might be helpful at different times. It makes sense that action-oriented strategies are more useful for clients who are in the later stages of change (for example, someone with a serious addiction to chocolate removing every stash of choc-olate bars from their home). On the other hand, strategies that help their clients contemplate the pros and cons of even making the change are useful for clients who are more ambivalent. There is certainly training available on MI, and it is very helpful to hone one's techniques, but it is also a way of working that is very accessible to people already in the field. Following are some specific skills that the MI therapy uses.

OARS

OARS is an acronym that captures the basic interaction techniques that the therapist uses; you'll notice that these are borrowed from client-centered therapy. You'll recognize that this way of working keeps the ther-apist in a very open, non-judgmental stance, which is optimal for building the relationship with clients quickly, gathering accurate information, and supporting them through even miniscule efforts to change and the inevitable relapses.

O is for open-ended questions, *A* is for affirmations of the client's strengths, *R* is for reflective listening to deepen emotional intensity, and *S* stands for summaries that capture essential elements and invite correction. Keeping OARS in mind helps you use therapeutic skills that will be the most pro-ductive in this approach, avoiding responses that might convey incredulity, disappointment, or advice. It also provides a nice metaphor for the steady effort that MI encourages clients to make—with oars for your boat you go a long way!

Decisional Balance

This technique is great for getting clients to bring all their pros and cons about making a change into the daylight. At the same time, it gives the therapist a chance to show that he or she accepts the client's ambivalence as reasonable. The idea is this: You draw a square on a piece of paper and divide it into four boxes. In these boxes, the client lists all the benefits or pros of changing, the costs/cons of changing, and then the benefits/pros of *not* changing and the costs/cons of the same. This helps clients figure out their own reasons for making a change, versus doing something they "should" or "have to" do.

As you might imagine, having everything displayed on paper gives clients a different view of the issues. Just completing this exercise often increases motivation for those who are only beginning to contemplate change. It can also help the client and the therapist with ideas about where to direct their next efforts to make a small change.

FOR A CLASS ACTIVITY

Divide into groups of two or three people. One will be the client, one the therapist, and one the observer/therapist's assistant. The client will choose some aspect of their behavior that they have had a hard time changing (perhaps their long-lost New Year's resolution from the previous reflection activity). The therapist will hear about the client's goal and his or her struggles with it, and then ask the client to try out the decisional balance exercise: Take a sheet of paper and fold it in half twice to make four zones. Write the desired change at the top (i.e., going to the gym or stopping procrastinating tendencies). Then, elicit from the client everything they can think of regarding (a) good things about going to the gym, (b) bad things about going to the gym, (c) good things about remaining a couch potato, and (d) bad things about remaining a couch potato. Have them write their answers down in each of the four boxes as you go along. After exploring all around their goal this way, check to see if their motivation for making their desired change has increased or decreased. Almost always, after doing this exercise, people feel more clear about the issues involved and are often motivated to experiment with at least a small change.

Scaling to Target Small Changes

As you will recall from an earlier chapter, scaling is a great technique for getting clients to be specific and clear about changes they want to make.

Let's take, for example, a client whose physician has referred him to you for help in making some lifestyle changes. As described before, we start with giving the client some anchors, using 0 and 10, to describe a continuum as in the following example.

THERAPIST: So, on a scale of 0 to 10, with 0 meaning you never get out and get any exercise or go to the gym—you're the classic "couch potato"—and 10 being you're getting some serious cardio for at least 30 minutes five times a week, where are you now?

CLIENT: Oh, well, I'm at least getting to the gym one day a week, and I try to ride my bike around the neighborhood once on the weekend ... so I guess it's a 4. But I need to get to a 10, or I'll be in really serious trouble with my doctor, my wife, and my kids! But even just for myself ... I don't want to have another heart attack. So, I've got to get into a routine of going to the gym right after work, every day, and riding the bikes for at least 30 minutes.

Now you can use scaling for a couple of follow-up questions:

1. How ready are you to make this change?
2. What is your level of confidence that you actually can make this change between now and the next session?

In our example, here we would ask our client, "Given that you are at a 4, and 10 is where you want to be, what would it take to get you to a 5 next week?" The next time you see the client, you ask, "How'd it go with moving up to a 5?"

What about if the client wanted to jump from a 4 to a 7 or 8? In other systems of therapy, this might be seen as great progress, but in MI, the therapist would discourage such a big jump. Why? This could set the client up for failure. Instead, small, incremental changes are encouraged as the very best way to make lasting change.

Another important key here is to use person-centered skills (including OARS, primarily) as you set up scaling and as you process whatever the client tells you were the results. Whatever happens is just interesting; the therapist reflects whatever the client reports with great empathy and curiosity about the details. It's important that you never act like you are disappointed that the client didn't follow through so as not to engender resistance (which we discuss next). The client is at all times the person who is deciding what needs to be done, when, and how often. As you might imagine, taking this stance encourages the client to be honest rather than exaggerating their progress.

Rolling With Resistance

Resistance is part and parcel of working with clients who are ambivalent about changing. But there is a technique that can be particularly useful with clients who present in a highly oppositional manner and who seem to reject every idea or suggestion. The idea in this type of therapy is to "roll with it" rather than to trying to dismantle it or oppose resistance (both fruitless tactics that usually make clients cross their arms, dig in their heels, and either walk out or stop talking!). Suppose the client in the example comes back and says, "Just couldn't do it. Still at a 4." The idea is that the therapist simply agrees with the client that changing may not be the thing to do now, in spite of some probable advantages. There is a paradoxical feel to this, because it often brings the client back to the side of change. Here is an example:

CLIENT: But I can't stop gambling. I mean, that's all me and my friends do when we get together on the weekends—we hit the casinos!

COUNSELOR: Well, yes; it may just be that at the end of our sessions you'll decide that it's worth it to you to continue gambling.

	It may be too difficult to make a change right now. That will be up to you.
CLIENT:	Hmm. OK. But if I keep it up, I'm going to go broke.
COUNSELOR:	(Laughs.) I see. Well, that's a pretty good reason to see what you can do sooner, rather than later!

Our examples highlight how MI is particularly good for getting people into action and working on their health-related problems and addictive behaviors. The main driver, though is *motivational enhancement* and keeping clients attuned to their own reasons for wanting to change.

MI has been applied to many kinds of client problems and settings. Because it can be easily adapted to a brief format, it is particularly useful in primary health care settings (D'Amico, et al., 2018) and is even being taught to medical students (Edwards, Bannatyne, & Stark, 2018). It is a great approach for working with teens because it preserves their autonomy and allows them to determine what changes they want to make and how fast they want to make them (Monti, Colby, & Tevyaw, 2018). Increasingly, it is now being used in schools to address issues such as bullying, dropout prevention, and behavior issues and with working with families of students to support their learning and success (Rollnick, Kaplan, & Rutschman, 2016).

MI is also a way of working that can be integrated with other approaches you've studied to help the therapist manage ambivalence and resistance to change. For example, cognitive behavioral therapy often uses techniques such as assigning homework involving applying new skills. However, some clients repeatedly return the next week without having done their homework! In this case, backing off and "rolling with resistance" can break this pattern as the therapist returns to motivational enhancement strategies (Westra & Norouzian, 2018). Incorporating MI techniques within other approaches can help resistant clients re-engage and improve.

SOME FINAL THOUGHTS

Brief, action-oriented approaches have become the standard operating procedure for many therapists much of the time. Yet it is also true that most of the theories presented throughout this book have been adapted for limited time and resources that are common in many settings today. As managed care continues to exert its influence on the profession, we will continue to feel pressure to operate as swiftly and efficiently as possible—bringing the client's focus to action, rather than on developing insight.

There will always be a market for longer-term, insight-oriented treatments, as well. Therapy and counseling are about more than merely solving problems and curing symptoms. They are also designed to help people understand themselves better, to work through long-standing personal struggles, to find greater meaning in life, to meet needs for intimacy, and to feel heard and understood.

Brief, action-oriented therapies and long-term treatments are also not mutually exclusive. Frequently, in fact, you will work on cases in which initial presenting complaints, once resolved, lead to other issues that arise. Often clients will return to you, months or even years later, with merely an excuse to resume the relationship. What is obvious is that they miss the ongoing opportunity to reflect on their lives, to be pushed and stimulated to go after something more in their work or their primary relationships.

Any competent therapist or counselor in today's climate must become proficient in both brief, action-oriented approaches and lengthier, insight-oriented treatments, depending on what the situation calls for and what the client needs most.

VOICES FROM THE FIELD

As brief therapists, we consider ourselves disentanglement consultants. Rather than focusing on clients' problems per se (as would befit someone wishing to nail down proper DSM diagnoses), we attend to people's *relationships* to their problems. Asking how our clients have been handling what's vexing them, we listen for ways their efforts at severing the relationship may have tightened it into knots. We think of therapy as a process of loosening and untying, rather than cutting through, such tangles. That is, we assume that a relationship is most viable when the *relata*—the parts at either end of it—are free to change or stay stable in coordination with each other. Therapy is, for us, the process by which we facilitate, encourage, and enhance the possibility for such relational freedom.

—Douglas Flemons, LMFT, and Shelley Green, LMFT
Context Consultants, Fort Lauderdale, FL

SUGGESTED READINGS

Arkowitz, H., Miller, W. R., & Rollnick, S. (Eds.) (2017). *Motivational interviewing in the treatment of mental health problems.* New York, NY: Guilford.

DiClemente, C. C. (2018). *Addiction and change: How addictions develop and addicted people recover.* New York, NY: Guilford.

Haley, J. (1984). *Ordeal therapy: Unusual ways to change behavior.* San Francisco, CA: Jossey-Bass.

Haley, J., & Richeport-Haley, M. (2007). *Directive family therapy*. New York, NY: Haworth.

Hoyt, M. F. (2017). *Brief therapy and beyond: Stories, language, love, hope, and time*. New York, NY: Routledge.

Hoyt, M. F., Bobele, M., & Slive, A., Young, J., & Talmon, M. (2018). *Single-session therapy by walk-in or appointment*. New York, NY: Routledge.

Miller, G. (2017). *Becoming miracle workers: Language and learning in brief therapy*. New York, NY: Routledge.

Miller, W. R., & Rollnick, S. (2012). *Motivational interviewing: Helping people to change* (3rd ed.). New York, NY: Guilford.

O'Hanlon, B. (2004). *Change 101: A practical guide to change in life or therapy*. New York, NY: Norton.

Rollnick, S., Kaplan, S. G., & Rutschman, R. (2016). *Motivational interviewing in schools: Conversations to improve learning and behavior*. New York, NY: Guilford.

Rosengren, D. B. (2017). *Building motivational interviewing skills: A practitioner workbook* (2nd ed.). New York, NY: Guilford.

Zieg, J. (2018). *Eriksonian therapy now*. Phoenix, AZ: Zieg, Tucker & Theisen.

CHAPTER 11

Mind–Body and Experiential Approaches: Just Breathe

LEARNING OBJECTIVES

After reading this chapter, you should be able to do the following:

1. Describe how neurologically informed discoveries are influencing therapists' understanding of mental health, trauma, and change.
2. Identify the association between attachment issues and psychological trauma.
3. Recount the key features of mindfulness approaches, their benefits, and how they can be taught to clients.
4. Identify therapeutic elements of three approaches that target clients' emotional and behavioral regulation.
5. Describe the key elements of several psychotherapeutic approaches that emphasize action and experience over talk therapy.
6. Evaluate the evidence supporting several experiential therapies, as well as their strengths and potential limitations.

One of the most delightful (and challenging) aspects of our profession is the ever-changing nature of our theories. Every few years, there is another stage of evolution in which some models disappear and others arrive on the scene. Theories that once enjoyed prominence a decade ago are now relics of another era. New approaches continue to rise in popularity.

Remember that at one time every theory was on the edge of respectability. Freud was branded a charlatan and his psychoanalytic approach equated with a form of witchcraft. Likewise, every other new therapy that has emerged since then has had to fight major battles to be taken seriously.

In this chapter, we introduce you to a few other theories that have come into clinical prominence in recent decades. Most of these approaches arose out of frustration with the existing tools for processing and working through clients' traumatic experiences. We predict you will be hearing more about these approaches over time. Recent gains in cognitive neuroscience have emphasized how little of what our brains process is under our conscious control; therefore, logic and "talk" about what we think is going on has its limits. The alternative treatments described here embrace the "felt sense" of experience in addition to conscious experiences as fruitful foci of therapy, and so are consistent with what we are learning about the neurological basis of psychological problems and their resolution.

FOR PERSONAL REFLECTION or CLASS ACTIVITY

Working together in teams, talk about theories that once were held in great esteem in our culture but are now considered obsolete.

Make a list of many other theories that are now no longer valued or taken seriously.

However, we must issue this review with a warning label: Many of the theories in this chapter are not often included in a text like this, except in passing. Some theories are still so novel or unusual that they have yet to receive wide acceptance. Others are growing in popularity and influence but have yet to find their way into mainstream practice, at least on a large scale. Our review of relatively new approaches is not intended to be comprehensive or exhaustive but merely to give you a flavor of other approaches that you are likely to encounter. You will have many other opportunities to study some of these approaches at a later time, if you so choose.

Do they work, you might be wondering? In most cases they are too new to have been subjected to the years of rigorous scrutiny it takes to become an evidence-based practice. But as every new law student learns: "Absence of evidence is not evidence of absence." Just because there's little data (yet) for a particular approach doesn't mean that it doesn't work (or that it does). It might hold up well in future studies or it might not; we just don't know yet. But even cognitive behavioral theory, now established as addressing certain symptoms quite well, was once in this "unproven and controversial" category.

In the following sections you will be introduced to a few of these theories that are gaining in prominence. With necessary space limitations, we were forced to select just a few of the options including neurologically informed approaches to attachment therapy; various expressive therapies that involve movement, art, music, play, or drama; acceptance and commitment therapy (ACT); dialectical behavior therapy (DBT); body and energy approaches; eye movement and desensitization reprocessing (EMDR); and animal-assisted therapy.

NEUROLOGICALLY INFORMED APPROACHES

This new influence in our field is gaining impetus and will likely continue to take on tremendous momentum during your career. It may help to unify many of our ideas about how and why therapy works. Scientists with backgrounds in neurobiology, genetics, anthropology, evolutionary psychology, memory, attachment, and complex systems theory have gotten together to come up with "pan-theoretical mechanisms of change"—in other words, some all-encompassing explanations about why people are mentally healthy, or not. To do this, some of them study the psychotherapy process up close and at multiple levels—what is going on in the talk, the eye gazes, the synchrony of interaction, and the biological arousal of both therapist and client, for people with different disorders and for therapists from various theoretical persuasions (Cozolino, 2017). The hope is to build an interdisciplinary view of mental well-being and a common framework that depicts how psychotherapy heals at the neurobiological level.

One important aspect of this work is the concept of embodiment. Long ago, when the philosopher Descartes pronounced, "I think, therefore, I am," Western societies embarked on the path that led us to talk about our mind and body as if they were separate entities. Some of the theories in this book have followed that trail to its end. You may recall that Gestalt therapy is one exception since Fritz Perls urged his clients to have sensory experiences in their bodies related to their presenting complaints. Since then, more researchers have discovered how our thoughts and perceptions are often shaped by embodied experiences. In other words, our brain and entire nervous system viscerally process our experiences of all sorts, including what we glibly refer to as our thoughts and our feelings (Clark, 2017). It seems that counseling and therapy help us use our minds to change our brains, but it also seems increasingly true that we can use our bodies to change our brains and our minds.

Perhaps an example is in order, here. Because technology now enables us to really see inside our brains and bodies as they are functioning, we can view images that correspond with what we describe as positive or problematic mental functioning. These graphics of brains and bodies at work are being mapped onto theoretical constructs we've long held dear. Take the concept of empathy: We aren't surprised to learn that the empathic capacity of the therapist is a key ingredient of therapy, regardless of the clinician's theory. But did you know that during moments of empathic connection, humans reflect or mirror each other's emotions, and their physiologies move on the same wavelength? Researchers have also found that, during moments of high shared positive emotion, both patients and therapists have similar physiologic responses, and these greater levels of similarity are related to higher ratings of therapist empathy by patients. Incidentally, this good stuff doesn't happen so much when therapists do most of the talking. Even outside of therapy, people who are in an empathic relationship have synced-up autonomic activity. This phenomenon can be observed in speakers and responsive listeners, members of a coherent group, and bonded pairs of social animals (Schore, 2018).

Even without the benefit of this scientific demonstration, our theories were built to make these kinds of moments happen more often, last longer, and occur over sustained interactions. Each theory leads us in a unique way into times when we and our clients have the sense that things are humming along nicely between us. The experience of feeling cared about in a relationship, including a therapeutic relationship, reduces the secretion of stress hormones and regulates the neuroendocrine system. So, it turns out there is a literal side to our intuitive expression, "good chemistry!" In therapy, clients learn or re-learn what it feels like.

Recently, there have been formulations of a new trans-theoretical model of psychotherapy called interpersonal neurobiology (Badenoch & Porges, 2017; Porges & Dana, 2018; Solomon & Siegel, 2017). They offer several key ideas that are significant:

- The structure and function of brain are shaped and reshaped by experiences, especially in emotional relationships. Mental health, defined as having a sense of well-being and fulfilling relationships, rests on a healthy, integrated brain, one in which thoughts and feelings are in clear communication.

- Right-brain to right-brain interactions between therapist and client, meaning the nonconscious, rapport-building communication that makes you both cross or uncross your legs at the same time, are enormously impactful even though they are out of our awareness.

- Therapists' own mental health and self-awareness are essential because we use our minds and brains to "hold" the client in the therapeutic relationship.

- The empathic awareness of the therapist brings healing interactions to life and thus reorganizes the client's brain in more healthy ways.

This may sound a little far out for those of you who weren't biology majors. On the other hand, this line of work will have some interesting implications for our field and will probably help us understand why psychotherapy usually works at least as well as or better than psychotropic medications and has longer lasting effect. After all, change for the better—whether it is attitudinal, behavioral, biochemical, neurological, or all of these—is our business!

Early Trauma and Attachment Issues

Findings in neuroscience are especially intriguing as they offer a new way to think about the impact of trauma and how these experiences might be healed, or at least more comfortably processed. Psychotherapists have long observed that many who turn up in our offices report early life experiences that were far from optimal. We now have an abundance of studies that show that *adverse childhood experiences* (ACEs) can have a cumulative impact on adult mental health and daily functioning (Merrick et al, 2017). In addition, the more adverse experiences one has, the more likely that problems may emerge such as heavy drinking, drug use, depression, and even suicide attempts. Traditionally, early trauma has been challenging and time consuming to treat, often requiring years of psychotherapy and prescribed medications. The hope of neurologically based approaches is that therapists can help clients find new ways of processing and regulating upsetting emotions by working with their embodied brain (Badenoch, & Porges, 2017; Dana & Porges, 2018). Clients are taught to become better attuned to how their entire body reacts to emotionally salient experiences and how to use techniques of that calm the body to soothe themselves.

Attachment issues can often be related to adverse childhood experiences. Some infants and children experience inconsistent or even punitive connections with adults, resulting in insecure, avoidant, or disorganized attachment styles that persist into adulthood. Interpersonal neuroscience perspectives propose that in therapy the client can be provided with optimally attuned experiences that reshape the client's mind and brain toward greater security in relationships (Wilkinson, 2010). Importantly, parents also often have important attachment work to do because their child's emotional behavior often triggers their own tendencies to be emotionally reactive due to their own deeply embedded memories of parent–child interactions that were painful. Increasing attention is being devoted to how an understanding of the neurobiology of attachment can help both parents and therapists enhance connection and trust with children and adolescents (Baylin & Hughes, 2016; Brown & Elliot, 2016).

MINDFULNESS APPROACHES

"Mindfulness" is a term being used to describe when the mind's focus of attention is simply on the present moment. This may sound familiar to the "focusing" technique we described in the chapter on humanistic approaches, and it is. It's interesting that when we focus on an experience in the present moment, our mind is too preoccupied to lapse into rumination, speculation, justification, blaming, and all the other things that can lead to misery. Rather than refuting dysfunctional thoughts, the client learns to simply notice and then ignore them, not letting them build momentum. With practice and training, clients learn to make this mental shift more and more quickly (Segal, Williams, & Teasdale, 2018).

Mindfulness is an ancient technique that has recently made a big splash in the realm of psychotherapy. Mindfulness and other Eastern meditation techniques were brought to the attention of Westerners by teachers such as Thich Nhat Hanh (1975) and were rendered understandable for our very different culture by scientists and teachers such as Jon Kabat-Zinn (1990) and Jack Kornfield (1993). Those who practice mindfulness find that by intentionally letting the mind rest on the rich potential in small moments each day, and being fully present with the body, life experience becomes richer and less stressful (Siegel, 2017).

You are probably wondering what mindfulness looks like, exactly. Essentially, the mind is directed to the present moment. Sounds easy, but it is not, because our minds have strong habits of replaying past events, worrying about the future, and everything in between. Some have called this tendency the "monkey mind"—and this is an image that I (Marilyn) find helpful; when I feel anxiety revving up, I try to stop and notice how my thoughts are wildly jumping from image to image, usually only tangentially related, and I kindly observe that my mind is acting like a bunch of monkeys in the Amazon swinging excitedly from tree to tree.

FOR A CLASS ACTIVITY

Many of us who help others are particularly drawn to a practice called the loving-kindness meditation. It is a way to remind ourselves that we must first extend compassion to ourselves, then to others.

Here is one way to do it. Sit in a quiet place, close your eyes, and gently slow down your breathing. When you feel ready, with each breath, inwardly say, "May I be happy. May I be peaceful. May I be healthy and strong," and so forth. Notice the emotion of compassion growing within you. Then move your thoughts to someone you love very much and repeat the words, "May she be happy. May he be peaceful ..." Then move your attention to someone who is suffering and whom you would like to help. Lastly, for a challenge, think of someone who irritated you or hurt you. Breathing gently and steadily, wish them happiness, peace, and health as well. Then return your compassion to yourself. Relax and rest a few moments as you notice your compassion for yourself. Then take a few deep breaths, open your eyes, and return to your daily activities renewed.

Mindfulness practices are very compatible with the positive psychology movement, which focuses on optimal functioning and the flourishing of people and groups. Through this avenue, clients have been introduced to mindfulness techniques as an "adjunctive technique" (an add-on to therapy) to reduce stress. Specifically, mindfulness-based stress reduction (MBSR) was developed at the University of Massachusetts during the 1980s and has since then been found to be effective in reducing many symptoms (such as dependence on pain medication, depression, and anxiousness) and increasing aspects of well-being (such as self-esteem and positive moods). As a result, workshops on mindfulness practices have sprung up everywhere and are now routinely taught in many hospitals around the world. Essentially, mindfulness has been embraced as a form of complementary medicine with many benefits for mind and body (though of course, the two are seen as inseparable in this approach).

Mindfulness practices easily combine with other psychotherapy theories (and we will give you a couple of examples of this in the next section). Gestalt therapy, with its emphasis on awareness of the here and now, is a natural cousin. So are the cognitive therapies, with direct attention to exactly what the mind is up to and how it is influencing us each moment. Mindfulness has been successfully integrated into other therapeutic approaches, most notably, cognitive therapy (MBCT). In fact, an entire center has been created for testing and refining the approach and assessing how clients can best use it. A number of studies have shown that MBCT is very helpful in treating depression and preventing relapses in depression. Essentially, it has proven to be another effective way to help clients develop their cognitive skills for regulating their distressing thoughts and emotions (Farb et al., 2018).

A great deal of research has been done on mindfulness practices during the last two decades, finding that in addition to reducing stress, they relieve anxiety and depression, recurring suicidal behavior, and substance dependence (Segal, Williams, & Teasdale, 2018). With these very promising results, we expect you'll continue to hear more about this approach for a long time to come.

EMOTIONAL AND BEHAVIORAL REGULATION THERAPIES

Some of the toughest cases we deal with involve working with individuals who find their own emotional states overwhelming. What others say or do, or even their own thoughts, result in such excruciating pain that they resort to cutting themselves, starving themselves, drowning themselves in mind-altering substances, or attempting suicide, just for a little relief. Some recent therapy approaches incorporate mindfulness techniques with more traditional approaches to help these individuals. These are sometimes characterized as "third wave" cognitive therapies (Hayes & Hoffman, 2017), which focus more on the individual's relationship to their thoughts and resulting feelings than on the content of the thoughts themselves.

Acceptance and Commitment Therapy

This approach, also known as ACT, is the brainchild of a behaviorist, Steven Hayes, and others with expertise in behavior analysis. Because of their background, Hayes and his colleagues described thoughts, feelings, memories, and sensations as "private events." (This may remind you of how some behaviorists became more comfortable working with cognitions by calling them a kind of "mental behavior.")

The main idea is that psychological suffering is usually caused by experiential avoidance (for example, steering clear of things or thoughts that you believe might make you anxious) or cognitive entanglement (having thought habits that recreate your problems and give you excuses for not solving them). Either or both of these tendencies result in a paralyzing psychological rigidity that leads to a failure to take needed behavioral steps. By changing this pattern of avoidance or over-involvement, clients gain something important: psychological flexibility (Chin & Hayes, 2017).

Unlike the cognitive therapies we studied earlier in which dysfunctional thoughts are challenged, refuted, or vigorously disputed, in ACT the client is taught to simply "let them be" or even embrace them. For example, someone with chronic pain from a sports injury might ordinarily tense up and begin thinking depressing thoughts such as, "Oh no! Here it is again. Why did this have to happen to me? I'll never ride my bike again, and all my cycling friends will forget who I am. I'll be left alone in my misery." ACT uses mindfulness techniques to teach such clients to "just notice," accept, and embrace their inner experiences. Similar to a meditative exercise, the client simply observes the pain: "Hmm, there's that stabbing sensation in my knee again. I wonder how long it will last? I'll try to breathe into it."

The client thus learns to practice mindful tolerance and acceptance of distressing thoughts rather than trying to change them (Harris & Hayes, 2019). This loosens up the FEAR and increases psychological flexibility so that clients can become unstuck in those patterns.

- **Fusion** with your thoughts ("Oh, I can't stand this!")
- **Evaluation** of experience ("I'm such a ninny; why can't I power through this?")

- **A**voidance of your experience ("Can't I take something to make it go away?")
- **R**eason giving for your behavior ("Anybody in my shoes would be grumpy!")

Once the client is more accepting of his or her thoughts and experience, he or she finds it easier to make behavioral changes. But the behavioral steps can't be just action for action's sake. Before taking action, a person must clarify his or her personal values. When actions are consistent with personal values, people experience more vitality and life feels like it has meaning and is worth living. In the previous example, the injured athlete might need to clarify that the important thing about competitive cycling wasn't just the win, it was also belonging to a group and the fun of being outside and getting active early in the day. With values clarified, the person is better set to take a healthy alternative, which is to ACT:

- **A**ccept your reactions and be present ("Ah, my pain is coming back. Interesting.")
- **C**hoose a valued direction ("I still want to stick with my plans to see my friends."
- **T**ake action ("I'll keep on schedule with my meds, and I'll call Jake and Marie.")

As you might expect, with their background in behavior analysis, ACT therapists are particularly well suited for helping people change what they do. Through the course of therapy, clients are helped to build patterns of "committed action" in line with their values of what makes a life most worth living (Hayes, 2016).

The originators of this approach are dedicated to investigating its effectiveness in research studies. So far, ACT has been effective for a broad range of problems, including managing chronic pain, chronic physical conditions, addictions, smoking cessation, depression, anxiety, psychosis, workplace stress, and diabetes management (A-tjak et al., 2015). As more and more therapists are trying it, we expect you'll see more training opportunities for doing this approach.

Dialectical Behavioral Therapy

This modern therapy is likely one you've heard most about, as its founder, Marsha Linehan, has been writing about it since the 1990s. Many clinicians are drawn to DBT because it is designed to help clients with entrenched mental health problems and distressing behaviors such as self-harm and offers many specific techniques that counselors can use with their clients. It has also been shown to help clients moderate intense emotional experience.

DBT is similar to ACT in that practitioners are carefully nonjudgmental as they tune into clients' private experiences, sometimes simply becoming an observer of them. At other times, particular private experiences or behaviors may be targeted for change.

Marsha Linehan developed DBT for treating clients with borderline personality disorder (BPD) (Linehan, 1993). She found that some clients got frustrated with cognitive behavior therapy and just couldn't get results. Borrowing ideas from cognitive therapy, behavior analysis, and her own practice of Zen meditation, she began formulating a new integrative approach. DBT combines standard cognitive-behavioral techniques for emotion regulation and reality testing with concepts of mindful awareness, distress tolerance, and acceptance. You might be wondering how the "dialectical" part comes in—it is the process of going back and forth between acceptance, on the one hand, and change, on the other hand. Weaving both together is thought to be necessary for a healthy life with a reasonable amount of happiness.

DBT maintains that some people, due to experiencing an invalidating environment during their growing up years and various neurobiological factors, are very reactive to emotional stimuli. When they encounter a situation that they perceive as threatening, this triggers a physiological response in which their neuroendocrine system (which governs stress hormones, heart rate, etc.) responds much more quickly, peaks at a higher level, and takes more time to return to baseline than it does in other individuals. (This explains why individuals with borderline personality disorder have emotions that shift rapidly and lives that seem to bounce from one crisis to the next.) Because of their past invalidation, they aren't good at self-soothing and calming themselves after these sudden, intense surges of emotion. DBT is a method for teaching skills that help individuals develop these strategies and build them into their daily lives (Lenz & Del Conte, 2018).

Like ACT, DBT is guided by an integration of philosophies and therapies that have been refined over the years. DBT workbooks and training manuals offer many acronyms that both counselors and clients can learn and remember in the heat of the moment, when distressing events (overt or private) have arisen, or for staying on track with healthy practices (Linehan, 2014).

Also like ACT, DBT makes use of acronyms to help therapists and clients keep focused on change processes. For example, when on the verge of being overwhelmed by unpleasant intense emotions, clients can remember to distract themselves with ACCEPTS, which stands for specific skills that the client learns. ACCEPTS breaks down the following suggestions:

ACTIVITIES: Identify and do positive activities that you enjoy.

CONTRIBUTE: Help out others or your community.

COMPARISONS: Compare yourself either to people who are less fortunate or to how you used to be when you were in a worse state.

EMOTIONS: Shift to a different emotion by doing things that tickle your sense of humor.

PUSH AWAY: Put your situation on the back burner for a while. Put something else temporarily first in your mind.

THOUGHTS: Force your mind to think about something else.

SENSATIONS: Do something that has an intense feeling other than what you are feeling, such as enjoying a spicy candy or sucking on an ice cube.

DBT involves a lot of homework and in-vivo coaching during tough moments. It also takes time: Clients are typically involved in once-a-week sessions with an individual therapist and weekly group sessions in which concepts are taught and reinforced. The therapist and the client often contract to work together for a year. Research indicates that in addition to effectively treating BPD, DBT is also effective for clients who have a variety of symptoms and behaviors, including those associated with mood disorders, self-injury, eating disorders, and sexual abuse (Lenz & Del Conte, 2018) and for adolescents with similar issues (Hunnicut, Hollenbaugh & Lenz, 2018). Some controversies have arisen as the originator of the theory and certain followers call for strict adherence to the original theory, while other practitioners seek to innovate and incorporate new research and ideas. But this is a story you've heard before—a story at least as old as Freud.

Eye Movement Desensitization and Reprocessing (EMDR) Therapy

This theory could easily have been included in the chapter on cognitive therapies because it clearly capitalizes on internal thinking and imagery processes in its treatment. We have chosen to include it here because it incorporates physical as well as cognitive methods, and its primary focus is on memories of adverse life events that have been inadequately processed by the brain. A growing number of studies show that this approach works for reducing PTSD and many other trauma-related symptoms, but studies that adequately explain how and why it works are few.

Francine Shapiro (1989) first developed EMDR as a way to help people recover from posttraumatic stress. This disorder is commonly seen among survivors of child abuse, combat fatigue, disasters, or other calamities that subject humans to high-stress situations from which they have difficulty recovering. These individuals are typically plagued by haunting images, nightmares, and disturbing thoughts that limit their healthy functioning.

Interestingly, EMDR may remind you of other approaches you've studied because it takes elements from many of them and proposes a new Adaptive Information Processing (AIP) model for how change can occur. It is cognitive in that it works through thinking processes. It resembles the psychoanalytic approach in dealing with unconscious and unresolved issues of the past. It is behavioral in seeking to recondition people to respond differently to internal stimuli. And it has also been called a kind of hypnotic induction procedure in which clients are introduced into hyper-suggestive states so they become more amenable to surrendering dysfunctional behaviors. The overall goal is to reduce "pathogenic memories" (Hase, Balmaceda, Ostacoli, Liebermann, & Hofmann, 2017), which are considered to be at the base of variety of mental disorders.

A woman arrives at the therapist's door incapacitated by debilitating symptoms. She has suffered terrible physical and sexual abuse as a child that continues to impact her life. She has continual nightmares and exhibits extremely anxious reactions to any new situation she might confront. She is very mistrustful of others and has been unable to have a satisfying intimate relationship with a partner throughout her life.

FOR PERSONAL APPLICATION

What are some examples from your own life in which you are haunted by traumatic, disturbing images? When your guard is down, when you are tired or distracted, when you drift off to sleep, when you least expect it, your mind feels invaded by painful memories that you would prefer to forget.

Think about how your own unresolved, painful experiences from the past continue to plague you in the present and limit your functioning in several areas.

The therapist asks the client to bring to mind one of the most disturbing, recurring images. She is urged to focus on the worst part of the memory and to describe it in detail, all the while she identifies exactly when and where she feels the most debilitating symptoms. During this narrative, the client is asked to follow the therapist's finger with her eyes, back and forth, as it is moved in front of her face. The therapist continues this consistent movement, guiding the client's eyes from one side to the other.

The eye movements are introduced as "sets," during which time the client is asked to bring up the disturbing image again, but this time erasing it in the process. Again and again this process is repeated, and each time the client is asked to describe what is happening internally. Eventually, clients report that the image loses its power altogether and they no longer have such disturbing thoughts.

FOR PERSONAL REFLECTION

Based on the theories you already learned about, how would you explain the process by which EMDR helps people deal with pathogenic memories? As a hint, you might go back and look at behavior therapy and the concept of desensitization, or psychoanalysis and its notion of unresolved conflicts, or perhaps cognitive therapy and the process of restructuring.

Other explanations that have been offered include the neuropsychological changes that take place as a result of bilateral eye stimulation, the benefits of eye movements that simulate REM sleep, brain activation in certain cortical centers, counter-conditioning, and something Shapiro (2018) calls adaptive information processing, which most closely relates to hypnotic methods. Shapiro concludes her review of possible theories and mechanisms through which EMDR works by stating that it is all very complex. Indeed, it is.

Thousands of practitioners swear by this approach to therapy, claiming miraculous improvements within a matter of weeks for anxiety, stress, trauma, eating disorders, depression chronic limb pain, and distress associated with borderline personality disorder (Shapiro, 2018). It is even being used with children and teens (Adler-Tapia & Settle, 2017). Evidence from systematic studies does indicate that EMDR is more effective than CBT for addressing PTSD symptoms, and also is effective in reducing anxiety and depression, but with important caveats: Longer treatment sessions were more effective than shorter ones and experienced therapists got the best results (Chen, Xhang, Hu, & Liang, 2015).

It seems as if this is one of those treatment procedures that currently defy our ability to explain thoroughly how it works. The latest hypothesis uses information processing theory to reason that it helps clients reconsolidate dysfunctionally stored memories into larger adaptive cognitive networks—an explanation that still involves a fair amount of mystery. If you really think about it, however, most theories in this book are based on a degree of faith.

One of the things that gave EMDR such a skeptical reception in the profession is that therapists had to pay large sums of money to buy their training from approved teachers and then sign contracts saying they wouldn't reveal what they learned. As more and more therapists have experimented with this method, there is considerable enthusiasm for its use even though they cannot explain exactly how it works. From their perspective, you shouldn't argue with success.

Body and Energy Psychotherapies

Based on the work of Wilhem Reich (1945), a psychoanalyst who used breathing work in his therapy, Alexander Lowen (1958) created a therapy to heal the split between mind and body. "The body will heal itself," writes Lowen (1997), "if one surrenders to it" (p. 144). This means trusting not only what one thinks and feels, but also what one senses and experiences in the body.

There are many recent variations on this theme, roughly grouped into areas called "body psychotherapy" and "energy psychology." These approaches—and there are many variations of them—hold that the body and the energy that flows through it are the principal determinants of all we see, feel, think, and perceive (Mollon, 2018).

Because the goal of these approaches is the integration of body and mind so that the client experiences a fuller sense of self, clients may be instructed in the use a variety of techniques, including physical exercises, deep-breathing techniques, and massage, to free up body energy (Lowen & Friedman, 2006). Clients are helped to work through blocks that get in the way of expressing themselves. Although the intent of cathartic expression parallels what psychoanalysts had in mind, these therapies sidestep the "talk" aspect of therapy. Because it is thought that core energy flows not only at the level of mind and emotion, but also through the body, spirit, and will, this kind of work bypasses the intellect in favor of a more direct form of experience. For example, a therapist would assist someone who had built a "fortress" with bodily and psychological defenses due to experiences with early childhood trauma to dismantle the fortress that keeps him or her protected but isolated, using an assortment of techniques involving the body as well as the mind (May, 2018).

One recent variation that is receiving some attention is called the *emotional freedom technique*. Similar to other approaches in this section, talking about one's problems is seen as less useful than more active forms of learning that directly affect the brain. This technique is a simple one, involving keeping one's painful memory or sensation in awareness while also tapping one's fingers on particular body points with the purpose of rebalancing the body's energy, similar to the ancient Chinese medicine practice of acupuncture and acupressure (Christine, 2017). It is regarded most favorably by those who seek complementary and alternative medicine approaches to health and mental health and is particularly attractive because it can be taught as a self-help aid.

What's the bottom line with these new body-energy models? Similar to all approaches, it is likely that some of their positive effects are due to clients' expectations that they will work (the placebo effect). It is also true that bringing any memory to mind over and over again, particularly doing something a bit weird and requiring concentration (whether that is a body posture, particular eye movements, or tapping) changes the memory's neural encoding and thus reduces its power to create feelings of distress (Leuzinger-Bohleber, 2015).

EXPRESSIVE THERAPIES

Although hardly new or even necessarily separate from other theories already covered, expressive therapies are somewhat innovative in their emphasis on different facets of the therapeutic experience. Unlike verbal and didactic therapies that rely on speech and instruction, expressive therapies access primary experience through more active forms of learning.

Drama, dance, music, art, and other expressive forms follow the earliest healing practices of our ancestors (Degges-White & Davis, 2018). Most expressive therapies hold the following beliefs:

1. Talk is not enough.
2. Active methods involving a person's mind, heart, and soul will have a greater impact than those that use only the intellect.
3. Language as a secondary experience (a translation of inner states) is not always an accurate or complete representation of experience.
4. Creativity and movement are critical to self-expression and growth.
5. The goal of therapy is to facilitate growth toward higher levels of personal development and enlightenment.

The conceptual base for expressive approaches is diverse, stemming from a number of different sources such as the healing rituals that have been employed by indigenous healers around the world since the beginning of recorded history. There is an emphasis on integrating talk with movement. More contemporary experiential family therapies, psychodrama, transpersonal approaches and Gestalt techniques are examples. In each case, the goal is to move beyond mere conversation to include forms such as art, dance, music, drama, or spiritual transcendence (Degges-White & Davis, 2018). Instead of asking someone *what* he or she is experiencing, the person would be directed to *show* what he or she is experiencing.

FOR A GROUP ACTIVITY

It is perhaps hypocritical of us to tell you about expressive theories and then ask you to think about them. After all, this violates the major premise of this theory that stresses primary experience rather than the intellect.

People in general, and therapy/counseling students in particular, are often inhibited when it comes to using more creative forms of personal expression that involve acting out internal reactions rather than merely talking about them. Even if you will not practice these approaches in pure form, it is still useful to gain experience employing some of their methods.

In small groups, play with several different modalities together. Start off by drawing a picture that best represents the way you feel about therapeutic theories thus far. After you are done, talk about what came up for you.

Next, each of you should use some form of dance, movement, or sculpted posture to demonstrate the theory you favor most. After you have illustrated your preference, invite the other participants to guess what you were communicating.

Discuss ways that you might use various expressive therapies in your work.

Drama Therapy

At the beginning of the 19th century, at about the same time that Freud was refining his theories in Europe, J. L. Moreno (1946) spent his time watching children interacting on playgrounds. Although this might be the sort of thing that would get you arrested today, Moreno was discreet in his observations, operating like an anthropologist who is studying the behavior of a foreign culture. In his field notes, Moreno became aware of the natural, spontaneous ways that children dramatized their feelings, expressing their emotions through various roles they played and scenarios they acted out. He wondered what would happen if adults could regain some of the creativity, spontaneity, and drama of their childhoods. Would such activities help them to work through problems, express feelings, and resolve struggles?

From such musings, a number of other theoreticians and practitioners (Jennings, 2014; Moreno, Blomkvist, & Rutzel, 2000) developed a field of drama therapy in which whatever comes to mind is played out. Images, stories, and fantasies are portrayed in real time—focused on the work of an individual, family, or whole group. First, a scenario is enacted spontaneously and then it is connected to what has occurred in one's own life.

The goals are as follows:

- Putting feelings and thoughts into action, creating or recreating direct experience
- Catharsis or release of tension
- Self-reflection, awareness, and insight
- Laboratory for experimentation
- Rehearsal of alternative strategies
- Vicarious learning

There are many variations in the structures and formats that are used, but generally the therapist serves as the director of the experience, helping to set the scene, choose the characters, and enact the scenario. The identified client is the protagonist, the hero of the show who faces some adversity that must be overcome. Another participant plays the antagonist who is the primary adversary in the story. This could mean an abusive spouse, a neglectful parent, a disrespectful boss, or a deceased ancestor. Other characters are chosen to play supporting roles in the story. Doubles and alter egos are also selected to give support to the protagonist or to reflect unexpressed or underlying feelings.

In the illustration to follow, the protagonist has been complaining about her timidity and passivity in various situations in her life. She rarely asserts herself at work, at school, or at home, preferring to play it safe. When asked to pick one scenario she'd like to enact, the client decided to pick the one that is most immediate: the classroom environment. Although she often has things she'd like to say in class, she holds herself back because of fears of being judged as stupid or inadequate.

After choosing one person to play the instructor, the authority figure whose approval she craves the most, she also picked individuals to play various consulting roles. One auxiliary ego would sit behind her and express the assertive part of her, while the other would speak out loud her fears. In the following dialogue, several characters are identified:

Protagonist—the woman who struggles with being assertive

Instructor—the authority figure whose approval she wants

Ghost—an amalgamation of her father, older sister, and fourth-grade teacher, none of whom approved of her the way she wanted

Approval seeker—the "perfect" classmate whom the instructor seems to like best. This woman always seems to say the right thing and earn smiles from the instructor

Teaser—another classmate who ridicules her and makes her feel self-conscious about her passivity

Assertive self—the auxiliary ego who will say out loud what the protagonist really wants to say but holds back

Fearful self—the auxiliary ego that expresses out loud the unexpressed fears

This seems complicated and chaotic, but when you actually see and experience such a dramatic enactment, it all comes together, as shown next.

INSTRUCTOR: Does anyone have anything to say about this?

PROTAGONIST: Um, well, I was thinking … I mean. …

FEARFUL SELF: See, there I go again. I'm making a complete fool of myself.

TEASER: Well, if you're done with your articulate statement, I have something to say.

PROTAGONIST: Well, OK, if you have …

ASSERTIVE SELF: (To teaser) Excuse me. But I am absolutely not done. And I'd appreciate it if you'd wait your turn.

GHOST: You might as well just give up. You don't belong in school anyway. You know you're not smart enough. I've been telling you that for years.

Well, you get the picture. They all have their say, expressing out loud the voices the protagonist hears inside her head every day. After the drama unfolds for a while, time will be taken to process what has occurred and give others a chance to share how they are identifying with various roles.

Psychodrama has been used since the 1930s to treat a variety of problems, but recently it has undergone more systematic evaluation. Studies have shown that it reduces symptoms of depression and increases social adjustment in individuals diagnosed with major depressive disorder, more so than medication only (Pitruzzella, 2016). Versions of psychodrama have recently been developed especially for use with children (Jennings, 2014). It is certainly an approach with staying power.

FOR A GROUP ACTIVITY

In a fishbowl in the center of the room, your instructor, a visiting expert, or an experienced drama therapist will demonstrate a psychodrama. Another alternative is to meet in small groups and use the foregoing example as a guide for structuring your own dramatic experiment. One of you will volunteer to be the director to lead the scenario while each of the others will take on a particular role as a character in the story or as an auxiliary ego. You can include not only those mentioned previously, but also consultants who are feeling communicators (saying out loud feelings that are sensed), doubters (who express self-doubts), or confidence boosters (who offer support and encouragement as needed).

As beginners, your job is not to be very skilled or adept at this modality, but rather simply to gain some basic experience in what it's like. Be patient with yourself because most therapists require years of training and supervised practice to become proficient in these therapies.

Art Therapy

Representative of another form of expressive therapy on the edge, art therapy encourages clients to express themselves through the media of drawing, painting, sculpture, clay, and collage. Although this approach is often used with children, the intellectually impaired, and older adults because it doesn't require verbal fluency, it can be adapted for a host of other populations.

Art therapy was originally designed as a diagnostic aid (Kwiatkowska, 1978), then later to promote insight (Rubin, 2009), and eventually as a more action-oriented method adapted for family therapy (Linesch, 1993; Riley, 1994). Natalie Rogers (1986), Carl Rogers's daughter, developed an approach to art therapy that incorporated the core conditions: "I base my approach to expressive arts therapy on this very deep faith in the innate capacity of each person to reach toward her [or his] full potential" (p. 3). She believed that person-centered expressive art therapy may be especially helpful for clients stuck in linear, rigid, and analytic ways of thinking and experiencing the world (Tudor, 2016).

Art therapy has also been explored as a way to get in closer touch with the unconscious mind. The idea is that both art and dreams speak to us in images and symbols, and help us access unconscious aspects of our "mindbrain" that we usually ignore (Blechner, 2018).

Art therapy has recently been included in studies to see if it can improve well-being for individuals with health problems. For example, a number of studies examining the effects of art therapy on anxiety and depression in women with breast or gynecological cancer have found improved psychological outcomes and coping skills (Hertrampf, & Wärja, 2017). It has also been explored as an innovative medium for treating depression.

FOR PERSONAL REFLECTION or A CLASS ACTIVITY

Draw a picture of your family. This could be a representation of your family of origin or your current family. (If you have time, do both.)

Draw your family doing something or involved in an activity that best captures the spirit of what you are trying to portray. Don't worry about your artistic accuracy. Use stick figures if you want.

When you are done, write down a few of the things that family members might be saying to one another or to you.

Talk to someone about what this exercise revealed to you.

Dance and Movement Therapy

Same idea, different domain of expression. This time, rather than expressing themselves through art, people are encouraged to do so through movement.

Almost all human cultures from the beginning of time have used dance to mark rituals, celebrate ceremonies, prepare for war, or entertain citizens. It has also been used to produce altered states of consciousness similar to hypnotic trance states. Dance therapy as an official treatment originated in inpatient psychiatry. In the 1940s, some psychiatrists in Washington, DC noticed that some of their patients—many whom had been traumatized by war—improved after attending the dance classes of Marian Chace, a dancer and choreographer who was influenced by psychiatrist Carl Jung (Pies, 2008). Subsequently, dance therapy was adapted for many other inpatient settings. Dance therapists now seek to help people develop a nonverbal language that allows them to tune into and express what is going on in their bodies in a setting that is safe and nonjudgmental.

Dance therapy is currently experiencing a surge of popularity worldwide. It is used in a variety of settings with people who have social, emotional, cognitive, or physical concerns. Often, it is prescribed as part of the recovery process for people with chronic physical or mental illness. Clients, whether in individual, group, or family settings, are helped to express their inner states through body movement.

Like any of the other expressive therapies, this modality is linked to a variety of other theories you have studied such as psychoanalytic, humanistic, and Gestalt therapies (Chaiklin, & Wengrower, 2016). Dance and movement therapists don't teach clients to dance. Rather, they dance with the client.

Similar to client-centered talk therapy, the client leads the movements and the therapist empathically mirrors and senses what the client is trying to express. Over the course of a session, the dance therapist might echo movement themes, expand on dynamics, or wait in silence.

Play Therapy

There are probably as many different versions of play therapy as there are theories of counseling and psychotherapy. We include them here because their popularity continues to grow, as therapists innovate with basic ideas and find new applications for them, with new populations and new problems. For example, as more and more children are diagnosed with attention and behavioral regulation problems, therapists have found ways to address these problems through play, which is children's natural medium of expression. But nonverbal techniques, including play, are also useful for other kinds of clients, as we have seen in the review of expressive therapies.

The early days of play therapy began when psychoanalysts and Jungian therapists realized that talk therapy, however free and unrestricted, was just not going to work very well with children. There are good reasons for this—children have not yet developed the cognitive apparatus to think about themselves in abstract ways or to be reflective and thereby gain insights into their behavior.

Nevertheless, they have a very rich emotional world and benefit from sharing it with caring adults. In play therapy, an adult provides a safe space that includes toys representing everyday activities (such as kitchen tools, baby dolls, school materials, play money, etc.) and expressive materials (such as costumes, puppets, clay, and paint). In nondirective play therapy, which is probably the form most often practiced, the therapist makes accepting and reflecting responses (similar to talk therapy, but the therapist reflects the child's play actions rather than narrative themes) (Landreth, 2012). Play therapists with a psychodynamic bent also include some interpretive responses, with the aim of helping a child integrate painful experiences from which they usually distance themselves (Landreth, 2012).

Play therapy can also be more directive, as when particular social skills such as turn-taking are reinforced through playing games, either with the therapist or as part of a group approach. Some play therapists use primarily behavioral techniques to teach impulsive children how to defer immediate gratification, using praise to reward children's attempts at behavioral regulation. These kinds of approaches are the ones most commonly used in schools, where behavior management is often a pressing priority.

FOR PERSONAL REFLECTION

If you've never observed or done play therapy, it can be a little hard to imagine. So, let us tell you about Jolie. Jolie, age 9, had been virtually mute during scheduled sessions. Regardless of the questions asked, she would only shrug or nod her head. It was more than being shy; she was obviously very troubled. After a few attempts to engage Jolie in some kind of interaction, the therapist asked her if she'd like to play instead. The first glimmerings of a smile showed on the corners of Jolie's mouth; then she nodded her head.

"Go ahead and pick something off the shelf," the therapist invited, pointing to a closet where there was a wide selection of toys, blocks, dolls, games, hats, and puppets.

After carefully reviewing the choices, Jolie took out a dollhouse that came equipped with an assortment of figures and props. She set the structure on the floor and began exploring the various rooms.

"Why don't you show me your family and where they stay in your house."

Jolie explained that they didn't have a house. Instead, her father, mother, sister, and brother all lived in one room.

"Go ahead and arrange the furniture the way it is where you live," the therapist suggested. "And put all the people where they belong."

During the next half hour, Jolie was mesmerized by the assignment, moving her family members around, trying out various rooms, all the while chattering to herself as if the therapist wasn't in the room. As time was drawing to an end, the therapist announced that it was time for the family to go to bed so maybe she could put them all asleep before they stopped the session and cleaned up.

Jolie had set up three single beds in the room. She placed her mother and father in one bed, her sister in another, and then lay the figure that represented herself on the third bed with her brother placed on top of her.

"That's how you sleep, Jolie? Your brother sleeps in your bed with you? You said he's 14, right?"

Jolie looked down at her hands but didn't answer.

In the span of 30 minutes of play time, the therapist was able to assess the possibility of sexual abuse in Jolie's home (not just with her, but also her sister), as well as to forge a closer relationship with her client. In subsequent sessions, even though Jolie would rather not talk about what was going on in her life, she had no difficulty acting out the struggles through play.

Filial Play Therapy

There is a relative newcomer on the play therapy scene that is increasingly popular because it addresses both the parent and the child in the context of their ongoing relationship—filial therapy. "Filial" refers to familial relationships, and filial therapy was developed by Bernard and Louise Guerney in the 1960s as a way to teach family members to affirm and connect with each other through person-centered techniques (Guerney, 1964; Guerney & Ryan, 2013). Essentially, the therapist models for the parent how to act "therapeutically" with their child—not in the sense of treating a disorder, but by giving the child safe places and times to be expressive, with clear boundaries, and an attentive adult who simply observes and appreciates the child's expression of himself or herself through play. Essentially, the therapist teaches the parent the skills of nondirective play therapy. The parent is instructed on how to have regular play therapy sessions with their child at home, but at very particular places and times. By keeping to this "frame," parents must practice setting limits with their child. They also practice a way of interacting with their child that is fully present—in other words, very different from the half-listening style that parents frequently employ as they go about assembling the day's lunches and hustling kids off to school. Children typically respond well to this fully present attention. Their behavior improves, and parents are reinforced for shifting out of their ignore-indulge-screech-spank parenting methods into ones based on acknowledgement of feelings and logical limit-setting.

Sandplay Therapy

One very popular form of play therapy involves playing in a sandbox to act out issues in a child's life, in much the same way that the therapist worked with Jolie in the preceding session.

Margaret Lowenfeld, a child psychoanalyst during the 1930s, was the first therapist to put sand into trays with water and miniature figures nearby in her consulting room so that her child patients had a means of nonverbal expression. Her "world technique," as she came to call it, was further developed by Dora M. Kalff, who had studied with Carl and Emma Jung, referred to sandplay as game without rules, played in "a free and protected space" (Kalff, 2003, p. xiv). Certified sandplay (or sandtray) therapists are members of national and international sandplay organizations, and they strongly believe that you need to have experienced sandplay as a client before you can learn to do it as a therapist.

You can tell you are in a sandplay therapist's office by noticing the characteristic box of sand with a blue bottom and sides, and shelves on the wall filled with intriguing miniatures of human, animal, and fantasy figures and objects. You, as the client, would be invited to create a scene in any way you wanted, picking and choosing from the miniatures and placing them in the sand (Homeyer & Sweeney, 2017). As you selected your figures and shaped the sand, your conscious, planful mind would take a back seat. The therapist would not interpret, interfere, or give you suggestions, but would maintain a receptive and accepting attitude, freeing you to explore your inner world and bring unconscious material into consciousness. The act of making your scene would, literally and figuratively, give you a new outlook on your life. When you were done, you'd both step back, admire your creation, and take a picture. The creation itself would not be interpreted immediately, but later, during a talk therapy session (Hong, 2010), sometimes using Gestalt techniques (Timm & Garza, 2017).

Because it is a creative way of working that does not rely on "talk" therapy, sandtray work is thought to facilitate exploration of deep emotional issues. It is suitable for both children and adults and allows them to reach a deeper insight into, and resolution of, a range of issues in their lives such as deep anger, depression, abuse, or grief. It has been used in inpatient settings to treat psychoses, borderline syndromes, psychosomatic illnesses, and addictions (Zoja, 2004). Sandplay seems to access areas of human suffering that have otherwise resisted psychotherapeutic treatment. Recent neurobiological research supports the fact that emotional memories and traumatic sensory experiences are stored in the midbrain's limbic system while nonverbal sensory experiences and sensations are stored somatically. At the same time, the areas of the brain responsible for speech and executive function are often compromised as a result of traumatic experience (van der Kolk, 2014). Nonverbal therapies like sandplay are the most effective ways to access and release these "unconscious" feelings and experiences that have never been articulated in words into a form shaped by the hands. Thus, it is thought, the inexpressible can be seen and touched, and therefore, it can be transformed.

ANIMAL-ASSISTED THERAPY

This approach may seem rather strange but will probably make inherent sense to animal lovers. Some early versions of this were what are now called "animal-assisted activities." Think of the positive moods and pleasant interactions that happen in a petting zoo, for example. Now, animal-assisted therapy (AAT) is a bona fide approach with its own standards of practice, certifications, and a growing body of research supporting it. It involves using an animal that meets specific criteria, whether dogs, cats, horses, rabbits, dolphins or "pocket pets," and is an integral part of the treatment process (Chandler, 2017).

You can probably imagine how this might work. A therapist approaches a reluctant client in a shelter or invites a shy child into the playroom; their eyes light up when they see a calm and friendly animal, and the stress of the first interaction is eased. Therapy animals can provide a point of connection and relief for individuals who are confined in a shelter, prison, hospice, or inpatient setting, giving the therapist a point of entry for beginning to establish trust. The therapist can also use the life history of the animal to establish a connection with the client. For example, an animal that was abused or abandoned can open a discussion with children with similar histories (Fine, 2015).

AAT can be done in both individual and group setting and has been used increasingly in schools. A growing number of studies indicate that it can reduce distress, depression, loneliness, anxiety, post-traumatic stress, grief reactions, conduct problems, attention problems, and attachment-related problems, while increasing self-esteem, appropriate touching behavior, and interpersonal skills such as reciprocity and mutuality (Chandler, 2017). It is also helpful for reducing behavioral and psychological symptoms of dementia, especially depression and agitation, in patients with cognitive impairment (Hu, Zhang, Leng, Li, & Chen, 2017). As a nice side benefit, it seems to be promising for reducing therapist distress and burnout as well, especially for those working in the toughest of human conditions.

In Summary

This concludes our treatment of major therapeutic approaches. In this chapter, we have examined those novel and contemporary approaches that seek to move beyond conventional conversational treatments. This was a mere sampling of the options currently available since there are many others such as video game therapy (Curtis, Phenix, Munoz, & Hertlein, 2017), music therapy (Silverman, 2018), global traditional and complementary systems of healing (Gureje et al., 2015), biofeedback (Fish, 2018), and positive mental imagery training (Blackwell et al., 2018). We suspect you are already pretty flooded and overwhelmed by the variety of therapeutic approaches already introduced, certainly enough to get you started.

It is natural at this point that you might be feeling more than a little bewildered by all the new concepts, terms, and different ways of looking at human difficulties and their resolution. In the last two chapters of the text, we will help you to pull everything together, look at common elements, and integrate what you have learned into a framework for guiding your practice.

SUGGESTED READINGS

Badenoch, B., & Porges, S. W. (2017). *The heart of trauma: Healing the embodied brain in the context of relationships.* New York, NY: Norton.

Chandler, C. K. (2017). *Animal-assisted therapy in counseling* (3rd ed.). New York, NY: Routledge.

Cozolino, L. (2017). *The neuroscience of psychotherapy: Healing the social brain* (3rd ed.). New York, NY: Norton.

Degges-White, S., & Davis, N. L. (2018). *Integrating the expressive arts into counseling practice: Theory-based interventions.* New York, NY: Springer.

Harris, R. M. & Hayes, S. C. (2019). *ACT Made Simple: An easy-to-read primer on acceptance and commitment therapy* (2nd ed.). Oakland, CA: New Harbinger.

Homeyer, L., & Sweeney, D. S. (2017). *Sandtray therapy: A practical manual.* New York, NY: Routledge.

Linehan, M. M. (2014). *DBT skills training manual* (2nd ed.). New York, NY: Guilford.

Luoma, J. B., Hayes, S. C., & Walser, R. D. (2017). *Learning ACT: An acceptance and commitment therapy skills training manual for therapists.* Oakland, CA: Context Press.

Rubin, J. A. (2016). *Introduction to art therapy: Theory and technique.* New York, NY: Routledge.

Segal, Z. V., Williams, J. M. G., & Teasdale, J. D. (2018). *Mindfulness-based cognitive therapy for depression* (2nd ed.). New York, NY: Guilford Publications.

Shapiro, F. (2018). *Eye movement desensitization and reprocessing (EMDR) therapy* (3rd ed.). New York, NY: Guilford.

Siegel, D. J. (2018). *Aware: The science and practice of presence.* New York, NY: Tarcher Perigee.

van der Kolk, B. (2014). *The body keeps score: Brain, mind, and body in the healing of trauma.* New York, NY: Penguin.

CHAPTER 12

Integrative Approaches to Doing Therapy

LEARNING OBJECTIVES

After reading this chapter, you should be able to do the following:

1. Describe four common ways that practitioners integrate theories to benefit clients.
2. Identify potential pitfalls associated with particular integrative practices.
3. Explain why integrating theories of counseling and psychotherapy has become a common practice.
4. Articulate ways in which Lazarus's multimodal therapy exemplifies the integrative practice of technical eclecticism.
5. Identify the common factors that facilitate clients' improvement across many therapeutic approaches.
6. List key elements of therapeutic process that take place across theoretical approaches.
7. Speculate about how your own theoretical preferences and allegiances may change over the course of your career.
8. Describe practices that you can undertake to further your development as a thoughtful clinician.

Therapists are fond of claiming that talk is cheap. Clients go on and on about the changes they intend to make, the things they want to do, and the plans they have, but all this means little if they do not act on their intentions. Furthermore, people often describe themselves in a way that has little to do with their actual conduct in the world.

If you are nodding your head in agreement, remember that this same pattern occurs with therapists as well. What practitioners say they do in their sessions isn't necessarily what they are really doing behind closed doors. Each of us could tell you our favored theory, the one that demands our loyalty. We can read all the appropriate literature in that specialty, attend the conferences and workshops devoted to it, hang out only with those professionals who share our theoretical beliefs, and tell anyone who will listen how much better our theory is than all others. Nevertheless, when we are with our clients, we might behave far more flexibly than we would lead anyone (including ourselves) to believe. Like so many practitioners, we might call ourselves a true believer of one theory but actually practice far more integratively and eclectically than advertised.

Most clinicians use techniques from several different theories in their practice, particularly after they have been in practice a while (Norcross, Goldfried, & Zimmerman, 2016). Just think about the challenges this presents! It is hard enough to truly come to terms with only one of these complex models, much less try to employ several of them at different times in the same session. It is for this reason that you must not only develop mastery of a theory's content, but also of its essence. This allows you to combine the best features with other models you find most appealing.

Both of us are frequently asked what kind of therapist we are, theoretically speaking. When someone puts us on the spot like this, we are never quite sure what to say. In some ways, I (Jeffrey) am proud of not knowing what I am and just as pleased that critics can't guess either. In some reviews of my books, I have read that I am everything from a psychoanalyst or existentialist to a cognitive theorist. I plead guilty to all three, plus a dozen others that strike my fancy. I (Marilyn) just keep making the rounds of the theories, and every time I learn more about one through a workshop, book, or new colleague, the more impressed I am of its wisdom and the more I try to incorporate it in my work. Do these confessions reveal that we are integrative therapists at heart?

Almost from the very beginning of the profession, when there were only two main approaches—psychoanalysis and behaviorism—practitioners such as French (1933), Kubie (1934), and Rosenzweig (1936) tried to combine the theories into a single, comprehensive, approach. As we've mentioned previously, Alfred Adler created another integrative theory; after practicing psychoanalysis as a disciple of Freud's, he eventually adapted the approach by combing features he considered important. Many years later, theorists and practitioners of all stripes are still trying to put together the most advantageous combinations of theories and techniques.

Likewise, there are several ways that you might integrate the various theories into a workable system. Each one allows you to customize the theory to fit your particular style and needs of your clients just as we have done. This is often better than *syncretism*, which is a haphazard amalgamation of one's favorite techniques implemented unsystematically and with usually without training. Like its culinary equivalent, "hash," syncretism doesn't get much respect. To guide you to more satisfying and respected results, we will review four of the main ways that theory integration is often accomplished most effectively.

First is an approach wherein practitioners combine two or more theories into a single conceptual approach with hopes that the new *theoretical integration* will be greater than the sum of its parts. A second option, *assimilative integration*, describes those who are grounded in one theory but incorporate techniques or interventions borrowed from other approaches. Third, and actually the least theoretically grounded, is *technical eclecticism*, in which any variety of techniques are chosen on the basis of what might fit a particular client or treat a particular symptom. Finally, there are those who seek to find processes common to many different approaches, building a working theory based on these "*common factors.*" Each of these approaches has certain advantages as well as limitations that we will discuss. But before we begin our review, we want to give you an illustration from a master integrator who brought technical eclecticism to the foreground—Arnold Lazarus.

ARNOLD LAZARUS AND MULTIMODAL THERAPY

Arnold Lazarus could have fit into the chapter on behavior therapies because he owes much of his allegiance to this approach. But after practicing many years, he stepped away from his theory of origin and began to advocate for a systematic model for assessing and treating problems that he called multimodal therapy (Lazarus, 1971, 1989, 2006). Although he was sometimes criticized for being "a-theoretical" he considered himself a pragmatist. After broadening his focus to include many aspects of the client's experience, he wrote, "To attempt a theoretical rapprochement is as futile as trying to picture the edge of the universe. But to read through the vast array of literature on psychotherapy, in search of techniques, can be clinically enriching and therapeutically rewarding" (Lazarus, 1967, p. 416).

Although today his theory retains its strong behavioral roots with its emphasis on behavior assessment and homework assignments, he included other dimensions of affect, imagery, relationships, physiology, and cognitions. Although it might seem that his theoretical integration is a mashed jumble of techniques, Lazarus preferred the term *technical eclecticism* because he advocated a systematic, consistent framework to choose interventions from a variety of approaches to address multiple needs of clients.

Foundational Ideas

Multimodal therapy has at its core an assessment process that includes most facets of human experience. In this BASIC ID model, each of seven different modalities plays a role in the diagnosis and treatment process. You will notice that cognitive and behavioral components are included, naturally, but Lazarus also takes pains to include other aspects of functioning that might play a part in the presenting problem and its resolution (see table 12.1).

TABLE 12.1. Profile of BASIC ID

Code	Modality	Description	Example
B	Behavior	Observable behavior that includes habits and actions	Drinking and smoking too much; acting aggressively
A	Affect	Feelings that result from thinking and behavior	Depression; helplessness; anger; loneliness
S	Sensation	Body sensations or anything significant from the five senses	Numbness; sense of isolation; disconnection from outside world
I	Imagery	Fantasies, dreams, or any strong images	Suicidal ideation; fantasies of lashing out; poor body image
C	Cognition	Thinking processes	"I'm stupid." "I'll never beat this thing." "Nobody likes me."
I	Interpersonal relationship	Relationship problems; inter-actions with others	Conflict with coworkers; estrangement from family; isolation
D	Drugs/Biology	Medical or physical conditions; medications or drugs used	Headaches; high blood pressure; excessive drinking

You can appreciate just how clearly and systematically a therapist can map out a client's presenting problems with this model, not only related to the original complaint, but also any other factors that might be relevant. Just as you would use this profile to make a thorough assessment of the client's issues, your treatment plan would also follow the same format. Based on the identification of areas, a treatment plan such as this could be designed:

BEHAVIOR   Curtail drinking and smoking. Apply assertiveness training to change behavior to more appropriate responses to stress. Begin exercise program.

AFFECT   Acknowledge and work through anger. Talk about sense of helplessness and powerlessness. Use therapeutic relationship to work on intimacy issues.

SENSATIONS   Spend time outside to reconnect with natural world. Work on fuller engagement with others to reduce numbness.

IMAGERY   Substitute fantasies with others that are more positive and optimistic. Practice imagery rehearsal of constructive actions that can be taken.

COGNITION	Dispute irrational beliefs. Confront exaggerations and overgeneralizations.
INTERPERSONAL RELATIONS	Reduce conflicts at work. Reach out to others. Initiate new friendships.
DRUGS	Reduce stress levels. Find alternatives to self-medication. Get a physical exam to rule out organic causes.

In this form of eclectic practice, you can see how easy it would be to use almost any method you want to address particular client issues. Multimodal theory is heavily steeped in behavioral and cognitive aspects, but you can borrow interventions from any other model. The great part of this multimodal framework is that you can integrate any combination of features or techniques you want, to best serve the client's needs.

Lazarus put a priority on making the ideas of multimodal therapy accessible to people who might prefer self-help to investing in an ongoing therapeutic relationship, giving, for example, advice on how people can rid their minds of toxic ideas or practice relaxation. Others, too, have taken the ideas of multimodal therapy—or its practices—and run with them.

FOR A GROUP ACTIVITY

Get together in groups of three. One person role plays a client who has a host of personal difficulties. The other two partners, working as a team, ask a series of focused, pointed, open-ended questions designed to elicit as much information as possible in the shortest period of time (15 to 20 minutes).

After you have conducted this intake interview, work together to create a BASIC ID profile for the client, listing symptoms present in each area (10 to 15 minutes) and plan for addressing each of them.

We will say more about simpler methods of integrating theory. Right now, it might occur to you that it is daunting enough to think about mastering one theory, much less the expectation in this approach that you would have reasonable fluency in several of them. Multimodal therapy is, therefore, best for more advanced practitioners after you have had considerable training in multiple approaches.

THEORETICAL INTEGRATION: BLENDED FAMILIES

One approach involves combining the ideas and methods of two or more different theories and reconciling their differences so that the goal is a new blend of both. This is like mediating a dispute between opposing factions in which you help the parties focus on what they have to offer one another instead of dwelling on their differences.

There have been a number of successful attempts to blend theoretical families, some of which we have mentioned in previous chapters. There have been marriages between psychoanalysis and behavior therapy (Wachtel, 1997), cognitive and behavior therapy (Lazarus, 1971, 2006), cognitive and humanistic therapies (Greenberg & Safran, 1987), cognitive and constructivist therapies (Mahoney, 2000), client-centered and Gestalt therapies (Prouty, 1994), and many others. More recently, we have seen marriages of psychodynamic and brief therapy, (Levenson, 2017), mindfulness with cognitive therapy (Segal, Williams, & Teasdale, 2018), object relations and psychodrama (Holmes, 2015), and behavior and family therapy (Falloon, 2015). You could almost take any two theories you wish and figure out a way to combine their best features into a comprehensive combined model.

To blend two or more theories, the challenge is to find compatible features that would complement one another without sacrificing the integrity of their essential contributions. This challenge is usually beyond the capability of beginners since it requires a deep understanding of the approaches that may take many years to develop. On the other hand, this is a slow evolutionary process that begins one small step at a time: You are firmly entrenched in one particular approach but then decide one day (or in one session) that it would be interesting to borrow a concept/idea/strategy from another model you read or heard about. Or, you become frustrated with how your chosen theory doesn't address a particular issue that another theory does address. So, you weave together key aspects of the two theories. Then, over time and through trial and error, you refine your ideas about how the new integration works. In other words, you come up with your own integrated theory of working that feels more complete and comprehensive to you, and the new whole feels like much more than the sum of its parts.

ASSIMILATIVE INTEGRATION: BORROWING AN IDEA NOW AND THEN

This approach describes those who are working from the base of one favorite theory, but occasionally borrowing a technique from another theory to accomplish certain goals with a client. For example, a cognitive behavior therapist might routinely work from this approach but employ the Gestalt two-chair technique to help a client resolve some opposing core beliefs that continue to give the client trouble. Or, you might imagine how someone who works from a narrative therapy framework might integrate some existential ideas to zoom out and help clients see the big picture of their story and make decisions about where they want to take the remaining chapters.

An intriguing example of this approach is described by two psychodynamic therapists who decided they needed to begin assigning homework to their clients with depression (Nelson & Castonguay, 2017). Psychodynamic practitioners are sometimes concerned that their clients have trouble translating the insights they gain to other issues in their lives. Logically, then, homework activities could help them build this bridge. Although homework is not elaborated as a conceptual technique in psychodynamic therapy, it certainly is in cognitive behavioral therapy, where it is used to provide clients with opportunities for practicing new skills. From within the perspective of psychodynamic therapy, the homework gives the client opportunities for reality testing and yielding information both the client and the therapist can use to foster new insights. Nelson and Castanguay (2017) felt that their depressed clients benefitted from this integration.

TECHNICAL ECLECTISIM: THE TOOLBOX APPROACH

One of the reasons that most therapists adopt an integrative framework is because their clients' needs demand it. Clients present a whole variety of problems in need of attention, everything from relationship difficulties (with family, friends, or co-workers), debilitating emotions (depression, anxiety, loneliness), learning disabilities, and disturbing thoughts or images (illusions, delusions, hallucinations, irrational thoughts) to disillusionment (emptiness, meaninglessness) or dysfunctional behaviors (compulsions, addictions, self-defeating actions). They also arrive with all different levels of motivations for change, as we discussed in Chapter 10. Some are very reluctant customers and some have reached their last straw and you couldn't stop them from getting better if you wanted to (Prochaska & Norcross, 2018). The point is that some clients do not do well when therapists try to apply a cookie-cutter approach. Would you really expect to treat someone with career indecision the same way as you would someone who is severely depressed and actively suicidal? Would you adopt the same approach with an 80-year-old Chinese woman who complains of disappointment in her grandchildren as you would a Mexican American teenager who wants to extricate himself from a gang? Of course not. You have to be light on your feet and ready to roll with the punches, so to speak, to meet clients where they are and with what they need most.

Evidence-Based Eclecticism

It is almost impossible to be in any field these days and not hear about "evidence-based practice." The words imply that there need to be good reasons, backed up by some sort of evidence, for choosing one way of intervening versus another. It sounds great in principle, but there are a lot of politics and money involved—not to mention underlying values about what is "evidence" and what makes good "practice"—and these are not always out in the open. So, we want to spend some time here looking at what it means (and doesn't mean) for therapists.

One of the consequences of the managed care movement in North America has been an emphasis on using integrative, time-limited, case-specific treatments that have empirical research support for their effectiveness. There is some merit to this because some approaches you have studied *do* work better for specific kinds of problems than others. In other words, the therapist must decide *what* (empirically supported theory and techniques) will likely work *for whom* (the client with specific preferences and needs). This means that practitioners are expected to select their treatments for a given client depending on what is recognized as a best practice according to the studies that have been done.

This is not unreasonable. If, for example, someone comes into an emergency room complaining of abdominal pain, the physician asks a series of questions to determine where it is located and whether it is merely indigestion or perhaps something more serious such as pancreatitis, colitis, or an appendicitis. After an examination, medical history, and series of tests are administered, a diagnosis is assigned (presumably the same diagnosis that almost any other doctor present would arrive at), and treatment is recommended. Of course, if more than one physician is present, there might be some debate and disagreement, but eventually they could settle on a prescribed course of action.

Assuming this model is feasible for mental health (and there is by no means a consensus that it is), our work will increasingly resemble contemporary medicine where clinicians select specific procedures according to what symptoms are presented. You might, for example, follow a treatment manual that is largely cognitive-behavioral to treat reactive depression, or one that draws on structural family therapy to treat a case of oppositional defiant disorder. Some hold a vision that someday, just like doctors, therapists will simply use their handheld device to indicate the particular symptoms that are presented, upload a client profile, and instantly receive the preferred treatment plan for downloading.

Along these lines, some in our field have devoted themselves to developing these shareable therapeutic regimens and manuals for specific emotional ailments. Typically, these involve an eclectic set of techniques drawn from a variety of theories with a "use whatever works" mentality. These treatment manuals are necessary for a therapeutic regimen to be systematically, empirically validated because all the researchers and clinicians testing an intervention have to be operating strictly from the same page. Ideally, they also give other clinicians like us reliable directions to follow when treating certain symptoms.

During the last couple of decades, enormous amounts of money have gone into developing treatment protocols for common complaints. A number of evidence-based programs and practices are available on the U.S. Department of Health and Human Services Substance Abuse and Mental Health Administration (SAMSHA) Evidence-Based Practice Resource Center website.

Skeptical readers will have already cocked an eyebrow, noting that clinical researchers who favor behavioral and cognitive behavioral therapies probably had the heaviest hand in setting up the rules for what is considered "evidence based." Theories that require treatment goals that are observable and measurable are thereby deemed the most "scientific"—in other words, they are the winners—while therapies that focus on "meaning" or "relational capacities" define themselves in terms that are not easily captured by that which can be counted, and are therefore the losers in the evidence game.

Don't get us wrong—we are very impressed with the long-term diligence and expense that it takes to systematically test a treatment or approach that is officially designated as "evidence based." However, we'd like to make two points. First, each of these approaches has only been established for a specific problem and a specific type of client (only certain races or ethnicities, age ranges, gender, etc.). There are many, many people out there who have problems for which there currently is no evidence-based program or practice. Second, note this: To plan on getting the same results, you'd have to implement the clinical procedures *exactly* as they were developed and specified in the treatment manual that the researchers used. Sometimes—oftentimes—this is simply not feasible.

So, what's a therapist to do? Suppose you've just met a client who needs your help; your first impressions suggest that she has some generalized anxiety. After your intake session do a little research to make sure you have some background on the latest recommendations for this particular problem. Maybe you find that there's nothing very definitive out there, or there is, but it was certainly not tested on anyone like your aging, Middle-Eastern client who immigrated from a war-torn country a few years ago and has a heart condition. What do you fall back on for guidance? Your theories, your own personal experience, and your ability to do what all master therapists are great at—building a relationship with this client and providing a tailored approach of your favorite techniques. You won't have a manual; instead, you'll be the one responsible for developing your own approach that is elastic enough to embrace a variety of interventions and styles depending on the client, situation, problem, and stage of treatment. This framework could be based on any one of a dozen different philosophies. It could be existential, Adlerian, psychoanalytic, client centered in nature, as well as many others, or a combination of these. Chances are, if you earnestly go to work and employ the tools that all well-prepared therapists have in their bag of tricks, your client will likely improve.

COMMON FACTORS: THE HEART OF THE MATTER

We're sure you've been wondering as you've read this book how different theoretical approaches, developed at different times by very different theorists, used by themselves or in combination with techniques from other approaches, could all will be helpful. How is it possible that all these theories could really work as well as their authors and advocates say they do? Is it really possible that you can help someone by reflecting their feelings or disputing their beliefs or uncovering their unconscious fears or helping them set goals *or …* ? You get the point.

The "common factors" integrative approach, as its name suggests, involves making connections between diverse theories and especially looking at what they all have in common. There are several ways to account for the similar effectiveness of approaches that seem to be so different:

1. The approaches aren't that different after all. They are really just doing the same essential things. And these things, whatever they are, help clients get better.
2. What practitioners actually *do* in their sessions is more generic than their espoused beliefs would appear. If you watched all of them, you might conclude that the theory guiding the therapist is more in his or her mind than in what they say to the client.
3. There are many different paths to achieve the same outcome. As the old saying goes, "There's more than one way to skin a cat."
4. There really are major differences, but the research measurements aren't sensitive enough to pick them up. After all, the "outcome" is usually measured by the absence of symptoms, but that's just a part of what people usually mean when they say they feel like a new person.

The most logical explanation (read: the one we like best) is that various theories are really far more alike than it would seem. Despite their radical divergences in therapist role, underlying philosophy, identified goals, and preferred techniques, there are indeed elements they share in common.

What does this mean for you as a beginner? Instead of only looking at the ways that theories are different from one another (which is the emphasis in a theories class), start considering what they have in common. What has got to be at work here are some universal therapeutic ingredients that are present in all these different theories. Aren't you just a little curious what those might be?

Quite a number of studies have been undertaken to identify the factors common to all forms of therapy. Beginning with the early effort of Rosenzweig (1936), continuing with Frank's (1973) seminal work to present-day efforts (Kottler, 2017b; Prochaska & Norcross, 2018; Wampold, 2015; Watkins, 2017), there have been several universal variables that have been identified. These are the ingredients that you would find present in almost all the theories you have studied. They include the following:

1. *Hope and expectations.* Clients bring with them certain attitudes and beliefs that influence the potential outcome.
2. *Relationship.* The particular kind of alliance may vary among approaches, but all agree that some type of relationship is needed to offer support and use as leverage to get compliance to treatment.
3. *Therapeutic techniques.* All the approaches do something, and certainly what they do has some impact on the proceedings (although probably not as much as practitioners think).
4. *Outside factors.* The client's motivation, personality style, presenting complaints, family influences, job situation, and other variables also play an important role.

These main ingredients can be supplemented with several other factors that can be recognized in most other theories currently in use. Several of these features may seem familiar to you.

Therapist Presence

What clients say is important in therapy is often quite different than what their therapists say is important. We, of course, believe it is our masterful interventions that make all the difference. Clients, on the other hand, most frequently mention the following (Egan & Reese, 2019; Wampold, & Imel, 2015):

1. Having a private place to talk and the structured time to share one's concerns
2. The therapist's personality, especially someone who is understanding, caring, and supportive
3. Having someone help to understand oneself and one's situation

There isn't much of a surprise in these findings. But it's important to remember that who you are is as important as what you do.

Use of Self

All your techniques, skills, interventions, and strategies are filtered through your personality and interpersonal style. The unique ways that you see the world and communicate to others are what give power and life to your therapeutic work.

We have long believed that one way to explain how professionals as diverse as Sigmund Freud, Fritz Perls, William Glasser, Virginia Satir, Albert Ellis, Alfred Adler, and Carl Rogers could all be so potent in their work, even though they seem to be doing such different things, is because they are really all capitalizing on the same factor. Think about it: What do they all have in common?

It isn't the sort of relationship they developed with clients, or the methods they employed, or even the types of things that they would talk about. What each of these professionals had in common was their charisma—the power of their selves. There is no way that you could spend time with any of them in a room for very long that you wouldn't come out of different from when you first walked in. This isn't because they reflected your feelings, disputed your beliefs, or interpreted your dreams, but because they all possessed a self that was charismatic, persuasive, and influential.

The Placebo Effect

In introductory psychology classes you first learned about the power of expectations to promote cures. Patients who were given sugar pills (especially tiny green ones) often improved just as rapidly as those who received actual medication—if their physician programmed their reactions by telling them that they would be helped.

In therapy, as well, the professional's positive expectations for a cure operate as very powerful medicine indeed. If you believe strongly that what you are doing is going to help your clients, and you are persuasive in convincing them that this is the case, then almost whatever you do within reason may be useful.

Both Jerome Frank (1973) and Jefferson Fish (1973) wrote extensively about this effect in therapy, noting how critical it is that you communicate your enthusiasm about the methods you are using. Imagine, for instance, that you visit a therapist for the first time. You are wracked with guilt, loneliness, and despair after the breakup of your marriage. You have little hope that you will ever find happiness again. Your life seems over.

The therapist listens to your sad story, nods her head in sympathy, and then says to you, "I want you to know that your experience is familiar to me. I have seen hundreds of people in your situation, and I have been able to help almost all of them in some way. How quickly we make progress and how far you go are up to you, but I can reassure you that what you are experiencing lends itself to improvement rather quickly. In fact, you will notice that you are already feeling some relief. For the first time in a while, you are feeling the barest glimmer of hope. I am very good at what I do and I know how to help you. With your cooperation and commitment, we should make progress very rapidly."

Obviously, your spirit would be lifted by such an introduction to therapy and you would be set up with expectations that are intended to maximize hope and optimism. If you believe that what the therapist is offering to you will be useful, you are much more likely to respond favorably to the intervention (Wampold, 2018).

Altered States

Another universal feature of most therapeutic systems is that they place clients in an altered state of consciousness in which they are more amenable to being influenced. It is like a hypnotic state in which people become hyper-suggestible; they won't do anything they wouldn't do otherwise, but they have much less resistance.

You can easily test this out for yourself. Notice when your instructor (or author) says something to you in class, you pay very close attention. You listen carefully, take notes, and (hopefully) put great confidence in your instructor's (and author's) expertise. Now, what do you think happens when we go home or hang out with our friends? Do you really believe that anyone listens to us, or does what we say, any more than they would for you?

One explanation is that when we are in our professional mode, in our own domain, we can control the environment and atmosphere as carefully as any faith healer. The books on the wall and framed diplomas all attest that we know things. Our manner and style communicate a kind of smug confidence, as if we have the secrets to life that are there for the asking. Then, we use our voices and manner to soothe clients, to reassure them, to lead them along in such a way that they will follow. We actually place them in a kind of hypnotic state in which they are far more likely to receive what we have to offer (Erickson & Keeney, 2006). Or, said another way, we exert a great deal of social influence on our clients by virtue of being seen as expert, attractive, and trustworthy (Strong, 1968; Wampold, 2015).

Helping Relationship

It is worth mentioning this universal ingredient again because it is so important. You have learned about several different models for how the therapeutic relationship should best be constructed so as to optimize benefits.

In the psychoanalytic approach, you have an arrangement in which the therapist appears neutral and objective so as to maximize the projections of the client. The transference can be worked through precisely because the therapist tries so hard to be disengaged; whatever the client experiences in the relationship must be the result of his or her own perceptions based on resolved relationship issues.

Carl Rogers presented a very different sort of relationship, one in which warmth, genuineness, and empathy prevailed. Rather than appearing as an aloof, disengaged parental figure, a new model was built on an egalitarian exchange of mutual respect and trust. Other models of the helping relationship conceive of the encounter as one that is essentially a teacher-student arrangement, or that of a coach or consultant working with someone one on one. To some, this relationship is not so much a projected fantasy as it is a very real encounter between two or more people. More accurately, the working alliance is composed of both a real relationship and a projection (Gelso, 2019; Norcross & Lambert, 2018).

In whatever form it takes, the helping relationship provides support and encouragement to people during a time of need. They have a private place to unload their troubles and a regular structure in which to speak of their concerns. In this relationship, they feel heard and understood, a marvelously restorative experience.

Several authors (Capuzzi & Gross, 2011; Corey, 2019) have described somewhat universal developmental stages in the therapeutic process. In the first part of the process, boundaries are negotiated and trust is built by discussing confidentiality and gathering basic information. The partners in the process get to know one another. Stage two involves more extended exploration in which goals are established, extensive assessment is conducted, and preparations are undertaken to begin change efforts. The third stage is characterized by collaboration and problem solving, experimenting with alternative behaviors within the safety of the supportive relationship. In the last stage, plans are made to separate from one another in a way designed to maintain the momentum.

FOR PERSONAL REFLECTION

Think about the stages in the therapeutic process. Come up with between four and six different stages that essentially include a beginning, in which the relationship is first formed, problems and background are explored, and a diagnosis is agreed on; a middle stage in which the work is done; and an ending stage in which the client is launched back into the world with suitable closure and preparation to deal with setbacks.

Given the specific objectives, challenges, and tasks of each stage in the therapeutic process that you have identified, would you really think that you would maintain the same sort of relationship and adopt the same strategy throughout the entire process? Would you not want to employ one kind of style in the beginning that might be different from the middle and end? Would you likely use procedures in the working stage that you wouldn't be inclined to rely on in the others?

Just as you might be inclined to customize a therapeutic approach for each individual client that takes into consideration the problem presented, cultural background, the time allotted, and so on, wouldn't you also individualize the treatment according to which stage you were in? Perhaps you would be more client centered in the beginning when you are first establishing a supportive relationship and then far more directive later. Or, maybe you would deal with affective material in the first stages when catharsis is important and then move on to cognitive and behavioral material later.

Depending on which stages you have settled on, how would you alter your style over the length of your relationship?

Feedback

Where else can someone go to hear the truth? In almost all the systems you have reviewed, the therapist attempts to be as honest, sincere, and straightforward as possible. Clients report on the things they are doing and act in the sessions just as they would in the outside world. It is our job to provide them with accurate, clear, and nonthreatening reactions to what we observe (Hill, 2014).

According to each theory, the therapist might comment on a different aspect of the interaction. The reality therapist points out the ways someone is avoiding responsibility for a poor choice that was made. The existential therapist might do the same thing but in a very different way. The cognitive therapist would provide feedback on the dysfunctional thoughts that are keeping him stuck. A client-centered therapist might talk to him about how he comes across in their own relationship, a Gestalt therapist might point out the inauthenticity in the way the feelings have been expressed, and a narrative therapist would offer observations on how he has internalized messages from his culture that might not be his own. In all these instances, the theory suggests that clients should be confronted with certain aspects of their behavior that are less than fully functioning. Then they are offered alternative ways of responding instead.

The feedback goes both ways, of course. Regardless of the approach taken, one of the best predictive variables of a positive outcome is when the therapist takes the time to ask clients (in session or in follow-ups) what they like best or least and what they would like to change about the way things are going (Wampold, 2018).

Finding Meaning

Existential, cognitive, and constructivist therapies aren't the only ones that help clients find meaning in their lives. Even the most action-oriented brief therapist might concentrate mostly on presenting symptoms but still can't help but address the inevitable questions clients ask: "Why me? And why now?"

Human beings are extremely curious creatures. We can't help searching for answers to questions that plague us. Even when the therapist does not make this exploration an explicit part of the treatment, the client may be doing this sort of work on his or her own (Hill, 2018).

There are so many ways that therapists facilitate this search for meaning. It can be called consciousness raising, facilitating insight, or meaning making, but in all these forms the client makes a cognitive shift in the way things are viewed. In the following table some specific examples are provided for each of a few sample theories.

TABLE 12.2. How types of meaning pursued in several theories

Theory	Type Of Meaning Making	Client's New Realization
Psychoanalytic	Search for underlying and unconscious reasons for present problems	"The reason that I keep picking losers in my love relationships is that I am following the template established by my own parents."
Constructivist	Realize that reality and personal narratives are constructed from cultural indoctrination	"It is not true that I am really a worthless alcoholic; that is the image I inherited from what the media, my family, and the dominant culture have told me."
Cognitive	Understand how negative emotions stem from irrational thoughts	"I am so upset about this relationship ending, not because of what he said to me, but due to what I've been telling myself about that."
Reality	Look at current actions and the impact the have on life's most important goals and priorities	"The reason I keep getting in trouble at school is because I keep doing the same thing over and over even though it isn't getting me what I say that I want."
Client centered	Access, understand, and communicate unexpressed feelings	"I walk around with so much anger inside me because I have never really told others how I feel."
Strategic	Reframe presenting problems in another way that makes them more amenable to change	"It's not that I am basically a shy person, just that I sometimes hide behind a safe persona when the situation calls for it."

In all its present forms, the act of helping clients create or find meaning in their experiences is an enterprise that is quite universal. However, it is likely that some types of meaning making will appeal more to you and your clients than others.

Rehearsal

Most therapies also share a strong belief that clients need opportunities to practice new ways of behaving and being. Sometimes this rehearsal is structured in sessions under the guise of role-playing; other times it is part of explicit or implicit homework assignments. Some approaches (behavioral, cognitive, narrative, strategic, problem solving) are far more deliberate about including rehearsal, and practice as part of their methods. Yet, even those models that may not give a lot of overt attention to action strategies (existential, psychoanalytic, client centered) still encourage clients to take what is being done in sessions and apply it in their lives.

There would be considerable disagreement about what exactly should be done and how it should best be practiced. A Gestalt therapist or Satir family therapist would structure enactments right in session, whereas an Ericksonian or strategic therapist is much more concerned with what the client does outside of the sessions. An REBT therapist would role-play a client's new behavior in the session, with the expectation that it would be completed outside the session and then reported on the next week. Thus, task facilitation is also an important part of many (but not all) therapeutic systems in which clients are expected and encouraged to complete assignments that are considered good for them. This could be as simple as writing in a journal or blog, reading an assigned book or article (bibliotherapy), or could be as complicated as prescribing tasks that include paradoxical elements (those that are designed to be disobeyed).

FOR A FIELD STUDY

Ask three experienced practitioners how they treat acute anxiety differently from prolonged depression. Find out as much detail as possible about how they adjust their relationship, methods, and treatment procedures. What do they think works, and why?

The Process

One final way that most therapeutic systems are alike is in their organizing process. Regardless of the specific ways they go about their work, most models follow a sequential process that consists of several stages (Brew & Kottler, 2017; Wachtel, 2012; Young, 2016):

1. *Listen to the client.* Engage him or her in the process. Assess what is going on. Construct a diagnosis and treatment plan. Negotiate goals. Decide who would be best to work with and what sort of relationship is indicated. Plant favorable expectations. This all takes place in the first few sessions.

2. *Build and deepen the relationship.* Work on trust issues. Explore presenting complaints in the context of the client's life. Gather relevant history. This stage can last anywhere from two sessions to two years, depending on the time available, the style of treatment, and client needs.

3. *Promote insight.* There are lots of ways to do this—explore secondary gains of the symptoms, uncover unconscious motives, construct personal meaning, dispute irrational beliefs, and a dozen other options. This stage can also last anywhere from a few sessions to a very long time. Much depends on the client's readiness, motivation, and openness, the therapist's preferred model, and the circumstances that led the person to seek help.

4. *Use modeling and rehearsal to introduce ideas of new ways to think, feel, and behave.* This is not so much a discrete stage in the process as it is a consistent presence throughout the experience. Be who you want your clients to be.

5. *Plan and implement interventions in sessions.* Depending on the type of concern, the situation, and the time available, you might use any one of the models presented in this text. Such interventions can last a few minutes or many sessions. In each case, you would monitor very carefully how the client responds and what sort of outcome is produced.

6. *Consider assigning homework.* Most approaches employ some sort of therapeutic task that takes place outside of sessions. This can involve formal homework, therapeutic tasks, or reflective activities. Basically, the idea is that people don't really change unless they can apply what they are learning in therapy to their lives in the real world.

7. *Finally, remember to follow up.* Select and follow up on a change that involves a transfer of learning to other situations outside therapy. You must assess the relative effectiveness of your interventions in helping the client make real-world changes.

FINDING YOUR OWN WAY

One of the ways that we both have stayed excited by our work is by constantly experimenting with new approaches and evolving our own theoretical orientations. I (Jeffrey) mentioned in the introduction to this text that I was at one time an avid, passionate, true believer of rational-emotive therapy. I read every book I could get my hands on and subscribed to specialist journals in REBT. I volunteered to be a client during one of Ellis's demonstrations. I associated myself with other like-minded therapists and practiced this approach exclusively for several years. I found it incredibly helpful and effective with a wide range of clients. Furthermore, I loved the ways I could be provocative, challenging, and dramatic in sessions disputing irrational beliefs and imitating my mentors. The only problem is that, after a while, I grew tired of identifying the same irrational beliefs, following the same routines, and applying essentially the same interventions.

The next time I saw Ellis in action, he looked bored, too, as if he had been through this a thousand times before (which he had). Members of the audience asked him the same questions in every city. He followed the same routines with every workshop. I had even heard him use the same examples before. During a break, I mentioned to him that he looked bored much of the time and asked him if that was the case. He looked at me with a smile, shrugged, and then said this was all about converting people to his way of thinking. He believed so strongly that what he was doing was important and valuable to learn that his own boredom didn't matter.

Well, Ellis might not have felt he had a choice because of his commitment to promote REBT around the world, but the rest of us assuredly do. Since that time of being an exclusive practitioner of the cognitive approach, I have tried a dozen others. And I like them all. Throughout my career, I have changed theories the way someone else might add to their wardrobe every few years. Even though the clothes you already have are perfectly serviceable, sometimes it feels good to wear something new.

Upon reflection, I (Marilyn) notice that my theoretical developments have been influenced by where I was living (and thus the types of therapists I was around for supervision and camaraderie); I suspect they will be for you, too. In my earliest days I was around a very innovative group of family therapists who had a lot of fun trying out surprising and strategic interventions that knocked their clients off guard and into better systemic relations with their significant others. So, my work with children and their parents bore some resemblance to constructivist and strategic family therapy. I also had one professor (and later, supervisor) who was the quintessential Rogerian, moving me to tears on more than one occasion with the sweet warmth of his truly unconditional positive regard. I naturally strove to emulate his way of reaching people's core in the very first session (and still do). I also blended in my developmental background and thought I was all set with my nice integration of systemic, client-centered, developmentally appropriate therapy. Then I moved to the East Coast and found myself in the midst of a lively group of psychodynamic therapists who meet regularly to psychoanalyze movies and art, conduct training, and lead the local movement to serve veterans and their families. (I had thought that Freud was dead and the few remaining followers he had were stuffed away in musty institutes; on the contrary, they do intense therapy with difficult cases by day and are flamenco dancers and rock musicians by night!) Naturally, I've picked up a few depth techniques from this sincerely dedicated and compassionate crowd.

FOR A FIELD STUDY

Interview a few experienced therapists who have been practicing for at least 10 years, preferably longer. Ask them to tell you about the development of their beliefs regarding therapy, including the models they have used, the practices they have evolved over time, and the ways their theoretical allegiances may have changed over time.

During your conversations, ask them to begin with their earliest experiences as students, when they first encountered the diverse viewpoints in the field. Then trace the progressive stages they have since gone through—internship, their first job, the mentors and supervisors that pushed them in particular directions, up until the present.

Based on what you learn from these interviews, think about what might lie ahead for you in your own professional development.

There's Too Much Good Stuff Out There

It's true. Almost every year, there is some new innovation in our profession that adds greater options to our work. When you limit yourself to only one theory, you make a decision to focus your attention on the contributions and improvements in that particular system. For busy professionals, that is often the only reasonable choice to make. You may end up working in a setting that has adopted a particular therapeutic approach, or you may work with colleagues who all share an interest in the same model. Or you may simply find yourself enamored with one theory that seems to fit you like a glove. It feels good to master one system well and to be able to apply it in a variety of situations. It is kind of like the best in a monogamous relationship:

Why wonder what it would be like to have multiple partners when you are already satisfied?

If that is the situation in which you currently find yourself, read no further. You are indeed fortunate to select a compatible theory that fits with your values and style. You will find lots of support from other professionals who feel the same way. If, on the other hand, you are always wondering what else is out there, if you continue searching for more and better strategies to help your clients, then you are probably going to have to look way beyond a single model.

It is sometimes the case that a client will leave your office dissatisfied with what you offered. There may be a number of reasons for this, many of which have little to do with you. The client may enjoy some benefits to remaining stuck. In some cases, there may actually have been substantial changes, but for one reason or another, the client won't admit it. Another possibility is that it sometimes takes a period of time to gather a clear and objective assessment of how therapy works, a kind of delayed reaction.

As much as therapists might prefer one of these preceding reasons to explain why a client left unhappy, there are also times when the reason is due to our own ineptitude, mistakes, misjudgments, or poor training. Sometimes we fail our clients because we don't know enough, or we couldn't do enough. (Sometimes we also try to do too much.) But this gives us an excuse to learn more! One of the very best things about this profession is that we will never know enough, never become as thoroughly competent as we would prefer. You can't possibly keep up on all the innovations and developments each year, much less catch up to what has already been done. Both of us really love this and it's why we can't imagine ever getting tired of this work. Just when you think you understand what is going on, some new idea comes on the scene that turns everything upside down. Or, even more powerful, a client teaches you something about yourself that you never knew was possible.

Sending Recall Notices

Every so often, a client we haven't seen in a while returns for a booster session or perhaps because of another set of problems. It would be perfectly reasonable for this person to expect that we would proceed according to a plan similar to the one that worked well last time. After all, we appear to be the same professionals we used to be. The office looks basically the same. And the client has fond memories of our previous visits, proud of the struggles we endured together and the terms we negotiated. The only problem is that in the intervening years, or even months, we have continued to evolve as therapists, abandoning old methods in favor of new ones we have since learned or invented.

"So," the client begins, beginning where he remembers we left off last time, "I suppose you'll want me to tell you about some of the disturbing thoughts I've had lately that have been interfering with my intimate relationships."

We cringe at the language he is using. Did we once talk that way? We have since moved on in our theory development. We might look the same, a little older perhaps, but we don't do therapy the way we used to. We sigh inwardly, thinking that this would be a whole lot easier with someone brand new who doesn't come with expectations for what we will be doing together.

Sometimes we feel exhausted by all the changes that take place in the field. It reminds us of the experiences we all have with software updates. Your phone works perfectly, doing just what you want it to do. (Of course, you only use about 5% of its complicated features, but that's plenty to get the job done.) Then every couple of months you get badgered into updating your operating system, which then doesn't work with some of your favorite apps. Sometimes you don't even have a choice in the matter—your phone will insist on the latest version! Then there are the inevitable glitches, crashes, and annoyances that occur.

We think of the developments in therapy the same way. We have been perfectly content working with clients in the usual way; they seem like satisfied customers as well. Then just about every year, we get a notice in a professional journal, or a flyer in the mail, announcing that some new therapy has been (re)invented and we had better get with the program, learn this new stuff, or we'll get left behind. So, we dutifully order the latest books, attend the obligatory workshops, and discover that whatever we have been doing up to this point is obsolete, old-fashioned, downright wrong, and probably dangerous. We are told that instead of doing one thing, we should be doing another (often the exact opposite of our current strategy).

This reminds us of car manufacturers that send out recall notices to their customers, informing them that there has been some defect and that they had better bring their vehicle in, forthwith, or it might catch fire, blow up, fall apart, or accelerate unexpectedly. To keep our sense of humor, we joke about whether we should send such notices to all our ex-clients letting them know that whatever we once did is no longer considered the optimal treatment. And whatever gains they thought they had made were really just illusionary. They'd better come back immediately so we can fix whatever we now understand was wrong and apply the newest treatment strategy.

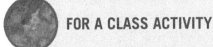

FOR A CLASS ACTIVITY

One good reason to be integrative in your therapeutic approach is to look at your own experiences of transformation. In small groups, talk to one another about the most dramatic changes that you have undergone in your life and how they came about. After each person has had a chance to tell one brief life-changing story that happened as a result of an encounter with a teacher, therapist, serendipitous event, tragedy, or other life experience, look at some of the underlying mechanisms that were most responsible for acting as catalysts.

Classify your experiences according to the therapeutic ingredients that seemed most influential.

Talk to one another about the possibility of any single theory being useful to explain how your changes transpired. Which one or two come closest? If you were to combine theories, which integration would give you the best "theory of change" for your own efforts?

HOW TO BE INTEGRATIVE

Assuming that you decide to adopt an integrative framework (if not now, then sometime later in your career), here is some advice that might be useful to you in your journey. We warn you that such a road taken is not an easy one. It feels good to be part of an exclusive club of people who all share similar beliefs. Nevertheless, in today's climate of practice, even those who choose one theory as a home base still must become skilled at using an assortment of strategies that are borrowed from other approaches.

But What's the Right Answer?

Before we provide you some thoughts on how to be integrative, there's another question that we should address first. Some of you may feel that being integrative is just a tricky way to avoid answering the tough but obvious question: Which theory is best? Surely with all modern scientific methods we have at our disposal, some theories have been proven to work better than others, and this book could have been a lot shorter! Why did we have to confuse things, you might be thinking, by giving homage to all these different theories when some of them are surely outdated and ineffective?

It's a good question, and certainly one that has been asked ever since behaviorism rose to challenge psychoanalysis. In fact, Saul Rosenzweig kicked off the common factors movement in psychotherapy by writing an article that famously quoted *Alice in Wonderland* in an epigraph: "At last the Dodo said, '*Everybody* has won, and *all* must have prizes.'" Recall that in *Alice in*

Wonderland, the animals get soaked when Alice cries, so they stage a race to dry off (Carroll, 1865/1962). But the animals run off crazily in every direction so the race is called off. The dodo bird is asked who won. He ponders and finally proclaims the "dodo bird verdict" as it is now called. In citing the dodo bird verdict, Rosenzweig foreshadowed the conclusion of modern research that has lined up various theories for a "horserace."

VOICES FROM THE PAST: SAUL ROSENZWEIG

It has often been remarked that no form of psychotherapy is without cures to its credit. Proponents of psychoanalysis, treatment by persuasion, Christian Science and any other number of other psychotherapeutic psychologies can point to notable successes. The implication of this fact is not, however, unequivocal. The proud proponent, having achieved success in the cases he mentions, implies, even when he does not say it, that his ideology is thus proved true, all others false. More detached observers, on the other hand, surveying the whole field tend, on logical grounds to draw a very different conclusion.

... Pursuing this line of inquiry it is soon realized that besides the intentionally utilized methods and their consciously held theoretical foundations, there are inevitably certain unrecognized factors in any therapeutic situation—factors that may be even more important than those being purposely employed. It might be conceivably argued that psychoanalysis, for example, succeeds, when it does, not so much because of the truth about psychoanalytic doctrines ... but rather because the analyst, in the practice of his method, quite unwittingly allows the patient to recondition certain inadequate social patterns in terms of the present situation—a phenomenon better explained by Pavlov's than by Freud's theories. Granting for the purpose of argument that this is the case, then the concepts of Freud are far less proved true by the successful analysis of a patient than are those of Pavlov—and therapeutic result achieved cannot uncritically be used as a test of theory advanced!

Source: Rosenzweig, 1936, p. 412.

So, who wins the race? Generally, studies that have been undertaken over the years comparing the theories and their associated therapies have shown that, especially in the everyday world outside research clinics, there is little difference in their effectiveness. For example, Wampold and Imel (2015) reviewed existing studies and drew some conclusions. Focusing primarily on studies done with depressed patients, they concluded the following:

- Psychotherapy is indeed effective
- The type of treatment is not a factor

Saul Rosenzweig, "Some Implicit Common Factors in Diverse Methods of Psychotherapy," *American Journal of Orthopsychiatry*, vol. 6, no. 3, pp. 412. Copyright © 1936 by American Psychological Association.

- The theoretical bases of the techniques used and the strictness of adherence to those techniques are both not especially important
- The therapist's strength of belief in the efficacy of the technique is crucial
- The personality of the therapist is a significant factor
- The alliance between the patient(s) and the therapist (meaning affectionate and trusting feelings toward the therapist, motivation and collaboration of the client, and empathic response of the therapist) is a key feature

There is Value in Most Approaches

Since apparently all our theories have good, effective aspects, then integrating the ones that appeal to you most makes sense. However, not all your instructors and supervisors will share this philosophy. They may quite legitimately suggest that as a beginner it is far more appropriate for you to stick with just one model until you become comfortable with it. Then perhaps later in your career you can add on additional layers.

Whether you begin your integrative efforts now, or at some later time, you still must see merit in most approaches. This means being respectful of those who have perspectives that are different from your own. It means being a critical consumer of research. It means trying out as many different methods as you can get your hands on. And it means resisting the impulse to remain safe and secure in your comfortable world, reluctant to venture out to discover what others are doing. This is much more difficult than it sounds.

Imagine that you settle on an excellent way to do therapy. You feel confident in your approach, get lots of good support for your efforts, and most importantly, see clear and compelling evidence that your clients are improving. Moreover, when you read research studies in the literature, you find solid support demonstrating the effectiveness of your methods.

Now, picture further that you come across someone at a conference or professional gathering who does therapy in seemingly the diametrically opposite way that you do; however you choose to work, this therapist appears to do something completely different. Furthermore, there seems to be research support for the effectiveness of this approach as well.

You may react critically and defensively to this encounter; after all, this alternative reality could very well threaten the validity of your own perceptions. On the other hand, you could also embrace such differences, intrigued with the possibility that there are many alternative paths to arrive at the same destination.

FOR A GROUP ACTIVITY

Each student will select the three theories that he or she likes the most. Rank order them according to your preference from 1 to 3.

Divide into partnerships (or small teams) in which people with the same choices work together in work groups.

Decide between you which two theories you will integrate and work together to combine their best features into a system that emphasizes their strengths but also overcomes their perceived weaknesses.

Give your new theory a name. Present it to the class.

Be Skeptical of Truth

A lot of other people are going to try and sell you their ideology. All of them may very well be convinced that they have discovered the "true" way to seek enlightenment, and they believe with all their hearts that the world would be a much better place if only others would adopt their beliefs. Of course, the Crusades was begun for just such a reason in which members of one religious system set out to convert or kill all those who didn't share their vision.

Hopefully, nobody will try to harm you because you don't adopt their preferred theory, but be forewarned that some people become mighty upset if you practice in a way that contradicts what they value most. In some cases, as a low person in the staff hierarchy, you might very well have to use the methods favored by the institution or those in power.

There are some professionals who are utterly convinced that they have discovered the truth and that others are flat-out wrong for operating in different ways. I will tell you a little secret: As of yet, nobody really understands the complexity of how and why therapy works. Some professionals may *think* they know what's going on, but rest assured they are as confused as everyone else.

Get Outside Your Discipline

To be truly integrative, you have to look far beyond your own field of psychology, psychiatry, nursing, family therapy, social work, counseling, or human services. When you read the biographies of the most prominent theoreticians, you will notice that they studied widely in fields outside their own. Many of the leaders of our profession were able to move way beyond the status quo and create new models because of their familiarity with multiple disciplines.

Recall that Freud was an amateur archaeologist and this contributed significantly to his metaphor of healing through excavation of the past. He spent a good portion of his free time traveling to other cultures, not to mention delving in other fields such as literature, philosophy, art, and the sciences. Albert Ellis and Rollo May were avid students of philosophy. Jung was fascinated by world religions and alchemy. Many of the other influential therapists read widely in the sciences, humanities, and fiction to broaden their education and widen their visions. You would do well to follow their lead.

Get Outside Your Culture

The more experiences you accrue living, working, and traveling in cultures different from your own, the more sensitivity and flexibility you'll have to connect with diverse clients. You develop yourself as a therapist not only by the professional books you read and workshops you attend, but also through life experiences that make you more worldly and wise.

The more time you spend traversing social environments different from your own, the more flexibility and sensitivity you can access in your work. Most of the impetus for my (Jeffrey's) own ideas about helping arose during my work living in Asia, Europe, Latin America, and various regions of North America. When running groups in Iceland, Nepal, Singapore, Peru, Turkey, Hong Kong, England, Australia, New Zealand, Vietnam, Brazil, Ghana, or Romania, I was forced to throw away a lot of what I thought I knew and understood to adapt to a different set of values and norms. So it has been with every agency and setting in which I've practiced: I have learned to continuously question my most cherished assumptions about what works and instead to pay closer attention to the way my clients respond to interventions.

The more opportunities you can find to immerse yourself in "foreign" cultures, whether they are within your own community or in far-flung places around the world, the more you can field-test and adapt what you do best. This sort of culturally rich reflective practice will help you refine and adapt your favored approach to make it more responsive to the needs of diverse people. You learn to stretch yourself in new ways since you can't rely on favored strategies that may have worked within your own culture. That is one of the marvelous things about this type of work we do: Every client you see requires you to enter a culture that is often alien to you. If you hope to make contact with people, you have to get outside of yourself and what is familiar.

Doing therapy is one of the most exciting adventures you can undertake, whether you are practicing in the neighborhood where you grew up or in a very foreign country. It isn't really an option to be integrative in your work; it is a necessity if you ever hope to make sense of what you're doing.

Avoid Thinking in Boxes

Look at the big picture beyond your individual cases. As part of your training, you will be taught the skills of differential diagnosis and systematic clinical assessment. That is one way to think about things, but there are others as well. You may be drilled in the methods of collecting data, formulating hypotheses, settling on diagnoses, and writing out treatment plans, but there are alternative ways to think about your cases. You can use intuition as well as logic, your heart as well as your head. You can ask yourself not only where this client fits in the *DSM*, but also whom he or she reminds you of and what part of yourself you can recognize in his or her experience. Take a step outside the usual parameters from which you make sense of things. Find alternative viewpoints to scan the territory. Look at cases from multiple angles. See every one of your clients as unique.

FOR PERSONAL REFLECTION

Hold onto this exercise for a time after you see a client, or after you have practiced therapy in a role-played situation. Teach yourself to be reflective after every session you conduct. Once you are done with the required paperwork—writing progress notes and case summaries, filling in log-books, filing folders—take a few minutes before your next appointment or meeting and ask yourself the following questions:

- What really happened in this session? If I go beyond what my notes say, what was the core of the experience?
- What worked best with this client? What did I do that seemed least helpful?
- If I could have approached this session differently, what might I have done instead?
- What did I learn about this client today? What did I learn about myself? What did I learn about the way that therapy works?

It is probable you will address many of these questions in supervision, but even so it is always profitable to consider them within the privacy of your own mind.

Resist the Urge to Label Yourself

We have already warned you that you will be asked often what sort of therapist you are. You could say, "A good one!" but that will only buy you a little time.

"No," the person will say with a nervous laugh, "you know what I mean. What kind of therapy do you do?"

Again, you can try to sidestep the query with a clever riposte: "I do whatever the client needs most at the time," but that won't work either.

"Oh," the person will say with recognition, "you're one of those eclectic types."

You almost can't avoid being labeled by others. Both colleagues and clients alike will try to "diagnose" you by putting you in one of their established categories. You have little choice except to play along with the routine and tell the person something that fits expectations. But that doesn't mean you have to believe what you are saying. You can tell others that you are a brief therapist, or a Gestalt therapist, or an addictions counselor, or a neo-psycho-analytic postmodern feminist grief specialist.

The consequence of such a label is that people then have certain expectations for how you are supposed to behave. You may become limited by these perceptions. When you think of yourself as integrative, you don't fit in any category—except your own.

One Additional Thought

Earlier in the chapter we offered several different explanations to account for why no single theory is superior to the others, and why they all seem to work. If you recall, one favored reason was that regardless of their espoused beliefs, most good therapists do essentially the same things with their clients.

One other interesting hypothesis contends that the reason various theories appear to work equally well, even though they approach things so differently, is that they each provide opportunities for clients to solve their own problems. As long as therapists don't get in the way too much by insisting that clients comply with their rigid agendas, the results are usually satisfactory (Bohart, 2017). In one sense, the job of a therapist is not to change people but to create an atmosphere that is conducive for them to change themselves (Bohart & Tallman, 2010).

To support this idea, they use the example of exercise methods. It doesn't matter so much whether you run or swim or bicycle or cross-country ski or take an aerobics class as long as you get your cardiovascular system in shape and do it on a regular basis. Of course, there are certain conditions that must be met—getting your heart rate into a certain range, sustaining the exercise for a minimum of 20 minutes, and repeating the process a minimum of several times per week, but other than that, what you do is less important.

Although it may be a bit early in your career to think about integrating theories that you have just learned, it is helpful to think of these frameworks as working models that must be adapted to your unique style of practice and the individualized needs of your clients.

SUGGESTED READINGS

Berman, P. S. (2015). *Case conceptualization and treatment planning: Exercises for integrating theory with clinical practice* (3rd ed.). Thousand Oaks, CA: SAGE.

Corey, G. (2019). *The art of integrative counseling* (4th ed.). Alexandria, VA: American Counseling Association.

Kottler, J. A. (2017). *Secrets of exceptional counselors.* Alexandria, VA: American Counseling Association.

Kottler, J. A. (2018). *Living and being a Therapist: A collection of readings.* San Diego, CA: Cognella.

Lazarus, A. A. (2006). *Brief but comprehensive therapy: The multimodal way.* New York, NY: Springer.

Norcross, J. (2011). *Psychotherapy relationships that work* (2nd ed.). New York, NY: Oxford University Press.

Prochaska, J. O., & Norcross, J. C. (2018). *Systems of psychotherapy: A transtheoretical approach* (9th ed.). Pacific Grove, CA: Brooks/Cole.

Sprenkle, D. H., Davis, S. D., & Lebow, J. L. (2013). *Common factors in couple and family therapy: The overlooked foundation for effective practice* (2nd ed.). New York, NY: Guilford.

Stricker, G. (2012). *Psychotherapy integration.* Washington, DC: American Psychological Association.

Wampold, B. E., & Imel, Z. E. (2015). *The great psychotherapy debate: The evidence for what makes psychotherapy work.* New York, NY: Routledge.

Wachtel, P. L. (2013). *Therapeutic communication: Knowing what to say when* (2nd ed.). New York, NY: Guilford.

CHAPTER 13

Personalizing and Customizing Theory for Clients and Settings

LEARNING OBJECTIVES

After reading this chapter, you should be able to do the following:

1. Compare several theoretical approaches in how their therapists interact with clients, what they target for change, and how they operate to promote positive change.
2. Assess your alignment with key dimensions underlying common families of theories.
3. Discuss how the therapists' own values and beliefs impact effective implementation of a theoretical approach.
4. Describe how your own interpersonal style influences your choice of your key theoretical approach.
5. Assess your own strengths, beliefs about change, affinity for particular theories, and the types of therapy you plan to do as guidance for defining your own preliminary theoretical framework.
6. Analyze the limitations of theory with respect to how it can help or hinder effective practice.
7. Describe how therapist expertise develops and make a plan for how you will hone your therapeutic approach and expertise throughout your career.

Lord Chesterfield, the 17th-century English statesman, claimed that the world can never be known by a theory. It provides the beginner with a general map with which to navigate through "mazes, windings, and turnings." It distills the wisdom of experienced travelers into a coherent model that can be used as a guide. But it is *only* a guide. Just that. Nothing more.

You will recall that Carl Jung, one of the earliest rebels to secede from the orthodoxy of Freud's psychoanalytic theory, went on to establish his own school of thought that has grown in influence. Yet Jung saw the limits of theory without personalizing it to the demands of a clinical situation and the needs of a client. Furthermore, theories can even insulate you from the uniquely magical encounter that often happens during therapeutic sessions.

"Learn your theories as well as you can," Jung (1954) advised, "but put them aside when you the touch the miracle of the living soul" (p. 73).

With this humble acknowledgement that having a theory isn't everything, and probably not even the most important thing, framing your work within a theory can help you and your clients in many ways. So, in this chapter we offer you some ideas for developing a personal model of counseling or therapy. This is the model that you will bring with you as you begin to see clients. But, you might be wondering, how do I decide what to do? There are a number of ways you could make this decision; here, we present a few, based on our years of teaching and supervision:

a. Wing it. Do whatever comes to mind.

b. Use techniques from your supervisors' favorite theory; it will keep them happy.

c. Look for the handouts from the last workshop you attended on the hottest new approach and give that a try.

d. Choose a theory that fits with how you see the world and how you like to work with people, read up on it, watch demonstrations of therapists doing it, and then try it yourself.

Obviously, we think the last approach is the most promising for you and your clients. In this chapter we will give you some ideas for how you might make the important decision of the first theory in which you will invest your time and energy.

FOR PERSONAL REFLECTION or A GROUP ACTIVITY

It should by now be readily apparent that each of the theories presented offers something of use to most practitioners, regardless of specialty area. Identify each of the following contributions with the theory (or theories) you have studied that are most often associated with each idea.

- Only by coming to terms with the past can you hope to understand problems in the present.
- Each individual's perception of reality is shaped by his or her unique experience.
- People suffer most from a lack of personal meaning in their lives.
- You must uncover dysfunctional thinking and beliefs to restore healthy emotional functioning.
- It is the therapeutic relationship that heals most, especially one that is open, honest, and trusting.
- You must look at any behavior within a larger context that takes into consideration relationship patterns.

- It is not what you understand that matters most but what you put into action.
- If you try something and it doesn't work, try something else.
- People must be held responsible for their behavior and accountable for the consequences of their actions.

IT ALL LOOKS THE SAME TO ME: COMPARISONS AND DIFFERENCES

One of the most important tasks in your effort to learn theories of counseling and therapy is to be able to see ways that each approach is related to several others, as well as to understand ways they are different. This is not an easy assignment, especially considering that the inventors of each system go out of their way to emphasize the uniqueness of their approach, often masking the ways they say the same things as others in slightly different language.

There are a number of ways to consolidate what you have learned so far. You can spend considerable time studying each of several favorite models, reading the original sources and secondary sources. You can also make an effort to put theories into practice, either by applying them to your work with clients or your own personal struggles. As preparation for both of those strategies, we would first suggest that you pull things together by trying to group the major theories according to their most significant features.

Before we get more deeply into the universal features of the theories you have studied, let's first examine some of their differences. In Table 13.1 you can see highlighted the ways that each approach differs from others in terms of (a) treatment goals, (b) underlying philosophy, and (c) favorite techniques.

TABLE 13.1. Summary of Therapeutic Approaches

Theory	Goals	Philosophy	Techniques
Psychodynamic Sigmund Freud Carl Jung Heinz Kohut Otto Kernberg	Resolve conflicts from the past; change character; promote insight; strengthen ego	Past determines the present; basic drives; role of the unconscious; developmental history	Transference; catharsis; uncover defenses; analyze resistance; interpretation
Person centered Carl Rogers Natalie Rogers Gerald Pine Eugene Gendlin	Create authentic relationship; increase awareness; express feelings; development of self	Humans are growth oriented; increased awareness of self and others to improve self-esteem and personal functioning	Empathic resonance; active listening; deep reflection of feelings; search for meaning; group interactions

(continued)

TABLE 13.1. Summary of Therapeutic Approaches (*Continued*)

THEORY	GOALS	PHILOSOPHY	TECHNIQUES
Gestalt Fritz Perls Laura Perls Miriam Polster Ewing Polster	Increase self-awareness in present; integrate split between conflicting selves	Explore unfinished business through direct experience; people as fragmented and cut off from core selves	Confrontation; role-playing and psychodrama; enactments; group interactions; risk taking
Behavioral B. F. Skinner Joseph Wolpe Albert Bandura John Gottman	Identify target behaviors; modify dysfunctional behaviors; learn adaptive responses	People shaped by environment and experience; all behavior is learned and reinforced	Goal setting; contingency contracting; skills training; reinforcement; relaxation training
Cognitive Aaron Beck Albert Ellis Donald Meichenbaum Arnold Lazarus	Increase awareness of cognitive activity; identify and challenge irrational beliefs; teach adaptive behavior	People learn maladaptive patterns; thinking precedes feeling and action; problems stem from core beliefs	Dispute irrational beliefs; confront distortions and exaggerations; introduce alternative thinking
Reality William Glasser Robert Wubbolding	Assume greater responsibility; become more skilled at meeting needs	People motivated to meet needs; greater self-control is possible; focus on success	Examine consequences of choices; challenge people to be accountable; develop action plans
Existential Rollo May Irvin Yalom Victor Frankl Jim Bugental	Explore core issues that give life meaning; address barriers to increased freedom and responsibility	Search for underlying meaning; struggles with personal responsibility, isolation, angst, death, and freedom	Collaborative, authentic relationship; being in the moment; focusing; confrontation; eclectic methods
Adlerian Alfred Adler Rudolph Dreikurs Jon Carlson Don Dinkmeyer	Provide support and increase motivation; challenge dysfunctional beliefs; work through feelings of inferiority	Birth order and early family experiences shape personality and social behavior; lifestyle a function of social interest	Conduct lifestyle assessment; interpret early recollections; explore mistakes and core fears; develop action plan
Systemic Murray Bowen Salvador Minuchin Carl Whitaker Virginia Satir	Identify underlying structures and patterns; realign system so that it is more healthy for members	Individual behavior and problems a function of larger context; families are living systems that seek stability	Reconceptualize problems; set boundaries; restructure power and control; improve communication
Constructivist Kenneth Gergen Michael White Tom Andersen Michael Mahoney	Identify societal influences and personal narratives; re-story life circumstances in more helpful ways	Cultural influences shape individual perceptions; subjective nature of reality; problems exist in language	Collaborative conversations; externalizing problems; examine cultural influences

Brief	Produce symptom-	Problems result from	Reframe problems;
Milton Erickson	atic relief; limited,	repetitive, maladap-	use directives;
Jay Haley	specific, and focused	tive patterns; forget	action plans and
Steve de Shazer	goals; discover	about how they	homework; focus on
William	patterns and change	developed and work	what works; flexible,
O'Hanlon	them	to change them	pragmatic methods
Feminist	Examine issues of	Personal problems	Support cultural and
Carol Gilligan	power and gender	have political and	gender differences
Rachel Hare-	roles; explore themes	contextual roots;	in relationship; chal-
Mustin	of marginalization	freedom and power	lenge and confront
Laura Brown	and oppression; work	have different mean-	stereotypes; use of
Lenore Walker	to change systems	ings for women than	empowerment
		men	

FOR PERSONAL REFLECTION or **A CLASS ACTIVITY**

Review the theories summarized in Table 12.2. Instead of concentrating on how each model is different from the others, look at their common features.

After you have studied the convergences rather than divergences, take all the theories and group them into three main categories that make sense to you.

After you have placed each theory in one of three categories, give each of the groups a name that describes the principal feature they share in common.

Consider other ways that you could group the theories according to dominant characteristics and shared beliefs.

Discuss your informal factor analysis with classmates to compare your different conceptions.

Insight Versus Action

One obvious way to think about the theories of intervention is in terms of the relative importance they place on the value of promoting some degree of understanding as opposed to stressing action. You will recall, for example, that strategic, behavioral, problem-solving, and other brief therapies tend to minimize the role of insight in the change process, preferring instead to work solely on a level of constructive behavior: It isn't what you say or understand that matters but what you *do*.

In direct contrast to this emphasis on doing, you have read about other approaches that work at a level of promoting greater self-awareness and understanding. It is believed that such personal revelations become transformative when clients are helped to apply their insights to their daily lives.

Psychoanalytic, existential, and client-centered theories most closely fit this style. They might approach matters with clients in a very different way, but they all share the conviction that "truth" will set you free. Note that most practitioners now develop competencies in both kinds of approaches since clients have different needs at particular times and with particular problems. Imagine, for example, trying to employ existential or psychodynamic therapy with someone in the throes of a panic attack; likewise, picture the inappropriateness of insisting on a problem-solving approach with a client who wishes to explore the lack of meaning in his life.

FOR PERSONAL REFLECTION

Like any of the polarities mentioned in this context, dividing theories based on insight or action is a gross simplification. After all, some theories fit right about in the middle. If you could imagine that any theory can be located on a continuum of insight versus action, which ones would you nominate to place approximately in the center?

_____

INSIGHT   BRIEF

    You could easily make a case that theories such as cognitive, narrative, Adlerian, Gestalt, and multimodal include features that promote both insight and action. Which others do you think belong in the middle of the line?

    In addition, which theories that you read about could you legitimately place on either end of the continuum, depending on the way the approach is interpreted and practiced?

Cognitive Versus Affective

Another obvious way to compare therapeutic approaches is to look at the relative emphasis they place on thoughts or feelings. Cognitive, existential, constructivist, and psychoanalytic approaches tend to be fairly intellectual, uncovering internal thought processes that may be dysfunctional or counterproductive. They might have very different names for the problems and choose to focus on different facets of cognitive processes, but they all agree that changing the way you conceptualize your world will dictate the ways you respond.

    In marked contrast to this cognitive, intellectual, rational, logical, traditionally male way of seeing the world, other theories stand at the opposite end of the continuum. According to client-centered, Gestalt, and expressive therapies, therapists should be spending their time helping people access their unacknowledged feelings, understand their origins, and then express them fluently and constructively. You can visualize, therefore, that the first set of theories claims that controlling thoughts alters feelings, whereas the second group believes that dealing with feelings changes underlying cognitive structures. Whereas once upon a time, therapists felt forced to choose between one or the other, nowadays practitioners may adapt their approach to focus primarily on thoughts or feelings (or behavior), depending on the clients presenting complaints, strengths, weaknesses, preferences, and goals.

FOR HOMEWORK and GROUP DISCUSSION

In an earlier chapter you reflected on where you stood on a set of dimensions that reflected assumptions and beliefs underlying theories of psychotherapy (Table 3.1). Look at these assumptions again and make a list of your beliefs. Now identity two or three theories that align best with your own world view.

Now share your conclusions with your peers. Do they agree that the theories you've identified align with your personal beliefs? What do they see as similarities and points of difference?

Present Versus Past

Again, you have heard considerable debate between combatants about whether the better approach is to deal with unresolved issues in the past or to concentrate primarily on what is going on in the present. In one corner, weighing in with the psychoanalytic schools of thought, there is the very strong conviction that real change is not possible unless you deal with the underlying origins of the presenting problem. This approach is also shared by some family systems theorists, such as Murray Bowen, who believe that present family interaction patterns are often influenced or perhaps even inherited from previous generations.

In the other corner, shaking their heads in amusement at how misguided the past-oriented theorists are, are those who believe that the only valid focus of treatment is to remain in the present. Anything else is, at best, a waste of time. Theories that must immediately come to mind in this regard form an improbable alliance. Just imagine, for instance, that behavioral, reality, and strategic approaches share this corner with Gestalt and client-centered models. All essentially minimize what has happened previously and keep pushing the client to stay in the here and now.

Flexible Versus Rigid Roles

Although there are several other ways to categorize the theories, the last one examined here looks at the degree of freedom the therapist has to improvise and operate pragmatically. In other words, how carefully prescribed are the clinician's therapeutic options? How much flexibility and pragmatism are permitted in practicing this system without abandoning the core ideas?

Again, there are some strange bedfellows. It may be apparent that a theory such as psychoanalysis has a very rigid set of rules for how the practitioner may behave, but so does the client-centered, behavioral, and rational-emotive therapist. In each case, the clinician is expected to apply the theory by following the established procedures.

Contrast these theories with others in which the therapist is allowed, even encouraged, to be as flexible, pragmatic, and eclectic as possible; any intervention is permitted as long as it gets desired results. Reliability of methods is far less important than creativity and flexibility. You will remember, for example, that the existential theory really has no techniques at all: Its practitioners follow a consistent philosophy but in any way they want. Then there are models such as Gestalt and strategic therapy that are absolutely loaded with practical strategies borrowed from every conceivable source. Finally, there are eclectic and integrative approaches such as multimodal therapy that encourage clinicians to borrow methods from all other theories.

Making Further Comparisons

These four ways of organizing the theories can get you started thinking in both convergent and divergent ways. First, with each approach, you ask yourself the following:

- What else does this remind me of?
- How does this resemble other ideas with which I am already familiar?
- What are some common threads that appear to be running throughout each approach?

Second, you can sort the theories by emphasizing the ways they differ from one another. In some ways, this might be harder to do because it requires you to understand enough about all the approaches that you can begin to recognize their unique contributions. When you combine both sorting strategies, you are well on your way toward completing the difficult task of integrating what you have learned this semester.

FOR PERSONAL REFLECTION or A GROUP ACTIVITY

Cheston (2000) offers one paradigm that organizes the theories into four main groups according to the practitioner's role and presence (way of being), chosen knowledge base (ways of understanding), and clinical methods (ways of intervening). Cover the left-hand column and then read the descriptions of different ways of being, understanding, and intervening. Highlight the words that you resonate with most at this time (realizing that you might be a little different in different clinical situations). Now uncover the left-hand column. Which row has the most highlighted words? Does it make sense to you that the theory group in that row would be a good place to begin your journey toward theoretical expertise?

	Therapist's Way of Being is...	Ways of Understanding Include...	Ways of Intervening include...
Psychodynamic	Neutral; even-handedly attentive to facilitate transference; quietly supportive	Searching for unconscious motives and unresolved core issues; discovering new insights	Increasing awareness of hidden, repressed material; working through transference
Humanistic	Warm, caring, authentic; focused on the present	Understanding client's world; increasing self-awareness and self-expression	Promoting insight and awareness of underlying feelings
Cognitive-behavioral	Assertive, active, challenging, teaching, and information	Examining reinforcers and underlying thinking patterns/scripts	Disputing irrational beliefs; assigning behavioral homework
Systemic	Mediational, persuasive, curious, experimental	Examining the structure and dynamics of interactions	Altering family structure; assigning paradoxical tasks

A CUSTOM FIT

Now you know where you stand in general, but there is more work to do. Theories are not like ready-to-wear clothes but rather outfits that must be custom made. Depending on your size, build, posture, and preferences, the clothes must be taken in a little here, let out a little there, and shaped to fit your form and preferences. It is the same with theories. You can pick one off the rack that fits you pretty closely, but you will still need to make some alterations to have a proper fit.

It is also crucial to remember that these theories not only need to be customized for your unique personality and interaction style, but also for the individualized background of each client. Just imagine how differently you would need to adapt your favored approach to the specific needs of the following clients:

1. An African American corporate executive who finds herself "lonely at the top"
2. A homeless man, addicted to meth, who once enjoyed the privileges of wealth until his company folded and his son died after a long struggle with leukemia
3. A Native American teenage girl who struggles between the pull of her boyfriend who wants her to be more like his friends and the influence of her more traditional parents and culture
4. An Iraqi War veteran who lost most of his sexual functioning in a battle wound and has been unable, ever since, to enjoy any sort of intimacy with a woman
5. A Mexican American family with a history of depression that is currently being manifested in the social withdrawal of two of their children
6. A racially mixed lesbian couple that experiences disapproval from both of their families and discrimination from many other sources
7. A Japanese exchange student who has become so Americanized during his stay that he cannot picture himself ever fitting in again back home

FOR A CLASS ACTIVITY

In small work groups, select two different theories with which you are fairly familiar. Make sure one approach is somewhat insight oriented and the other is more action focused.

Review each of the seven cases that have been listed, talking about the ways you may need to adjust your style of practice and approach according to the unique backgrounds of these clients.

No doubt, with each of these clients, you would approach matters with respect, compassion, and empathy. You would also most likely follow the usual process with which you are most comfortable and experienced to assess presenting problems and formulate a treatment plan. Recall the "golden thread" we described in Chapter 2 of this book, and how using a theory can tie together your ideas about what went wrong and what can be done about it—what "better" will look like (see figure 13.1 for one example). But remember also how important it is to form diagnostic impressions and treatment plans not only according to standard practices, but also by taking into consideration the cultural backgrounds of the cases. Moreover, the specific way that you apply your preferred theory would depend on how the specific client sees things.

FIGURE 13.1. The golden thread: CBT applied

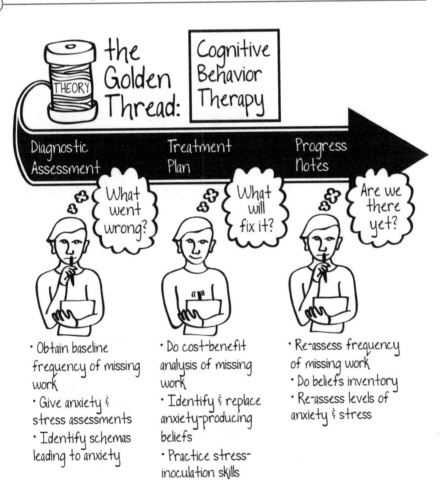

Clients Have Theories, Too

This is a book primarily about the theories of counselors and therapists. What about those of our clients? After all, they come to us with their own strong convictions about how change should and does take place (Howell, 2017). These certainly impact what happens, too.

Unless you are prepared to hear, understand, and honor the client's theory, instead of insisting your own view is correct, you are likely to be fired. The challenge is to negotiate with clients so that your preferred theory of change becomes acceptable to them, or adopting a more personalized approach, you agree to work within the parameters of their perceived reality.

Every person who comes to see you has a fairly definite idea of the following:

- What the problem is
- What needs to be done to fix it
- What you can do to be of service

Of course, most of the time there is no way you could ever subscribe to the client's framework, especially when the most common theory presented is something such as the following:

- "It's not *my* fault. The problem is my spouse/parent/boss."
- "What I want you to do is to get others off my back, let me talk a lot and don't interrupt me, and don't nag me about my drinking."
- "You should agree with me and tell others that I am right and they are wrong."
- "This is God's will that I suffer. Who am I to challenge His will?"

As part of your initial assessment, you must find out the client's theory by asking how the client believes that change will occur. Such a dialogue sounds something like this:

THERAPIST:	So, you've been saying that you've been depressed for quite a long time, ever since you can remember.
CLIENT:	Well, maybe not always, but on and off for a while.
THERAPIST:	How and when did this all begin?
CLIENT:	I think it started when I spent so much time sick in the hospital. I was just out of it for a long time.
THERAPIST:	You were pretty immobilized and helpless, depending on almost everyone else to take care of you.
CLIENT:	That's for sure. My doctor says there's nothing wrong with me, but I've just never been the same since then.
THERAPIST:	Say some more about how your life changed after that.

In this preliminary exploration, the therapist is helping the client articulate when the symptoms first began. Next, time can be spent finding out when and where the depression is better or worse, what seems to help and what doesn't, and what has already been tried previously to make things better. Just as importantly, the therapist needs to find out more about the client's ideas for what will help. If you don't discover those expectations and address them, you can do what you think is the best job in the world but it will all be useless if the client doesn't feel like a satisfied customer.

THERAPIST: You've talked a lot about those times when you've felt more in control than others, and especially when you start to fall apart. Maybe you could tell me what you'd like from therapy. What are you hoping that I can do to help?

CLIENT: [Laughs] You don't have a magic wand or something, do you?

THERAPIST: Wish I did. But I've got the next best thing.

CLIENT: What's that?

THERAPIST: Oh, lots of effective strategies to help you to combat your depression and feel more in control. But before I tell you about that, I'd like to know more about what *you* think will help most.

CLIENT: I guess it would help if you'd hear me out. Most people in my life are sick of listening to me. They say I whine too much and feel sorry for myself.

THERAPIST: What do you think?

CLIENT: Maybe so, I guess. But I think that people just don't understand what I'm going through.

THERAPIST: So, you are hoping that I'll understand in ways that others never have. And then maybe help you to understand better as well.

CLIENT: Sure. But most of all, I feel like I've just got this disease still in me from when I was sick a long time ago, and it just won't let go.

The client's theory is beginning to be teased out. Although it sounds like he wants an exorcist rather than a therapist, it is not at all unusual that expectations would be different from what the therapist hopes to deliver. Still, with depression, it is always a good idea to rule out physical maladies that could be contributing to the problem. In many cases, such as the diagnosis of an endogenous or long-term depression (as in this instance), it is generally advisable to have a psychiatric evaluation to see if medication might be useful as an adjunct to therapy. But all of that is further down the line; for now, your job is to help the client speak as frankly as possible about how the problem is conceived and how it is best resolved.

During this process of negotiation in the initial phase, keep in mind the following principles:

1. Ask the client how he or she believes change will occur.
2. Don't argue or disagree too much in the beginning or your client won't return.
3. Avoid imposing your alternative theory on the client without respecting the person's worldview, cultural values, and expectations.
4. No matter which theory you favor, remember that it must be adapted to fit the unique context of each client.
5. Speak in the client's language instead of professional jargon.
6. Negotiate with the client to find a common ground that you can both live with, one that is consistent with your professional strategy as well as the client's values.

The Real-Time Practice of Therapy

As we have mentioned, the boundaries between theories are becoming blurred. Therapists who were once avid humanists later merged with cognitive theory to call themselves cognitive-behavior therapists. Then they embraced constructivism and decided to include themselves as part of that school of thought. This same process of affiliation and integration is happening within other theoretical families as well. Mindfulness-based concepts are merged with cognitive therapy. Psychodynamic theory is linked to feminist ideas for a more contemporary approach. Existential philosophy is integrated with more practical behavioral techniques. As we've pointed out many times in this book, we have reached a point where very few clinicians adopt any kind of "pure" theory in their work: As experienced therapists grow and evolve, they continuously adapt their dominant model to incorporate new ideas, concepts, research, and strategies. This has been the policy ever since Freud's time in which most of his followers, such as Alfred Adler, Carl Jung, Harry Stack Sullivan, Anna Freud, and Karen Horney, went on to develop their own visions.

The whole idea of developing your own theory may sound daunting, if not impossible. After all, you have enough on your plate just trying to figure out the rudimentary principles of any single theory you have studied. You have been asked to learn the history and the major concepts of your profession. Then you were tested on the material and asked to write papers demonstrating your mastery of the material. Your head has, at times, become so full of content to the point that it feels like it would burst. Now for the next challenge. ...

Your first client walks in for help. Quick, what do you do?

The simple answer to this question is that you do whatever you can. You size up the situation as best as possible. With only a second or two between verbalizations, there is really no time to think much; you must react by instinct and training. Much of this preparation comes not only from your theory courses, but also from the instruction in core therapeutic skills. After you leave the session, you'll have to write up what you did using whatever version of treatment planning software you have.

Although from this class you might have gotten the distinct impression that therapists and counselors don't agree on very much, that is really not the case at all. There might be differences in one's preferred conceptual framework, but very little variation exists in the skills that are used in session. By skills, we are referring to the specific therapist behaviors that are used to respond and intervene in session.

If you would watch live or recorded sessions of therapists from different theoretical orientations, you would notice remarkable similarity in the skills they used. You would hear and see them asking questions and responding to client statements with what sounds like restatements or at least rephrasing what clients said. You would notice the use of summary statements occasionally, in which the therapist ties together several ideas. You would witness some interpretations in which the therapist introduces alternative ways of looking at things. Meanwhile, you would observe lots of head nodding, "uh-huhs," and nonverbal behavior to communicate that the therapist is listening intently. You would also hear the therapist probe and explore certain issues by framing questions in particular ways. You would see other skills as well that are virtually universal: confronting clients by pointing out discrepancies, setting goals, role-playing, and structuring therapeutic tasks. And in many cases, you would see pretty universal agreement about what constitutes exceptional therapeutic work (Hill et al., 2018; Kottler & Carlson, 2008).

FOR HOMEWORK and A GROUP PROJECT

Your university library or department most likely has a collection of demonstration videos in which noted theorists and practitioners show how they apply their ideas with clients. You have probably seen a few of these in class, although there are hundreds of others that you could watch in your spare time.

There is no better way to learn about the various therapeutic approaches, compare their differences, and integrate their commonalities than to watch as many videos as you can. It is for this reason that I would strongly suggest that you organize a video club in which you invite a few classmates to watch various therapy films together and then talk about your reactions.

One series for example, is called *Psychotherapy with the Experts*, in which each of several different theories are demonstrated and discussed (existential, solution focused, reality, mind–body, multimodal, feminist, systemic, integrative, object relations, cognitive, Adlerian, and person centered). A dozen other publishers also produce their own video series that cover similar ground. It doesn't even matter so much which videos you see because each one will highlight things that you like and dislike about that particular approach. The most important part of this exercise is what takes place afterward—how you process what you observed and what you learn from it. That is one reason it is preferable to see the sessions with others so that you can make sense of what you witnessed.

Your Own Inimitable Style

When it comes time to personalize the way you do therapy, this will not come about on a conceptual level alone, but also the way you practice in terms of your basic skills and therapeutic behaviors. We remember when, in our first courses, we actually sat and practiced for a whole class period how to sit with a client—leaning forward, making easy eye contact, learning attending behaviors. This felt a little silly at the time, but it is an example of the kinds of habits you will be taught to develop.

It is interesting the way different therapist training and counselor preparation programs handle these generic skills. You may already have taken a course in counseling techniques or therapeutic skills before this one. In other curricula, theory is offered first and then skills follow. In some programs, theory, skills, and practice are all integrated into one unit. This is more consistent with how professional helpers are prepared in other cultures because it does not make sense to break up learning into discrete units. Among indigenous peoples, for example, it is common that the role of healer includes not only the role of psychological interventionist, but also spiritual guide, medical practitioner, moral sage, and life coach (Kottler, Carlson, & Keeney, 2004). By contrast, in most psychotherapy and counseling programs, beginners are initially introduced to theories. Next, they practice the skills and techniques that come from that theory (reflective listening as part of client-centered theory or goal setting as part of behavioral theory). Finally, they apply the theory and skills with clients in the field. Then they move on to the next approach.

Regardless of which sequence you are following, whether you have already had a skills class, are taking it at the same time as this course, or will take it next, you should know that it is at this level that you will end up personalizing your practice the most. You may get drilled in the "correct" way to ask open-ended questions or the most opportune way to confront people without eliciting defensiveness. This is consistent with the way any new skills are taught, whether it is the proper grip for holding a backhand in tennis, the prescribed position of your knees when making a snowplow turn in skiing, or the proper breath control needed to hold a long note in an operatic aria.

Soon after you commit these skills and behaviors to memory and habitual responding; you will begin to adapt them to fit your unique interpersonal style. This is a very important stage in your evolution as a clinician, that which makes you come across as natural and comfortable rather than wooden and stiff. Your job in the coming years will be to take the generic therapeutic behaviors that are considered somewhat universal and integrate them into your unique style of communication.

DECIDING ON A STARTING POINT

In many cases, you won't have a choice about which theory you use in your practicum, internship, or first job—your supervisors may require you to follow a particular framework that they believe is best suited for beginners, most appropriate for the setting, or simply their most favored model. At some point in your career, however, you will have the chance to pick the theory you like the best and then later to adapt or integrate it with other things you learn.

In making your choice, you may wish to consider the following questions:

1. *What are your personal strengths and how do they fit best with a theory that seems well suited to your style?* If you are low key, nurturing, and warm, you might select an approach that is different from someone who is more flamboyant, provocative, and confrontive. You have read about theories in which the therapist's role is to be a teacher/coach as opposed to a parent/mentor, consultant/tutor, or provocateur. Start with a framework that seems most natural to you.

2. *What are your beliefs about how change takes place?* Do you think that real change takes a long time or that it can occur very quickly? How important do you think the past is in dealing with present problems? How much responsibility should the client have in the relationship as compared to that of the therapist? Does change take place most effectively at the level of feelings, thoughts, or behavior? Each of these questions signals a distinct preference you might have to choose

one theory over another. If you haven't yet made up your mind in these areas (which is entirely appropriate), you might wish to pick a framework that allows for maximum flexibility.

3. *What sort of work will you be doing?* Depending on where you will be working and whom you will be helping, you will find some approaches better than others. You would not want to use a long-term approach if you working with substance abusers or in a crisis intervention clinic. You also would not want to use a complex, intellectual approach with hospitalized schizophrenics or elementary school children, nor would you attempt a form of brief therapy with someone who has major depression or a personality disorder.

4. *Which approaches that you studied appeal to you most?* You must have some strong reactions, one way or the other, to the ideas you read about. Which ones speak to you? Which ones feel compatible with the way you live your life? A theory should feel like "home," a comfortable place for you to sort things out.

5. Once you settle on one theory as a starting point, how will you need to personalize it in such a way that it becomes part of your own style? Don't think of your choice of therapeutic approach as the end of your search but as the beginning. A theory is a tool, just like a computer. You acquire it in its generic form, with the default settings arranged according to the preferences of the original programmer. Then it is up to you to customize the instrument so that it fits your needs and responds to your most frequent commands.

6. *Which dimensions of a few other therapeutic approaches might you like to blend into your primary framework?* Once you have picked a central theory, that does not mean you must exclude the attractive features of other approaches you have studied. As you were surveying each of the options available, you probably kept inventory (in the form of mental or written notes) of ideas that you found especially useful. You will find ways to include many of these strategies in your chosen framework after you make the adjustments that are more consistent with the model. If you were existentially inclined, for instance, you would not want to simply start adding goal setting to your therapy without first thinking through how this structure contributes to your overall treatment objectives.

7. *Whom might you consult for supervision and additional training in your preferred model?* It can easily take a lifetime or two to master the intricacies of any single theoretical framework. Every year there are new refinements in the basic ideas, as well as innovations in research, technique, and applications. You can't learn this by reading alone.

You must practice the model with a variety of clients, reflect on your relative effectiveness, and get lots of feedback from more experienced practitioners about ways you could improve. Fortunately, a little Internet research will yield communities—in your locale, on the Web or both—to whom you can connect for additional training, dialogue, and encouragement. The people who form such groups or sites are very enthusiastic about their theory and typically welcome newcomers.

Once you have your general idea of which theory, or family of theories, you particularly resonate with, and which techniques from other approaches that you would like to blend in, you will need to do more thinking about your personal approach to counseling so that you will have your map firmly in hand when you land in the territory of seeing clients. Your clients will settle down and get to work more quickly when they sense that you are a confident guide. You will probably end up in treatment team meetings right away, where your peers will want to know what your plan is for each client and why you think it the best chance of succeeding.

By the way—we strongly believe there is merit to formally writing down your views as you conclude your first journey through the theories of counseling and psychotherapy. Not only will doing so help you feel clear and calm as you encounter the unexpected (and you will), but as the years pass you'll find it quite interesting to look back on the place where you began.

FOR HOMEWORK

In your journal answer the questions about your core beliefs and values. This will give you the basic workings of a personal theory in development.

Describe your worldview about the nature of people, how and why they do well or develop problems, and what needs to happen for them to get back on track. Include your basic life philosophies and spiritual views, as well as what you've learned in school. Then describe what therapists can do to assist in this process and how they would work with a client to accomplish positive change. When you are done, capture these ideas in a statement that is no more than a page. Then, share it with others and get their reaction to it; use their feedback to polish what you've said.

Many states require a therapist to maintain and distribute a *professional disclosure statement* that describes their philosophy and approach. Now you've got your first draft.

LIMITATIONS OF THEORY

In this text you have learned about many of the major theoretical frameworks currently in use by therapists. All of them are built on the assumption that understanding change is knowable. Therapists and counselors, as a group, share the strong belief that it is usually possible to figure out why people do the things they do. More to the point, we also believe that it is feasible to (a) guide people in desired directions, then (b) discover a reasonable and accurate explanation for why and how it happened and (c) how this can be replicated in the future. Although it is indeed entirely possible to push people toward particular outcomes, and do so consistently, it isn't necessarily the case that we can ever be sure what actually happened and why.

In physics and the sciences, there are theories that can be empirically tested in such a way that almost all variables can be controlled. Outcomes can be predicted time after time with almost perfect accuracy. This is not nearly the case with theories of human personality development and change. First, human behavior is far too complex to ever be truly understood. Second, even if we had a theory that consistently and completely explained why people have personal problems and what could be done to resolve them, the human practitioners could never apply it consistently in such a way that it would always produce the same outcome.

As you know, there are medical specialists who also treat emotional problems with medications and other surgical procedures. These psychiatrists and neurologists have been achieving rather successful outcomes prescribing psychoactive drugs to treat depression, panic disorder, and other severe mental disorders, although there are no magic bullets that work even close to 100% of the time—in fact, 50% of the time is considered good! So far, even the most advanced science cannot explain or predict exactly why, when, or to what extent any pharmacological or neurological treatment will work for a particular person, and this suggests that we have a long way to go in understanding the particular why's and how's, or "mechanisms," by which cures for psychological problems work. For example, electroconvulsive therapy, better known as shock treatment or ECT, has demonstrated dramatic benefits, achieving a success rate approaching 80% with chronic depression when given three times a week, usually for 2 to 4 weeks (Tor et al., 2015). As impressive as the results might be of these medical treatments, no one knows for certain how ECT helps treat severe depression and other mental illnesses. Saying that it is the rapid firing of neurons in the brain that recalibrates the neurological system is not entirely satisfactory. Researchers *theorize* that when ECT is administered on a regular basis, these chemical changes build on one another and somehow reduce symptoms of severe depression or other mental illnesses, but no one can demonstrate this at this point.

Similar points can be made regarding the proposed mechanisms implicit in all the theories of psychotherapy. Exactly how does a deep and emotional insight about disturbing incidents in one's past turn into a more hopeful outlook for the future? How does talking to oneself with more optimism than pessimism result in more optimal neurohormonal functioning, which apparently leads to "feeling better"? How does replacing an old behavioral repertoire with a new one result in a stronger sense of self-efficacy, since there's no "self-efficacy" gland anywhere in the brain? You get the point, no doubt. But it is hard to argue with success!

FOR PERSONAL REFLECTION

Think about phenomena in our world that are explained by theories that you consider inadequate. For example, meteorologists apply all that is scientifically known about weather patterns to try and predict what will occur several days in the future. They collect extensive data on wind, atmospheric conditions, and every possible variable. They rely on historical patterns that have been collected over the past century. They use the fastest supercomputers to collate all the information, examine patterns, and forecast what is on its way. Yet with all this know-how, technology, and data available, they are still wrong a significant number of times. Several times a year, they fail to predict a storm that takes everyone by surprise. They miss developing hurricanes. They say it will be a nice day and then it rains. Clearly, their theories of weather forecasting are missing some crucial elements.

What are some other aspects of daily life that also have limited theories to explain things? What does this mean for the therapeutic process?

MOVING ON

Recently, popular interest has grown in studying the masters in a field to see what makes them unique. (See, for example, Coyle, 2012; and Eriksson & Pool, 2017). The bottom line is encouraging because the key processes are available to all of us. "What the evidence shouts most loudly is striking, liberating news: that great performance is not reserved for the few. It is available to you and to everyone" (Colvin, 2018, p. 224).

What will it take for you to be really great therapist? First, it will take lots of experience. Look back on the great therapists, past and present, included in this book: Each of them put in lots of time trying to help others while also talking to colleagues, writing things down, hashing out their ideas, and honing them in every session. Nothing is stopping you from doing the same!

However, the most recent studies show that it is not just putting in hours, but rather a kind of deliberate reflective practice that makes all the difference. The time spent can't be passive, and it can't be casual. It must involve choosing a specific skill or technique, learning about it, implementing it, and using the feedback to make continuous changes for the better. As Coyle (2012) pointed out, parents who play "Baby Mozart" videos for their toddlers may be disappointed to learn that Mozart became Mozart by working furiously hard. You've likely encountered therapists who have put in the time—even decades—doing therapy, yet have remained quite mediocre in their results with clients and their standing with other professionals in the community.

Another key that will help you develop expertise is something that the study of theories will help you with quite a bit: a process that psychologists call pattern recognition. To explain this concept, Coyle (2009) recounts the story of a Dutch psychologist, De Groot, who liked to play chess in his spare time. He got curious about the master players in his chess club: What were they doing that enabled them to make such winning moves? De Groot set up some experiments and discovered that master players recalled the pieces and their arrangements four to five times better than ordinary players—no surprise here, right? You are probably thinking they had the advantage of a photographic memory. But no—when he challenged the experts to remember *random* placements of pieces, they were no better than novices. Similarly, as Coyle (2009) puts it, "the difference between an experienced baseball fan (who can take in a game with an ascertaining glance—runner on third, two out, bottom of the seventh inning) and the same fan at his first cricket match (who spends the game squinting baffledly) … consists of identifying important elements and grouping them into a meaningful framework" (p. 77). Translating this skill to your work as a therapist, your chosen theory will give you this precise advantage: It will help you recognize patterns and make quick sense of what is going on between you and your client, instead of feeling lost in a blooming, buzzing, confusion.

There is much emphasis in our field right now about what constitutes therapeutic expertise (Hill, Hoffman, Kivlighan, Spiegel, & Gelso, 2017). A great deal of attention and software development money is going into apps that clients can use to rate their satisfaction with every session. This allows therapists to compete with themselves and their colleagues in their "outcomes" scores (Duncan, 2014). However, it may not make the best sense to decide how good you are simply based on how your clients score you. After all, clients could have many reasons to rate a session the way that they do that has nothing to do with you—they might be in a bad mood because they have indigestion, or they might give you a positive report because they know you'll be talking to their parole officer, or because they have a crush on you. For these and other reasons, many supervisors in our field have concluded, based on years of experience observing and training therapists, that expertise in our field is also seen in personal qualities such as courage, willingness to innovate, honest self-evaluation and reflection, and their own efforts to grow as people as well as therapists (Hill et al., 2017).

What more can we learn from master therapists themselves? For the past decade, Kottler and Carlson (2003, 2006, 2007, 2008, 2009, 2011, 2015) have conducted a series of interviews with the most prominent theoreticians and practitioners in the field representing a diverse sampling of orientations and styles. These include not only those most well-known within the scope of Western psychotherapy, but also spiritual leaders and indigenous healers in other cultures. Based on these interviews with master therapists, there are several themes that emerged and we'd like to mention them as a way to bring closure to this book and study of theory:

1. Most theorists don't follow their own theories exclusively. They are far more flexible and pragmatic, borrowing ideas from colleagues, blending concepts from other approaches to fit the situation and client needs.

2. The practice of pure theories is mostly obsolete. Because of the interactions and collaborations that take place at international conferences and symposia, almost all clinicians borrow ideas from each other and take them home to try.

3. Prominent therapists are distinguished by their creativity and willingness to continually evolve their ideas and style or practice.

4. It was failures and negative outcomes with particular clients that led them to develop their new ideas and go beyond what they already knew and understood.

5. Breakthroughs in their theoretical development took place when they were stuck, when they ran out of options and had to invent something entirely new, sometimes in an act of desperation.

6. Despite their reputation for innovation in techniques or strategies, most of them valued the quality of their relationships with clients as the most important variable.

7. Most reported their clients as their most valuable teachers.

A Final Thought
We leave you with the humbling thought that the theories you have read about in this text and others you will most likely study in your lifetime represent only

approximations of truth. They don't really explain the way people function, nor do they describe comprehensively how therapy works. Nevertheless, they are the best models we have at the time, and they are always getting better.

The next step belongs to you. One of the exciting aspects of our young field is that there is still so much more room for growth and development. Your responsibility as a practitioner does not end with only helping your clients; you also have a professional obligation to further the advance of knowledge. You may decide not to publish your ideas and innovations in journals or present them at conferences (although we would strongly urge you to do so), but you are highly likely to discover things about therapeutic practice that have never been understood previously. Of course, you may not realize this at the time, or maybe ever, unless you decide to share your experiences with others.

A FINAL ASSIGNMENT

Rather than the end of your study of theory, this is just the beginning. A course such as this represents a conceptual foundation that you will need to understand the basic principles of helping others from multiple frames of reference.

If you have not already begun a journal in which to record your thoughts, reflections, insights, struggles, and confusions as a beginning practitioner, now is the time to do so. Once the formal requirements of this class are over and the assignments, papers, and tests are completed, you can concentrate more fully on your own personal and counselor or therapist.

Make it a habit to write to yourself on a regular basis about the current status of your theory development and practice. Focus on areas that perplex you the most. Highlight the things you read, hear, and see that don't make sense to you. Talk to trusted colleagues about your struggles and invite them to do the same.

Who knows? Perhaps a few decades from now, it will be *your* theory that is profiled in a text like this.

SUGGESTED READINGS

Bemak, F., & Coyne, R. K, (Eds.) (2018). *Journeys to professional excellence: Stories of courage, innovation, and risk-taking in the lives of noted psychologists and counselors.* Thousand Oaks, CA: SAGE.

Coyle, D. (2012). *The little book of talent: 52 tips for improving your skills.* New York, NY: Bantam.

Kottler, J. A., & Carlson, J. (2008). *Their finest hour: Master therapists share their greatest success stories* (2nd ed.). Bethel, CT: Crown.

Kottler, J. A., & Carlson, J. (2009). *Creative breakthroughs in therapy: Tales of transformation and astonishment*. Hoboken, NJ: Wiley.

Kottler, J. A., & Carlson, J. (2015). *On being a master therapist: Practicing what we preach*. Hoboken, NJ: Wiley.

Prochaska, J. O., & Norcross, J. (2018). *Systems of psychotherapy: A transtheoretical approach* (9th ed.). New York, NY: Oxford University Press.

Yalom, I. (2009) *The gift of therapy: An open letter to a new generation of therapists and their patients*. New York, NY: Perennial.

IMAGE CREDITS

Fig. 13.1: Illustration by Liesl McCormick.

References

A-tjak, J. G., Davis, M. L., Morina, N., Powers, M. B., Smits, J. A., & Emmelkamp, P. M. (2015). A meta-analysis of the efficacy of acceptance and commitment therapy for clinically relevant mental and physical health problems. *Psychotherapy and Psychosomatics, 84*(1), 30–36.

Abedtash, H., & Holden, R. J. (2017). Systematic review of the effectiveness of health-related behavioral interventions using portable activity sensing devices (PASDs). *Journal of the American Medical Informatics Association, 24*(5), 1002–1013.

Ackerman, N. W. (1958). *The psychodynamics of family life.* New York, NY: Basic Books. {Original work published in 1937)

Adams, N. & Grieder, D. (2014). *Treatment planning for person-centered care: Shared decision making for whole health* (2nd ed.). Waltham, MA: Academic Press.

Adler, A. (1931). *Guiding the child.* New York, NY: Greenberg.

Adler, A. (1938). *Social interest: A challenge to mankind.* London, UK: Faber & Faber.

Adler, A. (1959). *Understanding human nature.* New York, NY: Premier Books.

Adler-Tapia, R. & Settle, C. (2017). *EMDR and the art of psychotherapy with children.* New York, NY: Springer.

Ahktar, S. (2009). *Comprehensive dictionary of psychoanalysis.* London, UK: Karnac.

Ahktar, S. (2014). *Good stuff: Courage, resilience, gratitude, generosity, forgiveness, and sacrifice.* Plymouth, UK: Jason Aronson.

Akerele, E., & Yuryev, A. (2017). Single session psychotherapy for humanitarian missions. *International Journal of Mental Health, 46*(2), 133–138.

Alves, D., Neimeyer, R. A., Batista, J., & Gonçalves, M. M. (2018). Finding meaning in loss: A narrative constructivist contribution. In E. Bui (Ed.), *Clinical handbook of bereavement and grief reactions* (pp. 161–188). New York, NY: Springer.

American Psychiatric Association. (2013). *Diagnostic and statistical manual of mental disorders* (5th ed.). Arlington, VA: Author.

Anderson, W. T. (1990). *Reality isn't what it used to be.* San Francisco, CA: HarperCollins.

Ansbacher, H. L., & Ansbacher, R. R. (1956). *The individual psychology of Alfred Adler.* Oxford, England: Basic Books.

Aponte, H. J., & Ingram, M. (2018). Person of the therapist supervision: Reflections of a therapist and supervisor on empathic-identification and differentiation. *Journal of Family Psychotherapy, 29*(1), 43–57.

Aponte, H. J., & Kissil, K. (Eds.). (2016). *The person of the therapist training model: Mastering the use of self.* New York, NY: Routledge.

Arkowitz, H., Miller, W. R., & Rollnick, S. (Eds.) (2017). *Motivational interviewing in the treatment of mental health problems.* New York, NY: Guilford.

Badenoch, B., & Porges, S. W. (2017). *The heart of trauma: Healing the embodied brain in the context of relationships.* New York, NY: Norton.

Bandler, R., & Grinder, J. (1975). *The structure of magic.* Palo Alto, CA: Science and Behavior Books.

Bandura, A. (1969). *Principles of behavior modification.* New York, NY: Holt, Rinehart, & Winston.

Bandura, A. (1977). *Social learning theory.* Englewood Cliffs, NJ: Prentice Hall.

Barnett, L., & Madison, G. (2012). *Existential therapy: Legacy, vibrancy, and dialogue.* New York, NY: Routledge.

Bateman, A., Target, M., & Fonagy, P. (2018). The mentalization based approach to psychotherapy for borderline personality disorder. In P. Williams (Ed.), *The psychoanalytic therapy of severe disturbance* (pp. 53–98). New York, NY: Routledge.

Bateson, G. (1979). *Mind and nature: A necessary unity.* New York, NY: Dutton

Bateson, G., Jackson, D. D., Haley, J., & Weakland, J. H. (1956). Toward a theory of schizophrenia. *Behavioral Science, 1*(4), 251–264.

Baylin, J., & Hughes, D. A. (2016). *The neurobiology of attachment-focused therapy: Enhancing connection and trust in the treatment of children and adolescents.* New York, NY: Norton.

Beck, A. (1967). *Depression: Clinical, experimental, and theoretical aspects.* New York, NY: Harper and Row.

Beck, A. (1997). Cognitive therapy: Reflections. In J. Zeig (Ed.), *Evolution of psychotherapy: The third conference.* New York, NY: Brunner/Mazel.

Beck, A. (1999). *Prisoners of hate: The cognitive basis of anger, hostility, and violence.* New York, NY: Harper Collins.

Beck, A. T. (2018). Recovery-oriented cognitive therapy for schizophrenia: A personal perspective. In R. L. Leahy (Ed.), *Science and practice in cognitive therapy: Foundations, mechanisms, and applications.* New York, NY: Guildford.

Beck, A. T., Davis, D. D., & Freeman, A. (2015). *Cognitive therapy of personality disorders* (3rd ed.). New York, NY: Guilford.

Beck, A. T., & Haigh, B. (2014). Advances in cognitive theory and therapy: The generic cognitive model. *Annual Review of Clinical Psychiatry, 10*, 1–24.

Becker, A. (2018). *What is real? The unfinished quest for the meaning of quantum physics.* New York, NY: Basic Books

Becvar, D. S., & Becvar, R. J. (2018). *Systems theory and family therapy: A primer* (3rd ed.). Lanham, MD: Hamilton.

Bell, T. J. (2018). Career counseling with Black men: Applying principles of existential psychotherapy. *Career Development Quarterly, 66*(2), 162–175.

Bemak, F., & Coyne, R. K, (Eds.) (2018). *Journeys to professional excellence: Stories of courage, innovation, and risk-taking in the lives of noted psychologists and counselors.* Thousand Oaks, CA: Sage.

Benveniste, D. (2015). *The interwoven lives of Sigmund, Anna, and W. Ernest Freud: Three generations of psychoanalysis.* Astoria, NY: CreateSpace.

Bennett, S. T., Flett, R. A., & Babbage, D. R. (2014). Culturally adapted cognitive behaviour therapy for Māori with major depression. *The Cognitive Behaviour Therapist, 7*(e20), 1–17.

Berg, I. K. (1994). *Family-based services: A solution-based approach.* New York, NY: Norton.

Berg, I. K. (2001). *Tales of solutions: Tales of hope-inspiring stories.* New York, NY: Norton.

Berg, I. K., & Kelly, S. (2000). *Building solutions in child protective services.* New York, NY: Norton.

Berg, I., K., & Steiner, T. (2003). *Children's solution work.* New York, NY: Norton.

Berg, I. K., & Szabo, P. (2005). *Brief coaching for lasting solutions.* New York, NY: Norton.

Bernard, M. E., & Dryden, W. (2018). *Theory, research, and practice of REBT.* New York, NY: Springer.

Bertalanffy, L. von (1968). *Organismic Psychology and Systems Theory* Worcester, MA: Clark University Press.

Blackwell, S. E., Westermann, K., Woud, M. L., Cwik, J. C., Neher, T., Graz, C., Nyhuis, P. W., & Margraf, J. (2018). Computerized positive mental imagery training versus cognitive control training versus treatment as usual in inpatient mental health settings: Study protocol for a randomized controlled feasibility trial. *Pilot and Feasibility Studies, 4*(4), 133.

Blechner, M. J. (2018). *The mindbrain and dreams: An exploration of dreaming, thinking, and artistic creation.* New York, NY: Routledge.

Bloom, B. L. (1997). *Planned short-term psychotherapy: A clinical handbook.* Boston, MA: Allyn and Bacon.

Bohart, A. C. (2017). A client-centered perspective on "psychopathology." *Person-Centered & Experiential Psychotherapies, 16*(1), 14–26.

Bohart, A. C. & Tallman, K. (2010). Clients: The neglected common factor in psychotherapy. In B. L. Duncan, S. D. Miller, B. E. Wampold, & M. A. Hubble (Eds.). *The heart and soul of change: Delivering what works in therapy* (2nd ed.) (pp. 83–111). Washington, DC: American Psychological Association.

Bowen, M. (1974). *Toward the differentiation of self in one's family of origin.* London, UK: Jason Aronson.

Bregman, O. C., & White, C. M. (2011). *Bringing systems thinking to life: Expanding the horizons for Bowen family systems theory.* New York, NY: Routledge.

Brew, L. & Kottler, J. K. (2017). *Applied helping skills: Transforming lives*. Thousand Oaks, CA: SAGE.

Brown, L. S. (2010). *Feminist therapy*. Washington, DC: American Psychological Association.

Brown, D. P., & Elliot, D. S. (2016). *Attachment disturbances in adults: Treatment for comprehensive repair*. New York, NY: Norton.

Brubacher, L. L. (2018). *Stepping into emotionally focused couple therapy: Key ingredients of change*. New York, NY: Routledge.

Buber, M. (1996). *I and Thou* (W. Kaufman, Trans.). New York, NY: Scribner.

Buirski, C. K. & Buirski, P. (1994). The therapeutic mobilization of mourning in a young child. *Bulletin of the Menninger Clinic, 58*(3), 339–354.

Cain, D. (2010). *Person-centered psychotherapy*. Washington, DC: American Psychiatric Association.

Caligor, E., Yeomans, F. E., Clarkin, J. F., & Kernberg, O. F. (2018). *Psychodynamic therapy for personality pathology: Treating self and interpersonal functioning*. Washington, DC: American Psychiatric Association.

Capra, F. (1975). *The Tao of physics*. Boston, MA: Shambala.

Capuzzi, D., & Gross, D. R. (2011). *Counseling and psychotherapy: Theories and interventions* (5th ed.). Alexandria, VA: American Counseling Association.

Carkhuff, R. R., & Berenson, B. G. (1967). *Beyond counseling and psychotherapy*. New York, NY: Holt, Reinhart, and Winston.

Carlson, J. & Englar-Carlson, M. (2017). *Adlerian psychotherapy*. Washington DC: American Psychological Association.

Carlson, J. & Knaus, W. (2014). Albert Ellis revisited. New York, NY: Routledge.

Carr, A. (2018). Family therapy and systemic interventions for child-focused problems: the current evidence base. *Journal of Family Therapy, 4*, 1–61.

Carroll, L. (1865/1962). *Alice's adventures in Wonderland*. Peterborough, Ontario, CA: Broadview Press.

Carveth, D. L. (2018). *Psychoanalytic thinking: A dialectical critique of contemporary theory and practice*. New York, NY: Routledge.

Chaiklin, S. & Wengrower, H. (2016). *The art and science of dance/movement therapy: Life is dance* (2nd ed.). New York, NY: Routledge.

Chandler, C. K. (2017). *Animal-assisted therapy in counseling* (3rd ed.). New York, NY: Routledge.

Cheston, S. E. (2000). A new paradigm for teaching counseling theory and practice. *Counselor Education and Supervision, 39*, 254–269.

Chiappetta, L., Stark, S., Mahmoud, K. F., Bahnsen, K. R., & Mitchell, A. M. (2018). Motivational Interviewing to Increase outpatient attendance for adolescent psychiatric patients. *Journal of Psychosocial Nursing and Mental Health Services, 56*(6), 31–35.

Chen L., Zhang G., Hu M., & Liang X. (2015). Eye movement desensitization and reprocessing versus cognitive-behavioral therapy for adult posttraumatic stress disorder: Systematic review and meta-analysis. *Journal of Nervous and Mental Disorders, 203*(6), 443–451.

Chi, L. (2017). Satir Theory and sculpting in social work education: Helping people to help themselves. *Satir International Journal, 5*(1), 61–66.

Chin, F., & Hayes, S. C. (2017). Acceptance and commitment therapy and the cognitive behavioral tradition: Assumptions, model, methods, and outcomes. In S. G. Hoffman & G. J. G. Asmundson (Eds), *The science of cognitive behavioral therapy* (pp. 155–173). London, UK: Academic Press.

Chow, E. O. (2018). Narrative group intervention to reconstruct meaning of life among stroke survivors. *Neuropsychiatry, 8*(4), 1216–1266.

Christine, M. (2017). *Introducing emotional freedom techniques.* New York, NY: Routledge.

Christenson, J. D., & Miller, A. L. (2016). Slowing down the conversation: The use of letter writing with adolescents and young adults in residential settings. *Contemporary Family Therapy, 38*(1), 23–31.

Clark, A. (2017). Embodied, situated, and distributed cognition. In Bechtel, W., & Graham, G. (Eds.), *A companion to cognitive science* (pp. 506–517). Hoboken, NJ: Wiley.

Colapinto, J. (2016). Structural family therapy. In T. Sexton & J. Lebow (Eds.) *Handbook of family therapy* (2nd ed.) (pp. 120–133). New York, NY: Routledge.

Cole, P. H., & Reese, D. (2018). *New directions in Gestalt group therapy.* New York, NY: Routledge.

Colvin, G. (2018). *Talent is overrated.* New York, NY: Penguin.

Comstock, D. L., Hammer, T. R., Strentzsch, J., Cannon, K., Parsons, J., & II, G. S. (2008). Relational-cultural theory: A framework for bridging relational, multicultural, and social justice competencies. *Journal of Counseling & Development, 86*(3), 279–287.

Conlin, S. E. (2017). Feminist therapy: A brief integrative review of theory, empirical support, and call for new directions. *Women's Studies International Forum, 62,* 78–82.

Cooper, M., O'Hara, M., Schmidt, P. F., & Bohart, A. (2013). *The handbook of person-centered psychotherapy and counselling.* Hampshire, UK: Palgrave.

Corey, G. (2019). *The art of integrative counseling* (4th ed.). Alexandria, VA: American Counseling Association.

Coyle, D (2009). *The talent code: Greatness isn't born. It's grown. Here's how.* New York, NY: Bantam.

Coyle, D. (2012). *The little book of talent: 52 tips for improving your skills.* New York, NY: Bantam.

Cozolino, L. (2017). *The neuroscience of psychotherapy: Healing the social brain* (3rd ed.). New York, NY: Norton.

Crews, F. (2017). *Freud: The making of an illusion.* New York, NY: Metropolitan Books.

Crone, D. E., Hawken, S. L., & Horner, R. H. (2015). *Building positive behavior support systems in schools.* New York, NY: Guilford.

Csikszentmihalyi, M., (2014). *Flow and the foundations of positive psychology.* Dordrecht, NL: Springer.

Curtis, M., Phenix, M., Munoz, M., & Hertlein, K. M. (2017). Video game therapy: Application of the couple and family technology framework. *Contemporary Family Therapy, 39*(2), 112–120.

D'Amico, E. J., Parast, L., Shadel, W. G., Meredith, L. S., Seelam, R., & Stein, B. (2018). Brief motivational interviewing intervention to reduce alcohol and marijuana use for at-risk adolescents in primary care. *Journal of Consulting and Clinical Psychology, 86*(9), 775–791.

Daod, E. (2018, June 20). How we can bring mental health support to refugees? [Video file]. Retrieved from http://www.ted.com/talks/essam_daod_how_we_can_bring_mental_health_support_to_refugees

Davis, E. S., Pereira, J. K., & Dixon, A. (2015). Introducing reality play therapy: Reactions and perceptions from elementary school counselors. *Journal of Creativity in Mental Health, 10*(4), 402–422.

Degges-White, S., & Davis, N. L. (2018). *Integrating the expressive arts into counseling practice: Theory-based interventions.* New York, NY: Springer.

DeMille, S. M., & Montgomery, M. (2016). Integrating narrative family therapy in an outdoor behavioral healthcare program: A case study. *Contemporary Family Therapy, 37*(4), 17–25.

de Shazer, S. (1982). *Patterns of brief family therapy: An ecosystemic approach.* New York, NY: Guilford Press.

de Shazer, S. (1985). *Keys to solutions in brief therapy.* New York, NY: Norton.

de Shazer, S. (1991). *Putting difference to work.* New York, NY: Norton.

de Shazer, D., & Dolan, Y. (Eds.) (2007). *More than miracles: The state of the art of solution-focused brief therapy.* New York, NY: Taylor & Francis.

Demorest, A. P. (2004). *Psychology's grand theorists: How personal experiences shaped professional ideas.* New York, NY: Taylor & Francis.

Denborough, D. (2014). *Retelling the stories of our lives: Everyday narrative therapy to draw inspiration and transform experience.* New York, NY: Norton.

Dewan, M. J., Steenbarger, B. N., & Greenberg, R. P. (Eds.). (2017). *The art and science of brief psychotherapies: A practitioner's guide.* Washington, DC: American Psychiatric Association.

DiClemente, C. C. (2018). *Addiction and change: How addictions develop and addicted people recover.* New York, NY: Guilford.

Dillon, A., Timulak, L., & Greenberg, L. S. (2018). Transforming core emotional pain in a course of emotion-focused therapy for depression: A case study. *Psychotherapy Research, 28*(3), 406–422.

Dinkmeyer, D., Carlson, J., & Michel, R. E. (2016). *Consultation: Creating school-based interventions.* New York, NY: Routledge.

Dishion, T., Forgatch, M., Chamberlain, P., & Pelham III, W. E. (2016). The Oregon model of behavior family therapy: From intervention design to promoting large-scale system change. *Behavior Therapy, 47*(6), 812–837.

Dobson, D., & Dobson, K. S. (2018). *Evidence-based practice of cognitive-behavioral therapy.* New York, NY: Guilford.

Dobson, K. S., Poole, J. C., & Beck, J. S. (2018). The fundamental cognitive model. In R. L. Leahy (Ed.), *Science and practice in cognitive therapy: Foundations, mechanisms, and applications,* 29–47. New York, NY: Guilford.

Dominitz, V. A. (2017). Gestalt therapy applied: A case study with an inpatient diagnosed with substance use and bipolar disorders. *Clinical Psychology & Psychotherapy, 24*(1), 36–47.

Dreikurs, R. (1967). *Psychodynamics, psychotherapy, and counseling.* Chicago, IL: Alfred Adler Institute.

Druck, A. B. (2018). *Modern structural theory.* In A. B. Druck, C. Ellman, N. Freedman, & A. Thaler (Eds.), *A new Freudian synthesis: Clinical process in the next generation.* New York, NY: Routledge.

Duncan, B. (2014). *On becoming a better therapist: Evidence based practice one client at a time.* Washington, DC: American Psychological Association.

Edwards, E. J., Bannatyne, A. J., & Stark, A. C. (2018). Twelve tips for teaching brief motivational interviewing to medical students. *Medical Teacher, 40*(3), 231–236.

Egan, R., & Reese, R. J. (2019). *The skilled helper* (11th ed.). Boston, MA: Cengage.

Enns, C. E., & Williams, E. M. (2012). *The Oxford handbook of feminist multicultural counseling psychology.* Oxford, England: Oxford University Press.

Ellis, A. (1962). *Reason and emotion in psychotherapy.* Secaucus, NJ: Citadel.

Ellis, A. (1996). *Better, deeper, and more enduring brief therapy: The rational emotive behavior therapy approach.* New York, NY: Brunner/Mazel.

Ellis, A. (1997). The evolution of Albert Ellis and rational emotive behavior therapy. In J. Zeig (Ed.), *Evolution of psychotherapy: The third conference.* New York, NY: Brunner/Mazel.

Ellis, A. (2001). *Overcoming destructive beliefs, feelings, and behaviors: New directions for rational emotive behavior therapy.* New York, NY: Prometheus.

Ellis, A. (2007). *Overcoming resistance: A rational emotive behavior therapy integrate approach* (2nd ed.). New York, NY: Springer

Ellis, A. & Bernard, M. (2005). *Rational emotive behavioral approaches to childhood disorders: Theory, practice, and research.* New York: Springer.

Ellis, A. & Dryden, W. (2007). *The practice of rational emotive behavior therapy* (2nd ed.). New York, NY: Springer.

Ellis, A., & Ellis, D. J. (2011). *Rational emotive behavior therapy*. Washington, DC: American Psychological Association.

Ellis, A., & Harper, R. A. (1961). *A new guide to rational living.* No. Hollywood, CA: Wilshire Book Company.

Ellis, A., & MacLaren, C. (2005). *Rational emotive behavior therapy: A therapist's guide.* Atascadero, CA: Impact.

Ellis, D. J. (2019). The power and compassion of rational emotive behavior therapy (REBT). In N. R. Silton (Ed.), *Scientific concepts behind happiness, kindness, and empathy in contemporary society* (pp. 178–189). Hershey, PA: IGI Global.

Erickson, M. (1954). Special techniques of brief hypnotherapy. *Journal of Clinical and Experimental Hypnosis, 2*(4), 109–129.

Erickson, M. (1964). The confusion technique in hypnosis. *American Journal of Clinical Hypnosis, 6*(3), 183–207.

Erickson, B. A., & Keeney, B. F. (Eds) (2006). *Milton H. Erickson, M.D.: An American healer.* Philadelphia, PA: Ringing Rocks Press.

Eriksson, A., & Pool, R. (2017). *Peak: Secrets from the new science of expertise.* New York, NY: Houghton Mifflin.

Evans, A. M., Kluck, A., Hill, D., Crumley, E., & Turchan, J. (2017). Utilizing existential meaning-making as a therapeutic tool for clients affected by poverty. *International Journal of Existential Psychology and Psychotherapy, 6(*1), 16.

Ewen, V., Mushquash, A. R., Mushquash, C. J., Bailey, S. K., Haggarty, J. M., & Stones, M. J. (2018). Single-session therapy in outpatient mental health services: Examining the effect on mental health symptoms and functioning. *Social Work in Mental Health, 16(*5), 1–17.

Eysenck, H. (1952). The effects of psychotherapy: An evaluation. *Journal of Consulting Psychology, 16*(5), 319–324.

Falloon, I. R. (2015). *Handbook of behavioural family therapy.* New York, NY: Routledge.

Farb, N., Anderson, A., Ravindran, A., Hawley, L., Irving, J., Mancuso, E., … & Segal, Z. V. (2018). Prevention of relapse/recurrence in major depressive disorder with either mindfulness-based cognitive therapy or cognitive therapy. *Journal of Consulting and Clinical Psychology, 86*(2), 200–204.

Farmer, R. F., & Chapman, A. L. (2016). *Behavioral interventions in cognitive behavior therapy: Practical guidance for putting theory into action.* Washington, DC: American Psychological Association.

Field, T. A., Jones, L. K. & Russell-Chapin, L. A. (2017). *Neurocounseling: Brain-based clinical approaches.* Alexandria, VA: American Counseling Association.

Fine, A. (2015). Incorporating animals in outpatient psychotherapy: Guidelines and suggestions for therapists. In A. H. Fine (Ed.). *The handbook on animal assisted therapy* (4th ed.), (pp. 141–153). San Diego, CA: Elsevier.

Fisch, R., Weakland, J. H., & Segal, L. (1982). *The tactics of change: Doing therapy briefly.* San Francisco, CA: Jossey-Bass.

Fish, J. M. (1973). *Placebo therapy: A practical guide to social influence in psychotherapy.* San Francisco, CA: Jossey-Bass.

Fish, M. T. (2018). Gaming for stress: Application of a commercially available biofeedback system for at-risk young adolescents. *American Journal of Recreation Therapy, 17*(1), 37–42.

Flemons, D. (2012). Hypnosis and brief family therapy. In. In A. Rambo, C. West, A. Schooley, & T. V. Boyd (Eds.), *Family therapy review: Contrasting contemporary models* (pp. 123–128). New York, NY: Routledge.

Flemons, D., & Gralnik, L. M. (2013). *Relational suicide assessment: Risks, resources, and possibilities for safety.* New York, NY: Norton.

Flemons, D., & Green, S. (2018). *Quickies: The handbook of brief sex therapy.* New York, NY: Norton.

Fonagy, P. (2018). *Attachment theory and psychoanalysis.* New York, NY: Routledge.

Frank, J. D. (1973). *Persuasion and healing.* Baltimore, MD: Johns Hopkins University Press.

Frankl, V. (1962). *Man's search for meaning.* New York, NY: Washington Square.

Frankl, V. (1997). *Victor Frankl recollections: An autobiography.* New York, NY: Perseus.

Franklin, C., Zhang, A., Froerer, A., & Johnson, S. (2017). Solution focused brief therapy: A systematic review and meta-summary of process research. *Journal of Marital and Family Therapy, 43*(1), 16–30.

French, T. M. (1933). Interrelations between psychoanalysis and the experimental work of Pavlov. *American Journal of Psychiatry, 89,* 1165–1203.

Friedberg, R. D., & McClure, J. M. (2015). *Clinical practice of cognitive therapy with children and adolescents: The nuts and bolts.* New York, NY: Guilford.

Freud, S. (1900). *Interpretation of dreams.* London, UK: Hogarth Press.

Freud, S. (1920). *Beyond the pleasure principle* (Vol. 14). New York, NY: Norton.

Freud, S. & Breuer, J. (1895). Studies on hysteria. In J. Strachey & A. Strachey, (Trans.); J. Strachey, A. Strachey, and A. Richards (Eds.), *Pelican Freud library.* (Vol. 3) (pp. 190–201). London, UK, Penguin.

Fulkerson, M. H. (2015). *Treatment planning from a reality therapy perspective.* Bloomington, IN: iUniverse.

Garrido, G., Penadés, R., Barrios, M., Aragay, N., Ramos, I., Vallès, V., ... & Vendrell, J. M. (2017). Computer-assisted cognitive remediation therapy in schizophrenia: Durability of the effects and cost-utility analysis. *Psychiatry Research, 254,* 198–204.

Gelso, C. J. (2019). *The therapeutic relationship in psychotherapy practice: An integrative perspective*. New York, NY: Routledge.

Gendlin, E. (1981). *Focusing*. New York, NY: Guilford.

Gendlin, E. (1986). *Let your body interpret your dreams*. Wilmette, IL: Chiron.

Gendlin, E. (1996). *Focusing-oriented psychotherapy: A manual of the experiential method*. New York, NY: Guilford.

Gerson, B. (Ed.). (1996). *The therapist as a person: Life crises, life choices, life experiences, and their effects on treatment*. New York, NY: New York Analytic Press.

Gillihan, S. J. (2016). *Cognitive behavioral therapy in 7 weeks: A workbook for managing depression and anxiety*. Berkeley, CA: Althea Press.

Gillihan, S. J. (2018). *Cognitive behavioral therapy made simple: 10 strategies for managing anxiety, depression, anger, panic, and worry*. Berkeley, CA: Althea Press.

Gladding, S. T. (2015). *Family therapy: History, theory, and practice* (6th ed.). Upper Saddle River, NJ: Pearson.

Glasser, W. (1965). *Reality therapy: A new approach to psychiatry*. New York, NY: Harper and Row.

Glasser, W. (1969). *Schools without failure*. New York, NY: Harper and Row.

Glasser, W. (1976). *Positive addiction*. New York, NY: HarperCollins.

Glasser, W. (1990). *The quality school: Managing students without coercion*. New York, NY: HarperCollins.

Glasser, W. (2001). *Counseling with choice theory: The new reality therapy*. New York, NY: HarperCollins.

Glasser, W. (2003). *For parents and teenagers: Dissolving the barrier between you and your teen*. New York, NY: HarperCollins.

Glasser, W. (2013). *Take charge of your life: How to get what you need with choice theory psychology*. Bloomington, IN: iUniverse.

Glasser, W., & Glasser, C. (2007). *Eight lessons for a happier marriage*. New York, NY: HarperCollins.

Glasser, W., & Wubbolding, R. E. (1995). Reality therapy. In R. J. Corsini & D. Wedding (Eds.), *Current psychotherapies* (5th ed.) (293–321). Itasca, IL: F. E. Peacock.

Goldenberg, I., Stanton, M. & Goldenberg, H. (2017). *Family therapy: An overview* (9th ed.). Belmont, CA: Wadsworth.

Goodcase, E. T., & Love, H. A. (2017). From despair to integrity: Using narrative therapy for older individuals in Erikson's last stage of identity development. *Clinical Social Work Journal, 45*(4), 354–363.

Gordon, T. (1975). *Parent effectiveness training*. New York, NY: New American Library.

Gordon, T. (1986). *Leader effectiveness training*. New York, NY: Bantam.

Gordon, T. (1987). *Teacher effectiveness training*. New York, NY: David McCoy.

Gostečnik, C. (2017). *Relational family therapy: The systemic, interpersonal, and intrapsychic experience.* New York, NY: Routledge.

Gottman, J. M., & Peluso, P. R. (2018). Dynamic models of social interaction. In Strawinska-Zanko & Liebovitch (Eds.,) *Mathematical modeling of social relationships* (pp. 17–29). New York, NY: Springer.

Greenberg, L. S. (2002). Integrating an emotion-focused approach to treatment into psychotherapy integration. *Journal of Psychotherapy Integration, 12*(2), 154–189.

Greenberg, L. S. (2017). *Emotion-focused therapy.* Washington, DC: American Psychological Association.

Greenberg, L. S., & Goldman, R. N. (2008). *Emotion-focused couples therapy: The dynamics of emotion, love and power.* Washington, DC: American Psychological Association.

Greenberg, L. S., & Goldman, R. N. (2018). *Clinical handbook of emotion-focused therapy.* Washington, DC: American Psychological Association.

Greenberg, L. S., & Safran, J. D. (1987). *Emotion in psychotherapy: Affect, cognition, and the process of change.* New York, NY: Guilford Press.

Greenberg, L. S., & Tomescu, L. R. (2017). *Supervision essentials for emotion-focused therapy.* American Psychological Association.

Greenberg, L. S. & Watson, J. C. (2005). *Emotion-focused therapy for depression.* Washington, DC: American Psychological Association.

Greenberg, L., Rice, L, & Elliot, R. (1993). *Facilitating emotional change.* New York, NY: Guilford.

Grills, C., Villanueva, S., Anderson, M., Corsbie-Massay, C. L., Smith, B., Johnson, L., & Owens, K. (2015). Effectiveness of choice theory connections: A cross-sectional and comparative analysis of California female inmates. *International Journal of Offender Therapy and Comparative Criminology, 59*(7), 757–771.

Guerney, B. (1964). Filial therapy: Description and rationale. *Journal of Consulting Psychology, 28*(4), 304–310.

Guerney, L., & Ryan, V. (2013). *Group filial therapy: The complete guide to teaching parents to parents to play therapeutically with their children.* Philadelphia, PA: Jessica Kingsley.

Gureje, O., Nortje, G., Makanjuola, V., Oladeji, B. D., Seedat, S., & Jenkins, R. (2015). The role of global traditional and complementary systems of medicine in the treatment of mental health disorders. *The Lancet Psychiatry, 2*(2), 168–177.

Halbur, D., & Halbur, K. V. (2014). *Developing your theoretical orientation in counseling and psychotherapy* (3rd ed.). Upper Saddle River, NJ: Pearson.

Haley, J. (1963). *Strategies of psychotherapy.* New York, NY: Grune & Stratton.

Haley, J. (1967). *Advanced techniques of hypnosis and therapy: Selected papers of Milton H. Erickson.* New York, NY: Grune & Stratton.

Haley, J. (1973). *Uncommon therapy: The psychiatric techniques of Milton H. Erickson.* New York, NY: Norton.

Haley, J. (1976). *Problem solving therapy*. New York, NY: Harper and Row.

Haley, J. (1984). *Ordeal therapy*. San Francisco, CA: Jossey-Bass.

Haley, J. (1987). *Problem solving therapy* (2nd ed.). San Francisco, CA: Jossey-Bass.

Haley, J. (2003). *The art of strategic therapy*. New York, NY: Brunner/Routledge.

Haley, J., & Richeport-Haley, M. (2007). *Directive family therapy*. Binghamton, NY: Hawthorne Press.

Harris, R. M. & Hayes, S. C. (2019). *ACT made simple: An easy-to-read primer on acceptance and commitment therapy* (2nd ed.). Oakland, CA: New Harbinger.

Hase, M., Balmaceda, U. M., Ostacoli, L., Liebermann, P., & Hofmann, A. (2017). The AIP model of EMDR therapy and pathogenic memories. *Frontiers in Psychology, 8*, 1578.

Hayes, S. C. & Smith, S. (2005). *Acceptance and commitment therapy: Get out of your mind and into your life*. Oakland, CA: New Harbinger.

Hayes, S. C., & Hofmann, S. G. (2017). The third wave of cognitive behavioral therapy and the rise of process-based care. *World Psychiatry, 16*(3), 245–246.

Hayes, S. L. (2016). Acceptance and commitment therapy, relational frame theory, and the third wave of behavioral and cognitive therapies. *Behavior Therapy, 47*(6), 869–885.

Hayes, S. L., Strosahl, K. D., & Wilson, K. G. (2012). *Acceptance and commitment therapy: The process and practice of mindful change* (2nd ed.). New York, NY: Guilford Press.

Hays, P. (2016). *Addressing cultural complexities in practice: Assessment, diagnosis, and therapy* (3rd ed.). Washington, DC: American Psychological Association.

Havighurst, R. (1972). *Developmental tasks and education*. New York, NY: Mackay.

Henden, J. (2017). *Preventing suicide: The solution focused approach*. Hoboken, NJ: Wiley.

Hertrampf, R. S., & Wärja, M. (2017). The effect of creative arts therapy and arts medicine on psychological outcomes in women with breast or gynecological cancer: A systematic review of arts-based interventions. *The Arts in Psychotherapy, 56*, 93–110.

Hill, C. E. (2014). *Helping skills: Facilitating exploration, insight, and action* (4th ed.). Washington, DC: American Psychological Assocation.

Hill, C. E. (2018). *Meaning in life: A therapist's guide*. Washington, DC: American Psychological Association.

Hill, C. E., Hoffman, M. A., Kivlighan, D. M., Jr., Spiegel, S. B., & Gelso, C. J. (2017). Therapist expertise: The debate continues. *The Counseling Psychologist, 45*(1), 99–112.

Hobson, R. P. (2016). *Brief psychoanalytic therapy*. Oxford, UK: Oxford University Press.

Holmes, J. (2009). *Exploring in security: Towards an attachment informed psychoanalytic psychotherapy*. London, UK: Routledge.

Holmes, P. (2015). *The inner world outside: Object relations theory and psychodrama.* New York, NY: Routledge.

Homeyer, L., & Sweeney, D. S. (2017). *Sandtray therapy: A practical manual.* New York, NY: Routledge.

Hong, G. (2010). *Sandplay therapy: Research and practice.* New York, NY: Taylor & Francis

Horney, K. (1945). *Our inner conflicts.* Oxford, UK: Norton.

House, R., Kaslisch, D., & Maidman, J. (Eds.) (2018). *Humanistic psychology: Current trends and future prospects.* New York, NY: Routledge.

Howell, A. J. (2017). Believing in change: Reviewing the role of implicit theories in psychological dysfunction. *Journal of Social and Clinical Psychology, 36*(6), 437–460.

Hoyt, M. F. (2008). *Brief psychotherapies: Principles and practices.* Phoenix, AZ: Zeig, Tucker, & Theisen.

Hoyt, M. F., & Andreas, S. (2015). Humor in brief therapy: A dialogue. *Journal of Systemic Therapies, 34*(3), 14–25.

Hoyt, M. F. (2017). Brief therapy and beyond: Stories, language, love, hope, and time. New York, NY: Routledge.

Hoyt, M. F., Bobele, M., & Slive, A., (2018). Single-session/one-at-a-time walk-in therapy. In M. F. Hoyt, M. Bobele, A. Slive, J. Young, & M. Talmon (Eds.), *Single-session therapy by walk-in or appointment* (pp. 27–48). New York, NY: Routledge.

Hoyt, M. F, Bobele, M., Slive, A., Young, J., & Talmon, M. (Eds.) (2018). *Single-session therapy by walk-in or appointment.* New York, NY: Routledge.

Hu, M., Zhang, P., Leng, M., Li, C., & Chen, L. (2017). Animal-assisted intervention for individuals with cognitive impairment: A meta-analysis of randomized controlled trials and quasi-randomized controlled trials. *Psychiatry Research, 260*, 418–427.

Hunnicutt Hollenbaugh, K. M., & Lenz, A. S. (2018). Preliminary evidence for the effectiveness of dialectical behavior therapy for adolescents. *Journal of Counseling & Development, 96*(2), 119–131.

Jackson, J. B., Pietrabissa, G., Rossi, A., Manzoni, G. M., & Castelnuovo, G. (2018). Brief strategic therapy and cognitive behavioral therapy for women with binge eating disorder and comorbid obesity: A randomized clinical trial one-year follow-up. *Journal of Consulting and Clinical Psychology, 86*(8), 688–714.

Jarrett, T. A. (2013). Warrior resilience and thriving (WRT): Rational emotive behavior therapy (REBT) as a resiliency and thriving foundation to prepare warriors and their families for combat deployment and posttraumatic growth in Operation Iraqi Freedom, 2005–2009. *Journal of Rational-Emotive & Cognitive-Behavioral Therapy, 31*(2), 93–107.

Jennings, S. (Ed.). (2014). *Dramatherapy with children and adolescents.* New York, NY: Routledge.

Jewell, J. A., & Brown, C. S. (2014). Relations among gender typicality, peer relations, and mental health during early adolescence. *Social Development, 23*(1), 137–156.

Johnson, C. (2018). *Implementing effective behavior intervention plans: 8 steps to success.* New York, NY: Routledge.

Johnson, S. (2019). *Attachment theory in practice: Emotionally focused therapy (EFT) with individuals, couples, and families.* New York, NY: Guilford.

Johnson, S., & Greenberg, L. (1985). Emotionally focused couple therapy: An outcome study. *Journal of Marital and Family Therapy, 11(3),* 313–317.

Jones-Smith, E. (2018). *Culturally diverse counseling: Theory and practice.* Thousand Oaks, CA: SAGE.

Jools, P., Byrne, N., & Berg, J. (2017). *Working with developmental anxieties in couple and family psychotherapy: The family within.* New York, NY: Routledge.

Jordan, J. V. (2017) *Relational cultural therapy.* Washington, DC: American Psychological Association.

Jung, C. (1933). *Modern man in search of a soul.* New York, NY: Harvest.

Jung, C.G. (1954). Development of personality. In *Collected Works of C.G. Jung,* Volume 17. Princeton, N.J.: Princeton University Press.

Kabat-Zinn, J. (2005). *Coming to our senses: Healing ourselves and the world through mindfulness.* New York, NY: Hyperion.

Kalff, D. M. (2003) *Sandplay: A psychotherapeutic approach to the psyche.* Cloverdale, CA: Tenemos Press.

Kaliebe, K., & Weigel, P. (2018). *Youth Internet habits and mental health.* Philadelphia, PA: Elsevier.

Kearney, A., (2015). *Understanding applied behavior analysis: An introduction to ABA for parents, teachers, and other professionals* (2nd ed.). Philadelphia, PA: Jessica Kingsley.

Kearns, A. (2007). *The mirror crack'd: When good enough therapy goes wrong and other cautionary tales for humanistic practitioners.* New York, NY: Routledge.

Keeney, B. (20010). *The creative therapist: The art of awakening a session.* New York, NY: Routledge.

Kernberg, O. F. (1984). *Severe personality disorders.* New Haven, CT: Yale University Press.

Kernberg, O. F. (1997). Convergences and divergences in contemporary psychoanalytic technique and psychoanalytic psychotherapy. In J. Zeig (Ed.), *Evolution of psychotherapy: The third conference.* New York, NY: Brunner/Mazel.

Kernberg, O. F. (2012). *The inseparable nature of love and aggression: Clinical and theoretical perspectives.* New York, NY: American Psychiatric Association.

Kerr, M. E. (2019). *Bowen theory's secrets: Revealing the hidden life of families.* New York, NY: Norton.

Kim, J. S. (2013). *Solution-focused brief therapy: A multicultural approach to working with minority clients.* Thousand Oaks, CA: SAGE.

Kirschenbaum, H. (2009). *The life and work of Carl Rogers.* Alexandria, VA: American Counseling Association.

Kohut, H. (1977). *Restoration of the self.* New York, NY: International Universities Press.

Kohut, H. (1984). *How does psychoanalysis cure?* Chicago, IL: University of Chicago Press.

Kolmannskog, V. (2018). *The empty chair: Tales from Gestalt therapy.* New York, NY: Routledge.

Kongstvedt, P. R. (2015). *Health insurance and managed care: What they are and how they work* (4th ed.). Sudbury, MA: Jones & Bartlett.

Kornfield, J. (2014). *A lamp in the darkness: Illuminating the path through difficult times.* Boulder, CO: Sounds True.

Kottler, J. A. (2015). *The therapist in the real world: What you never learn in graduate school (but really need to know).* New York, NY: Norton.

Kottler, J. A. (2017a). *On being a therapist* (5th ed.). New York, NY: Oxford University Press.

Kottler, J. A. (2017b). *The secrets of exceptional counselors.* Alexandria, VA: American Counseling Association.

Kottler, J. A. (2018). *Living and being a therapist: A collection of readings.* San Diego, CA: Cognella.

Kottler, J. A., & Balkin, R. (2017). *Relationships in counseling and the counselor's life.* Alexandria, VA: American Counseling Association.

Kottler, J. A., & Carlson, J. (2003). *The mummy at the dining room table: Eminent therapists reveal their most unusual cases and what they teach us about human behavior.* San Francisco, CA: Jossey-Bass.

Kottler, J. A., & Carlson, J. (2006). *The client who changed me: Stories of therapist personal transformation.* New York, NY: Brunner/Routledge.

Kottler, J. A., & Carlson, J. (2007). *Moved by the spirit: Discovery and transformation in the lives of leaders.* Atascadero, CA: Impact.

Kottler, J. A., & Carlson, J. (2008). *Their finest hour: Master therapists share their greatest success stories* (2nd ed.). Bethel, CT: Crown.

Kottler, J. A., & Carlson, J. (2009). *Creative breakthroughs in therapy: Tales of transformation and astonishment.* New York, NY: Wiley.

Kottler, J. A., & Carlson, J. (2011). *Duped: Lies and deception in psychotherapy.* New York, NY: Routledge.

Kottler, J. A., & Carlson, J. (2009). *Creative breakthroughs in therapy: Tales of transformation and astonishment.* Hoboken, NJ: Wiley.

Kottler, J. A., Carlson, J., & Keeney, B. (2004). *An American shaman: An odyssey of ancient healing traditions.* New York, NY: Brunner/Routledge.

Kottman, T., & Meany-Walen, K. (2016). *Partners in play: An Adlerian approach to play therapy.* Alexandria, VA: American Counseling Association.

Kramer, G. M., Kinn, J. T., & Mishkind, M. C. (2015). Legal, regulatory, and risk management issues in the use of technology to deliver mental health care. *Cognitive and Behavioral Practice, 22*(3), 258–268.

Kubie, L. S. (1934). Relation of the conditioned reflex to psychoanalytic technique. *Archives of Neurology and Psychiatry, 32*, 1137–1142.

Kwiatkowska, H. (1978). *Family therapy and evaluation throughout.* Springfield, IL: C. C. Thomas.

Kuss, D., & Lopez-Fernandez, O. (2016). Internet addiction and problematic Internet use: A systematic review of clinical research. *World Journal of Psychiatry, 6*(1), 143–176.

Landreth, G. L. (2012). *Play therapy: The art of the relationship* (3rd ed.). Philadelphia, PA: Brunner/Routledge.

Lazarus, A. A. (1967). In support of technical eclecticism. *Psychological Reports, 21(2)*, 415–416.

Lazarus, A. A. (1971). *Behavior therapy and beyond.* New York, NY: McGraw-Hill.

Lazarus, A. A. (1989). *The practice of multimodal therapy.* Baltimore, MD: Johns Hopkins University Press.

Lazarus, A. A. (1995). Different types of eclecticism and integration: Let's be aware of the dangers. *Journal of Psychotherapy Integration, 5(1)*, 27–39.

Lazarus, A. A. (2006). *Brief but comprehensive therapy: The multimodal way.* New York, NY: Springer.

Lebow, J. L. (2016). Empirically supported treatments in couple and family therapy. *Family process, 55*(3), 385–389.

Leahy, R. L. (2017). *Cognitive therapy and techniques: A practitioner's guide* (2nd ed.). New York, NY: Guilford.

Leahy, R. L. (2018). *Science and practice in cognitive therapy: Foundations, mechanisms and applications.* New York, NY: Guildford.

Leichsenring, F., & Steinert, C. (2017). Further evidence for short-term psychodynamic therapy in major depressive disorder: Updating the Canadian Network for Mood and Anxiety Treatments 2016 Guidelines. *Canadian Journal of Psychiatry, 62*(1), 75–76.

Leichsenring, F., Luyten, P., Hilsenroth, M. J., Abbass, A., Barber, J. P., Keefe, J. R., … & Steinert, C. (2015). Psychodynamic therapy meets evidence-based medicine: a systematic review using updated criteria. *The Lancet Psychiatry, 2*(7), 648–660.

Lenz, A. S., & Del Conte, G. (2018). Efficacy of dialectical behavior therapy for adolescents in a partial hospitalization program. *Journal of Counseling & Development, 96*(1), 15–26.

Leslie, P. J. (2014). *Potential not pathology: Helping your clients transform using Ericksonian psychotherapy.* London, UK: Routledge.

Leuzinger-Bohleber, M. (2015). *Finding the body in the mind: Embodied memories, trauma, and depression.* London, UK: Karnac.

Levenson, H. (2017). *Brief dynamic therapy* (2nd ed.) Washington, DC: American Psychological Association.

Lichtenberg, J. D., Lachmann, F. M., & Fosshage, J. L. (2016). *Self and motivational systems: Towards a theory of psychoanalytic technique.* New York, NY: Routledge.

Lindley, O. R., Skinner, B. F., & Solomon, H. C. (1953). *Studies in behavior therapy.* Waltham, MA: Academic Press.

Linehan, M. M. (1993). *Cognitive-behavioral treatment of borderline personality disorder.* New York, NY: Guilford.

Linehan, M. M. (2014). *DBT skills training manual* (2nd ed.). New York, NY: Guilford.

Linesch, D. (1993). *Art therapy with families in crisis.* New York, NY: Brunner/Mazel.

Lowen, A. (1958). *The language of the body.* New York, NY: Macmillan.

Lowen, A. (1997). My evolution as a body-mind therapist. In J. Zeig (Ed.), *Evolution of psychotherapy: The third conference.* New York, NY: Brunner/Mazel.

Lowen, A., & Friedman, H. (2006). *The language of the body: Physical dynamics of character structure.* Alachua, FL: Bioenergetics Press.

Madanes, C. (1981). *Strategic family therapy.* San Francisco, CA: Jossey-Bass.

Madanes, C. (1984). *Behind the one-way mirror: Advances in the practice of strategic therapy.* San Francisco, CA: Jossey-Bass.

Madigan, S. (2011). *Narrative therapy.* Washington, DC: American Psychological Association.

Madison, G. (2014a). *Theory and practice of focusing-oriented psychotherapy: Beyond the talking cure.* London, UK: Jessica Kinsley.

Madison, G. (2014b). *Emerging practice in focusing-oriented psychotherapy: Innovative theory and applications.* London, UK: Jessica Kingsley.

Mahrer, A. (2004). *The complete guide to experiential psychotherapy.* New York, NY: Bull Publishing.

Mahoney, M. (2000). Behaviorism, cognitivism, and constructivism: Reflections on persons and patterns in my intellectual development. In M. R. Goldfried (Ed.) (2000). *How therapists change: Personal and professional reflections* (pp. 183–200). Washington, DC.: American Psychological Association.

Manfrida, G., Albertini, V., & Eisenberg, E. (2018). Psychotherapy and technology: Relational strategies and techniques for online therapeutic activity. In *Clinical interventions in systemic couple and family therapy* (pp. 119–137). Cham, Switzerland: Springer.

Martin, G., & Pear, J. (2014). *Behavior modification: What it is and how to do it* (10th ed.). Upper Saddle River, NJ: Pearson.

Marzi, A. (2018). *Psychoanalysis, identity, and the Internet: Explorations into cyberspace.* New York, NY: Routledge.

Maslow, A. (1954). *Motivation and personality.* New York, NY: Harper.

Masters, W. H., & Johnson, V. E. (1970). *Human sexual inadequacy.* Toronto; NY: Bantam.

Masterson, M., Rosenfeld, B., & Breitbart, W. (2018). Meaning-centered psychotherapy for cancer patients with advanced and terminal illness. In R. Allen, B. D. Carpenter, & M. K. Eichorst (Eds.), *Perspectives on behavioural interventions in palliative and end-of-life care* (pp. 80–102). New York, NY: Routledge.

May, K. (2018). Collaborating with the fortress around early childhood trauma: A depth psychotherapy process. *Perspectives in Psychiatric Care, 54*(1), 39–45.

May, R. (1983). *The discovery of being: Writings in existential psychotherapy.* New York, NY: Norton.

McDowell, T., Knudson-Martin, C., & Bermudez, J. M. (2018). *Socioculturally attuned family therapy: Guidelines for theory and practice.* New York, NY: Routledge.

McGoldrick, M. (2016). *The genogram casebook.* New York, NY: Norton.

McNeil, C. B., & Hembree-Kigin, T. L. (2011). *Parent–child interaction therapy* (2nd ed.). New York, NY: Springer.

Merrick, M. T., Ports, K. A., Ford, D. C., Afifi, T. O., Gershoff, E. T., & Grogan-Kaylor, A. (2017). Unpacking the impact of adverse childhood experiences on adult mental health. *Child Abuse & Neglect, 69*, 10–19.

Mickel, E. (2013). African-centered reality therapy parenting: An alternative paradigm. *Journal of Human Behavior in the Social Environment, 23*(2), 278–286.

Miller, G. (2017). *Becoming miracle workers: Language and learning in brief therapy.* New York, NY: Routledge.

Miller, J. B., & Stiver, I. (1997). *The healing connection: How women form relationships in therapy and in life.* Boston, MA: Beacon Press.

Miller, W. R., & Rollnick, S. (2012). *Motivational interviewing: Helping people to change* (3rd ed.). New York, NY: Guilford.

Miltenberger, R. G. (2015). *Behavior modification: Principles and procedures* (6th ed.) Boston, MA: Cengage.

Minuchin, S. (1974). *Families and family therapy.* Boston, MA: Harvard University Press.

Minuchin, S. (1998). Where is the family in narrative family therapy? *Journal of Marital and Family Therapy, 24*(4), 397–403.

Minuchin, S., & Fishman, H. C. (1981). *Family therapy techniques.* Cambridge, MA: Harvard University Press.

Minuchin, S., Nichols, M., & Lee, W. (2006). *Assessing families and couples: From symptoms to system.* New York, NY: Pearson.

Minuchin, S., Reiter, M. D., & Borda, C. (2014). *The craft of family therapy: Challenging certainties.* New York, NY: Routledge.

Mollon, P. (2018). Attachment and energy psychology: explorations at the interface of bodily, mental, relational, and transpersonal aspects of human behaviour and experience. In *Talking Bodies* (pp. 65–88). New York, NY: Routledge.

Monk, G., Winslade, J., Crocket, K., & Epston, D. (1997). *Narrative therapy in practice.* San Francisco, CA: Jossey-Bass.

Monti, P. M., Colby, S. M., & Tevyaw, T. O. (2018). *Brief interventions for adolescent alcohol and substance abuse.* New York, NY: Guilford.

Moreno, J. L. (1946). Psychodrama and group psychotherapy. *Sociometry, 9*(2/3), 249–253.

Moreno, Z. T., Blomkvist, L. D., & Rutzel, T. (2000). *Psychodrama, surplus reality, and the art of healing.* Philadelphia: Brunner/Routledge.

Mosak, H. H., Schneider, L. E., & Mosak, L. E. (2012). *Life style: A workbook.* Chicago, IL: Alfred Adler Institute.

Moschini, L. B. (2018). *Art, play, and narrative therapy: Using metaphor to enrich your clinical practice.* New York, NY: Routledge.

Moustakas, C. (1986). *Being-in, being-for, being-with.* Northvale, NJ: Jason Aronson.

Napier, A., & Whitaker, C. (1978). *The family crucible: The intense experience of family therapy.* New York, NY: HarperCollins.

Neenan, M., & Dryden, W. (2015). *Cognitive therapy: 100 key points and techniques* (2nd ed.). New York, NY: Routledge.

Neimeyer, R. A. (2009a). *Constructivist psychotherapy.* New York, NY: Routledge.

Neimeyer, R. A. (2009b). Survivors. In *The art of longing: Selected poems* (pp. 22–23). Charleston, SC: BookSurge.

Neimeyer, R. A. (Ed.) (2016). *Techniques of grief therapy: Assessment and intervention.* New York, NY: Routledge.

Nelson, D. L., & Castonguay, L. G. (2017). The systematic use of homework in psychodynamic-interpersonal psychotherapy for depression: An assimilative integration approach. *Journal of Psychotherapy Integration, 27*(2), 265–281.

Nelsen, J., Lott, L., Glenn, H. S. (2013). *Positive discipline in the classroom: Developing mutual respect, cooperation and responsibility in your classroom* (4th ed.). New York, NY: Three Rivers Press.

Nichols, M. P. (2017). *Family therapy: Concepts and methods* (11th ed.). Boston, MA: Pearson.

Norcross, J. C., & Lambert, M. J. (2018). Psychotherapy relationships that work III. *Psychotherapy, 55*(4), 303–315.

Norcross, J. & Popple, L. M. (2016). *Supervision essentials for integrative psychotherapy.* Washington, DC: American Psychological Association.

Norcross, J. C., Goldfried, M. R., & Zimmerman, B. E. (2016). Integrative psychotherapies in historical perspective. In A. J. Consoli, L. E. Beuler, & B. Butler (Eds.), *Comprehensive textbook of psychotherapy: Theory and practice* (2nd ed.) (pp. 188–204). New York, NY: Oxford University Press.

Oberst, U. E., & Stewart, A. E. (2014). *Adlerian psychotherapy: An advanced approach to individual psychology.* New York, NY: Routledge.

O'Hanlon, W. H. (1993). *Solution-oriented therapy.* New York, NY: Norton.

O'Hanlon, B. (2004). *Change 101: A practical guide to change in life or therapy.* New York, NY: Norton.

O'Hanlon, B. (2009). *A guide to trance-land: A guide to trance land: A practical handbook of Ericksonian and solution-oriented hypnosis.* New York, NY: Norton.

O'Hanlon, B. (2010). *Quick steps to resolving trauma.* New York, NY: Norton.

Paris, B. J. (1996). *Karen Horney: A psychoanalyst's search for self-understanding.* New Haven, CT: Yale University Press.

Patterson, G. R., Chamberlain, P., & Reid, J. B. (2016). A comparative evaluation of a parent-training program. *Behavior Therapy, 47*(6), 804–811.

Pies, R. (2008). Summoning the muse: The role of expressive arts therapy in psychiatric care. *Psychiatric Times, 25*(10), 12–19.

Pipher, M. (2016). *Letters to a young therapist: Stories of hope and healing.* New York, NY: Basic Books.

Pitruzzella, S. (2016). *Drama, creativity and intersubjectivity: The roots of change in dramatherapy.* New York, NY: Routledge.

Pope, K. S., & Vasquez, M. J. T. (2016). *Ethics in psychotherapy and counseling: A practical guide* (5th ed.). Hoboken, NJ: Wiley.

Polster, E., & Polster, M. (2000). *From the radical center: The heart of Gestalt therapy.* Hillsdale, NJ: Analytic Press.

Popkin, M. H. (2014). Active parenting: 30 years of video-based parent education. *Journal of Individual Psychology, 70*(2), 166–175.

Porges, S. W., & Dana, D. A. (2018). Clinical applications of the Polyvagal Theory: The emergence of polyvagal-informed therapies. New York, NY: Norton.

Prochaska, J. O., & DiClemente, C. C. (2005). The transtheoretical approach. In J. C. Norcross & M. R. Goldfried (Eds.), *Handbook of psychotherapy integration* (2nd ed.), pp.147–171. New York, NY: Oxford University Press.

Prochaska, J. O., & Norcross, J. C. (2018). *Systems of psychotherapy: A transtheoretical analysis* (9th ed.). New York, NY: Oxford University Press.

Prouty, G. (1994). *Theoretical evolutions in person-centered/experiential therapy.* Westport, CT: Praeger.

Prouty, G., Werde, D. V., Portner, M. (2002). *Pre-therapy: Reaching contact-impaired clients.* Midsommer Norton, UK: Bookcraft.

Quick, E. R. (2011). *Core competencies in the solution-focused and strategic therapies.* New York, NY: Routledge.

Racker, H. (2018). *Transference and countertransference.* New York, NY: Routledge.

Rakowska, J. M. (2015). Brief strategic therapy in first myocardial infarction patients with increased levels of stress: A randomized clinical trial. *Anxiety, Stress, & Coping, 28*(6), 687–705.

Rancour, P. (2017). The emotional freedom technique: Finally, a unifying theory for the practice of holistic nursing, or too good to be true? *Journal of Holistic Nursing, 35*(4), 382–388.

Rawowska, J. M. (2015). Brief strategic therapy in first myocardial infarction patients with increased levels of stress: A randomized clinical trial. *Anxiety, Stress, & Coping, 28*(6), 687–705.

Reich, W. (1945). *Character analysis.* New York: Farrar, Straus & Giroux.

Reiter, M. D. (2017). *Family Therapy: An Introduction to Process, Practice and Theory.* New York, NY: Routledge.

Richeport-Haley, M., & Carlson, J. (Eds.) (2010). *Jay Haley revisited.* New York: Routledge.

Richeport-Haley, M., & Haley, J. (2012). *Directive family therapy.* New York, NY: Routledge.

Riley, S. (1994). *Integrated approaches to family art therapy.* Chicago, IL: Magnolia Street Publishers.

Rivett, M., & Buchmüller, J. (2017). *Family therapy skills and techniques in action.* New York, NY: Routledge.

Rodda, S. N., Lubman, D. I., Cheetham, A., Dowling, N. A., & Jackson, A. C. (2015). Single session Web-based counselling: A thematic analysis of content from the perspective of the client. *British Journal of Guidance & Counselling, 43*(1), 117–130.

Rohrbaugh, M. J., & Shoham, V. (2015). Brief strategic couple therapy: Toward a family consultation approach. In A. S. Gurman, D. K. Snyder & J. Lebow (Eds.), *Clinical handbook of couple therapy* (5th ed.) (pp. 335–357). New York, NY: Guilford.

Rogers, C. (1931). *A test of personality adjustment.* New York, NY: Association Press.

Rogers, C. (1939). *The clinical treatment of the problem child.* Boston, MA: Houghton Mifflin.

Rogers, C. (1957). The necessary and sufficient conditions of therapeutic personality change. *Journal of Consulting Psychology, 21(2)*, 95–103.

Rogers, C. (1980). *A way of being.* Boston, MA: Houghton Mifflin.

Rogers, C. R., & Russell, D. E., (2002). *Carl Rogers: The quiet revolutionary—An oral history.* Granite Bay, CA: Penmarin.

Rogers, N. (1986). Express yourself. *Self & Society, 14*(4), 171–174.

Rollnick, S., Kaplan, S. G., & Rutschman, R. (2016). *Motivational interviewing in schools: Conversations to improve learning and behavior*. New York, NY: Guilford.

Rollnick, S., Miller, W. R., & Butler, C. B. (2008). *Motivational Interviewing in health care: Helping patients change behavio*r. New York, NY: Guilford.

Root, M. P., & Brown, L. (2014). *Diversity and complexity in feminist therapy*. New York, NY: Routledge.

Rosengren, D. B. (2017). *Building motivational interviewing skills: A practitioner workbook* (2nd ed.). New York, NY: Guilford.

Rosenzweig, S. (1936). Some implicit common factors in diverse methods of psychotherapy. *American Journal of Orthopsychiatry, 6(3)*, 412–415.

Roth, M. S. (2016). Freud: At the individual level. *Psychoanalytic Psychology, 33*, 19–33.

Roubal, J. (2016). *Towards a research tradition in Gestalt therapy*. Newcastle upon Tyne, UK: Cambridge Scholars.

Roudinesco, E. (2016). *Freud: In his time and ours*. Boston, MA: Harvard University Press.

Rubin, J. A. (2009). *Introduction to art therapy: Sources & resources*. New York, NY: Routledge.

Russell, G. I. (2018). *Screen relations: The limits of computer-mediated psychoanalysis and psychotherapy*. New York, NY: Routledge.

Russo-Netzer, P., Schulenberg, S. E., & Batthyany, A. (Eds.). (2016). *Clinical perspectives on meaning: Positive and existential psychotherapy*. New York, NY: Springer.

Satir, V. (1978). *Your many faces*. Berkeley, Calif: Celestial Arts.

Satir, V. (1988). *The new peoplemaking*. Palo Alto, CA: Science and Behavior Books.

Sauerheber, J. D., Graham, M. A., Britzman, M. J., & Jenkins, C. (2016). Using reality therapy to facilitate successful aging in clinical practice. *The Family Journal, 24*(2), 174–181.

Schneider, K. J., & Krug, O. T. (2017*). Existential-humanist therapy*. Washington, DC: American Psychological Association.

Schore, A. N. (2018). The right brain implicit self: A central mechanism of the psychotherapy change process. In G. Craparo, & C. Mucci (Eds.), *Unrepressed unconscious, implicit memory, and clinical work* (pp. 73–98). New York, NY: Routledge.

Schwartz, J. (2017). *Counseling women across the lifespan: Empowerment, advocacy, and intervention*. New York, NY: Springer.

Scott, B. G., & Weems, C. F. (2013). Natural disasters and existential concerns: A test of Tillich's theory of existential anxiety. *Journal of Humanistic psychology, 53*(1), 114–128.

Segal, Z. V. Williams, M., & Teasdale, J. (2018). *Mindfulness-based cognitive therapy for depression* (2nd ed.). New York, NY: Guilford.

Seubert, A. (2018). Becoming known: A relational model utilizing gestalt and ego state-assisted EMDR in treating eating disorders. *Journal of EMDR Practice and Research, 12*(2), 71–86.

Shapiro, F. (1989). Eye movement desensitization: A new treatment for post-traumatic stress disorder. *Journal of Behavior Therapy and Experimental Psychiatry, 20(3),* 211–217.

Shapiro, F. (2018). *Eye movement desensitization and reprocessing: Basic principles, protocols, and procedures (3rd ed.).* New York, NY: Guilford.

Shedler, J. (2010). The efficacy of psychodynamic psychotherapy, *American Psychologist, 65*(2), 98–109.

Sheldon, C. (2014). *Gestalt as a way of life: Awareness practices.* Bellingham, WA: CreateSpace.

Sherman, R., & Dinkmeyer, D. (2014). *Systems of family therapy: An Adlerian integration.* New York, NY: Routledge.

Siegel, D. J. (2017). *Mind: A journey to the heart of being human.* New York: Norton.

ilverman, M. J. (2018). Staff and administrators' perceptions of music therapy with acute care mental health inpatients: A qualitative investigation. *Journal of Creativity in Mental Health, 13*(2), 206–219.

Simon, G. M. (2015). Structural couple therapy. In A. S. Gurman (Ed.), *Clinical handbook of couple therapy* (5th ed.) (pp. 358–384). New York, NY: Guilford.

Skinner, B. F. (1938). *The behavior of organisms: An experimental analysis.* New York, NY: Appleton-Century.

Skinner, B. F. (1945, October). Baby in a box—Introducing the mechanical baby tender. *Ladies Home Journal, 62,* 30–31, 135–136, 138.

Skinner, B. F. (1948). *Walden two.* New York, NY: Macmillan.

Sklare, G. (2014). *Brief counseling that works: A solution-focused approach for school counselors and administrators* (3nd ed.). Thousand Oaks, CA: SAGE.

Slife, B., O'Grady, K. A., & Kosits, R. D. (2017). *The hidden worldviews of psychology's theory, research, and practice.* New York, NY: Routledge.

Solomon, M., & Siegel, D. J. (2017). *How people change: Relationships and neuroplasticity in psychotherapy.* New York, NY: Norton.

Sommerbeck, L. (2014). Combining person-centered therapy and pre-therapy with clients at the difficult edge. In P. Pearce & L. Sommerbeck (Eds.), *Person-centered practice at the difficult edge* (pp. 67–73). Ross-on-Wye, UK: PCCS Books.

Sonstegard, M. A., & Bitter, J. R. (2004). *Adlerian group counseling and therapy: Step by step.* New York, NY: Brunner Routledge.

Spinelli, E. (2015). *Practising existential therapy: The relational world* (2nd ed.). Thousand Oaks, CA: SAGE.

Steinert, C., Munder, T., Rabung, S., Hoyer, J., & Leichsenring, F. (2017). Psychodynamic therapy: As efficacious as other empirically supported treatments?

A meta-analysis testing equivalence of outcomes. *American Journal of Psychiatry, 174*(10), 943–953.

Stern, D. N. (2018). *The motherhood constellation: A unified view of parent-infant psychotherapy.* New York, NY: Routledge.

Strong, S. R. (1968). Counseling: An interpersonal influence process. *Journal of Counseling Psychology, 15*(3), 215–231.

Sweeney, T. J. (2015). *Adlerian counseling and psychotherapy: A practitioner's approach* (5th ed.). New York, NY: Routledge.

Szapocznik, J., Duff, J. H., Schwartz, S. J., Muir, J. A., & Brown, C. H. (2015). Brief strategic family therapy treatment for behavior problem youth. In T. L. Sexton & J. Lebow (Eds.), *Handbook of family therapy* (pp. 286–304). New York, NY: Routledge.

Talmon, M. (1993). *Single-session solutions: A guide to practical, effective, and affordable therapy.* New York, NY: Addison-Wesley.

Taubner, S., Fonagy, P., Bateman, A., & Rabung, S. (2017). Psychodynamic treatment of violence and aggression: Empirical evidence and new approaches. In P. Sturmey (Ed.), *Wiley handbook of violence and aggression,* (pp. 1–11). Hoboken, NJ: Wiley.

Thase, M. E., Wright, J. H., Eells, T. D., Barrett, M. S., Wisniewski, S. R., Balasubramani, G. K., ... & Brown, G. K. (2017). Improving the efficiency of psychotherapy for depression: Computer-assisted versus standard CBT. *American Journal of Psychiatry, 175*(3), 242–250.

Thich Nhat Hanh, T. (1975). *The miracle of mindfulness.* Boston, MA: Beacon Books.

Thomas, L. (1974). *Lives of a cell: Notes of a biology watcher.* New York, NY: Viking.

Thorn, B. E. (2017). *Cognitive therapy for chronic pain: a step-by-step guide* (2nd ed.). New York, NY: Guilford.

Thorne, B. (2013). *Carl Rogers* (3rd ed.). Thousand Oaks, CA: SAGE.

Timm, N., & Garza, Y. (2017). Beyond the miniatures: Using Gestalt theory in sandtray processing. *Gestalt Review, 21*(1), 44–55.

Titelman, P. (2015). Differentiation of self: Bowen family systems theory perspectives. New York, NY: Routledge.

Tor, P. C., Bautovich, A., Wang, M. J., Martin, D., Harvey, S. B., & Loo, C. (2015). A systematic review and meta-analysis of brief versus ultrabrief right unilateral electroconvulsive therapy for depression. *Journal of Clinical Psychiatry, 76*(9), 1092–1098.

Truax, C. B., & Carkhuff, R. R. (1967). *Toward effective counseling and psychotherapy: Training and practice.* Chicago, IL: Aldine.

Tudor, K. (2016). Natalie Rogers (1928–2015): A personal appreciation. *Self and Society, 44*(1), 48–50.

Turner, M. J., & Davis, H. S. (2018). Exploring the effects of rational emotive behavior therapy on the irrational beliefs and self-determined motivation of triathletes. *Journal of Applied Sport Psychology, 30,* 1–20.

Ullman, D., & Wheeler, G. (2009). *Cocreating the field: Invention and practice in the age of complexity.* London, UK: Routledge.

van der Kolk, B. (2014). *The body keeps score: Brain, mind, and body in the healing of trauma.* New York, NY: Penguin.

van Deurzen, E., & Arnold-Baker, A. (2018). *Existential therapy: Distinctive features.* New York, NY: Routledge.

Vasquez, M. J., & Vasquez, E. (2017). Psychotherapy with women: Theory and practice of feminist therapy. In A. J. Consoli, L. E. Beutler, & B. Bongar (Eds.), *Comprehensive textbook of psychotherapy: Theory and practice* (pp. 299–314). New York, NY: Oxford University Press.

Vetere, A., & Dowling, E. (Eds.). (2016). *Narrative therapies with children and their families: A practitioner's guide to concepts and approaches.* New York, NY: Taylor & Francis.

von Glahn, J. (2018). Operationalizing the actualizing tendency. *Person-Centered and Experiential Psychotherapies, 17*(1), 37–53.

Wachtel, P. L. (1997). *Psychoanalysis, behavior therapy, and the relational world.* Washington, DC: American Psychological Association.

Wachtel, P. L. (2013). *Therapeutic communication: Knowing what to say when* (2nd ed.). New York, NY: Guilford.

Wampold, B. E. (2015). How important are the common factors in psychotherapy? An update. *World Psychiatry, 14*(3), 270–277.

Wampold, B. E. (2018). *The basics of psychotherapy: An introduction to theory and practice* (2nd ed.). Washington DC: American Psychological Association.

Wampold, B. E., & Imel, Z. E. (2015). *The great psychotherapy debate: The evidence for what makes psychotherapy work.* New York, NY: Routledge.

Watanabe, S. (2001). Van Gogh, Chagall and pigeons: Picture discrimination in pigeons and humans. *Animal Cognition, 4*(3–4), 147–151.

Watanabe, S. (2010). Pigeons can discriminate "good" and "bad" paintings by children. *Animal Cognition, 13*(1), 75.

Watanabe, S., Sakamoto, J., & Wakita, M. (1995). Pigeon's discrimination of paintings by Monet and Picasso. *Journal of the Experimental Analysis of Behavior, 63(2),* 165–174.

Watkins, C. E., Jr. (2017). Convergence in psychotherapy supervision: Common factors, common processes, common practices perspective. *Journal of Psychotherapy Integration, 27*(2), 140–155.

Watson, J. C., & Greenberg, L. S. (2017). *Emotion-focused therapy for generalized anxiety.* Washington, DC: American Psychological Association.

Watson, J. B. (1924). *Behaviorism.* Chicago, IL: University of Chicago Press.

Watter, D. N. (2019). *Narrative sex therapy: Using patients' stories to inform practice.* New York, NY: Springer.

Watzlawick, P. (1978). *The language of change: Elements of therapeutic communication.* New York, NY: Basic Books.

Watzlawick, P. (1997). Insight may cause blindness. In J. K. Zeig (Ed.), *The evolution of psychotherapy: The third conference.* New York, NY: Brunner/Mazel.

Watzlawick, R., Weakland, J., & Fisch, R. (1974). *Change: Principles of problem formation and problem resolution.* New York, NY: Norton.

Weiner, L., & Avery-Clark, C. (2017). *Sensate focus in sex therapy: The illustrated manual.* New York, NY: Routledge.

Weissman, M. M., Markowitz, J. C., & Klerman, G. L. (2017). *The guide to interpersonal psychotherapy.* Oxford, UK: Oxford University Press.

Weisz, J. R., & Kazdin, A. E. (2017). *Evidence-based psychotherapies for children and adolescents* (3rd ed.). New York, NY: Guilford.

Wenzel, A. (2017). *Innovations in cognitive behavioral therapy: Strategic interventions for creative practice.* New York, NY: Routledge.

Westra, H. A., & Norouzian, N. (2018). Using motivational interviewing to manage process markers of ambivalence and resistance in cognitive behavioral therapy. *Cognitive Therapy and Research, 42*(2), 193–203.

Wheeler, G., & Axelsson, J. (2015). *Gestalt therapy.* Washington, DC: American Psychological Association.

White, R. C. (2018). *The stress management workbook.* San Antonio, TX: Althea.

White, M., & Epston, D. (1990). *Narrative means to therapeutic ends.* New York, NY: Norton.

Whitebook, J. (2017). *Freud: An intellectual biography.* New York, NY: Cambridge University Press.

Wiederhold, B. K. (2018). Stop scrolling, start living: The growing reality of internet addiction disorder. *Cyberpsychology, Behavior, and Social Networking, 21*(5), 279–280.

Wiener, N. (1948). Cybernetics. *Scientific American, 179*(5), 14–18.

Wilkins, P. (2016). *Person-centered therapy: 100 key points* (2nd ed.). Oxon, UK: Routledge.

Wilkinson, M. (2010). *Changing minds in therapy: Emotion, attachment, trauma, and Neurobiology.* New York, NY: Norton.

Wincze, J., & Weisberg, R. B. (2015). *Sexual dysfunction: A guide for assessment and treatment* (3rd ed.). New York, NY: Guilford.

Winnicott, D. W. (1958). *Through pediatrics to psychoanalysis.* London, UK: Tavistock.

Winslade, J. M., & Monk, G. (2007). *Narrative counseling in the schools: Powerful and brief* (2nd ed.). Thousand Oaks, CA: Corwin.

Winslade, J. M., & Monk, G. (2008). *Practicing narrative mediation: Loosening the grip of conflict.* San Francisco, CA: Jossey-Bass.

Winter, D. A. & Neimeyer, R. A. (2014). Constructivist psychotherapy. In E. Neukrug (Ed.), *Encyclopedia of theory in counseling and psychotherapy* (pp. 216–225). Thousand Oaks, CA: SAGE.

Wright, J. H., Brown, G. K., Thase, M. E., & Remiriz Basco, M. (2017). *Learning cognitive-behavioral therapy: An illustrated guide.* Washington, DC: American Psychological Association.

Wolpe, J. (1958). *Psychotherapy by reciprocal inhibition.* Stanford, CA: Stanford University Press.

Wolpe, J., & Plaud, J. J. (1997). Pavlov's contributions to behavior therapy: The obvious and the not so obvious. *American Psychologist, 52*(9), 966–984.

Wood, A. G., Barker, J. B., Turner, M. J., & Sheffield, D. (2018). Examining the effects of rational emotive behavior therapy on performance outcomes in elite paralympic athletes. *Scandinavian Journal of Medicine & Science in Sports, 28*(1), 329–339.

Wubbolding, R. E. (2017). *Reality therapy and self-evaluation: The key to client change.* Alexandria, VA: American Counseling Association.

Wubbolding, R. E., & Brickell, J. (2017). *Counselling with reality therapy* (2nd ed.). New York, NY: Routledge.

Wubbolding, R. E., Casstevens, W. J., & Fulkerson, M. H. (2017). Using the WDEP system of reality therapy to support person-centered treatment planning. *Journal of Counseling & Development, 95*(4), 472–477.

Wurmser, L. (2015a). Mortal wound, shame, and tragic search: Reflections on tragic experience and tragic conflicts in history, literature, and psychotherapy. *Psychoanalytic Inquiry, 35*(1), 13–39.

Wurmser, L. (2015b). Primary shame, mortal wound and tragic circularity: Some new reflections on shame and shame conflicts. *International Journal of Psychoanalysis, 96*(6), 1615–1634.

Yalom, I. (1998). *The Yalom reader: Selections from the work of a master therapist and storyteller.* New York, NY: Basic Books.

Yalom, I. (2005). *The theory and practice of group psychotherapy* (5th ed.). New York, NY: Basic Books.

Yalom, I. (2009). *Staring at the sun: Overcoming the terror of death.* San Francisco, CA: Jossey Bass.

Yalom, I. (2017). *The gift of therapy: An open letter to a new generation of therapists and their patients.* New York, NY: HarperCollins.

Yang, M. C. (Ed.). (2017). *Existential psychology and the way of the Tao: Meditations on the writings of Zhuangzi.* New York, NY: Taylor & Francis.

Yontef, G., & Schulz, F. (2016). Dialogue and experiment. *British Gestalt Journal, 25*(1), 9–21.

Young-Breuhl, E. (2008). *Anna Freud: A biography* (2nd ed.). New Haven, CT: Yale University Press.

Young, M. E. (2016). *Learning the art of helping: Building blocks and techniques* (6th ed.). New York, NY: Pearson.

Zeig, J. K. (Ed.). (1982). *Ericksonian approaches to hypnosis and psychotherapy.* New York, NY: Brunner/Mazel.

Zeig, J. K. (Ed.). (1985). *Ericksonian psychotherapy.* New York, NY: Brunner/Mazel.

Zieg, J. (2010). The brief brief therapy of Milton H. Erickson. In Richeport-Haley, M., & Carlson, J. (Eds.), *Jay Haley revisited* (pp. 281–283). New York, NY: Routledge.

Zieg, J. (2018). *Eriksonian therapy now.* Phoenix, AZ: Zieg, Tucker & Theisen.

Zoja, E. P. (Ed.). 2004). *Sandplay theray: Treatment of psychopathologies.* Einsiedein, Switzerland: Diamon Verlag.

Zubala, A., & Karkou, V. (Eds.). (2018). *Arts therapies in the treatment of depression.* New York, NY: Routledge.

Zukav, G. (1979). *The dancing Wu Li masters: An overview of the new physics.* New York, NY: Bantam.

Index

A

abbreviated treatments, 17–18
"ABCs" (antecedents, behaviors, and consequences), 114
ABC theory
  activating event, 173
  disputing the irrational beliefs, 175
  emotional consequence, 174
  irrational belief, 174
  new emotional effect, 175–176
absolute judgments, 172
acceptance and commitment therapy, 292–293
ACCEPTS, 294–295
Ackerman, Nathan, 203, 210
"acting as if,", 182
action-oriented therapies, 180, 261–262, 276–278
Adaptive Information Processing (AIP) model, 296
Adler, Alfred, 55, 76, 159–160, 203, 261, 312, 322
  human capacity for overcoming disabilities, 182
  theory of individual psychology, 180
Adlerian therapy, 180–190
  basic concepts, 182–183
  birth order, 183
  common fears presented by clients, 187–188
  helping process, 184–187
  limitations, 189–190
  plan of action, 188–189
  social interest and mutual respect, 183
  strength and flexibility, 189
adverse childhood experiences (ACEs), 289
affective contact, 154
aggression, 57
aggressive and sexual instincts (id), 58–59
Alexander, Franz, 76
altered state of consciousness, 323
American Psychoanalytic Association (APA), 56
angst, 126
animal-assisted therapy (AAT), 286, 308–309
animal magnetism, 20
antisocial behavior, 163
applied behavior analysis (ABA), 114–115
artificial intelligence (AI) therapist, 33
art therapy, 303
assessment and diagnosis, 25–26
assimilative integration, 313
a-theoretical, 26
attachment-based therapy, 77
attachment, neurobiology of, 289

avoidant behavior, 163
awfulizing, 172, 178

B

Bandura, Albert, 93
Bateson, Gregory, 204
Beck, Aaron, 160–166
  belief patterns for personality disorders, 163
  cognitive schemas, 161
  dysfunctional styles of thinking, 161–162
  generic cognitive model, 160
behavioral medicine, 114
behavioral theories of intervention, 87
behavior intervention plan (BIP), 111–112
contemporary developments, 112–115
contingency contracting, 108–111
focus on specific actions, 98–99
goal setting, 101–104
history of behaviorism movement, 88–94
importance of therapeutic relationship, 114
incremental movements, 97–98
measurement of progress and outcomes, 98
reinforcing and discouraging of target behaviors, 96
relaxation training, 104–107

sensate focus exercises, 107–108
strengths and limitations, 114–115
techniques, 100–112
behavioral therapy, 48
behavior intervention plan (BIP), 111–112
behavior support plan (BSP), 111
being for, 121
being in, 120, 130
being with, 121
Berg, Insoo Kim, 247
Bertalanffy, Karl von, 203
  general systems theory, 203
  Organismic Psychology and Systems Theory, 203
bipolar disorder, 166
blend families, 316
body psychotherapy, 298–299
borderline behavior, 163
borderline personality disorder (BPD), 294
Boszormenyi-Nagy, Ivan, 210
boundaries of subsystem of families, 214
Bowen, Murray, 203, 210
  family therapy, 210–211
Breuer, Josef, 18, 54
brief psychodynamic psychotherapy, 78–80
brief strategic family therapy (BFST), 267, 273
brief strategic solution-oriented therapy, 267
brief therapy
  background and history, 261–262
  defined, 256–257
  insight vs action, 259–260

theory behind, 257–259
Buber, Martin, 123, 128
Bugental, James, 123

C
Camus, Albert, 124
career development, 41
Carkhuff, Robert, 151
catastrophizing, 162
catharsis, 64–65
central relational paradox (CRP), 246
Charcot, Jean-Martin, 20
chronic pain, 166
circle of security, 77
circular causality, 202, 204–207
circular interactions, 200
classical conditioning, 89, 94
client's projections (subjective perceptions), 67
client–therapist cultural differences, 23
cognitive behavior therapy (CBT), 44
  differences between cognitive therapy and, 167–168
  strengths and limitations, 168–169
cognitive development, 40
cognitive rehearsal, 168
cognitive theory, patterns of thought distortions, 161–162
cognitive therapy, 160–162
  application to common psychological complaints, 165–166
  differences between cognitive behavior therapy (CBT) and, 167–168
  limitations, 166

person-centered approach, xxiv
principles of, 164
commitment therapy (ACT), 286
"common factors" integrative approach, 320–328
  adopting an integrative framework, 333–340
  altered state of consciousness, 323
  assessment of therapy, 330–331
  effectiveness of approaches, 320
  feedback, 325–326
  finding meaning, 326–327
  helping relationship, 323–324
  importance of therapist's personality and presence, 321–322
  placebo effect, 322–323
  rehearsal, 327
  sending recall notices, 331–332
  sequential process, 328
  use of self, 322
communicative contact, 154
competence, 22
Comprehensive Dictionary of Psychoanalysis, 56
computer-assisted (or computer-mediated) therapy, 30–31
  advantages and disadvantages, 31–32
computer simulations, 30
concentration camps of Nazi Germany, 36
confidentiality, 22

conscience and moral beliefs (superego), 58–59
conscious aspects of psyche, 57
constructivist theories, 230–231
assumptions, 231–232
constructivist therapy, 180
contingency contracting, 108–111, 168
core family therapy techniques, 209
corrective emotional experience, 65–66
countertransference, 70–71
"crazy-making" families, 210
critical thinking, 33
cultural diversity, 23–24
cultural identity development, 41
cultural worldviews, 42–45
customizing/personalizing theory and settings, 349–357
approach to specific needs of clients, 350
deciding on starting point, 357–359

D

dance therapy, 304–305
death, 126
defense mechanisms, 61–63
denial, 63
of worth, 186
dependent behavior, 163
depression, therapeutic approaches for, 32, 76, 165
DeShazer, Steve, 247
developmental stages, 60
developmental tasks, 40

developmental theories, 41–42
Diagnostic and Statistical Manual (DSM-5), 25
dialectical behavior therapy (DBT), 286, 294–295
dichotomous thinking, 162, 172
didactic method, 177
differential reinforcement, 168
differentiated self, 210
disqualifying, 178
doing "to" vs doing "with,", 190–191
Dostoyevsky, Fyodor, 124
double bind, 204
drama therapy, 300–302
dreams, 63–64
Dreikurs, Rudolph, 182
dual relationships, 22
dysfunctional styles of thinking, 161–162, 172

E

ego development, 40, 58–59
ego psychology, 72
Einstein, Albert, 202
Ellis, Albert, xxiv, 197–199, 261, 322
background, 170–171
dysfunctional beliefs, 172
rational-emotive therapy, 37, 169–180
emotional and behavioral regulation therapies, 291–299
emotional energy, 54
emotional freedom technique, 298

emotionally focused couples therapy (EFCT), 155
emotion-focused therapy (EFT), 155–156
empathic mutuality, 154
enactment, 77
energy psychology, 298–299
Epston, David, 232
Narrative Means to Therapeutic Ends, 232
erectile dysfunction, 108
Ericksonian therapy, 262–267
Erickson, Milton, 210, 262
as anti-theorist, 264–266
contributions, limitations, and contraindications, 266–267
sense of therapist power, 264
Erikson, Eric, 55
ethical practice, 21–22
evidence-based eclecticism, 318–320
evolutionary psychology, 39
existential psychotherapist, becoming, 132
existential theory, 123–133
background and history, 123–124
existential philosophy, 125–126
logotherapy, 124–125
existential therapy, 43, 127–128
application, developments, 131–132
applying being in, 130
being in the moment, 130

client–therapist relationship, 129–130
here-and-now engagement, 128
immediacy and "realness" of therapeutic encounter, 129
making connections with past, 130
primary relationships, 130
strengths and limitations, 132–133
therapeutic process, 129–130
expertise, developing, 362
expressive therapies, 299–308
extinction, 98
Eyberg, Sheila, 113
eye movement desensitization and reprocessing (EMDR) therapy, 286, 295–298
Eysenck, Hans, 91, 93

F
face-to-face therapy, 31
false goals, 186
family behavior therapy (FBT), 113
Family Process, 203
family therapy, 204
 assessment, 223
 conducting a family session, 220–222
 humanistic/experiential approaches, 211
 multicultural, 215–216
 reorientation, 224–225
 sociocultural approaches, 215–216
 stages, 222–226
 strategic approaches, 214–215

structural approaches, 212–214
 structural realignments, 226
faulty values, 186
fears
 of being imperfect, 187
 of being vulnerable, 187
 of disapproval, 187
 of responsibility, 187
feminist family therapy, 239
feminist postmodernism, 239
feminist psychoanalysis, 240
feminist standpoint theory, 239
feminist theory, 239
feminist therapy, 239–246
 aims, 245
 common beliefs, 240
 practical problems of women of color, 240
 viewpoint and set of values, 244–245
filial play therapy, 306–307
Fish, Jefferson, 322
focusing-oriented psychotherapy, 153
Framo, James, 210
Frank, Jerome, 322
Frankl, Victor, 36
 human freedom and making choices, 125
 logotherapy, 124–125
 Man's Search for Meaning, 125
free choice, 120
freedom, 126
Freud, Anna, 55
Freud, Sigmund, 18, 36, 56, 181, 322
 An Outline of Psychoanalysis, 56

Beyond the Pleasure Principle, 57
case of Katharina, 82–86
catharsis, 64–65
client reluctance or resistance, 61
conscious aspects of psyche, 57
consciousness, ideas about, 56–57
corrective emotional experience, 65–66
defense mechanisms, 61–63
dreams, 63–64
drives, ideas about, 57–58
early background, 54–55
early traumas, 60–61
id, ego, and superego, 58–59
Interpretation of Dreams, 56
optimal state of balance, 58
preconscious aspects of psyche, 57
psychoanalytic therapy, treatment procedures, 66–71
psychosexual stages, 59–60
structural theory, 58–59
The Psychopathology of Everyday Life, 56
unconscious aspects of psyche, 57
"friendship skills" intervention, 112
Fromm, Erich, 55, 123

G
Gemeinschaftsgefuhl, 183
gender development, 41
gender equality, 241

gender, mental health and, 241–243
Gendlin, Eugene, 153
generalized anxiety disorder, 166
generic cognitive model, 160
genograms, 209
Gestalt theory, 48
Gestalt therapy, 37, 233
   channels of resistance, 149
   choice of language, 149
   early background, 145–146
   empty chair technique, 149
   here and now, 148
   strengths and limitations, 150
   unfinished or unresolved business, 148
Gestalt two-chair technique, 316–317
Gilligan, Carol, 41
"giving in" behavior, 113
Glasser, William, 192, 261, 322
goal setting, 101–104
golden thread metaphor of theory, 16–17, 351
Goodman, Paul, 147
Gordon, Thomas, 151
Gostecnik, Christian, 210
grand theories, 3
Greenberg, Les, 155
growth orientation, 120

H

Haley, Jay, 204, 214, 261–263
Havighurst, Robert, 40
Heidegger, Martin, 123
Helms, Janet, 41
helping process
   establishing collaborative relationship, 184

exploring mistakes, 186–187
interpreting early recollections, 185–186
lifestyle assessment, 184
helping relationship, 323–324
helping, theory of, 36–37
Hoffman, Louis, 132
Horney, Karen, xxiv, 55, 74
humanistic psychology, 157
humanistic theories (existential), 119
   concerns and criticism of, 157–158
   contemporary extensions, 150–157
humanistic therapies, 43, 119
   background and history, 122–123
   basic assumptions, 120
   existential theory, 123–133
   free choice, 120
   growth orientation, 120
   primacy of experience, 120
   responsibility for self and others, 120
   shared beliefs, 119–121
hypnosis, 20, 54, 263
hypnotherapy, 266

I

"I" messages, 153
incremental movements, 97–98
inferiority complex, 181–182
informed consent, 21
integrative counseling, 2
International Psychoanalytical Association, 56

Internet addiction, 31–32
Internet-based conversations, 30
Internet-based dialogue, 30
interpersonal neurobiology, 288
interpersonal psychotherapy (IPT), 74–76
intgeration of theories, 33
intimacy, 77
isolation, 126
"I–Thou" relationship, 128
Ivey, Allen, 210

J

Jackson, Don, 204
James, William, 90
Jaspers, Karl, 123
Johnson, Susan, 107
Journal of Applied Behavior Analysis, 113
Journal of Individual Psychology, 189
Journal of Rational-Emotive and Cognitive-Behavior Therapy, 180
Jung, Carl, 55
Jungian therapy, 55

K

Kafka, Franz, 124
Kernberg, Otto, 74
Kierkegaard, Soren, 123
Klein, Melanie, 55
Kohlberg, Lawrence, 40
Kohler, Wolfgang, 146
Kottler, Jeffrey, 1–2, 49–50
   careers, 2–6
   crisis intervention counselor, 4
   psychoanalytic theory, 3–4

L

Lazarus, Arnold, 313–315
learned neuroses, 90
Lewin, Kurt, 146
liberal feminism, 239
libido, 57–58
life drive, 57
life isn't fair, 172
linear causality, 204
Locke, John, 20, 94
Loevinger, Jane, 40–41
logotherapy, 36, 124–125
Lowen, Alexander, 298
Lowenfeld, Margaret, 307

M

Madanes, Cloe, 214, 261
Mahrer, Alvin, 123
managed care, 26
Maslow, Abraham, 122–123
Masters, William, 107
mathematics, 202–203
May, Rollo, 123, 127
Mesmer, Anton, 20
mindful breathing, 113
mindfulness approaches, 289–291
   mindfulness-based stress reduction (MBSR), 291
mind reading, 162, 172
Minuchin, Salvador, 212–213, 262
misperceptions, 186
modeling, 168
Modern Man in Search of a Soul (Jung), 55
Montgomery, Marilyn, 2–3, 51
   careers, 2–3, 5–6
moral development, 40
motivational enhancement, 282
motivational interviewing, 278–282

contemplation stage, 278
decisional balance, 279
OARS, 279
resistant clients and, 282
scaling technique, 280–281
Moustakas, Clark, 123
movement therapy, 304–305
"moving against" strategy, 75
"moving away" strategy, 75
"moving toward" strategy, 75
"moving with" strategy, 75
multicultural family therapy, 215–216
multimodal therapy, 313–315
   BASIC ID model, 313
   foundational ideas, 313–314
muscle relaxation, 105
musturbating, 172

N

narcissism, 74, 157
   belief patterns in, 163
narrative of theory-in-action, 14–15
narrative therapy, 232–240
   approach to helping, 233
   common assumptions, 237
   externalizing conversations, 235
   mapping of influence, 235–236
   outcome questions, 236
   restorying, 236–237
   stages in narrative process, 235–237

strengths and limitations, 238–239
negative filters, 162
negative reinforcement, 109
Neimeyer, Robert, 234–235
neurologically informed approaches, 287–289
neurosis, development of, xxiv
neutral scientific inquiry, 35
Newton, Sir Isaac, 203
Nietzsche, Frederich, 36, 123
North American Society of Adlerian Psychology (NASAP), 189

O

OARS, 279
object relations, 72
object relations theory, 72–73
obsessive-compulsive disorder, 166
Oedipal stage, 59
Oedipus Rex, 59
operant conditioning, 90–91
optimal state of balance, 58
Oregon Social Learning Center, 113
outbreaks of psychological maladies, 19–20
overgeneralization, 161, 172, 186
overpersonalizing, 178

P

paradoxical directive, 108
paranoid behavior, 163
parent–child interaction therapy (PICT), 113

Pavlov, Ivan, 87, 93–94
  classical conditioning, 89, 94
Pedersen, Paul, 210
perfectionism, 178
Perls, Fritz, 37, 146–147, 182, 261, 287, 322
  gestalt therapy, 145–150
  Gestalt therapy, 37
Perls, Laura, 147
personality traits in adulthood, 59
personalization, 162, 172
personal meaning, 126
personal reflection, 147–148
  angry behavior, 62
  being in the moment, 130–131
  cognitive processes, 165
  common defense mechanisms, 63
  competence, 49
  contributions of theory/ theories, 342–343
  cultural worldview, 24–25
  excuse-making exercise, 193–194
  existential issues, 124
  experienced insight as a gestalt, 146
  eye movement desensitization and reprocessing (EMDR) therapy, 297
  family system, 209
  feminist perspective of autism spectrum disorder, 245
  group activity, 19
  history repeating, 54
  intimate relationship, 217
  irrational beliefs, 173

  levels of consciousness, 57
  maladaptive beliefs and thoughts, 161
  management of boundaries, 76
  neurotic coping strategies, 75
  on favorite theory, 39
  organization of theories, 346, 349
  peak experiences, 122
  playing back struggle or conflict, 15
  play therapy, 306
  probation, 171
  projection of feelings, 68
  representation of family, 304
  role-played situation, 338
  scope of competence, 22–23
  stages in therapeutic process, 324–325
  theoretical paradigms, 27
  therapeutic process, 21
  therapists' engagement in deception, 265
  togetherness between people, 212
  tracing origins of belief, 13
  transference and countertransference, 70
  women's roles, 243
Person-Centered and Experiential Psychotherapies, 143
person-centered therapy, 133
  authenticity, genuineness, transparency, and warmth, 139–140

  basic assumptions, 134–135
  contemporary revisions, 143–144
  core conditions, 136–139
  empathy and active listening, 140–141
  features of client-centered session, 139–142
  focus on affect and feelings, 142
  fully present and being attentive, 139
  openness and unconditional regard, 139
  strengths and limitations, 144–145
person's development, understanding of, 39
phobias, 166
Piaget, Jean, 40
play therapy, 305
pleasure principle, 58
positive reinforcement, 109
practicing therapists, personal and professional lives of, 38–45
practitioners, points of agreement among
  assessment and diagnosis, 25–26
  cultural diversity, 23–24
  ethical practice, 21–22
  managed care, 26
  working efficiently, 26–27
preconscious aspects of psyche, 57
pre-therapy, 153–154
primacy of experience, 120
problem-solving therapy, 267

process-experiential
     approach, 155
projection, 67
psyche
     conscious aspects of, 57
     preconscious aspects
          of, 57
     unconscious aspects
          of, 57
psychoanalysis, 18, 99
psychoanalytic framework,
     38
psychoanalytic theories,
     63, 180
     basic principles, 56–65
     dominance during the
          middle of 20th cen-
          tury, 94
     of personality and
          treatment, 55
psychoanalytic therapy, 43
     client's projections
          (subjective percep-
          tions), 67
     countertransference,
          71–72
     "evenly hovering atten-
          tion,", 66–67
     strengths and limita-
          tions, 80–81
     traditional approaches
          to, 78–79
     transference, 67–69
     treatment procedures,
          66–71
     working through, 67
psychoanalytic training
     centers, 56
psychodynamic systems,
     210–211
psychological contact, 154
psychosexual stages,
     59–60
psychotherapists, preferred
     theories of, 50
psychotherapy theories,
     assumptions and

beliefs underlying,
     47
Psychotherapy with the
     Experts, 356
punishment, 109

Q
quantum physics, 203

R
radical feminism, 239
Rank, Otto, 76, 261
rational emotive behavior
     therapy (REBT),
     169–180, 233, 329
     ABC theory, 173–175
     specific disputing strat-
          egies, 176–178
     steps in, 175
     strengths and limita-
          tions, 179–180
rational-emotive therapy,
     37
rationalization, 63
rational philosophy, 94
reaction formation, 63
reactive contact, 154
reality principle, 58
reality therapy/choice
     theory, 160, 191–
     196, 233
     approach, 191–192
     assumptions, 192
     happy or angry emo-
          tions, 193
     strengths and limita-
          tions, 195–196
     therapeutic process,
          194–195
     WDEP model, 195
real-time practice of ther-
     apy, 354–355
reciprocal inhibition, 92
regression, 63
Reich, Wilhem, 298
Reik, Theodore, 55

reinforcement, behavioral
     principles of, 108
reinforcing incompatible
     behavior, 109
reinforcing of target
     behaviors, 96
reinforcing stimuli, 90
relational cultural theory,
     5
relational cultural therapy
     (RCT), 246–247
relational family systems
     theory, 211
relational psychoanalysis,
     77
relaxation training, 104–
     107, 109, 168
repetition compulsion, 58
repressed (buried) trau-
     mas, 60
repression, 63
resistant or unmotivated
     clients, 46
respect for differences, 22
responsibility for self and
     others, 120, 126
Rogers, Carl, xxiv, 98,
     123, 133, 153, 261,
     322, 324
     memories from child-
          hood, 36
     person-centered ther-
          apy, 133–145
Roosevelt, Eleanor, 122
Rousseau, Jean-Jacques,
     20
Russell, Bertrand, 124

S
sandplay therapy, 307–308
Sartre, Jean-Paul, 123–124
Satir, Virginia, 211, 227–
     228, 322
schemas, 161, 167
Schweitzer, Albert, 122
secondary gains, 61
self-actualization, 157
self-awareness, 126, 157

self-centeredness, 74, 157
self-defeating thinking, 107
self-expression, 157
self-fulfillment, 157
self-psychology, 74
sensate focus exercises, 107–108
Shapiro, Francine, 295
Sherby, Linda, 72
shoulding, 172
sibling constellations, 182
single-session therapy, 274–276
  advantages and special problems, 275–276
Skinner, B. F., 87, 93–94, 98, 115–117
  "blank slates,", 91
  operant conditioning, 90–91
  Skinner Box, 91
  The Behavior of Organisms, 91
  Walden Two, 91
sleep disorders, 166
socialist feminism, 240
social learning theory, 93
Socratic method, 177
solution-focused therapy, 247–252
  common misconception about, 247
  core questions used in, 251–252
  discovering patterns and constructing new ones, 250–251
  flexible approach to therapeutic work, 248–250
  scaling questions, 252
  strengths and limitations, 253
  theoretical assumptions, 248
spectatoring, 107

stimulus control procedures, 108
stimulus discrimination, 92
stimulus generalization, 92
strategic therapy, 267–274
  assumptions of approach, 267–268
  directives, 270–271
  preparations, 270
  prevention of relapses, 272–273
  reframing a problem, 268–269
  strengths and limitations, 273–274
structural family therapy, 214
structure of family, 213
sublimation, 63
subsystems of families, 214
Sue, Derald, 210
Sullivan, Harry Stack, 55, 74–75
Super, Donald, 41
superiority complex, 182
syncretism, 312
synthesizing theories, 33
systematic desensitization, 48, 92, 168
systematic inquiry, 35
systemic approaches, 210
  family therapy, 210–211
  humanistic/experiential approaches, 211
  multicultural family therapy and sociocultural approaches, 215–216
  strategic approaches, 214–215
  structural approaches, 212–214
systemic theory, 200, 203
  psychoanalysis and, 203–204
systemic therapy, 44

systemic thinking, 201–204
  circular causality, 204–207
  family rules, 208–209
  principles of, 205–209
  rules of relationship, 207–209

T

"talk" therapy, 308
Talmon, M., 274
technical eclecticism, 313, 317
technology, impact of
  challenges for practitioners, 32
  ethical issues, 32
  on clients, 28–29
  on therapists, 30–32
The Inseparable Nature of Love and Aggression (Kernberg), 58
theoretical frameworks, understanding of
  confusion and ambiguity, 45–46
  evidence to support ideas, 48
  expanding opinions, 49–51
  fervor and zeal, 46
  points of departure, 47–49
  preferences and practices, 50–51
  preparation for main attraction, 51
  regional preferences, 51
  value relationships and process, 47
theoretical worldviews, 43–44
theories of counseling and therapy, comparisons and differences, 344–349

cognitive vs affective,
    346–347
flexible vs rigid roles,
    348
insight vs action,
    345–346
present vs past, 347
theory/theories, 363
    abbreviated treatments
        and, 17–18
    definition, 15
    for appeasing uncer-
        tainty and anxiety,
        16
    functions of, 16–17
    golden thread metaphor
        of, 16–17
    historical context of,
        18–20
    integration of, 32
    intersection of good
        and moral conduct,
        22

limitations of, 360–361
obsoleteness of, 17–18
of being and doing,
    147–148
of helping, 36–37
of intervention, 17,
    39–42
synthesis of, 32
trends, 28–33
therapist-client relation-
    ships, 44
Thomas, Lewis, 201
    communication of ter-
        mites and ants, 202
    Lives of a Cell, 201
transference, 67–69

U

unconscious aspects of
    psyche, 57

V

virtual therapist, 30

W

Watson, John, 87, 93–94
    case of "Little Albert,",
        90
    learned neuroses, 90
Watzlawick, P., 259–260
"WDEP" helping process,
    195
Weakland, John, 204
web-based counseling, 276
web-based interactions, 30
Whitaker, Carl, 211
White, Michael, 232
    Narrative Means to
        Therapeutic Ends,
        232
Wiener, Norbert, 202
Wolpe, Joseph, 91–93
women of color, practical
    problems of, 240
worldviews, 42–45
Wundt, Wilhelm, 94

CPSIA information can be obtained
at www.ICGtesting.com
Printed in the USA
FSHW020139101219
64904FS